THE FIELD GUIDE TO
HEALTHY
RELATIONSHIPS

Discovering and Applying Biblical Precepts to the Building of Lasting, Quality Relationships, Including Marriage and How to Find the Person Who Is Right for You!

RICHARD JOSEPH KREJCIR, PH.D.

PublishAmerica
Baltimore

First printing

All Scripture quotations unless otherwise stated are from The Holy Bible, New International Version, (North American Edition) by Zondervan Bible Publishers © 1973, 1978, 1987 International Bible Society. Used by permission of Zondervan Publishing House. Table of Contents

At the specific preference of the author, PublishAmerica allowed this work to remain exactly as the author intended, verbatim, without editorial input.

ISBN: 1-4137-7179-3
PUBLISHED BY PUBLISHAMERICA, LLLP
www.publishamerica.com
Baltimore

Printed in the United States of America

DEDICATION

I dedicate this work to the GLORY OF OUR LORD!

I have been crucified with Christ and I no longer live, but Christ lives in me. The life I live in the body, I live by faith in the Son of God, who loved me and gave himself for me. Galatians 2:20

Many thanks to all the people who have discipled and inspired me over the years, such as Steve Morgan, Chuck Miller, R.C. Sproul, Robert B. Munger, and of course, my friend and mentor, Francis A. Schaeffer. A special thanks to my editor Fran Smith who has worked very hard on the manuscript and the people in my Bible study who have encouraged, prayed, given me insights, and kept me sane on this journey.

And, of course, my utmost dedication is to my great love with appreciation for all of her help—my wife, MaryRuth, *"I found the one my heart loves"* Song of Solomon 3:4

Devote yourselves to prayer, being watchful and thankful. And pray for us, too, that God may open a door for our message, so that we may proclaim the mystery of Christ, for which I am in chains. Pray that I may proclaim it clearly, as I should. Be wise in the way you act toward outsiders; make the most of every opportunity. Let your conversation be always full of grace, seasoned with salt, so that you may know how to answer everyone. Colossians 4:2-6

TABLE OF CONTENTS

Preface 7
THE JOURNEY OF LOVE AND RELATIONSHIPS!
Chapter I 15
PREPARING FOR RELATIONSHIPS WITH THE RIGHT MINDSET
Chapter II 34
THE QUEST FOR AUTHENTIC LOVE
Chapter III 52
THE MYTHS OF LOVE
Chapter IV 62
KINDNESS: MAKING LOVE REAL IN OUR LIVES
Chapter V 73
UNDERSTANDING THE IMPORTANCE OF BEING GOOD!
Chapter VI 85
ATTITUDE: THE PRELUDE TO EFFECTIVE RELATIONSHIPS!
Chapter VII 96
THE CHARACTER OF FRIENDSHIP
Chapter VIII 115
HOW TO BUILD A GOOD PERSONALITY
Chapter IX 136
COURTSHIP ANYONE?
Chapter X 147
PREPARING FOR A SUCCESSFUL AND HAPPY MARRIAGE
Chapter XI 163
HOW TO SET BOUNDARIES
Chapter XII 177
WHAT THE BIBLE SAYS ABOUT SEX AND ROMANCE
Chapter XIII 192
LEARNING TO SEE IN RELATIONSHIPS
Chapter XIV 210
THE CALL OF FORGIVENESS

CHAPTER XV 231
HOW TO UNDERSTAND, SOLVE, AND PREVENT CONFLICT
CHAPTER XVI 248
LONELINESS
CHAPTER XVII 268
HOW TO DESTROY A RELATIONSHIP
CHAPTER XVIII 287
HOW TO DEAL WITH ANGER
CHAPTER XIX 305
RELATIONSHIPS IN THE WORKPLACE
CHAPTER XX 326
PUTTING IT ALL TOGETHER

APPENDIX I 349
HOW TO BUILD YOUR FAITH
APPENDIX II 355
ACCOUNTABILITY QUESTIONS
APPENDIX III 359
SCRIPTURE REFERENCES
APPENDIX IV 374
THE "ONE ANOTHER" PASSAGE
APPENDIX V 376
ABOUT INTO THY WORD MINISTRIES
APPENDIX VI 379
ABOUT THE MAN BEHIND THE WORDS

*Here there is no Greek or Jew, circumcised or uncircumcised, barbarian, Scythian, slave or free, but **Christ is all, and is in all**.* Colossians 3:11

THE JOURNEY OF LOVE AND RELATIONSHIPS!

We always thank God, the Father of our Lord Jesus Christ, when we pray for you, because we have heard of your faith in Christ Jesus and of the love you have for all the saints—the faith and love that spring from the hope that is stored up for you in heaven and that you have already heard about in the word of truth, the gospel that has come to you. All over the world this gospel is bearing fruit and growing, just as it has been doing among you since the day you heard it and understood God's grace in all its truth. Colossians 1:3-6

One way to look at the world of relationships is to see it as a journey in a big, dark, and foreboding jungle, with many paths we could undertake, each plotted with all kinds of options, potential traps, and dangers. As we venture into this jungle, we come face to face with our fears, doubts, and our conflicts with all kinds of opportunities and ideas. Coupled with these fears and discords, we may collide with others who are seeking the same path. When we are faced with so many paths and choices, we can become frustrated, and be led into the possibility of making wrong decisions. This, in turn, can become a string of lost and broken friendships that further direct our lives toward conflict and strife. Or, perhaps we find the right path, by chance, leading to a life of contentment, harmony, and love. Do we step back or do we proceed? If we stay off the path, we end up in loneliness and despair. If we take our chances, we can become lost and hurt. So, what do we do? We need to be willing to choose a direction, and move ahead on that path. Then, the questions become, *what is that direction? How can I find it?* We may ask, and even plead, *what do I do? Where do I go? With whom do I desire to share my life? Is there a Divine plan for me? Do I need to prepare myself first, or can we just dive right in according to our own whims?* Or, *Do I seek God's precepts, so I can take the path with more confidence?*

7

It is the goal of this book to help you in your journey through this dark jungle, to seek God's plan and the right approach to take. We will look at what God's Word has to say—His timeless, tested, and righteous path on which we can walk. We can go into that dark jungle armed with the Light of His Word so we can take risks, and make right decisions; we can find and form friendships that work! After all, the meaning of the Christian life is relationships—first with God, and then with the others around us. That is why we are on this earth. This is the only experience we take with us into eternity. When we are walking on His path, with His Light, we will experience the wonder and excitement of life. Let us be willing to look up and experience His Wonder!

I have been placed in a "catbird seat" for observing relationships from being in pastoral ministry for over twenty years and as many years of counseling. These observations, along with my education, and fueled by my own personal relationship journey (with all the mistakes I have made), have given me a plate full of observations concerning what works and what does not. And, what I have found, believe it or not, is that few Christians ever seek God or His help in their relationship choices; they just dive right into a pool that usually has no water in it. Choosing the right path through that jungle of dark apprehensions will be the most important decision we ever make, because this is what will echo into eternity. Relationship choices are far more important than our other daily decisions, including what school to attend or what career to undertake. Yet, few take this seriously.

When we venture into the shadowy jungle, getting ourselves entangled in the vines and thorn bushes of relationships, the options confronting us will cause us either to embrace others with eagerness, or become fearful and alone. One path may make us content, the other, bitter. These trepidations are a natural defense mechanism warning us away from dangerous situations. Added to these natural fears are all the various attitudes of our culture and the desires of our will, all diverging with one another, causing chaos and conflict. Meanwhile, Christ is seeking us, beckoning us to follow Him out of that deep, dark, dangerous jungle on to a path of solid, lasting relationships, where the vines become arms of love and the rose bushes lose their thorns. In this way, we can develop close friendships, date successfully, understand and give real authentic love, find the right spouse, and even develop a healthy marriage.

Relationships are important. Yes, there are other activities and goals that preoccupy us in life, such as our jobs, cars, hobbies, money, and having fun.

However, consider these thoughts: *When you are at the end of your sojourn on this earth, what will you have received from it? What will you take with you? Will it be that successful career? What about that hobby that took all of your time? Would it be the wealth that you accumulated?* I am not saying these things are not important to pursue; rather, they are just a few of the various means to do what really is important, and that is, *building relationships!* Career, material accumulation, activities, money, and having fun are not the goals in life; they are only portions of the means to the goal. The reason for, and meaning of life is, again, *relationships*—with God and then with others!

Relationships include a variety of options and challenges. We can easily see many choices, yet we have so little time to investigate them. So many ways, opportunities, and ideas to go about it, but in our heart we know there is only one real Truth. *How can one navigate this strange land? How can we find God's real purpose and plan? How can we turn our wrong choices into good ones? Can we learn how to build quality relationships, even if we have never experienced one? Does He have only one, precise person chosen to be my spouse? If so, how do I find that one? How can I develop a genuine best friend relationship that will last? How can I make my marriage work?*

My purpose in writing this book is to point you in the right direction, and provide for you solid, biblical insights from my more than twenty years of pastoral counseling and biblical investigations into this subject. It is my prayer and plan to give you a general overview of relationships, from the Bible's timeless perspective, to equip you for your journey. This is not a work based on the latest trends in psychology; rather, it is based on the understanding of the underlining spiritual principles that we all need to know and follow. *Field Guide* is meant to show you the right path to take you through the jungle of what all of us are to do and to be. Consequently, you can learn and gain the fullness of His empowerment and wisdom from God's Word in order to improve in all of your relationships and to glorify our Lord.

I did not just wake up one day, free from that jungle. I, too, had to struggle to keep myself from getting lost, and in trying to find my way out of ruthless situations. I had to overcome my fears from intense teasing as a child, overcome learning disabilities, dyslexia, ADHD, and a seriously embarrassing speech impediment that caused me to be the butt of many jokes while growing up. I am not even a natural extrovert; I prefer to study and be alone. At parties, at school, and social gatherings as an adult, I tended to be the "wall flower," a fish out of water, standing by the food, so it would seem I was a part of it and not out of it, which I was. Yet, God called me into relationships, and as a pastor, I cannot avoid them. So, I had to learn to reverse myself, to grow away from my natural tendencies to be alone. I was engaged once, and realized, after a lot of agony and pain, that this would be a wrong direction for me to go. I have spent so much time in my pastoral career and education that I have had, at times, few, and sometimes no relationships of any quality or depth. It is my intention to help you find the right path so you can discover and build healthy, quality relationships that are centered upon Christ as Lord. We will begin by looking at how to prepare ourselves with the right mindset, knowing what real love is, and learning about attitude and character so we can be prepared to bring about and build relationships that will last, as well as developing a good personality.

When we have prepared ourselves to better know ourselves and what God has to say to us, we can start to find and build relationships that work. We can start to see life as a pleasurable and exciting adventure, not a gloomy journey to endure, hoping something better comes along one day. When we find people with whom we can bond, we can start to see His abode of love and contentment emerging in our lives. Yes, we will have ups and downs, but the main anchor in our lives will be our solid, growing relationship with Christ, and His transforming presence imploring us to empower others.

Once we learn how to get ourselves on the right path, we will discover helpful tips and biblical ideas on how to form and build healthy, quality relationships. We can even learn how to find the love of a lifetime and be able to keep it. We will realize we have His best available to us. We will have real, authentic relationships that are centered upon Him because our lives and mindset have been aligned to His. This happens because we have yielded to Christ as Lord of our lives all of the time, so that we can see His path through the jungle and receive His best. We will sometimes make the wrong choices and get lost ourselves. However, if we are willing to seek His help, Christ will help us through it, and work our wrong choices for good.

Some stay put in that land of choices because it is fun, it is a party, and they enjoy it. Others feel that if you do that, you will put yourself in danger, which may lead into bad relationships. So, what do we do? How do we proceed?

What we need is a Tour Guide, to lead us through our journey in those jungles of confusing options and rough waters of wrong choices, so we can avoid the dangerous paths and not find ourselves living in the jungle of despair. Maybe, you wish and pray for some kind of *how to* guide that will cut through that jungle of despair and give you God's precepts. Perhaps, you want a guide that is not rooted in some counselor's experiences and theories, but in timeless, biblical values that are tried and true and real for you. You are holding it in your hand. It will show you how God's Word is a sword—a machete—that will cut that path for you.

This book is about seeking, from God's most precious Word, the right way to proceed into that jungle of developing friendships and dating choices. We will help prepare you to come through life not only with the right decision and the love of your life, but with the tools, character, and ability to make godly, Christ-centered relationships work, filled with God's blessings and purpose! This book is not just for singles! Many married people have found the precursor articles to this book very helpful in giving their marriage the boost it needs, and in developing romance. Even if you have done it all wrong, so to speak, God can and will turn your mistakes around when your attention becomes focused upon Christ and His precepts from His Word.

I urge you to seek God's will by recognizing God's love for you. In that way, you will be able to apply biblical principles to help you decide what is right or wrong in relationships and to find the love of your life. Additionally, if you are already married, you can use the principles of His Word to spruce up your marriage with a romantic makeover through self-discovery and character in action. You can take a look at what you have done wrong, and then correct it by removing your false thinking and behaviors.

The goal of this book is not to give you a set of rules to either "do" or "don't." Rules are not what this book is about; it is about finding God's best for you. Rules are just rules, and our determination and sinful nature tend to fight against, break, and reject them. Therefore, this will give you scriptural principles and reasons so you can think them through, examine them for yourself, and come to a better understanding of friendship, love, fellowship, sex, singleness, dating, and how to build Christ-like relationships that will last a lifetime.

We will be looking at qualities we should seek in a soul mate. *What should we avoid? How do we find that love that will last a lifetime? Is finding the right mate a matter of just being lucky, or being in the right place at the right time? Is it possible that someone else stole him or her from you? Does God really care, and does He have that special someone for you? How do you find out?*

We will discover that the current dating model most people use, from pre-teens to older adults, is ineffective at best and dangerous at worst. Our dating traditions result in a 50 percent plus divorce rate, which is the same in the church as it is in secular society (statistics are consistent from the *United States Census Bureau, Barna Research,* and *Focus on the Family*). This means people who attend a religious institution and who claim to be Christians have the same divorce rate as people who do not go to a church or as people who hang out in bars, showing their contempt for God. This translates that Christians have a problem with building and maintaining relationships. And, the relationships that do tend to last have major problems. Just ask any counseling pastor or Christian marriage counselor and they will say that a significant amount of the marriages that stay together are mostly miserable and dysfunctional. Something is definitely wrong.

What should we do? What do we need to consider and to avoid? For this quest, let us venture into God's most precious Word, and examine the Scriptures carefully to find His will. (In the back of this book is a section in the Appendix called "Scripture References" for each chapter and section.) For deeper insights and self-study, look up the Scriptures, read them, and ask: W*hat does this mean? How can I be changed because of these precepts? How will it affect my life if I do?* Then, do it! The Bible holds the truth for life today, including how and with whom you should be building that life. If you feel that the Bible is not the paradigm for your faith and practice or your standard for relationships, then you will find yourself disappointed and hurt in life. The perspective we are to have is a desire for what God wants, not what we want. Our focus is to be on Him because He has the best plan for us! Our plans will only lead us to make the wrong decisions and miss out on the best opportunities and situations He has for us.

I understand that what I am writing may not sit well with some people, because it goes against some of our popular notions and experiences. However, regardless of how we may feel about something, if you claim Christ as your Lord, you must always seek to follow God's model. In addition, you need to do this simply because it will be the best, most effective, and most fulfilling way—period! This book's purpose is not to burst your bubble or to cause you to end your current relationship; it is to challenge you to step back, seek His Word, and do what is His best—for you as well as the person or people you are presently with, or will be with. In so doing, you will be in the right relationships, and will experience the ultimate joys and opportunities in life— His best for you!

The first thing we must see is that God does care, and has a plan for you, even when you cannot see it. So, be willing to learn and develop your character.

Study the Word, seek wisdom, be prudent, and lean on the strength of the Lord! These things do not come to you by chance; they come by knowing and following Christ (Proverbs 12:4; 28:20; 31:10)!

So, I challenge you to search the Scriptures and see what is contained in this book. This book is not a collection of trendy opinions or distillations from popular psychology; rather, the focus is on timeless values that last and that work. If you are still not sure about what we are talking about, especially about courting versus dating, and what the Bible has to say, then read some other sources. You will find some good suggestions in our Scripture References and Bibliography sections at the end.

Consider this: without the right attitude and perspective on life, without glorifying God and following His will, you will not find the real, quality love relationship for your life! You will be taking a big gamble that you might miss what is priceless and precious.

May the Lord richly bless and keep you in His loving arms, and bless your search to find the relationship God has for you—even for the love of your life!

—Rev. Richard Joseph Krejcir M.Div., Ph.D.

The LORD bless you and keep you; the LORD make his face shine upon you and be gracious to you; the LORD turn his face toward you and give you peace. Numbers 6:24-26

CHAPTER I
PREPARING FOR RELATIONSHIPS WITH THE RIGHT MINDSET

And we pray this in order that you may live a life worthy of the Lord and may please him in every way: bearing fruit in every good work, growing in the knowledge of God. Colossians 1:10

One of the best activities I ever did when I was a Youth Pastor was taking the youth to rest homes. I would assign each of them to interview an elderly person. They would find out what was most important in that person's life, what they had learned and what they would have done differently. Did they have regrets? Did fear keep them from making good decisions? Did they throw away what was important, such as friends, a spouse, or children? Later, we would discuss their findings and determine what they had learned and could apply to their own lives. I would also ask them to think about what they did *not* hear the person say, which could also be very important.

During these countless interviews over a span of twenty years, I never encountered a person who regretted spending too much time with his or her family, regretted not having enough time for a hobby, or, who needed more money. In fact, after interviewing congressmen, industrialists, tradesmen, clergymen, businessmen, mothers who had never held a job outside the home, and many others from all walks of life, the biggest regret expressed was spending too much time at work in order to make money. They regretted the distance between them and their children, the lost relationships with friends, and the spouse they let go. They also expressed the desire to have a better disposition and personality. They all wished they could live their lives over, spending more time working on relationships, keeping their friends, and not losing out on what they finally figured out was important in life!

It is my prayer that we can carry out our lives with the right mindset of what is really important in life so we do not end up in loneliness and regret.

I wanted to let those young people know, while they were still in their youth, that they did not need to wait until they reach the age of seventy or eighty to see life in the right perspective; they could do it now. We do not need to miss out on what God has for us. We do not need to spend all of our energies chasing after what is fleeting while ignoring what is good.

Being strengthened with all power according to his glorious might so that you may have great endurance and patience, and joyfully giving thanks to the Father, who has qualified you to share in the inheritance of the saints in the kingdom of light. Colossians 1:11-12

Most young people do not look up to see what is really important; therefore, confusion and dysfunction have taken over their mindsets. Most live in the world of coffee houses, clubs, Internet dating, singles clubs, and personal ads. These things have become cultural icons, and are booming in our society. People are dazed and confused on who and what to look for in finding friendships and intimacy. Even the quest to find the love of one's life can be all consuming. This boom has even infiltrated the church, as we can easily see countless ads for Christians seeking Christians, and Christian dating services on the web, radio, and newspapers. There are even personal ads in church bulletins. People are so busy in this fast-paced society, there seems to be no time to date or even to make friends. There is no time to look up and see God's plan. Of course, in saving time by not looking up, we just end up spending decades in wrong choices and in the midst of dysfunction.

For he has rescued us from the dominion of darkness and brought us into the kingdom of the Son he loves, in whom we have redemption, the forgiveness of sins. Colossians 1:13-14

Perhaps, people have been hurt and do not want to do as they have done before. Many are fed up with the traditional dating scene and are searching for an alternative; perhaps this is true for you. If you think your busyness keeps you from finding the right people, once (and if) you do find someone, will you have time for a relationship? Almost certainly not! Something or someone needs to change. That someone is you, and that something is your attitude and outlook on life. No, we do not like to hear those words, do we? But, we do need to hear them. I know I do!

In our struggle to learn biblical character and apply it to our lives, we can cut through the thorny jungles of complicated choices to discover the means to having and building meaningful and intimate relationships. This is not only possible—it is for you! Yet, for many Christians, this is struggle number one! Consider singleness. Many people today are staying single longer due to career choices, fear of commitment, or an over-zealous party lifestyle. Perhaps, they are from a divorced family and do not want to go through what their parents did. However, there comes the time when they look and see the biological clock ticking away, then begin feeling lonely and wanting. After being too busy or too choosy about whom they might date while in their 20s, the 30s come and desperation takes over. They often end up in a mismatched relationship that possibly was not a part of God's best for them.

Humble yourselves, therefore, under God's mighty hand, that he may lift you up in due time. Cast all your anxiety on him because he cares for you. 1 Peter 5:6-7

The answer is not in the latest fad or service; it is in getting our priorities straight, then seeking out relationships! If your call and desire is to have a committed relationship, you will have to make room in your life for one. That means you will need to be willing to prepare yourself, emotionally and mentally, with the right biblical attitude and mindset. If not, then you will be gambling with the second most important decision and choice you will ever make. And, when it comes to a marriage, your choices and attitudes will have lasting repercussions for many people, and for many generations to come. It will become a crapshoot with much greater and higher odds for the "house" (where the "house" is a regretful and discontented life) than for you.

We all desire and seek love and companionship to fill that empty hole we think we have. For some singles, this is the driving force in their lives, as it was for me at one time. Yet, as Christians, our primary purpose in life is to grow in our relationship to our Lord. We need to serve and glorify God, and fulfill the call and the destiny that He gives us. This also translates into who we are, and how we should be in Christ. This is true in the arena of all relationships, even for finding the "love of your life." Thus, we need to find out what God's plan is for relationships, and then follow it. It seems simple on the surface, and it really is. The problem is that we have clouded God's plan with our superficial culture and desires. We seek that crapshoot rather than the stability of impacting faith and godly values.

BUILDING YOUR FOUNDATION WITH THE RIGHT BIBLICAL MINDSET

I have been crucified with Christ and I no longer live, but Christ lives in me. The life I live in the body, I live by faith in the Son of God, who loved me and gave himself for me. Galatians 2:20

The goal—from finding lasting friendships to finding the "love of your life" to building an exceptional marriage—is to live in undivided surrender and devotion to the Lord Jesus Christ. He is Lord, meaning that He is in charge of all areas of our lives. He is our first and primary love! That means your life must reflect the supremacy and glory of God, and serve as an example in a world of temptation and evil. Since He represented us in life and death and imparts to us His grace, this is our driving force, our number one reason in life and in eternity to come. Because of what He has done for us, we should have the desire to assemble our lives to glorify Him. That means to also strive toward our best in fullness of relationships. We have to be willing to take to heart that His will supercedes ours; His is the best, whereas our will and desires are limited in our understanding and knowledge. By surrendering our will to His will, we can build a foundation of trust, reliance, and obedience. These actions become the foundation upon which to build the rest of the house of character, values, and fortitude, and where a Christ-centered relationship can live and grow.

You will then be able to make healthy and wise decisions because the Lord, through His Word and the Spirit, is your Guide, as opposed to what the media, friends, your passions, and emotions may dictate. Because you are seeking His truth, you will be able to discern how to go about your life, your direction and plan, even who is right for you. Following these timeless, biblical precepts will help you make the right decisions, and avoid making the wrong ones. If for some reason you decide God's ways are not for you, be forewarned; as you lose yourself in the jungle of wrong decisions, you may never receive what He has and what is best for you. Thus, you may face the unpleasant prospect of venturing into a life of misery and strife. So, why do that?

We need to learn four primary attitudes that form the foundation for building effective relationships. These are like the footers to a skyscraper—massive, concrete platforms where the steel girders that hold up the entire building are placed. Just like the crossbeams that are bolted and welded on those girders, each of these aspects needs to be bolted onto the other. Each one produces the next one and is dependent on the previous one; thus, they all interlock collectively to work synergistically tighter together to form us into the person God has called us to be. These will be the groundwork upon which the character, maturity, and willingness to make right decisions are constructed. They will continue to assemble those relationships in the right direction, as they become the foundation for understanding God's will. The remainder of the precepts we investigate will build the skyscraper of relationships.

First: Understanding the Kingdom of God

Repent, for the kingdom of heaven is near! Matthew 3:2

Three penetrating questions that have been pondered by humanity since the dawn of time are *who are you? What do you want?* and, *Where are you going?* These form the foundation of the disciplines of philosophy and religious studies, affecting the humanities, sociology, and of course, psychology. These questions fuel what directs us, who motivates us to do what we do, and who motivates us to be who we are. This is the *meaning of life* stuff. Through understanding Christ and who we are in Him, these three ageless questions come alive to help sustain us and direct us in the right direction. As a result, we will center our motivations and directions on Him, on what is perfect and pleasing, and not on what we think. Our answers will only serve to get us lost. However, the key is to understand the answers to these questions that Jesus asks us in His Word. If we get the answers wrong, we get lost in that jungle of life; if we get them right, we stay on the right path. Are you thinking, *hey, that is not fair*, or, *is life just a big test?* Take this to heart; you have the answer sheet—His Word. He has written the answers in creation, in our hearts, and revealed them in His Word. We have no excuse not to know, but because of our Fall, the fog of our will and desires obscures them from view.

Take comfort in the awareness that God is not hidden, nor is His will so mysterious that we cannot find it. God's influence, glory, and presence are all around us; this is called "Mediated Revelation." This is not *pantheism*, which teaches that everything is God, that creation itself is God. Rather, God is *all present*, "omnipresent," and we have no escape from Him. He reveals His presence to us in countless ways.

These *meaning of life* questions also mean that we as humans are spiritual by nature and seek a higher purpose and order. God uses that nature to make

19

Himself known. "Mediated Revelation" means that God plants an innate sense of who He is in each of us, even without the Bible or missions. (However, remember that missions and evangelism are still a mandate from our Lord!) Coupled to God's revelation in nature and in our hearts, we have "special revelation," which is the Bible that God directly inspired, and is the ultimate source and superintendent of the original manuscripts, without any error. He used humans as the authors, and a word processor as a tool. Thus, we receive His will for our faith, and the practice of life, duty, law, grace, His plan, and our purpose.

Why the theology lesson? Because, we have to know from whence our direction in life comes. This is foundational for all aspects of who we are and what we do. What motivates us and creates in us our actions and behaviors will translate in our relationship with God and how we are with those around us. If you do not get this, that God has a plan for you, you will have tremendous issues and obstacles that you may never climb over in becoming the person that God desires and calls you to be. The best plans, the best adventures, contentment, and joys we can ever have in life can easily be missed if we become stubborn and refuse to look up at Him.

Here comes some more theology—essential theology—to know so that you can get yourself on the right path to know God better and to receive His direction.

Consider that every culture and people group since the beginning of time has had religion and some form of a civil government at the core of its society. Throughout recorded human history, humanity has gathered for trade and protection as well as for organizing the gathering of food, for hunting, and for forming relationships within a structure, which translates into control and government. The word *Kingdom,* in the *Kingdom of God* or *Heaven,* means government; it is the need to be organized for purpose and direction. Some people lead, others strive to obey; still others seek to destroy. This is a result of our fallen nature and criminal element. Nevertheless, we need leadership and direction for success in building relationships and a society. Biblically, we are called to have a civil government and obey it—within the parameters that there is actually only one true government and leader—and that is God. This means we are to yield to the exercise and implementation of our God's "Lordship," that He is our King, hence the name, "Kingdom of God." He is sovereign; He is the absolute monarch of the universe. His rule is absolute. When we refuse to be governed and controlled, anarchy and chaos will result because of our sinful nature, and will cause harm to others.

Thus, it is our responsibility to obey God and the others who have responsibility over us.

For through him we both have access to the Father by one Spirit. Ephesians 2:18

This theme, the *Kingdom of God*, is found throughout Scripture, and links the two Testaments. It exists now with God's reign of His people, and it will come to fulfillment in the future. It means God is supreme, sovereign, and Lord over all, including our lives. It infers who we are and what we are both in the real world and the spiritual world. God reaches out to us; we, as citizens of His Kingdom, are to reach out to others. God does not shut us out; thus, we are not to shut others out. This affects all we do, all of our relationships, past, present and future. Check out the passages on this subject in the "Scriptural References" in the back of this book. There are a lot of Scriptures, indeed; now you can start to see how important this is!

John the Baptist announced the *Kingdom* to us, with a sense of urgency, at the inauguration of Jesus' ministry on earth. It is now in its beginning, and will be fulfilled, as Jesus said, in the future. Thus, it is already running, and there is more to come with Christ's second coming. Exactly what, we do not know; we only have a glimpse. What we do know is that it will be consummated.

Jesus went throughout Galilee, teaching in their synagogues, preaching the good news of the kingdom, and healing every disease and sickness among the people. Matthew 4:23

Jesus preached the *Kingdom of Heaven*, which is both here and yet to come. The term, the *Kingdom of Heaven* means the same in Matthew as it does in the other three Gospels. They all refer to God's rule and sovereignty. They point to both the church today and our eternal future. Matthew used the expression, *Kingdom of Heaven*, almost exclusively, whereas the other gospels use the term *Kingdom of God*. The distinction lies in who the audience was. The Jews, to whom Matthew wrote, were reluctant to say the name of God because of their high reverence for His name. To the Gentiles and Greeks it did not matter. The Kingdom of Heaven will culminate with our Lord's second coming, bringing in a new heaven and a new earth.

But in keeping with his promise we are looking forward to a new heaven and a new earth, the home of righteousness. So then, dear friends, since you are looking forward to this, make every effort to be found spotless, blameless and at peace with him. 2 Peter 3:13-14

What does this boil down to? Our task in the church is to proclaim Christ as Lord as well as His character, righteousness, peace, and joy, all by the Holy Spirit. This will effectively be the catalyst to build quality, lasting, and effective relationships. The "coming of the Kingdom" in the Old Testament meant that a new stage in God's redemptive plan was coming—CHRIST. For us, it means our personal identification and relationship to our Lord and Savior! Our need is to bow to His Lordship for our betterment and growth! This will keep us going on the right path through that dark, foreboding jungle of the pandemonium of life!

Second: Applying the Mind-Set of Fullness

Be very careful, then, how you live—not as unwise but as wise, making the most of every opportunity, because the days are evil. Therefore do not be foolish, but understand what the Lord's will is. Ephesians 5:15-17

Fullness equals knowing who you are in Christ and what He did for you on the cross. This is paramount, because everything you do as a Christian is a response to what He has first done in you. With this knowledge, you will have the proper attitude and discernment to make correct decisions based on God's will. With this knowledge, you will ask the right questions and look for fullness, not merely fulfillment! The difference is that fullness is seeking Christ as Lord; fulfillment is seeking someone or something to meet your needs and wishes, or seeking to fill your own desires and lusts! Fulfillment is seeking what we want, and that often is not the best for us. It is filling our emptiness with the wrong filler. It is much like putting gasoline in a diesel-fueled truck; it is fuel, but it will not work, and will damage the engine. These passages testify to such as this. Sin and the desires of our lust can, and will consume us, taking us far away from God and His goodness. So, this pursuit of fulfillment will end up bringing us nothing but emptiness, the very thing we are trying to avoid. Sin will dig in us, causing our thinking to be skewed, and our decisions flawed.

Fullness is the filling we have. It is like we are "Twinkies" and He is the filling; Twinkies are not much without the filling! It is the realization that we are missing our "filling" and we are indeed *poor in spirit*. Being poor may conjure up ideas of physical and social poverty, but it actually means total dependence on God, and realizing our sinfulness! It is the realization that we are sinners without any righteousness of our own. We are saved by the grace and mercy of God alone! *Poor in spirit* applies to our daily lives as we strive to be humble and surrendered, where we do not look to ourselves, but to God. It is where we have a Christ-centered drive and not a self-centered drive to life and relationships; this is the "letting go and letting God" concept. So, we are able to see through our poverty and discover it is much better to be in Christ and His fullness and not in ourselves. It is letting go of our ways to surrender to His Way! The preface to the Matthew passage is the word *blessed* or *happy*, which means we are fortunate to realize who we are in Christ. We are overjoyed because of what Christ has done for us and this gives us our fullness; He is our fullness (John 8:32). We rejoice because we are a part of His Kingdom. See how this all fits together? The cure for physical and spiritual poverty is the realization of what really is important, and who we are in Christ! Humbleness is the fruit that shows fullness has taken hold in our lives.

Therefore do not let sin reign in your mortal body so that you obey its evil desires. Romans 6:12

The opposite of this concept is being prideful and self reliant, to the exclusion of allowing Christ to work in you, or allowing Him to use you to help others. In so doing, you are keeping yourself and others in spiritual and physical poverty, and oppression (Luke 18:9-14; Rev. 3:17-19)!)
Galatians, chapter five, gives us two sets of *fruit* that we can choose to produce.

There is the one found in verses 19 to 21 that is the rotten scum of life and that creates division and strife, or the one found in verses 22-23 which will produce goodness as we build one another up. In addition, verses 24-25 give us the reason for our motivation and pursuit. God's Word tells us that we choose the ways of adultery, fornication, and impure thoughts that make us eager for destructive behaviors, and pronounce them to be pleasure. These are what the Bible calls *uncleanness*. These are what create relationships filled with hostility, quarreling, jealously, anger, selfish ambitions, and divisions between people and God. The focus is on envy, drunkenness, wild parties, and all kinds of sin. This attitude conveys the idea that everyone else is wrong, and those who will agree with you become desired allies! The

Bible gives us a harsh warning that if we pursue these things, then workable relationships cannot be built. Nor can one be formed with God, as you will impede His presence with you. You will not inherit the kingdom of God!

Fullness is first seeking Christ and His work in you, so you are pursuing righteousness and all that is good as a way to glorify Christ as Lord. What we all need to be doing is applying fullness into our relationships; from our friendships to dating, we seek someone to be our complement—a helpmate in our service and mission for His glory. And, this is to be the same in dating as it is in marriage. This is real, authentic fullness that is essential—not only in our faith development, but also in how we are to prepare ourselves to build relationships and interrelate with others.

But seek first his kingdom and his righteousness, and all these things will be given to you as well. Matthew 6:33

This is serious business, as the "Kingdom of Heaven" directly relates to fullness as in living our lives because of who we are in Christ. That means that our identity—who we are, what we want, and where we are going—is fueled from our fullness in Christ. This is the quintessential aspect on earth we are to pursue after our salvation by what Christ has done. This was "inaugurated" for the Christian church at Pentecost and is spiritual in nature for the time being. It will "culminate" when Jesus returns, where it will involve the *Day of Judgment* and the *new heavens and new earth,* where we will be with God and Jesus for eternity! Both fullness and the Kingdom of God exist, and are concentrated in the Person and work of Jesus Christ. This means He is the one to rule our will and heart on earth, climaxing in eternity. This is where our fullness must reside! The Kingdom of Heaven produces the fullness; our completeness in Christ comes from our comprehension of who Christ is.

For he has rescued us from the dominion of darkness and brought us into the kingdom of the Son he loves. Colossians 1:13

When we are just self-seeking, we are selfish and unconcerned with eternal values or with serving our Lord. By being so, we fall into a trap—not because of God's vengeance, but because we are not doing as we should. As a result, natural consequences will take over. God's precepts are for our benefit and protection and are what is best, just as loving parents would do for their child. Fullness makes a relationship real, and is centered upon godly directions. Fullness will seek the love of 1 Corinthians 13, and will compel us with the desire to share our fullness and self with others. So, out of our fullness in Christ, we build ourselves up in Him, casting away what is wrong and replacing it with biblical character and values. This will be the foundation to create lasting bonds with others as we glorify our Lord.

Be very careful, then, how you live—not as unwise but as wise. Ephesians 5:15

Ephesians 5:15-21 gives us a picture of walking in that fullness, as people who are wise in the ways of the Lord are also on their guard against the ways of the world. We are to be careful how we live so we treat our lives and the lives of others with dignity and respect. We ought not to be careless with what is precious. We are to make the most of our lives and the opportunities He gives us. To waste it away is what a fool would do; so, let us not be fools! When we understand what the Lord wants us to do—and, by the way, this is not difficult—we will do well in life. It is not difficult because God is concerned with our character. We form our character from understanding and putting into practice this fullness.

Do not get drunk on wine, which leads to debauchery. Instead, be filled with the Spirit. Ephesians 5:18

Verse 18 tells us that we need to be filled with the Spirit, which means having great joy from our commitment to God (Nehemiah 8:10). It also means we are to seek His power with joy for the overcoming of our sins, and for the courage to witness and do ministry, even to people we do not like. This will flow into attitude number three. This joy means *radiant joy* that fills us up with the joy that flows among the Persons of the Holy Trinity. That very love which God the Father, God the Son, and God the Spirit have for one another will be in us. And, it will overflow from us to others around us! If we follow the first part of verse eighteen, we will miss out on what Christ has, because our purpose and direction will become cemented in sin, and not in Him.

This *joy* spoken of in Ephesians will become sealed in us as we mature in the faith and are filled with His Word. It is the power to enjoy Him in worship and as a lifestyle that affects all aspects of our life and the lives of others around us. It *then* empowers us for His service and for His glory. It literally means music flowing from our hearts!

This fullness creates joy. This is what fuels our friendships, our search to find our love, and in making the right decisions. This is what we are to seek so it can be repeated; we are not to seek it for our betterment or attention to ourselves, but rather, for Christ's sake! It is a fullness with which we are to be completely filled. This translates into *joy* that comes from being in His Word, and because we are in Christ! This is the extra power He gives us to glorify and serve Him, and the extra power that we need to make sure we are on the right track!

Will you be controlled by drunkenness, which is any kind of sin that takes you away from God? Or, will you allow yourself to be controlled by the Spirit? Remember, He does not force you; the choice is yours—and so are the consequences and rewards. We can ruin our lives or grow in fullness. Also, remember that what you do does not affect just you, but will touch all those around you, too.

Third: Reconnection and Confession

Do not conform any longer to the pattern of this world, but be transformed by the renewing of your mind. Then you will be able to test and approve what God's will is—his good, pleasing and perfect will. Romans 12:2

Take another look at those three ageless questions of "Who are you?" "What do you want?" and "Where are you going?" So, what do you want to do in your life? Does it correspond to God's Word? Our call in life is to please God. Will you seek His Kingdom; will you be filled with fullness? This can be our joy as well as our stumbling block. We have to realize that the Fall of man defaced everything in this world, including our thinking, relationships, and sexuality! Our sin will block any attempt to seek our Lord; that is why the cross was, and is, so essential. This applies to everyone; even those of us who are fortunate to be saved by Grace are affected by sin. Christ's atonement means He covered the sin, but it still remains—lurking, destroying, and causing us to replace good thinking with bad.

This essential third attitude will allow us to recognize, then confess our sins. Confession will motivate us to yield to the work of the Spirit within us. Our confession helps remove the blockage, to allow His work to flow. His work is there; it is done. He can force it, but normally, He will not. Yes, God did so with the apostle Paul, but who of us is Paul? We still have to respond to it by faith. Sin and confession are not popular subjects. Who wants to be bothered and confronted, let alone be convicted? But, for us to grow and mature, we have to, lest we remain in those sins—and how sad that would be! The sin will cloud everything. It will blind us to truth, and from seeing the will of God for our lives. We will, instead, be lost in that jungle of despair, and end up making very poor choices for our lives, especially in our relationships! Fullness will be choked off, as well as His Kingdom, making the distance too far for us.

We have to be willing to declare: *I, as a follower of Christ, bought and paid for by His shed blood, must acknowledge my own sinful nature*. If this is not in your practice and in your mindset, you will fall way short of His plan and possibly even His redemption for you. All of humanity is fallen from God, and, we are corrupt in our thinking and actions. Unless God's Grace is not only flowing in us, but is also being emphasized and utilized, we will fail to make the right decisions. Our sinful nature directly relates to friendships, marriage, our sexual choices, and even finding our true love (if you are still single.) Each of us must commit to ongoing confession in this area, from selecting relationships, to battling lust, to growing in your marriage.

The Israelites, during the time of the judges, were at a crucial juncture, as the Philistines had occupied their land and killed thousands of them. God was neglected, His law was refuted, and His people were in bondage, all because they refused to acknowledge Him as their Lord. Instead, they prostituted themselves to foreign gods who led them into sin and ruined their lives. They lived their lives *as they saw fit*. So, God raised up Samuel to be their leader and help them see that what they saw as *fit* really was not. He further showed them how false gods and pride devastated them, so they could turn from their sins and back to Him. Samuel calls to them, after many defeats and hopeless situations, to turn back to God. And, to do this, they had to renounce all of their idols and false gods, repent, and turn to the God who served, loved, and protected them. So, the Israelites repented and recommitted themselves to God. Thus, the people were spared from the Philistines and became ready to receive the blessing of God, for the land to be healed, and for prosperity to come.

To be willing and able to confess sin will renew your mind and prepare you to be more effective in relationships because you will have given yourself to God—mind and body. Just think through what He has done for you, the incredible amount of forgiveness you have received, and your response to what He has done. It should be gratitude that leads you to desire to purge yourself of sin. When we do as we see fit, all we bring on ourselves is strife and confusion that leads to endless hurt. When we have purged the sin, and continue to do so as an ongoing venture, we will have no desire to copy the evil ways of the world. Rather, we will desire to be further transformed and renewed by God. We will be new persons, infused by the Spirit, so that all we think and all we do is pointed in His direction and call. Because of this renewal, we will know what He desires for us, what is best, and what is pleasing and perfect.

Once you were alienated from God and were enemies in your minds because of your evil behavior. But now he has reconciled you by Christ's physical body through death to present you holy in his sight, without blemish and free from accusation—if you continue in your faith, established and firm, not moved from the hope held out in the gospel. This is the gospel that you heard and that has been proclaimed to every creature under heaven, and of which I, Paul, have become a servant. Colossians 1:21-23

We have to make a commitment to acknowledge our fallen nature, and be willing and able to confess our sin and repent, which means we do not do it again. It also means to have someone hold us accountable, and that we confess our sins to God.

When we are not accountable to God and to others such as a spouse, pastor, mentor, or friend, we are free to sin, which will lead to social and physical disaster. The sin of the Israelites led to their occupation and the loss of countless thousands, all from their desire to do *as they saw fit,* which was the refusal to see their sin and recant it. Their sin was pride; it is the root of most sins. Refusing to deal with your sin will lead to pornography, flirting, inappropriate lust, jealousy, and then sexual encounters, relationship breakdowns, and perhaps, the break-up of a marriage that God brought together. Just think how devastating sexual addiction can be. If you think because you are single you are OK, or, you have a good marriage and you do not need this, know this: it will lead you to betray your spouse, your future spouse, our Lord, and you may even acquire a disease and die!

Living a surrendered, redeemed life is about seeking the Lord's will, and seeking to glorify Him!

Fourth: Be Willing to Learn About Yourself

Let the wise listen and add to their learning, and let the discerning get guidance. Proverbs 1:5

One of the themes of the book of Proverbs is the contrast between the wise man and the fool. The Word tells us the right and just way, and then, the wrong and irrational way. We need to see the value and importance of being willing to be taught and to learn. Otherwise, we will keep repeating the same patterns of wrong thinking over and over again. By refusing to learn and grow, we place ourselves in the realm of what the Bible calls the fool! I hope it is not your desire to camp in that area. Because, when we do, we delude ourselves into taking the wrong direction in life, missing God's best for us.

We have to ask ourselves, *why would I want to be a fool and miss out on so much? Why would I want to do as I see fit, hanging on to patterns and ways that do not work, going from broken relationships to more failures and more broken relationships, causing hurt, pain, and loneliness as well as depression, dysfunction, and strife?* Why? Just to hang out in our own pride? Do people actually find fulfillment in this? Perhaps we get so blinded by our pride we just never look up to see what God has to offer us in the areas of growth, healing, and learning. So, why be the fool, and miss out on so much? Just to have a little fun? To do as you see fit? Remember, that did not work for the Israelites, did it? Have you ever seen it work? In over twenty years of pastoral ministry and counseling, I never have!

Just read through Proverbs, and let God's Word reveal to you what will happen. By reading just one chapter a day, you can get through it all in one month. You will spend less than five minutes a day, and be far wiser too! The sad fact is, too many of us will not spend the time needed in the Word. Too many Christians will put their minds in the ways of the fool and not in the ways of the wise. So, we do miss out. What makes a fool a fool? The fool refuses to learn; he does not want to be told that something is right or wrong; he just wants to do his own thing. This may sound like fun, but the lifestyle of the fool results in consequences of misery that we should all pray might never happen to us.

The fear of the LORD is the beginning of knowledge, but fools despise wisdom and discipline. Proverbs 1:7

Wise people are those who are willing to grow and improve themselves. It is not an IQ thing; intelligence has nothing to do with wisdom. Some of the most intelligent people I hung out with in college and grad school, even in *Mensa* meetings, did some really stupid things, and led lives of self-destruction. I have also seen people with little education who live their lives with real, practiced wisdom. The wisest people are not perfect and they make mistakes; but, there is one key aspect that keeps them wise and blessed. They are willing to learn. They are willing and able to look at their behaviors and past mistakes, and brainstorm through the guidance of God's Word to develop the needed skills of life, and be better than they were before. By doing this, they learn how to avoid those same mistakes in the future. The fool will keep repeating his mistakes over and over. This is why so many people go into numerous, varied relationships and marriages; they go from one that does not work, to the next one that does not work, and so on and so forth. They seem to never learn. They do not strive to make it work.

If you see yourself here, do not be dismayed. The fact that you can recognize your pride and your past refusal to learn becomes your first step. You must be willing to commit to improving yourself. These improvements are in the realm of our character, values, and ability to relate to others better, especially to our spouse and family.

You must be willing to learn about your personality and what you need to improve and work on. We will look at several key components of character in the coming chapters that will pave the way to building good, quality relationships, and a lifestyle that is pleasing to the Lord.

How do I begin to be a person who learns? Be a person who listens! Those of you in your teens and twenties—listen to your parents. Yeah, I know how hard that is! Most of the time, they know you better than you know yourself. Do not rely only on your friends, especially if they are less mature than you. Rather, seek older people with whom you can talk. Parents need to talk to children about their sexuality, about God's plan for them, and to help them improve their character development. Deuteronomy 6:6-7 says, "These commandments that I give you today are to be upon your hearts. Impress them on your children." The commandments referred to here are the *Ten Commandments*, which include the very one about sexuality that Jesus alluded to in the Sermon on the Mount. God's design is that sex education happen in the family. This does not mean to have just one talk about the facts of life, and get it over with. It involves an ongoing conversation about bodies and the physical changes young people are going through; it also includes dating, marriage, how they feel about people of the opposite sex, and responding to questions. It involves different kinds of conversations at each stage of the seasons of life and spiritual development.

So, no matter if you are 15 or 115, commit yourself to listen to others, and take the time to observe your own behaviors. You can do this by finding a good Christian mentor of the same sex as you, with whom you can talk and learn from. If you do not have parents that are mature, if you already missed that season of your life, or if growth and learning did not take place in you, do not be dismayed. It happens this way with many people. Make the commitment now to grow. The classic disciplines of the Christian faith are your keys too, as well as devotions, getting into the Bible, Bible study, good Christian fellowship, and being in a quality church where you can worship, and where God's Word is proclaimed with power, conviction, clarity, and truth.

Putting It All Together

But the fruit of the Spirit is love, joy, peace, patience, kindness, goodness, faithfulness, gentleness and self-control. Against such things there is no law. Galatians 5:22-23

Ask yourself, *am I really mature enough to share myself with someone else for the long run? Do I spend too much time at work? Are there other things cluttering my time and attention that are wrong, or need to be cut back? Are there unresolved issues? Am I clear of my past? Is my attitude and relationship with Christ employing and empowering me, or is it my will and determination? Are the first three attitudes permeating my life and infusing me with the Holy Spirit? If not, what is in the way?*

Once we get ourselves properly lined up with God and His will, a whole new world opens up. We will build the right character, maturity, and mindset as we emulate the Fruit of His Spirit. Then, His plan starts to become clear as we become more comfortable with and able to make the right choices in our relationships.

If you only seek what you can get, you will end up in despair! You will not be able to build quality relationships or compliment others because you are not seeking to bring yourself into the relationship as much as you are seeking to take or get from it. What we bring must come out of a life filled with Christ. Whether you are in ministry professionally or not, we all have the same job—to know Christ, to grow in Christ, and get the word out about the Word. To help you further in this pursuit, seek people who will bring out the best in you, and will be your partners and companions in the exciting, adventurous journey of life. This is especially important when it comes to your spouse or that special someone who will be your spouse. If you are married, your relationship priority is to make your spouse that special someone!

What we have been talking about may seem difficult, and perhaps even overwhelming, but take this to heart: *God does not call you to do anything that He has not empowered and enabled you to do!* The cross is the proof text of how far He will go for you!

Our God has rescued you from your sin through an event, the depths of which we can never fathom. We are not good enough on our own, but He makes us good enough! Our sins have built a chasm that totally cut us off from a relationship with and salvation in Him. In our election and acceptance of Jesus as Savior by faith alone, making Him Lord over all, we freely obligated ourselves to die (get rid of) to our old nature (sin), and be totally reborn (recreated) in the new nature that He offers us. His living a sinless life in our place, and His death on the cross to pay our penalty of sin not only purchased our redemption, but it also allowed us to identify with Him in an intimate way.

Thus, God Himself, from His immeasurable love, paid our debt and freed us from His wrath. So, we must ask ourselves, *what now? What do I do? How will I live? Will I do as I see fit* (God will let you), *or, do I go His way, the best way?* Do we allow Christ's love to motivate and control us, or do we go it alone? If we really, truly believe in Him with sincere trust and obedience, then results will come. We must allow that result of fruit (Galatians 5:22-25) to reside in us.

For Christ's love compels us, because we are convinced that one died for all, and therefore all died. And he died for all, that those who live should no longer live for themselves but for him who died for them and was raised again. 2 Corinthians 5: 14-15

I firmly believe that the Love He has demonstrated for us is the stimulant of life, the prime directive for us to live out, our model to follow, and what we are to show to others. We are secured in eternity; our life here is a learning experience, molding us for our life to come. What we do here will echo throughout eternity, so, let us make the most of it! By focusing on what is important, we are motivated to be much more than we could ever be on our own. What is it? *Relationships!* It is living out our lives, centered upon His glory, so our lives *ooze* Christ-like character and personal growth and striving for greater heights, good works, and personal growth. So, our goodness by what He has done for us becomes intertwined with distinction for one another. It is not because we earn anything, but because we are filled with gratitude which translates into compassion and friendship with others.

When we learn and apply these four primary attitudes, then Christ is glorified; moreover, quality relationships are built and are kept! This happens best when we realize that Christ paid our debt in full!

And he died for all, that those who live should no longer live for themselves but for him who died for them and was raised again.
2 Corinthians 5:15

CHAPTER II
THE QUEST FOR AUTHENTIC LOVE

One of the teachers of the law came and heard them debating. Noticing that Jesus had given them a good answer, he asked him, "Of all the commandments, which is the most important?" "The most important one," answered Jesus, "is this: 'Hear, O Israel, the Lord our God, the Lord is one. Love the Lord your God with all your heart and with all your soul and with all your mind and with all your strength.' The second is this: 'Love your neighbor as yourself.' There is no commandment greater than these." Mark 12:28-31

In the jungle of life and relationships, especially in marriage and the dating world, one of the key, essential paths we need to be on is that of love. But, what is it? How do we find it? Without knowing what to look for, we will not be able to navigate away from the dangers of life. We will confuse falsehoods of lust as love; we will rely on feelings that mimic love, but are not real, authentic love. We will build our relationships on confused feelings derived from false data, and, in so doing; we will not be able to build competence or eminence in our relationships. We will be left with shallow, meaningless, self-centered, one-way associations, without any depth or real meaning.

If we get love wrong, or confuse it with something else, we will end up with loose associations. We will not have in-depth relationships. We have to know what love is. It is essential to the world of relationships! This is the spotlight that will light our path through the jungle as Christ lights up our life, a spotlight to guide and show us where to go, where to turn, and what to avoid. This is paramount for all serious relationships, and essential in marriage. It is the light of love to show you the right path, and allow you to understand and practice real, authentic love. You need to be able to find, build, and maintain relationships and community because you cannot practice what you do not know.

HAVE YOU EVER WONDERED WHAT LOVE REALLY IS?

Surely goodness and love will follow me all the days of my life, and I will dwell in the house of the LORD forever. Psalm 23:6

What is love? Have you ever wondered if your understanding of love is the right understanding? Most people are emphatic that they know what love is, but if you ask them to define love, you will get either silence or lyrics from love songs. Whether you think you may be right or you feel you may not understand love at all, we all need to have a solid biblical view of love before we can effectively proceed to engage in, or build on a good, loving, Christ-centered relationship. If not, we will just rely on our feelings and what others and the media have to say. This will cause distortion in our thinking, creating disorientation and confusion that will adversely affect our ability to love and to discern who is right for our mate selection, or how to deal with our spouse. And, when we do get into a relationship, an unhealthy attitude of love will adversely affect our growth and ability to build that relationship. True love will be absent—in either the giving or receiving of it! So, what is love? So much poetry and beautiful prose have been written over the millennia of human experience to try to capture its purpose and meaning. All of humanity, in all cultures, places, and times has sought out the meaning of love. We have the incredible depth of the Shakespearian sonnets and poetry from master wordsmiths. But, even the greatest writers have defused their views through their personal experiences, emotionalism, experimentation, the seeking of desires, trying to add logic and reasoning, and seeking a higher being, to name a few. We hear contemporary songs that have no real, ponderous thinking to them at all, just mindless dribble from confused minds seeking rhymes and an audience—without any real, authentic meaning. It is ironic that most of these wordsmiths and artisans have messed up relationships themselves. So, how can we learn from them?

In my personal quest for love in my youth, I focused on music. Two of my favorite songs way back when I was dating were, "Love is a Many Splendored Thing" and, "I Want to Know What Love is." Both of these songs ask the question, *what is love?* As with many love songs, these two did so with high energy and enthusiasm. That "love" was exciting and inviting, and was only found in another person. Yet, these ideas of love from songs and friends left me confused, not really knowing what love was, yet thinking I did. Perhaps you, too, are confused. Through my experience in marriage counseling, I have found that most Christian couples and many pre-married couples have no real grasp of what biblical love is. Thus, they would be trying to dive in at the shallow end of a pool without having the deep waters of real love to smooth the impact.

Perhaps, you are thinking that the relationships you seek will fill that void of loneliness and add meaning and purpose to your existence. And, if you are dating or married, this comes as a foundation of whom and how you are and what you do. This means that how you handle biblical precepts will influence who and what you do in your mindsets, behaviors, and actions. Perhaps, you have a favorite love song that motivates and thrills you with feelings of anticipation and excitement. But, will you be practicing love? Will that be real, authentic love? The media and our culture have enslaved and confused many people into thinking that they know what love is. Have you considered that what our culture has to say about love is just a façade, with no real backing behind it? Like a house on a movie set, just the front part is built; so, there are no real rooms, no working plumbing, no utilities, no roof—when it rains, you get wet. Yes, it may look good, but there is nothing there to make it a home, not even a bed. Not having real love will leave you empty and alone in a house that is only a façade, and not a home.

When we are seeking, from friendships to romantic love and fullness, we will apply what we think love is, causing our relationships to be skewed. It will also flow to other areas of our thoughts and lives, causing further harm and confusion. We then pass all of this on to our progeny and others around us. The quest of love will eventually cross into theological love if we really desire to seek and apply what God has to say about it. But, we have to get this right, too. Many people have said, *God Himself is pure love,* to the point that all God is to them is love. They leave out the rest of His characteristics. Thus, love runs the full spectrum from romanticism and the quest for personal satisfaction, to God, and the meaning of life. When you have the wrong idea and definition of love, it will adversely impose on all those other areas in your life.

A new command I give you: Love one another. As I have loved you, so you must love one another. By this all men will know that you are my disciples, if you love one another." John 13:34-35

The other end of the quest for love is to ignore it, or use it wrongly. Not loving, or loving the wrong thing will lead us far away from God's truth and perfect plan for us. The wrong use of love can be sin. When we do something wrong against God, it not only affects us as an individual, but, it also affects everyone around us, such as our family, friends, and the rest of the body of Christ. Even God Himself, who is not affected by, but is hurt by our practice of sin, is included. God is Holy. His character and who He is remains unaffected. However, He is saddened that we choose to ignore Him and seek false truths and created things over the Creator. Sin is a disease that spreads and builds, one into another, just like cancer. It starts with a single cell that mutates, builds upon its self, then multiples and mutates further until it starts spreading into and throughout the whole system. Malignancy occurs because the spread is not reversible, and soon affects the entire body. In the case of the Christian, false love and pride will affect the whole life of the person— not just the physical body, but also the body of Christ. What does sin affect? What does improper love do? The body of Christ, the people who claim Jesus as Lord, and those with whom we are in fellowship together, can be affected and even destroyed. Then, the Gospel and the Truth are muted!

HOW IS LOVE SPELLED OUT IN THE BIBLE?

Do not love the world or anything in the world. If anyone loves the world, the love of the Father is not in him. 1 John 2:25

In the Old Testament, the Hebrew word most often used for love is *hesed*, and refers to a covenant of love that is promised or owed (Hosea 1:1). Sometimes, it refers to being merciful (Psalm 23:6). Throughout the centuries, Jewish commentators have stressed that it is God's love for Israel. It basically means because God promised to love you, you must (as in He commands it) respond in kind to others around you in His covenant (other Jews). It is a replicable relationship formed by God's covenant with us; thus, we respond to others as God has chosen to deal with us. Even in the Old Testament, this love could not be forced or compelled even though it was commanded; rather, it was freely and graciously given. That is how God deals with us—freely and graciously. It is a love, not based on feelings, but a choice, as in marriage, to say *I do* and follow through with *I will, and not only just when I feel like it!* This is what it means to Christians under grace: *because God loves me even though I do not deserve it, I can respond to His love in appreciation by loving others He has chosen to love.* He loves us; so we are to love others, even though we do not have to.

In the Greek, there are four words that we translate as *love*, two of which are found in the New Testament. The four words are *agape, phileo, eros*, and *stergo*.

The first is *phileo*, which means to have a brotherly love for others. It implies a deep-rooted affection. It means *brotherly love*, and is where we get our word for the City of Brotherly Love, Philadelphia (Matthew 19:19b). This word implies that we go beyond superficial relationships and strive for deep ones without being shallow or pretentious (Matthew 5:44).

The second word for love in the Bible is *agape*. This word was used in classic Greek literature to refer to someone who was generously favored by a god. It conveys the idea of a person giving all of his or her love or favor to someone else other than self. It is a love of self-sacrifice and response (John 21:15). It is a love that is not earned; rather, it is given freely. It also refers to parents giving all of their love to their child. In the New Testament, *agape* love is used to make a similar point, as God gives each of us all of His love. *Agape* is also the most common word used both as a noun and a verb in the New Testament. The greatest example of *agape* love is what our Lord Jesus Christ did when He died for our sins. God showed His love by taking our place, and the wrath and punishment for our sins. He paid that price through His sinless life and His sacrifice on our behalf. Consequently, God's *agape* love rescued us from the punishment that we deserved. We received His favor without earning it.

There are two other types of love in the Greek that are not found in the Bible. The first one is *eros*, which usually refers to sex and the love between a husband and wife. It is more than just sexual ecstasy because, in classic Greek, it also includes embraces, yearning, and caring. But, in passages such as Ephesians 5:25 where we are called to love our spouse romantically, the word used is not *eros*, rather, *agape*! So, as a Christian, we are to have a deeper love than what we see in the media and society, one that is not based on eroticism. *Eros* has noun and verb forms that we find in the New Testament for *lust*, such as *epithumeo* (1 John 2:16).

The second love that is popular in evangelical circles is *stergo*, also not found in the Scriptures. It normally refers to the love between parents and children, or the love between people and their leader who has responsibility over them. What we learn from these Greek words *agape*, and *phileo*, used in the Bible, is their emphasis of real, authentic love, without pretensions or expectations (1 John 4:7-11). The other two words imply strings attached, expectations needed to make them work. They refer to lust, which is a pretender to love, and the reason they are not used for *love* in God's most precious Word. They refer to a connection that must already be there, such as a parent and child. Parents do not love another's child as they do their own. As Christians, we may know all about love from books and sermons; yet half of us get divorced. We may know about it beyond knowledge and insight; but we are not being wise with it. We are not applying real love into our lives, connections, and marriages! Let us look to God's Word and ask ourselves, *am I applying this? If not, why not? How can I do so?*

Love According to 1 Corinthians 13

If I speak in the tongues of men and of angels, but have not love, I am only a resounding gong or a clanging cymbal. If I have the gift of prophecy and can fathom all mysteries and all knowledge, and if I have a faith that can move mountains, but have not love, I am nothing. If I give all I possess to the poor and surrender my body to the flames, but have not love, I gain nothing.
1 Corinthians 13:1-3

Most pastors have stated, in wedding homilies and sonnets, that this is the marriage passage, a love a man and woman share together in matrimony. This passage, of course, applies to marriages and we will be talking about that later. However, this passage had nothing to do with weddings and everything to do with how the people in the church were to treat one another! In fact, this passage is in the context of spiritual gifts, how each Christian is to operate in the world and in the church with the gifts and abilities God has chosen to give (1 Corinthians 12:1-14:40). These are the operational parameters to our behaviors. They are not limited to marriage; rather, this love is to be extended to all relationships. *Agape* love does not have a target; it only has a response and a choice. It does not have the boundaries that *hesed* had in the Old Testament. It does not apply to only those to whom we want to give it. It does not have attractiveness or even *like* in its sites; it is an expression of grace that has all of humanity as its audience!

When a computer is programmed, the program runs because the language has mandated what the program is to do. Within this language of computers, there are operational instructions called *parameters*, which tell the program what it can and cannot do. Thus, the program can only operate within its own guidelines, or *parameters*. In contrast, a virus is designed to do the opposite. That is why they are so destructive, and can eradicate files as well as the computer! We must look at this passage as our parameter, our guideline as to how we must execute the gifts we are given, exercise the passion of what Christ has done on our behalf, and proclaim the truth. Our operational parameter in relationships—how we operate and relate—is to be love. We must stay clear of viruses that will destroy it.

This passage is our template on how we must behave toward one another. We can do our best in trying to be a good person; we can be in a good church filled with wonderful programs and staffed with gifted people. We can be in a magnificent cathedral, reaching upwards, manifesting, and pointing to the glory of God. We can be pouring out our time and resources in serving Christ. However, if we are doing it for ourselves, out of selfish gain and not out of real love, we end up accomplishing nothing. We become just an annoying noise to the neighbors we are called to reach. Even having great faith is useless, and probably not even real, if love is not coupled with it. Without love, our relationships are shallow and ineffectual. And, we can even become the hated "ex" in the relationship. We can become a person who is broken and confused, prideful and arrogant, steeped in bitterness and dysfunction, all from failing to embrace what love is. Therefore, we will have haplessness, hopelessness, loneliness, and hurt as our guide, as our identity. How sad that can be!

First Corinthians 13:1-8 shows us the path and way for our Christian life and walk. As Christians, we are to imitate Christ, and work within His parameter, which is love. This passage is a character description of who Christ is, and it must be the character description of our actions and our behaving responsibly in all that we do.

For a Christian, the proper building of relationships is always within the parameters of love with no strings attached, just as God Himself works through all of His characteristics in love. By understanding love, we can also understand God, and who we are in Him; God is the source of love, and the example of what love is through Christ (1 John 4: 7-12). This is the love that binds us together in Christ, both with one another, and with the One to whom we commit our lives.

What Love Is, What Love Means, How Love is an Action!

Love is patient, love is kind. It does not envy, it does not boast, it is not proud. It is not rude, it is not self-seeking, it is not easily angered, it keeps no record of wrongs. Love does not delight in evil but rejoices with the truth. It always protects, always trusts, always hopes, always perseveres. Love never fails. 1 Corinthians 13:4-8

When God tells us that love is patient, He means love endures a long time. Love helps us endure extreme hardships as we keep our eyes upon our Lord. It is longsuffering, with the focus on accommodating others and not ourselves, so we can give others room to grow and time to accomplish the work that God is doing in them. When someone is abrupt with us, or when someone treats us wrongly, we are called to be patient; we cannot have everything our way all the time, every time. We cannot allow ourselves to become angry when others fail to live up to the expectations that we set for them. When our spouse angers or disappoints us, we are not to give up on him/her. Because God is patient with us, and God loves us, then we are to show patience with others. We need not become angry, but be content, for this is love. **Authentic love endures, never giving up on others!**

When God tells us that love is kind, He means it looks for a way to be constructive and useful, to invest honor, and declare others valuable. We are to look for the best in other people. We are to spend our energy and time encouraging and building up one another, not tearing others down. We are to bring the best out of our friends and spouse by always treating them with kindness. We are to tell them the truth in love and with care. You see, God takes the circumstances of our lives and uses them in a constructive way for personal growth and for better support for one another. God is not treating us as an object to be manipulated or controlled, because He has given us free will. We should do the same with one another. Therefore, we need to always be seeking the healing of relationships, and be cautious in our judgments toward others. **Authentic love cares more about others than it does about self!**

When God tells us that love does not envy, He means we need to be happy for whom and what we are. We are not to be comparing ourselves with others, nor are we to be jealous, spiteful, or possessive of others. God is in control, and He has a unique plan for each of us. When we hear that a friend receives a promotion before we do or gets something we wanted, we are to be happy for him/her. If we have a sibling who excels, we should be happy with him/her. If our neighbor has a brand-new car, we should be happy for him/her, and be thankful for the old wreck that we may drive. When our spouse is doing better than we are, we are to be happy for him/her. In other words, we are to be happy for someone else who has something we do not have, even if we do not like it. We must not become possessive, or control freaks, especially where it concerns others and our relationship with them. Being possessive and attempting to control others will cause the destruction of a church very quickly. We will soon lose our contentment, and run ourselves off into that jungle of despair, dejection, and desolation. At the very least, this will compromise its effectiveness. Love is letting go of our desires and will for a greater love we cannot receive on our own—grace. **Authentic love does not desire that which it does not have!**

When God tells us that love does not boast, He means we are not to go around bragging about our accomplishments and abilities. When this love is working, we will have no desire to impress others. Thinking that we are important is foolish, and distracting to our call and purpose in life. We are not to go around showing off our possessions. In so doing, we become patronizing to those who do not have such things. We are not to be so full of our accomplishments that we fail to see what others have accomplished. Because God loves us so much, we should have no need to impress one another. We are not to be condescending to others, especially our spouse, with pride, criticism, or contempt, nor are we to withdraw from them when they do not meet our approval. We must allow God to impress us with His greatness, because He is God and we are not. We can so relax and enjoy who we are in Christ, and that He approves us that we do not have to be in control or be the life of the party to feel secure. Nor, do we need the say—so of others since we have the approval of God, the Creator of the universe. Love is the security we have in Christ that needs nothing else for fulfillment. **Authentic love does not strut around!**

When God tells us that love is not proud, He means we are not to have inflated ideas about our significance. Being vainglorious is having a conceited mindset (the quintessential thing that God hates the most), so we must not be that way! Period! Being in Christ means we must be willing to be in relationships with all kinds of people, especially those outside our perceived likeness, such as background and/or race. We must not let our fears hold us back from one of life's most precious gifts—friendship. Not being proud means that when we make a mistake, we can own up to it and admit that we are wrong. We can go to our spouse with open hands and seek forgiveness. Pride will create contempt, arguments, misunderstandings, resentment, loss of community, and indifference. Because God loves us, He is on our side, and wants us to grow and mature in His love. We do not have to have an inflated ego about the perceived importance of ourselves. We need to seek others first and their well-being, not our arrogant and egocentric mentality. Love lifts up God, not us. **Authentic love does not puff up the giver or parade itself!**

When God tells us that love is not rude, He means that we must treat others with the respect and dignity that we would like in return. We are to concentrate on courtesy for people and property. We are to strive to have good manners, and model distinction and admiration for others. We are to treat our friends, and especially our spouse, with the utmost dignity and respect. Because God loves us, He sent His Son to cover us, and protect us from His wrath. Therefore, when we make everyday mistakes—or even the big mistakes—lightening bolts do not zap us. Because Christ loves us, we are not consumed by God's wrath, as we deserve. So, in return, we should not go around with pride or judgment, zapping others with evil looks, spitefulness, or condescending comments, thinking that we are "high and mighty," and better than everyone else. Never think of yourself as the capstone or the most important piece of the puzzle, because you are not. We should be grateful that God chooses to use us. Our goal is to worship Christ with passion and distinction. In so doing, we are to work together and not be little dictators, especially in our relationships. Love cannot be in the same room with pride or apathy, **Authentic love does not force itself!**

When God tells us that love is not self-seeking, He means that we are never to take advantage of others. We are to place others first, and ourselves after that. We are to be considerate, appreciative, and never critical. We are never to plot evil, or allow insults to get to us. We are to give allowances for the shortcomings of others. Our call is to lift one another up and be dignified, having good conduct, yet never dictating to one another our standards or demanding or manipulating others to get our way. Rather, we are to model Christ-like character, so it is contagious and inviting. Because God loves us so much, He never has a self-seeking attitude. If He did, He would never have sent His Son on our behalf. Every Christian must respect the rights and dignity of other people, and never force our will and thoughtless behavior onto others. We cannot force expectations or demands to our friends or our spouse. We need to be happy when others around us experience success and growth, and never be jealous. Love is the seeking of His truth, and finding a way to bring it to others. **Authentic love does not have a "me first" attitude!**

When God tells us that love is not easily angered, He means just that. We are not to be touchy, easily provoked, fretful, resentful, suspicious, or oversensitive with our feelings. We are to be very slow to get angry, and we are not to let little things cause us to "fly off the handle." Because God loves us so much, He did not allow His anger to wipe us out of existence when we so much deserved it. Instead, He allowed His drama of redemption to unfold throughout history, climaxing with the Person and work of our Lord Jesus Christ. We need to try to understand other people, and place ourselves in the shoes of another, respectfully. We need to listen, and not allow our hostile feelings to get the best of us. We are not to let the sun set before we extinguish our anger with our spouse. Since God is patiently working in us, we should reciprocate with the understanding of the debt we owe to God and the unfathomable love and concern He has for us. Love put us in another's shoes. **Authentic love is not touchy or resentful; it does not "fly off the handle!"**

When God tells us that love keeps no record of wrongs, He means we do not go around with a list, writing down or keeping track of the faults of one another. Rather, we are to look for the positive things that happen in our relationships, and to affirm others. We are to seek reconciliation and forgiveness, never strife or dissention. We should not go around with a negative attitude, but, rather, with one that is positive, enthusiastic, and equipping to God's people. We are not to keep track of the mistreatments or carry the baggage we may receive from friends or our spouse. Because God loves us so much, He does not keep a scorecard of our sins as long as we honestly repent of them. We do not need to reflect or gossip about the flaws of other people in order to elevate ourselves. God refuses to do that to us. Love lets things such as resentment and anger go, so they do not build up and destroy us and our relationships. **Authentic love does not keep a scorecard!**

When God tells us that love does not delight in evil, He means we should not enjoy it when bad things happen to others. When others plead or grovel, we should feel their plight and act upon it. We not only do not need to enjoy doing bad things to each other, but we must refuse to allow evil to happen. We should feel badly when we see others being hurt. Compassion is one of God's great characteristics, and we should strive to our fullest to model it to one another. We must be filled with compassion in all of our relationships, especially those with our family and spouse. We are to refuse to think evil or let any harm come to them, by word or deed. Because God loves us so much, He is deeply grieved when we do not follow His example and His will. We are not to put others down in order to make us feel good about ourselves. Love hurts even when an enemy is down. **Authentic love does not delight in evil!**

When God tells us that love rejoices in truth, He means when we see injustice corrected, and people treating others with respect, kindness, and honesty, we should feel wonderful. Because God loves us so much, we should live our lives so that we reflect a God of truth and justice. Thus, we should find delight when we see justice being played out in others. As Christians, we should get excited when justice prevails, and we should be mad enough to do something when injustice occurs, and we see the rights of others being violated. We should realize how much God rejoices when we personally stand up to the pressures of life, and prevail with integrity and truth. We should stand up, affirm, and support our friends and spouse, never lying to them or manipulating situations. God's Word is His love and truth. When we get into it and live it, we are showing Christ the love He deserves. **Authentic love takes pleasure in truth!**

When God tells us that love always protects, He means we should allow love and trust to endure. We are to accept and stand with others, believing in the best in others. We can swallow the bitterness that some relationships can bring us by coating them with the sugar of love. With this kind of love, we can feel protected, and, in return, protect those around us. This does not mean we become security guards; rather, it means our actions and attitudes should be such that they project protection, and not destruction. Because God loves us so much, He does not forsake us, even though others may do so. People will always disappoint us, and we will always be disappointing to those around us, but God will never disappoint us. Love perseveres, and is an easier route than running off and abandoning relationships to which we have made a commitment. We need to protect our friends and spouse, and realize that even though they will disappoint us, we should deal with it using the correct, encouraging attitude. We should realize how much God is grieved when we fail to walk in His path for our lives, and when we do not trust His protection. Love is always on the lookout for the best interests and protection of others, where gossip and strife cannot function. **Authentic love has staying power!**

When God tells us that love always hopes, then we should be assured He will give us a future. We should be confident that when things are going bad, they will always get better, and that there is hope because our circumstances will always change. We should never lose hope. Because God loves us so much, He always has hope for us. God is patiently working in us, and when we understand what God has truly done for us, we should have as much hope as we could ever need. We will be able to see the need and the potential of others, the hope that God gives them, and how we can be ambassadors of this hope. We will also see how we can bring our relationship with our spouse to a deeper level of love and commitment. Love will see the potential in other people, what they can accomplish and become, and not hold them back out of our jealously. **Authentic love always is enduring and points to the future!**

When God tells us that love always perseveres, He means that real love has staying power; it will last, and not fade or weaken. Thus, we can have confidence in God, and others, to hang in there and keep going strong, especially when things get tough. Because God loves us so much, He will stand with us, and even carry us through our difficulties and upsets. Even when we feel we have reached rock bottom and have no hope, when we are filled with despair, God is carrying us because He loves us. Real love will never fade or become obsolete. It will remain standing when all else has gone to ruin. This love will destroy rumors and gossip, and cause us to believe the best about one another until proven otherwise—by facts. We will be able to maintain our relationships with friends, and with our spouse, and not give up in times of dire stress and confusion. When we do not have preserving power in our love, we will fail at our relationships, especially our marriage! Love carries us to the ultimate hope, and points us to the cross and the eternity to come. This love will show us that what we do and learn here on earth will echo for eternity. **Authentic love refuses to quit!**

GOD'S LOVE MUST BE OUR MODEL FOR LIFE

Dear friends, let us love one another, for love comes from God. Everyone who loves has been born of God and knows God. Whoever does not love does not know God, because God is love. This is how God showed his love among us: He sent his one and only Son into the world that we might live through him. This is love: not that we loved God, but that he loved us and sent his Son as an atoning sacrifice for our sins. Dear friends, since God so loved us, we also ought to love one another. No one has ever seen God; but if we love one another, God lives in us and his love is made complete in us. 1 John 4:7-12

God, through His Word, is pronouncing to us that the effects and results of love will live far beyond the moments of our life. When we pass on into eternity, and our frail, mortal bodies are laid in the grave to rot, what we have done on this earth, and who we were, will still echo to all those whom we have touched. Such deeds of love will never rot. When real, authentic love is in our lives, it is endowed with an eternal quality, because God is empowering that love.

So, we need to take this seriously and with confidence to allow love to flow into us from Christ, and, in return, flow out from us to those around us. God's love is the ultimate power for the Christian. Character, and the love that infuses it, will be the only thing we produce that we will take with us into Heaven——the only thing that matters. Love has power that transcends human logic and emotions. So, while we remain here on this earth, let us perform our life with love! Allow your relationships to be built on love instead of the pride and spite we so often dish out.

If you are thinking, *wait, I might get hurt.* or, *I have been rejected after I spent so much of my time and energies on so-and-so.* Well, take to heart this valuable point; you did not waste your time. Giving love and time to others, even when we do not get anything back or even if we get hate thrown back at us, is never a waste of time. Emulating and fostering real love is never a waste, because we followed Him! Love is not about our circumstances; it is about Christ working in us. Remember, God has borne your hurt too!

When love is practiced, our relationships are certain to succeed. When we practice love, we are both trusting and obeying our Lord, doing His prime will. We can take to heart that the love we give will never be defeated, no matter how poorly people treat us in return, or, only appear to be playing their part. When we give love and it is not returned, the hurt and rejection we receive is not in vain. We may feel hurt, confused, and not understand what has happened or why we did not succeed. But, in God's eyes, we did succeed. Our time of giving love did not go to waste! We all, at some time, will experience love for someone who does not return it to us; perhaps you were once the one who did not return it to someone else. There are a multitude of reasons for that. Maybe the love was not meant to be; perhaps he/she was the wrong person for you. Maybe you got your signals crossed, or maybe you were too afraid to take the chance. Maybe the fear of being rejected consumed you, so, you are alone now. Your hurt has become your identity, while love and relationships go unmet and undone. If this is your life, remember: Love is never offered in vain. Your hurt has not been borne alone!

LOVE IS A SPIRITUAL FRUIT

Therefore, as God's chosen people, holy and dearly loved, clothe yourselves with compassion, kindness, humility, gentleness and patience. Bear with each other and forgive whatever grievances you may have against one another. Forgive as the Lord forgave you. And over all these virtues put on love, which binds them all together in perfect unity. Colossians 3:12-14

Love is a spiritual fruit that is built from real, godly character and commitment. It is the fiber of our moral center that stretches throughout our being, embracing and holding together our relationships when it is sealed as a choice and commitment, not just a feeling. Love will synergistically combine with the other characters of our Lord that flow from the Fruit of the Spirit (Galatians 5:22-23). This fruit will promote our ability to relate and grow in all of our relationships, to better others as well as ourselves.

Most people assume that love is the most important thing in a marriage, or the most important reason to get married! You will frequently hear people on TV, in the movies, out in the streets of life, and even in the church saying, *I do not need to work on love and relationships, it will just happen. And, if not, it was not meant to be. I can get out of it if it does not work out.* How sad that philosophy is! But, when you carefully examine love as seen in the Bible and not as seen on TV, you will find that love is a choice. Love is a choice—to have it and work on it. Love is a choice over our desires and over and against any feeling or aspiration of what we may want it to be or mean.

Love is a choice that also happens in a seemingly magical and metaphysical way, as poets have tried to explain throughout the millennia. But, is that it? As we discovered in the last chapter, the Bible tells us that love is more than a feeling; it has segments and characters to it. Love is also a choice, a decision that must be perused and worked on. In our human mind, we may see it as magical, as if it "just happened," but, without pursuing its true meaning and character, it will dispel and waste away. So, when we do receive that spark of love that we cannot explain, in order to keep that magic, that romance, that spark going, we are required to do something about it. If we do not work on it, the spark that was once there will vanish as quickly and as suddenly as it came. It will fade into the night, leaving us in the darkness of the jungle of relationships, lost and confused. We keep that flame from being blown out by our understanding and modeling of the character of love. So, as it becomes contagious and spreads, it flames and excites, burns and grows, so the winds of the ups and downs of a relationship will not blow it out!

We do not necessarily *fall in love* as the love songs and movies proclaim, because, you may well fall *out* of it faster than you fell *in* it! If you never choose to make a commitment with love, you will never have it; or, if you do, you will not keep it! Love is a verb; it requires action that is implied for being a verb—action to do something with it. What are you doing with it? Are the precepts of 1 Corinthians 13 being put into action with your friends, family, acquaintances, and your spouse? If not, what is in the way of that verb action?

If you ask most couples who are thinking about marriage, or who are already engaged, why they are getting married, they usually will say: "Why, we're in love." It has been through studying the Word, plus over twenty years of pastoral counseling experience that has prompted me to question the validity of this motive. Yes, love is essential and powerful! However, if that is all you have, you will end up with nothing! The number one mistake people make when they date is to look just for love. The number one mistake married couples make is thinking that their love is all they need. This puts their brains "on hold" from everything else. Yes, love is putting the precepts of 1 Corinthians 13 into action, but most people, including Christians, do not even know what real love is! So, the precepts they are using in the place of love, thinking it is love, are *fuzzies* at best or feelings and desires that mimic love. Choosing a life partner should never be based on love alone. A marriage cannot last on love alone. This may sound like crazy talk, but think it through. Have you ever seen a relationship work with just love? No, not for movie or TV stars who have everything going for them, not for the singers who sing about it, and not even for the Beatles! Because, they do not know what love is, so they cannot really put it into practice.

For although they knew God, they neither glorified him as God nor gave thanks to him, but their thinking became futile and their foolish hearts were darkened. Romans 1:21

Have you ever known someone to get married to a person they did not love (other than Anna Nichole Smith, the model born in 1967 who marred the billionaire oil tycoon J. Howard Marshall II, born 1904; married June 27, 1994; he was many decades her senior and he died a few months after the wedding), or Britney Spears' two day marriage? Most, if not all, people who get married, do it for love; yet, according to most statistical evidence, fifty percent will divorce in less than five years. So, what happened to the love? If love is all we need, should it not have worked out? Why did it not work? Because, there never was real love, they misunderstood what love is, they had nothing but love, or they had some real love, but did not work on it, so it dissipated. Perhaps, they let that spark of love flame out in neglect, so that there was a huge vacuum in their relationship! Love should not be the horse in front of the cart. Love alone cannot influence a relationship. Love needs to be a result of, not a cause for getting married. Love is the result of a good marriage, not the fuel to make one. Love is an attitude that is followed by action; when this does not happen, love will sit and go nowhere.

Just think this through: how much would your marriage, your family relationships, friends, or people at school or at the office improve if you were practicing these love truths—even if they were not! The world says that love must flow two ways, but God says otherwise. Yes, it is better when both parties in a relationship are practicing the elements of 1 Corinthians 13, but we are called to love even when others do not!

We are to be fueled and empowered by love through all situations. And the incredible news from His Word is that love is already deep within us. All we have to do is learn to let it come up to the surface as a fountain of *living water* (John 7:38), so it infuses us and touches others. God does not just command us to love; He has fashioned us to Love! We already can do it, we already have it at our disposal and He keeps giving love to us abundantly. He designed us to commune and to communicate, so when we fail at it, we fail because we are not working on, or in it.

Christian love is the turning of our backs to self-concerns and facing forward to our relationships with family, friends, and neighbors. It is the surrender of our will to His. Because, if love does not take us beyond our self-interests, then what we have is lust, and not love! Then, as the passage says, we are just noise that has no reason or purpose. Out of true love, God the Father gave us His Son, and the Son gave us His life as a replacement for ours. The Son sent the Spirit to save us, and we should be literally overwhelmed—consumed with extreme joy and gratitude by what God has done for us. Then, that can turn and spill onto others around us. If not, then read Romans 1:21!

The key to all of this? Be willing to apply **love** and **respect** the other person, and stay **committed** to these precepts! Ephesians 5:33 states, *However, each one of you also must love his wife as he loves himself, and the wife must respect her husband.* God's Word gives us the plan; we have to be willing (the hard part) and capable (what we already have at our means) to carry it out. Love and respect traverse genders and cross lives and must cross yours by His cross to others too!

Therefore, since we have been justified through faith, we have peace with God through our Lord Jesus Christ, through whom we have gained access by faith into this grace in which we now stand. And we rejoice in the hope of the glory of God. Not only so, but we also rejoice in our sufferings, because we know that suffering produces perseverance; perseverance, character; and character, hope. And hope does not disappoint us, because God has poured out his love into our hearts by the Holy Spirit, whom he has given us. Romans 5:1-5

CHAPTER III
THE MYTHS OF LOVE

Now it is God who makes both us and you stand firm in Christ. He anointed us, set his seal of ownership on us, and put his Spirit in our hearts as a deposit, guaranteeing what is to come. 2 Corinthians 1:21-22

Myths are powerful influencers in most cultures and societies—Americans, perhaps, being the most allured by them. You may think myths are just for primitive tribes of people living in the jungle, but, if you think it through, we all succumb to myths at some point in time. Most anthropologists and sociologists say that all belief systems have myths at their core and beginning, and it is those myths that fuel the beliefs and faith of the religion and items to which people adhere. I am not going to take the time to challenge that assumption as applied to Christianity, because it is my belief we do not have myth, but rather, fact at our core and beginning. But, this idea of myth does play into most people's mindsets.

Take love for example. The average *Joe* and *Joann* have certain ideas, certain presumptions about love that fuel their opinions and beliefs, and which affect their actions. Most of the time, what we think about love is not fact, as we found out in the last two chapters. So, consider that your idea of love and that of most people are, perhaps, rooted in ideas that are myths. That is, they are not based on fact, but on feelings and desires derived from songs and the media, or maybe from friends. So, are you ready to be challenged about what love *is not*? If so, you will be in a much better mindset to practice and develop real, loving relationships!

When the religious leaders challenged Jesus on what was the most important law, Jesus quickly pointed to Deuteronomy 6:5. This is what is called the *Shema*, meaning, "here the Lord is One." The Israelites used this word to proclaim our monotheistic God; God is One. Thus, we respond to God with all of our being, including our heart, mind, soul, and strength.

Jesus then has us focus on one of the primary emphases of the purpose of life, which should be our pursuit of real, authentic love. This love is to be directed to God, then to others around us. But, if we have it wrong, we will end up just spilling *junk* to God and *dysfunction* to others!

We have already explored what love is, and what God's Word has to say. However, what about the other influencers that may be rattling around in our heads? Do they measure up to Scripture, or are they myths? Let us look at some of the common sayings from American and Western culture that portray love:

- Love conquers all!
- Love is enough.
- All you need is love! (By the way, that did not work for the Beatles, did it?)
- If it is true love, you will know it right away!
- If you love me, you will _____.
- I want to know what love is!
- The perfect Mr. or Mrs. "Right" will fulfill you completely!
- Having a strong sexual attraction is a sign of true love!
- I'll do my half if you _____.
- If you really love someone, you will have sex with him/her within the first month of dating!

Music, TV, movies, friends, and fairy tales all teach us, in different and creative ways, how to love. But, have you considered that they teach us the *wrong* ideas of love and relationships?

A LOOK AT SOME "SAYINGS"

Put to death, therefore, whatever belongs to your earthly nature: sexual immorality, impurity, lust, evil desires and greed, which is idolatry. Colossians 3:5

Does love conquer all? Well, this is just not so! If it were, we would have a very low divorce rate, because, I have never seen a marriage take place where the couple was not *in love*, or at least thought they were in love. Yet, over fifty percent of them are divorced within five years! If love were enough, those marriages would work out; obviously, love is not enough! Love, by itself, cannot hold two people together. As we discovered in the last two chapters, most people do not know what love is, nor are they able or willing to apply the characteristics of love that we discussed in the last chapter. They forget that love will place the interest of the other first, and, they do not. The feelings and ideas of what they think love is take the place of working on the relationship. So, communication, as well as understanding and the willingness to work together to solve problems is left out of the relationship.

In reality, there is no *happily-ever-after* or riding off into the sunset together. Relationships require effort to make them work; they just do not happen. So, our favorite movies and the romance novels do not give us proper reality; in fact, they corrupt our perspectives and thinking so we make faulty decisions. When our reality is in line with God's, and we are following His precepts, then the adventure of the relationship becomes fun, and we can ride off into that sunset. We can enjoy life better. Just know that that sun will rise the next day, and you may still be in the jungle, lost and confused— perhaps, even hurt. The effort you put forth will help keep you on the right path of developing that good relationship, as well as finding and keeping the love of your life.

Is it true that all you need is love? Well, again, no! This is a big myth! When the friendship-seeking and dating adventure is over, and you find yourself outside of the jungle and on the right path, you still need to build your house of love. The house of love is built on the precepts of character and love that were already discussed, and further constructed with the materials we will be looking at in the coming chapters.

All who make idols are nothing, and the things they treasure are worthless. Those who would speak up for them are blind; they are ignorant, to their own shame. Isaiah 44:9

If all you have is love, and, let's say that it is real, authentic, biblical love, yes, you will be doing well. However, as I have already said, most people, even committed Christians, do not operate in all of those precepts all of the time. You will get bored when your friends never develop that relationship any further, and, you will, perhaps, go on to many more, skipping from one to another, and so forth. After you marry, just about the time you move in together, you will discover that you have traded your loneliness and quest of finding a mate, which you thought was your biggest problem, for a whole, new set of problems—bigger problems—unless you see it as bigger opportunities.

How are you going to relate to each other all of the time—from the toothpaste and toilet seat to sleeping together, sharing personal items, friends, relatives, in-laws, pets, cars, your future, career—and, in addition, handling money, and rearing children? You are no longer in the dating and friend scene, where you can go home to do whatever you want. You have gone from being strangers to each other to a committed relationship with responsibilities! Change can be very difficult for some, and, if you made the wrong decision to live together first, you entered into an entire, additional set of problems, as well. Love is *not* all you need, especially if you do not know what love is!

Will the perfect mate fulfill me? NO! Nothing can fulfill you completely. As we are filled with imperfections caused by sin, so we cannot have a mindset that is perfect and understanding like that of God, who is without sin. That is why understanding and applying the precepts from Chapter I, "Preparing for Relationships with the Right Mindset," are so important! When we accepted Christ's gift of grace, we did become complete in Him. But, not as most people think. We become *declared* complete. Thus, in God's eyes, we are pure; but, in reality and practice, our sinful state is still in practice, and is active. We can strive to become more mature, which is an aspect of sanctification, but, nonetheless, we are still imperfect beings. Sin affects all we do, including our mate selection and our relational skills. So, all we do is corrupt, even while trying to fulfill His will to the best of the ability and gifts He has given us. We are not even made for this world, but rather for the life to come.

Will my expectations of, "if you love me you will…" or, if you are only willing to do "my" half, help me? No! Because, you will have no real love-only your expectations to keep you company! These will only develop into pride, and then, loneliness. If you set conditions, such as saying "I'll do my half if you…." you will stifle any love that may be there, and your will and pride will take over. You will not be able to develop any kind of godly relationship if you set up conditions and expectations. Love does not put others in a stable made of the fencing of personal desires and expectations. It just will not work; it is not biblical. All those who try, end up hurt, jumping from relationship to relationship, distancing from friends. Trying this in marriage will land you in divorce court.

If you are only willing to go half-way, doing what you think is your part and no further, you are refusing to change. Do not go from one friendship to another until you get yourself straight, because you will cause too much hurt to others. Do not even think of getting married, messing up someone else's life and the lives of generations to come. You will be on the jungle road to disappointment, disillusionment, and divorce. Selfishness takes up all of the space of relationships, and has no room in a relationship. Stay alone, buy a cat, and stay single, because you will be far happier. Yes, this is harsh, and it is sad, but it is true. In addition, you will be saved from a lot of hurt as well as from hurting others. Relationships are far too valuable and important to fool with.

You have to be willing to bend; if not, you will break! And, it will not be just you, because it affects so many others, too. In marriage, it affects the families of both of you, and any kids you might have. You have to be willing to take chances with confidence. If you are operating in God's character, it is a chance worthy to take and make. Look up and see His wonder, the wonderful things He has for you! But, you will not be able to if your vision is skewed with anything except His precepts.

You have to be willing to give at least 95 percent. If you are not, you need to work on yourself. When you are willing to give that amount, it will not be long until you will be at a 50/50 partnership. But, the key is the effort and willingness to go far beyond what you think your part is! When they feel you are contributing, your friends and spouse will feel inspired to do so, too. You will be able to cut through the tall grasses of conflict, understanding the issues and problems that spring up. Be willing to be the mower of the weeds of fear and pride that cover up relationships.

Since I already know what love is, then, I do not need to learn. And, there are a lot of people who think this way. It is called "pride;" all you have to do is look up the word, "pride" in a concordance, and see what God has to say about it! If you think you do not need to learn, then you will find yourself….stupid! Some of the "Post Modern" people have a cynical attitude and feel that *there is nothing I can learn. I will just plug in and do it.* With this attitude, you would have better odds of winning the lottery and being struck by lighting at the same time than finding happiness and contentment in relationships. You will not learn how to communicate, solve problems, or be willing to work on the relationship to make it work. You will give up, move on to the next relationship, and so on and so on! If you are not a teachable person, one who is willing to learn and to work on yourself and your relationships, you will not have a good experience. So, why bother with the stress and strife? A little work, a little love, and a heart poured out to our Lord will lead you to the happy house of a good relationship. You will be so much happier; your friends and spouse will be so much happier—even your cat will be happier! Everyone wins! It really does not take as much work as you might think compared to countless hours of arguments, dysfunction, and chaos!

I cannot love someone unless they will love me first; if…. When you seek to make love conditional, expecting the other person to do or behave as you think they should, you will see a sure sign of a coming disaster! Because, what you are, in fact, doing is telling them, "I do not trust you! I will only like you, or love you if you like or love me first, or, if you…. then I will…" You will be communicating to the person whom you claim to love and whom you want to love you, "I do not care about you as a person—your feelings, wants, or needs—only how I think and feel!" Just think it through; how would you like to be treated in this way (Matthew 7:7-13)? There can be no real love in this mindset! Nor can you place unreasonable expectations on the other person; we all need to remember what love really is!

And do this, understanding the present time. The hour has come for you to wake up from your slumber, because our salvation is nearer now than when we first believed. The night is nearly over; the day is almost here. So let us put aside the deeds of darkness and put on the armor of light. Romans 13:11-12

The only way your friends, relationships at work, acquaintances, your spouse, or future spouse can know what you feel, need, want, desire, or think, is by your telling them. If you want to be heard, you have to be willing to listen. You have to be willing to put your share of the relationship out on the table first, rather than wait for the other person. Good communication is a must—essential to the understanding of one another. We will talk more about expectations in the coming chapters.

On the other hand, there is the opposite trend to think *my friend or mate will change. Once we get to know each other, he/she will see my position and make a change.* Or worse, *once we get married all will change!* NOT! The relationship will only get worse, since the motivation to change has been removed, and replaced with the reward of attaining the goal of friendship or marriage! Remember this important fact, we humans are motivated by two things—desire and fear—just like dog training! Take away the motivation and the dog will not learn, as it is with you and me!

You can never force a person to change; they have to desire to do so themselves. And, by the way, fear is never a way to motivate love. It is good for discipline when it is in the parameters of love, as with childrearing, but, not with friends or spouse. If your future spouse is going out with friends, and partying all of the time, and you think it will stop once you say, "I do," the simple answer is *no, it won't*. You will just get frustrated and hurt. He/she will keep doing it. You will both argue. He/she will get more relentless in their lifestyle, because, you are not dealing with it, and it continues—back, and forth. The only person you can change is **you**!

Unrealistic expectations will not magically be fulfilled once you say, "I do." Those are not magic words! They are the words to commitment, not to metamorphoses. Good relationships are built on a commitment that both of you are willing to be open, and improve yourself to please the other person. This means compromise, growth, and change. And, most importantly, you will be developing good biblical character to please our Lord. This will, in turn, develop your relationship with each other!

When we accept these love myths as fact, and these pursuits as what we should undertake, we will be heading down dangerous paths in the jungle where we will only find loneliness and hurt. Such myths will block the path of quality relationships that last, especially when it comes to love and dating. They will lead you so far off the godly path that you find yourself falling off the cliffs of life and into the realm of despair and discontentment. Your relationships will fall far short of what they could have been. When we have these ideas about love from troubled sources as a template on how we evaluate others or select a mate, we will be in as much trouble as the singers and actors who made these statements and sang those songs.

These false ideas of love will also cause a fairytale mindset rather than a biblical one, or reality-based thinking. We will think we are in love when we are actually filled with the wrong idea of love, coupled with lust and desire. Therefore, we believe these statements are possible, feasible, and real. Actually, they will cause us to make grave mistakes, and mislead not only us, but also all those around us!

Still not sure? Just watch the biographies of singers, actors, and other famous people on the cable TV biography shows, or read *People* magazine! Many of those who have proclaimed such statements have not found them to be working out in their very own lives! Most of these celebrities have led very disappointing and meaningless lives. With all of their wealth and fame, they have more divorces, dysfunctional relationships, and hurt than most of us regular folks. Because they jumped from one marriage to another and one relationship to another, they have never found the contentment or happiness they thought they could have from their philosophy. Rather, they have found turmoil, discontent, and hopelessness, instead. (This comes from their statements—not mine!)

Wrong ideas of friendship, dating, and love will have grave consequences that can last for generations, as it affects us, the other person, and, in marriage, any children, both families, the extended families, friends, the church, and, of course, our Lord! Your choice is not just your choice; It does not affect only you. Therefore, be careful that you always strive to conduct yourself in the parameters of real, authentic love. In dating, choose wisely; in friendships and marriage, operate in those godly characters, and base everything on Scripture rather than on false ideas and lust!

Yes, our God is a great God of grace, and forgiveness. He will eventually work things out in your life for good (Romans 8)! But, why place yourself in strife, when you can have it so much better when you start early?

Your objective is not just to seek fulfillment or desire, but to build relationships that last, and that are impacting and real. In dating, your commission is to choose a mate with whom you can live together with unbroken devotion to the Lord. This brings the fullness that we talked about in the first chapter, to make your house reflect God, serve for His glory, and be an example to those around you.

A question I am asked a lot in singles groups is, "What about attractiveness?" Well, if you are courting, following the biblical principles (which we will talk about later), and are not attracted to each other (which, from over twenty years of experience, I have only seen this once or twice out of hundreds of couples), that is a sure sign that something is wrong.

I would like you to be free from concern. An unmarried man is concerned about the Lord's affairs—how he can please the Lord. But a married man is concerned about the affairs of this world—how he can please his wife—and his interests are divided. An unmarried woman or virgin is concerned about the Lord's affairs: Her aim is to be devoted to the Lord in both body and spirit. But a married woman is concerned about the affairs of this world—how she can please her husband. I am saying this for your own good, not to restrict you, but that you may live in a right way in undivided devotion to the Lord. 1 Corinthians 7:32-35

1 Corinthians 7:32-35, gives us a picture of the magnitude and value of relationships with love in action, both in marriage and in preparing for marriage. We need to see life as an adventure, with no time to waste. The central focus, paying close attention to verse 35, is not being distracted by things that are false and misleading to us; rather, we are to focus on Christ,

and allow Him to provide us the motivation for godly living. His precepts must reign in us so our attention is on the right track. If not, those myths and *cares* of the world—including the myths of love—will overtake us, and bring us down into the world of bad decisions, that lead to bad relationships, that produce bad living.

What do I do? Learn about real love, as we previously discussed. Understand that Christianity is about growth. It starts with profession and conversion, and keeps building into maturity. The process of Sanctification comes into play here. We need to ask ourselves, a*m I willing to reduce myself down to merely "ME," as, who I am in Christ?* Are you determined enough to strip yourself of all that you are in the world, in your career, ministry, and your church, including what your friends think of you and what you think of yourself? Are you willing and determined to hand over your true self, your simple, naked self to God? Once you are, then He can begin to do greater work in you, and in others through you. Christ will immediately sanctify you completely, and your life will be free of distractions from His character and precepts. You can be determined and persistent toward glorifying God, and Christ as your Lord (1 Thessalonians 5:23-24)!

You can start by surrendering to Him in prayer (Galatians 2:20-21; Philippians 1:6; 3:10), *Lord, show me what sanctification means; help me live, as my life is yours.* He will show you! Sanctification means being made one with Jesus. Sanctification is not something Jesus puts in you; it is He, Himself, in us (2 Corinthians 1:39). The understanding of Sanctification will allow you to be discerning of yourself, and realize that no mere person can fulfill you! No ideal guy or gal will make you complete, or fill a hole that only Christ can! No friend can take the place of God.

To completely change the black, dirty oil of our mind with the new, golden anointing oil of His love, we have to surrender ourselves to Christ. When we become a Christian, the Spirit transforms us completely, all that we are, all that we do, our will, our plans, and our opportunities (2 Corinthians 3:18). However, we cannot do this unless we give our selfish will over to His (Galatians 2:20-21)! The incentive for us to surrender to Christ is that His way is better than ours! This will directly translate into who we are, and how we are in relationships. This means there can be no perfect person; you can only seek who is best for you and be willing to work on that relationship, and on yourself.

Remember, most of the ideas people have about love are artificial and insincere. We must be prepared to recognize the real fruit over the artificial one. If not, when we think we have found love, we will only have lust and insincerity. These artificial fruits will turn into hate and indifference. When this happens, we will not be even close to expressing any kind of love, in any form. Do not let this happen to you. Do not let yourself, or the ones you love, succumb to the myths of love that only produce false expectations, and lead into the dark, forbearing jungle path of despair! Songs and movies are nice entertainment; but, they are not the reality of life. Remember, relationships are a choice. It is your choice to succeed or fail. Are you willing to succeed, knowing that so many countless millions of friendships end, and marriages fail? Being willing and able to work to understand yourself, love, and God's precepts will motivate you, and provide commitment to build your house of love. Being willing to make the other person feel they are a priority and that they are special will make that house content, too.

If you are willing to live out the art of loving, then, you will keep your relationships alive!

And do this, understanding the present time. The hour has come for you to wake up from your slumber, because our salvation is nearer now than when we first believed. The night is nearly over; the day is almost here. So let us put aside the deeds of darkness and put on the armor of light. Let us behave decently, as in the daytime, not in orgies and drunkenness, not in sexual immorality and debauchery, not in dissension and jealousy. Rather, clothe yourselves with the Lord Jesus Christ, and do not think about how to gratify the desires of the sinful nature. Romans 13:11-14

Chapter IV
KINDNESS: MAKING LOVE
REAL IN OUR LIVES

I thank my God every time I remember you. In all my prayers for all of you, I always pray with joy because of your partnership in the gospel from the first day until now, being confident of this, that he who began a good work in you will carry it on to completion until the day of Christ Jesus. Philippians 1:3-6

The character of *kindness* is the willingness to allow the love within ourselves to be poured out to others, powered by God's grace and precepts. Character is the quintessential mechanism that tells others who we are. It is the springboard from which comes all we do and say in life. It is the proof text, measuring who we are to others by what we do to others. It is the storybook of our lives that tells of our personality, moral fiber, maturity, and faith. Developing solid biblical character in the face of our experiences, both positive and negative, setbacks and triumphs, then applying them to our daily lives, will make us better, richer, and more of use to God. We will be much better able to deal with others such as friends, relatives, coworkers, and all those we touch in life, especially our spouse—or, when he/she arrives on the scene.

When we develop character from adversity, it will be the essential component to make us grow in our faith and maturity, and the proof that we have an honest, tangible, growing relationship with Christ as the Lord of our lives! Character is not just having integrity or honesty, or even doing the right thing at the right time. It is not the only aspect of a personality. What is real character? It is the ensuring of a continual, constant, living, growing relationship in Christ, which produces a synergistic combination of the *Fruit of the Spirit* found in Galatians 5:22-23 and 1 Peter 1:5-11. This is what produces good, Christ-like temperament. It is not just what Christ would do, but what He would have us do.

Character is aligning our lives so our behaviors are Christ-like. It is the fruit that the vine of our abiding in Christ will produce. Thus, we look to the life of our Lord as our prime example. We seek to know more about our Lord and Savior, so we know how He handled situations, and what He taught, so it affects all that we do, and so we know what Jesus would have us do! This alignment of our will and ways to His ways is what produces the "Fruit of the Spirit" that we find in Paul's letter to the Galatians: *But the fruit of the Spirit is love, joy, peace, patience, kindness, goodness, faithfulness, gentleness, self-control.* (Galatians 5:22-23a)

The acts of the sinful nature are obvious: sexual immorality, impurity and debauchery; idolatry and witchcraft; hatred, discord, jealousy, fits of rage, selfish ambition, dissensions, factions and envy; drunkenness, orgies, and the like. I warn you, as I did before, that those who live like this will not inherit the kingdom of God. Galatians 5:19-21

The strange thing is that many Christians just do not get it; they live their lives in the pretext of the following verses of this passage (Galatians 5:19-21). Thus, the opposites of these characters, which this passage describes as *the works of the flesh,* become the rotten personalities and dispositions. These *works* become who we are to our friends and family, being spiteful, arrogant, pretentious, and counterfeit Christians who are the destroyers of relationships, and that cause us to repeat the same bad patterns over and over. We ignore our Lord, substituting our whims and pretensions, when we could have so much more and better, but our stubborn nature will not allow that goodness to come out. So, we choose our way, and substitute the *works* for the *fruit;* in so doing, we bring strife and dysfunction to our relationships instead of His love, call, and character.

We need to be aware of our natural, sinful nature that all of us have and all of us perpetuate. This sin contains these rotten tendencies that Paul describes in verses 16-21, in action. We see lust, adultery, fornication, lewdness, and revelry to name a few. You may think, *I do not have those*; but, look further and deeper to quarreling, jealousy, anger, selfishness, envy, pride, and such. The results of these rotten fruits will cause chaos and strife to any relationship, and preclude God's working in us. Extreme division will be wedged into any relationship, preventing your receiving any good or pleasing work, as well as any blessings. It will prevent God from using you to the fullest extent possible, especially in helping others. They are the "anti-kindnesses," which cause cruelty and destroy what God has for us. Kindness cannot exist in an atmosphere of strife. You will not be a real, functioning Christian with these works. (That is what God says, not me!) You have to be willing to counteract these rotten works by committing to the good fruit of keeping your goals and focus upon Christ and His Word, so you can develop them.

Be conformed to the image of God's Son. Romans 8:29

Obviously, we cannot re-enact His character with any kind of perfection or precision. However, we can strive to do our best by the power He gives us. The fact that our Lord was also fully human and lived a life of pure perfection should give us hope and encouragement for what is *theoretically* possible, even though no one has ever been able to do so. We can strive for a goal even though that goal may be impossible. Its impossibility is no excuse not to do our utmost to achieve it.

The character of kindness will be the bond to hold us together, to make us as we should be. Without it, a wedge will form, keeping us away from those good, quality, effective relationships. You can be the wedge of works, or, the light of fruit. Which will it be in your relationships?

Be imitators of God, therefore, as dearly loved children and live a life of love, just as Christ loved us and gave himself up for us as a fragrant offering and sacrifice to God. Ephesians 5:1-2

The simple definition of "kindness" is practicing benevolence with a loving attitude towards others. It encompasses all of the aspects of love we have talked about in the preceding chapters, and synergistically puts them into practice. It is allowing our interests and attitudes to be focused upon Christ's precepts, and pouring them out on others. Kindness is the essence that shows the world that we are indeed a Christian. This character is like the fragrance coming from a flower. It will show our sweet essence and aroma to others. It is being convicted with God's Word, and then modeling it to others. It is the medium through which Christ's love becomes tangible through us, so others can touch, feel, and see it. Kindness is the subject to the object of who we are in Christ!

Kindness will replace all the bitterness, malice, and slander—all that is wrong in relationships—if we are willing to receive it from above, and will allow it to be poured out from us. It is being willing to take the risk, and go for it—regardless of the outcome.

Ask yourself this essential question: *Is the character of kindness working in me?* If you are not sure, or, if you think you are kind to others, do others agree? Here is how you can find out. Take a careful look at this character and fruit of kindness from God's most precious Word by examining the passages in the back of the book. Ask yourself: *How do I exhibit kindness in my daily life? What can I do to develop more of an attitude of kindness? What blocks the practice of kindness in my life? How can I make kindness function better, stronger, and faster, even in times of uncertainty and stress?* Then watch how the Spirit will convict you and your life will change and your relationships will be infused with kindness and contentment!

We live in a world that relishes cruelty, and considers it as the thing to do to be "cool" and accepted. A funny put down, a sly remark, a good practical joke, and the ability to be "cool" are all desirable traits. Just look at TV and the movies. Can you imagine a movie where the latest and greatest action hero is going around being kind to everyone? It would not be much of a plotline; however, how would you like to be treated in the same way as that action hero treats others? This may be fun to watch, and good for the movies and entertainment, but not for real life! The Christian is called to be higher, and, at the same time, lower—higher in our character and lower in accepting of others (as long as it does not bring us down to their level!).

By the examples from the Bible, we can get a clear picture of how we are to be kind, and how we are *not* to act. What we are *not* to do is look to the models we see in the world and media. Television and movies are the prime sources many people today look to for their role models of behavior. They see their favorite characters, and think they look cool and fashionable with their humor, comebacks, snickering remarks, and putdowns. We have to take a step back, and look at it in His light, to be willing to seek God and ask, *is that what I really want in my life?* Think it through to its logical conclusion; what is funny on TV is not funny in real life because it hurts and causes division. We do not have a team of professional writers, actors, agents, stagehands, producers, publicists, and directors helping our outcome. However, what we have is so much more—the Holy Spirit. But, like the professional actors, who are only as good as their ability to receive the direction and the writing given to them, we are only effective by being sensitive to the Spirit, and God's Word, and allowing Him to rule our hearts and motivations, so it affects our actions and behaviors. Kindness is how we are to treat one another, especially the ones we love!

The opposites to the practice of kindness are cruelty, spitefulness, being mean, and holding grudges. This can range from intently seeking to harm someone to being cruel and rude so you seem funny, or just ignoring people you do not like. It may be that you are seeking to make friends by being humorous, but is it at the expense of others? There is nothing wrong with humor, as long as it does not tear some else down. Remember, it is only funny on TV, not in your life or the lives of others! Following the ways of the world in how we treat others will only create the rotten works of strife and dissension toward them. God created us for much more, and far greater purposes. Our greatest purpose is to build relationships with Him and with others; when we ignore this, we fail in the most important aspect in life, including our relationship in Him!

UNDERSTANDING GOD'S KINDNESS

Consider therefore the kindness and sternness of God: sternness to those who fell, but kindness to you, provided that you continue in his kindness. Otherwise, you also will be cut off. And if they do not persist in unbelief, they will be grafted in, for God is able to graft them in again. After all, if you were cut out of an olive tree that is wild by nature, and contrary to nature were grafted into a cultivated olive tree, how much more readily will these, the natural branches, be grafted into their own olive tree! Romans 11:22-24

To get a better understanding of kindness, let us look at how God is kind with us. When we have a grasp of the incredible thing He has done for us, we should have the inclination to respond with that knowledge. So, it builds our faith and maturity, and pours out that essence we have learned onto others with whom we are in contact.

We can know the value of God's love and allow it to affect us and flow to those around us. When we have this knowledge affecting our hearts and feet, we can know how to build and apply a value system to last a lifetime. That way, we are living in response to His love and in the value of love and kindness. Also, by knowing more about God's kindness, we will gain a picture of His providence. This means we can be assured that God is in total control; thus, we can trust our Lord completely, whatever unfolds before us. The ultimate love of God is that He laid down His life for His enemies!

Romans 11:16-24 gives us some stern words about pride, about *not* being kind, and how we are before God. This passage gives us a warning light that

66

the oven is on and it is hot, so do not touch it. Do not touch arrogance, and do not put kindness in the cupboard where it cannot be used. This passage is also an echo of Hell, a place where kindness is absent. When we refuse to practice goodness—as in kindness—we are, in fact, bringing an aspect of Hell to others. This is a further testament to the fact that we have no right ever to be arrogant or prideful. God took the Jew's blessing away and gave it to the Gentiles, not because they were better, rather, because of belief and faith. We are in danger of rejecting God by elevating ourselves in pride, just as the Jews did.

Paul crafts an image from the workings of a tree, its roots and branches, and then equates it to the role of the Gentile and Jew. Both have a future, hope, and purpose. If you are ever discouraged and feel left out in life, you are not! His kindness is at your grasp. We can have ultimate hope and peace in Christ with no fear of rejection, because, He will not reject us when we accept His gift of grace. Even when we reject Him first, He still seeks us out. If we still refuse to go His way, we will undergo the harsh reality of consequences due to our wrong decision to flee from Him. This is not because God is an unkind killjoy, but, because of the natural laws of the universe which are there to sustain us. The sharp knife that is designed to be a tool to prepare a meal can cut our hand by our misdirection. But, His love is always there, waiting on our faith to embrace Him; so, we can feel and know His embrace is already upon us! We may not be able to always explain or understand God, but we can have faith and trust, and praise Him because of His kind love for us.

We have been grafted into His grace, made His child, saved by His grace. Yet, somehow we allow arrogance to set in, push others away, and even say we do not need God. Therefore, we cut off our roots, and in so doing, choke off our true nourishment and ability to function with character and distinction. God is the One who supports us, and we need to see that fact as the reality of our life, nourish ourselves from His presence, and draw from His streams of living water (John 3).

We cannot stand alone, thinking we are the determinists of ourselves and the world. That school of thinking has not worked; it is what fuels the misery, violence, and corruption in the world and it leads to the destiny of poor relationships, marriage dysfunction, abuse, and the loss of community. The unbelief and arrogance creates fear and brokenness, and that leads to loneliness and despair. Can we really say God will spare us when we continually disobey Him and do as we please? These verses say *no*, yet, still point to His hope and kindness.

Then, with all the severity and wrath of God in this passage is His kindness. He gives us a way, a plan, a wonderful life to be had. He does not have to; yet, He does. So, when you read, "Behold the severity (sternness) of God," we all should do just that. The severity of God includes the truth about Hell as endless suffering, and the truth of His kindness poured out to us. Kindness is not just a personality trait; it is a call, and a result of our faith. God does not force us to exercise our faith; but, when we do not put faith in our relationships, we not only cause dysfunction and even destruction, but also take the chance of cutting relationships off. Having faith and putting our faith into action will be the essential component to fueling kindness into our relationships. Your growing faith will be the visible results of that faith, impacting others and producing character.

His winnowing fork is in his hand, and he will clear his threshing floor, gathering his wheat into the barn and burning up the chaff with unquenchable fire. Matthew 3:12

Just take a look at Matthew 3:12; 18:9; 25:41-46; Luke 16:24; Mark 9: 43-48; and Revelation 14:11. The point we are to get from all of these passages is that we are meant to shudder, and think about what we are doing. God warns us; so, heed to the "fear" of Him (Proverbs 3:5), as it is the beginning of your knowledge and practice of life. If you do not tremble and feel dread, your reality will be vacant of kindness. You will be, in fact, denying God in your life, fleeing from the arms of Jesus who died to save us all from ourselves and His severity. If we want God to be kind to us, we need to do something ourselves; we need to be kind, in return, to one another. One day, the disobedience of our will and heart will end. As Romans foretells that Israel will turn, so will the Gentiles and disobedient Christians. Repentance will be to our Lord's glory, as we turn from our wicked ways to His best ways! So, I urge you to follow a mindset that believes the Bible is real, impacting, and for daily practice, even though it may seem the reverse of the ideas of today. His ideas work best because His ways are true and eternal.

Because God is kind, we are to...

Get rid of all bitterness, rage and anger, brawling and slander, along with every form of malice. Be kind and compassionate to one another, forgiving each other, just as in Christ God forgave you. Ephesians 4:31-32

68

When we have the grasp of God's kindness and love, the response that must ooze from the pores of our soul is *kindness*. Ephesians 4:31-5:2 gives us not only the picture of this happening, but also the dangers of our pores getting clogged up with pride and anger, resulting in bitterness and slander. Remember, fruit and character cost dearly; they are not cheap. They are by and from the One who bought them for us, for our betterment and for His glory. We must not take for granted what cost Him so much! Just think through how much you are loved by God. Have you realized that Christ lived and died in your place? Are you fully confident that Christ loves you, and gave Himself up for you as a fragrant offering, a sacrifice to God? Do you fully realize the magnitude of the fact that God has forgiven all of your sins, all the sins you have ever committed and will ever commit? To know these truths is one thing; to believe them helps a slight bit further. But, you have to be willing to trust and obey because, for the Christian, there is no other way. The other ways are a slap in God's face, the One who has freely forgiven you by what Jesus Christ has done. When we know these essential truths in a deeper way, it affects who we are and what we do; when we let these facts change us, endow us, indwell in us, and transform us, we will be the people that Christ wants us to be. Then Ephesians 5:1, which tells us to be imitators of Him, will be lived out in our lives, transforming and renewing our relationships for His glory!

Be imitators of God, therefore, as dearly loved children and live a life of love, just as Christ loved us and gave himself up for us as a fragrant offering and sacrifice to God. Ephesians 5:1-2

When we are imitators of God, living our lives because we are as beloved children, we will walk in love *as a fragrant offering.* We will be kind to one another. Which would you rather have from people around you, anger and bitterness, or kindness and love? The answer is plain, lest some mental dysfunction has its grips upon you.

A lot of people wonder, where do we draw the line? How much kindness should I show? This answer is dispatched to us in Ephesians 4:31: for the reason that Christ forgave us! Because, when all the bad stuff is out of the way, all we have left is kindness and the rest of the characters, working in and through us. Real, impacting Christian kindness is to be all embracing, so it replaces all of the rotten fruits, such as spitefulness, slander, gossip, bitterness, and anger. These are the aspects of our fallen, sinful nature that is old and corrupt, and that we must put off. We will look at some of those "put offs," and what we can replace them with, later on in the next chapter.

When to be kind, and when not to be...

Jesus entered the temple area and drove out all who were buying and selling there. He overturned the tables of the money changers and the benches of those selling doves. Matthew 21: 12

You may be wondering, as a Christian, *do I have to be kind, even to those who will not repent, and who continue to do harm to others and to me?* As I have looked over all the uses of the word "kindness" in the Bible, paying special attention to Jesus, I have to be honest, and say that Jesus was not being kind to the Pharisees. They did not deserve kindness, as their deeds and words were destructive to the Jewish religion and culture, which is why Jesus was being severe with them.

Look again at Romans 11:22; you can see for yourself that there is a separation from the *kindness* of God and the *severity* of God. They are not polar opposites; rather, distinctions in His character that operate to the situation. So, kindness is not an absolute virtue all of the time. That means we are to be kind at all times; yet, at the same time, there are occasions when we do not act in kindness, such as a soldier in battle, or to a child who comes home drunk all of the time. Tough love may be necessary for the child, and war may be called for by our nation. The situation determines the response, but the other characters are in operation, too. We are never to play favorites, but we are also not to excuse unrepentant sin or bad behaviors that are repeated. We must take into account the good of the church; if it is in jeopardy, we must act with discipline toward the one who is disruptive and/or to false doctrine. To show kindness is not always the most loving thing. My brother-in-law, the Marine, who is kind to his family and friends, was not kind to the enemy solders in Iraq. In both cases, he did his job——one as a husband and father, and the other as a soldier. Yet, he exhibited kindness and respect to the Iraqis when they surrendered, and then provided food and water for them, which they did not do for his fellow soldiers. Kindness is to be exhibited in us all of the time, unless we come in contact with an evil that is so serious that we have to switch gears in our composure. We may have to hurt the other person so others in our care can be helped, such as, if an intruder were to come into our home.

In your anger do not sin. Do not let the sun go down while you are still angry. Ephesians 4:26

Ephesians 4:26 tells us that even when we come across evil, we still must not allow our anger to overwhelm and consume us. It is not necessary to become evil in order to fight evil. This theme can be seen clearly throughout Scripture. If we allow all the bitterness and malice to continue, it will flare up in our relationships—even our intimate situations; then the Devil will have his hold on us.

So, how can we be sure we will act with sternness at the right times, yet not let it become the works of destruction? Ask yourself his—will it glorify God? Do not let your emotions and indignation get the best of you, regardless of the situation. You are far better off to handle bad situations without anger, or, at least have your anger under control. A good soldier must be disciplined to control his/her anger, lest he be killed. He is even trained to harness his fear as a means of self-preservation and guided instinct. Seek His Word, and the leading of the Holy Spirit. That way, you will choose wisely.

Give yourself a deep self-examination; ask a good mentor to evaluate how you express anger as well as kindness.

1   Do I allow anger to be under God's control so it is my ally in crushing sin and holding up the cause of His truth and holiness?
2   How can I make sure that I do not allow my anger to be out of control?
3   How can I make sure that in all circumstances, kindness is properly shown?
4   If you still are not sure, ask yourself this simple question: *will God be glorified in that situation?*
5   If you are still not sure, then ask yourself if it is just about you or about His precepts? If it is just about you and not about His glory, then it probably is not just anger.

The point here is that real Christian kindness is not simply an outward change of our manners; it is an internal change of our hearts. Kindness is our tenderheartedness that we use because God has so touched us, therefore we are sensitive and compassionate toward others. We can react in a timely approach quickly and assuredly. If our heart is hard on the inside and we are trying to show our good manners on the outside, it is not biblical kindness, and it will not last. We will be neither tender nor sensitive, and we will not respond as we should. Kindness cannot be pretended, nor can it be superficial; it has to come from within as poured out to us from our Lord. It has depth that has been built from a consistent life of worship, devotion, and study, of being real and impacting, of learning, trying, and failing, yet continuing to be kind anyway.

The brother in humble circumstances ought to take pride in his high position. But the one who is rich should take pride in his low position, because he will pass away like a wild flower. For the sun rises with scorching heat and withers the plant; its blossom falls and its beauty is destroyed. In the same way, the rich man will fade away even while he goes about his business. James 1:9-11

The love of Christ given to us was sacrificial, costly, and self-denying, and ours should be, too. Yes, one of the hardest things about being a Christian is to show kindness—especially when that person has hurt us; but, see how much Christ was hurt on our behalf.

Kindness is beyond just being accepting, compromising, or being liberal or open-minded; it is thoughtful consideration to one another, putting ourselves in their shoes. We are called to be kind to enemies, to strangers, to family, and to outcasts (life of Jesus). Kindness is not something we confront; it is what we proclaim! We must change our behaviors in how we treat others— on the road, in our work, at school, and with family—to reflect how Christ treats us. As society gets more complicated and crowded, kindness will decrease more and more, which makes its need greater and greater. Let us step up to the plate of treating and serving others as Christ would. Then, watch our relationships improve!

As your mom may have said, "If you do not have anything nice to say, do not say anything at all." If so, she was very correct! Pay close attention to what we talked about concerning kindness. Kindness is contagious. Like tossing a small rock in a pond, it has a ripple effect that grows larger in an expanding manner from the original source. You can be that stone that sends the ripple of kindness to all those around you, even those you have never met!

My dear brothers, take note of this: Everyone should be quick to listen, slow to speak and slow to become angry. James 1:19

CHAPTER V
UNDERSTANDING THE IMPORTANCE OF BEING GOOD!

We are therefore Christ's ambassadors, as though God were making his appeal through us. We implore you on Christ's behalf: Be reconciled to God.
2 Corinthians 5:20

Goodness is another character listed as a Fruit of the Spirit that synergistically combines with kindness. This is what God calls *righteousness* throughout Scripture. This is what and how God has called us to be to one another. It comes when we are in a state of right being; this can only come about from a right relationship with God, which, in turn, only comes by accepting what Christ has done for us and applying it to our life by faith.

This goodness will be the quality to create an atmosphere of happiness, contentment, cooperation, and the closest we can get to living in real unity. It has the best potential of being a utopia on earth while we await the new kingdom. Perhaps it seems to be just pipe dreams and potential theory; nevertheless, it is real, and at our grasp if only we surrender our pride and sin and really live by what Christ has called us to.

This character of goodness is the cabinet that holds righteousness in plain view. It is the display case that shows the rest of the godly characters and Fruit of the Spirit. It helps make them real, seen, and used. It moves theory into action and theology into practical care and love. Goodness displays integrity, honesty, and compassion to others and allows us to do the right thing even when we do not feel like doing so. To see how this character is used in the field of life, just take a look at the life of Joseph (Genesis 37-50). Joseph was betrayed and sold as a slave; he was in a miserable situation of extreme desperation and urgency that most of us cannot fathom. Yet, he chose to make his situation into something good. He was able to focus on God and help and treat others better than he needed to. In return, he was greatly blessed and God used him to save his own family from famine, preserving the Israelites for countless generations to come. His life story still speaks loudly for us today and also gives us a model of how we can be.

Goodness is the representation for people to see how life can be, and how it should be. It lifts up our Lord and points to our depravity. It is a template for seeing our need for redemption and satisfaction, our need for salvation and growth in our Lord. It can help motivate a person to repent and accept Christ. Goodness transmutes itself into relationships, showing us how we are to treat one another, especially the one we love, our spouse! It does not augment or replace the Holy Spirit, but works with Him and His mission!

He must turn from evil and do good; he must seek peace and pursue it. 1 Peter 3:11

The opposite of being good is being bad, merciless, and unscrupulous! When we fight against one another in the church, especially in our personal relationships, we are, in fact, acting directly opposite to what God calls us to. No relationship will be healthy, and there will be no contentment or happiness in such an environment. We will end up imparting hurt, strife, dysfunction, and misery to all those around us while the misery boomerangs directly back upon us. We will be creating an ever so escalating circle of dysfunction and chaos, while outside of our circle of strife is Jesus with the call and how we can be better. We ignore Him, and therefore sink deeper into despair and dysfunction. We could have had it better; we just chose not to, rather letting our circumstances rule our life. It is so sad that so many people thrive in such situations, a testament to our fallen, sinful nature.

Joseph, being in a far worse environment than we could be, chose to make it into something good even in a dungeon of despair, and with no hope to see. His faith remained in God and God lifted him out of that pit. He can lift you up, too! You have to be willing to see how hurtful and even pathetic it is in God's eyes for you to ignore Him and go your own way in being bad! Perhaps then you can look outside the tornado of dirt and dysfunction that surrounds you, and see a potential, achievable, clean relationship filled with goodness and Christ's love.

Goodness is the fruit with which virtue and the rest of the characters combine to produce endearment. It is the character that makes people likeable, even lovable to others. It is what is attractive and alluring, what catches the attention and respect of others. It is virtue in action; it is being a role model and putting into practice excellence in all that we do, both to God and others. Remember, it is the display case of righteousness, how we are to be. Goodness enables us to be liked and enjoyed, even if an enemy comes against us. It is the taste of what is to come, the flavor of how we are to be. It is our expression of worship and gratitude to Christ played out in our lives, so we can enjoy Him, He can enjoy us, and so that life can be more enjoyable for all. Goodness is the energizer to help us develop and form good, quality relationships that are committed and impacting. Just think through how much better your relationships and future relationships would be with such characters flowing through you!

Remember, the Fruit of the Spirit is not what we do when we have the time or feel like it; it is what we are to do—period! It is how we are to be, regardless of our circumstances and abilities. It can be the hope we see, the example of our Lord, and our faith in action. It is essential for us to be relational beings. As God exhibits the fruit to us, we are to exhibit it to others, too!

PUTTING GOODNESS IN ACTION

For the eyes of the Lord are on the righteous and his ears are attentive to their prayer, but the face of the Lord is against those who do evil. 1 Peter 3:12

Have you ever wondered why some people have so many friends and why people naturally gravitate to them? Well, here you have a list coming from over 20 years of observing interpersonal relationships from a pastoral perspective. This list also includes my own frailties and what I often fail to do but wish I had. So, let us now look at some practical things we can do with these characteristics and godly traits so to be a person who attracts others for Christ and establishes better relationships. This short list gives us ways we can apply righteousness.

1. **Smile at people!** It takes seventy-two muscles to frown and only fourteen to smile. People love a smile! Think how you feel when someone smiles at you, and see how important it is to do so to others, too.
2. **Call people by name!** Take the time to remember a person's name, and use it. The sweetest music to anyone's ear is the sound of one's own name!
3. **Speak to people!** Take the chance! Step up to that plate and beyond your fears to engage someone in dialogue. Be willing to keep your friends

close but also go outside of your *clique* and comfort zone to talk to others. There is nothing as nice as a cheerful word or an honest, friendly greeting! You know it when you get a nice greeting; so, why not give one out to others?

4. **Be friendly and helpful!** Most people I have known and observed that have few, if any, friends do not make any effort to be a friend. If you would like to have friends, then, be friendly!

5. **Be genuinely interested in people!** Take the time to listen and show you care. Plan your schedule so you have time for people. If you are always in a rush, your relationships will suffer greatly. People whom God has brought to you will be ignored, wasting the help, ministry, and influence you could have given. Christian empathy means involvement and care!

6. **Be pleasant and cordial!** Be a person who is nice and engaging to others. Speak and act as if they are the most important persons in the room, and do so as if it is genuine pleasure!

7. **Be considerate with the feelings of others!** It will be appreciated. Each person is unique, created and loved by God. Acknowledge this and make your responses to others in this light.

8. **Be thoughtful of the opinions of others**. There are three sides to every controversy or disagreement: yours, that of the other person, and that of God (which is the right one!). We must not rely on our own presumptions and assumptions, because, we do not have all of the facts. Seek to know and understand the other person's perspective, and start your dialog with those agreements.

9. **Be generous with praise!** Seek to find something that person has done that is good—a personality trait, what they are wearing, or a smile that you

   noticed—and let them know. Be the person who takes the time to encourage

   others, but, do so honestly; no one likes a pretentious pretender.

10. **Be cautious with criticism!** No one likes to be condescended to or put down! There are times we are to correct others or motivate them in a better direction, but do so with an attitude of love and care, showing patience, respect, and tact.

11. **Be ready to give your service!** What counts most in life is who we are in Christ; we then respond with gratitude for what He has done for us by doing for others!

The power of our words

Let the peace of Christ rule in your hearts, since as members of one body you were called to peace. And be thankful. Let the word of Christ dwell in you richly as you teach and admonish one another with all wisdom, and as you sing psalms, hymns and spiritual songs with gratitude in your hearts to God. And whatever you do, whether in word or deed, do it all in the name of the Lord Jesus, giving thanks to God the Father through him. Colossians 3:15-17

To put all of this into action, we will remember to think before we speak so we are careful not to say things that could hurt someone or cause a fight or an argument. We will strive to not let bad influences and questionable activities enter into our lives, as they will manipulate us and pour garbage in our minds so garbage comes out of our words and deeds. We will not let our words or body language discourage others. We will know that showing respect to authority is right and biblical. At the same time, we have to be willing to stand up for what is right. This translates to: we will not ever gossip or talk negatively about others at work, school, home, church, or anywhere in the universe—period—if we claim Christ as Lord!

We must be willing and able to check our words before they leave our lips, and to think in good terms before we speak. We have to see the destruction that can come by inflicting anger and frustration, resulting in low self-esteem, loneliness, and despair. Our words can create success or they can create failure. We all have been positively and negatively motivated by someone's words uttered purposefully or as a slip of the tongue, a mistake. Words do hurt, as they cause anger, frustration, low self-esteem, feelings of emptiness, loneliness, emotional withdrawal, depression, and pain. And, if you think you are immune—think again. Or, if you like to use words as weapons, consider this; words have a boomerang affect. That means, *what you throw out will come back to hit you.* If you think you can duck them, well, you cannot; once you release those hurtful words, you cannot put them back any more than you can put the toothpaste back into the tube; it is out, and it is out for good.

We put no stumbling block in anyone's path, so that our ministry will not be discredited. Rather, as servants of God we commend ourselves in every way: in great endurance; in troubles, hardships and distresses; in beatings, imprisonments and riots; in hard work, sleepless nights and hunger; in purity, understanding, patience and kindness; in the Holy Spirit and in sincere love; in truthful speech and in the power of God; with weapons of righteousness in the right hand and in the left; through glory and dishonor, bad report and good report; genuine, yet regarded as impostors; known, yet regarded as unknown; dying, and yet we live on; beaten, and yet not killed; sorrowful, yet always rejoicing; poor, yet making many rich; having nothing, and yet possessing everything. 2 Corinthians 6:3-10

If you criticize others, then you will be criticized, too. If you lie to others, then you will be lied to, also. If you gossip about others, then others will gossip about you. If you cheat others, then others will cheat you. Do you see a pattern? It is a simple pattern; what you give out, you will soon get back. We have to realize deep down in our hearts and minds how powerful our words are as they shape and form us and others around us. Words have power to destroy people's lives, just as a spark can destroy an entire forest (James 3:1-12). Words also have the power to determine the direction of our lives, as well as that of others, just as a small rudder can move a large ship, and as a small bit can guide a horse. Words can make and shape us either for God's glory or Satan's plans. To show you how important this is, James uses the word *poison,* as in deadly cobra venom, the most powerful illustration that could be made in his time!

The issue of words is:

1.   Do you truly know the power your words have?
2.   How are words from your mouth being used?
3.   How are words guiding you?
4.   How are your words touching others?

Your words will reflect your true character! Your words have the power to change someone else's life for the better. The greatest gift you have is the ability to communicate; the greatest responsibility is using your ability to communicate with character and distinction within the parameters of God's call to you. The greatest message you will ever utter is the one that impacts others for our Lord. It is the power to communicate the gospel and love to those with whom you come in contact. To impact people's lives from your tongue and character is an awesome privilege and responsibility. Your character is the gospel that most people will read! Thus, your words will either help draw them to Christ or repel them away from Him.

Words are the trust of our communication. But, words are not the only means of our communication. Most experts in the field of communication say that 55 percent of our communication is from our body language, 38% is from our tone, and only 7 percent from our words. Our words reflect our body and tone, so, make sure you are aware of *you* when those words come out! The words and how we use them will make us either abusers or people who cherish others!

When you start to be careful with what you say and how you say it and are willing to change, then you will see your relationships blossom. Your life will change! How to do this? Well, it is really simple. Just as your mom or grade school teacher must have said, *think before you speak.* When we think first and speak later, we will be able to make positive affirmations and create happiness in and for others. When those words boomerang back to us, we will experience success in our life and, most importantly, God will be glorified. Plan ahead for what you will say, so you will have a clear idea of the words you will use. At the same time, be in prayer, asking God to help you say words that encourage and impact, and do not tear down, or cause gossip or distraction to Christ-like character. If you do not have encouraging words to say, then do not say anything. It is always best to say less and listen more. We have to guard what we are *not* to say as much as what we *do* say!

Here are some practical ideas on how we can make just minor changes to our words and reap much greater relationship skills. You will be able to help create friendship and confidence in others as well as yourself. You will be building people up and not tearing them down; you will be glorifying our Lord and not taking an axe to His church.

Here are some simple plans to put goodness in action by just watching how you use your words.

Do not repay anyone evil for evil. Be careful to do what is right in the eyes of everybody. If it is possible, as far as it depends on you, live at peace with everyone. Romans 12:17-18

Here are some replacement words you can use to create a better environment at work, school, church and home.

Substitute Negative Words	With	Positive Words
"I can't" and "I won't"	With	"I haven't yet."
"I don't know"	With	"I will find out for you."
"If I"	With	"When I."
"That will be a problem"	With	"That's going to be a challenge."
"I will try"	With	"I will do"
"You are...or, I am...a failure"	With	"We are a success because we learned something."

Here are some replacement words you can use to create a better environment at work, school, church and home.

How many more can you think of?

Who is going to harm you if you are eager to do good? But even if you should suffer for what is right, you are blessed. "Do not fear what they fear; do not be frightened." But in your hearts set apart Christ as Lord. 1 Peter 3:13-15

The ups and downs of relationships may get us down, and the arguments, tension, disagreements, gossip, treachery, betrayal, financial disasters, stress, and false accusations may take its toll on us. When life seems to rise up and wage war against us, our character can grow stronger and our relationships can improve. We can become even stronger and more loving—even more content. The choice is ours! On the other hand, these tough times can produce despair, confusion, anger, bitterness and loneliness. This will translate into how we use our words, and can escalate the problems into a revolving cycle of despair and chaos. If all that we see is failure and self-pity, cynicism will be produced rather than the person of character that God calls us to be. The same crushed grape will produce a good wine or sour vinegar. It all depends on how it is cared for and crafted. You are in control of your care and crafting when you keep your eyes on His care, and His crafting will enable you to produce the character of a fine wine, not sour vinegar.

The same scenario happens in our "self-thinking" with how we view and respond to ourselves. What we believe shapes what we do and say. That is why a healthy understating of doctrine and God's Word is so essential, as it will help shape our whole being. Again, this is also why the first chapter is so important as a foundation to understand fullness and the Kingdom of God as well as ourselves. If what we believe does not reflect the truth of what is in the Word of God, how we behave will fall way short of the character we are to emulate. If what we believe does not reflect His truth, then what we feel will not reflect the reality of Christ's love for us. If we do not have a healthy self-worth from the realization of who we are in Christ, it will adversely affect our ability to communicate and build relations with others!

Here are some replacement thoughts to help line up your thinking to God's reality.

Do not conform any longer to the pattern of this world, but be transformed by the renewing of your mind. Then you will be able to test and approve what God's will is—his good, pleasing and perfect will. Romans 12:2

Substitute Negative Thoughts	With	Positive Thoughts
I do not feel loved.	With	God loves me and nothing can buffet that. Romans 8:31; 38-39
I give up.	With	I can. Philippians 4:13
I am too weak.	With	The Lord is my strength. Psalm 27:1
I am a failure.	With	God does not abandon me. 2 Corinthians 4:8-9
I am worthless.	With	I am not worthless because God made me. Psalm 139 13-16
I am confused.	With	God has a plan for me. Jeremiah 29:11
I am afraid.	With	God gives me power, love and no fear. 2 Timothy 1:7
I feel alone.	With	God is with me. Matthew 28:20; Hebrews 13:5
I feel unfulfilled.	With	I can be content. Philippians 4:11
I do not know what to do.	With	God will give me wisdom. James 1:5

Positive thinking has been negatively viewed in Reformed and Evangelical circles due to its abuse by some preachers. Nonetheless, positive thinking is a call from our Lord. It does not replace His Spirit and Word, but it will impact all that we are and do.

Theology is our understanding of who God is and what He has done for us. This directly translates into who we are and what we do. If you think theology is not important in regard to relationships, consider how it relates to our feelings and how we view ourselves and others around us:

Theological Concepts	Theological Results
Justification means we are completely forgiven by God by what Christ has done! God's righteousness is covering us! There is nothing that we can add to it, such as good works or clean living. Thus, we have no balance to weigh a judgment on someone else! (Romans 2:5-16; 3:22; 5:1;10; 9:30; Philippians 3:4-14; I John 1:9).	My response to *justification* is I do not need to fear the expectations of others or my own failure because God accepts me! Therefore I do not need to withdraw, gossip, manipulate, or be overly driven to succeed; I do not need to please others for my self approval. My focus is on God's glory and His Kingdom!
Reconciliation means I am at peace with God because Jesus *reconciles me to God,* so I am not an enemy of God; I am accepted by Him and need not fear His wrath and punishment. Since I am at peace, I am no longer at war with God. I realize as a believer that I am in a fallen world that is still at war with God (2 Cor.5:18-21; Eph.2:16; Col. 1:20-22).	My response to reconciliation is realizing I have harmony in Christ. I do not need the approval of people when I have God's. I do not need to fear being rejected or not accepted by others. I can be an instrument of His peace and character regardless of what others do to me. I can relax and in Him and be vulnerable to build relations with others without fear.

Understanding who and what God has done for us affects all of our being, including relationships, goals, and the direction we take in life. We cannot rely on our own efforts, skills, personal connections, or beliefs. How we come across to others is directly related to how we see ourselves in Christ. If our relationship with Christ is on track and growing, so are our relationships!

Our self-esteem must come from who we are in Christ and what Christ has done for us. This should give us an enormous satisfaction and sense of worth. The King and Creator of the universe cares for me and loves me! He is living within, guiding, loving, and holding me! There is no adequate substitution for that! But, it is sad that we try so hard to substitute the wonders of the truth of what Christ did for us with stupid, insignificant lies.

Building and developing character is not just something we learn from a book or hear from a sermon. It does not come upon us in the night, or sneak up in the day. It does not come automatically, accidentally, or suddenly. It is a process that comes from being parented in it. Then it lays in us and in our motives. It is a slow process. You may not even realize you have it until others point it out in you.

Remember this. Character is not permanent once it is formed. It requires our continual grip and practice. There are many times when it falls away from great leaders through personal loss or personal sin. I have seen it nearly flee from me on many occasions from all that I have been through in life. But, when we remain in Christ, He remains in us; He even remains in us when we do not remain in Him!

Many great people have said this over the millennia, "Our strength is shown in the things we stand for; our weakness is shown in the things we fall for. People of genius are admired; people of wealth are envied; people of power are feared; but only people of character are trusted." Can you see yourself in those words? We create our world of relationships by our choices through our own use of words, so use them wisely!

"It is that particular wise and good God, who is the author and owner of our system, that I propose for the object of my praise and adoration. He is not above caring for us, being pleased with our praise and offended when we slight Him or neglect his Glory ... I love Him therefore for his goodness, and I adore Him for his wisdom. Let me then not fail to praise my God continually, for it is His due, and it is all I can return for His many favors and great goodness to me." Benjamin Franklin

Chapter VI
ATTITUDE: THE PRELUDE TO EFFECTIVE RELATIONSHIPS!

For by the grace given me I say to every one of you: Do not think of yourself more highly than you ought, but rather think of yourself with sober judgment, in accordance with the measure of faith God has given you. Romans 12:3

How do you deal with problems? Do you see them as opportunities? Or, do you just see the danger and not beyond that cloak of stress? Do the everyday problems of life get you so down that they control and consume your thoughts and motives? Does the stress of work, school, or relationships have you so boxed in, overwhelmed, and confused that you do not know what to do? We can either let bad situations control us, or we can allow ourselves to learn and grow by them. We can be masters of our attitude, or be controlled by the bad attitudes of others. A choice is given; an opportunity arises; it is up to us to respond. Attitude is essential for love to flow, for the characters to be exhibited so that effective relationships can be built.

The Chinese word character for *stress* is a combination of two words, *danger* and *opportunity*. This is a great illustration for us, as all problems and stresses can be refined into both categories—a potential danger and a potential opportunity. One key ingredient will help ensure that you make the right choice and weather out the storm, becoming better and stronger. This one word, which encompasses so much of how we are and what we do, is *attitude*. Attitude has the power to hold us, as well as others, captive. So, by knowing how to develop a positive Christian attitude in our lives will help our lives and relationships greatly!

How is your attitude? There is perhaps no person who truly feels, deep down, that attitude is not important. Just think about this: how do you feel when people have a good attitude toward you, when someone takes the time to smile and be kind? It is the person who takes the extra time to smile or show care and concern that will impact others positively. How do you feel when people take the time to listen, and have your best at heart? Now, consider how you are to your spouse, girl/boy friend, family, friends, acquaintances, strangers, and the people at church and at work. Are you the person who shows that they care? Are you even the person you think you are? Many people think they have good attitudes but, in reality, they do not realize how they come across to others. Do you just expect good attitude from others and do not try to put the effort in it yourself? You would be surprised at how many Christians I have known over the years who fit in this last category!

You should be wondering about how your attitude is; if not, you may have a deeper issue regarding pride. To find out how your attitude is, spend some significant time in prayer, seeking to know if your attitude is in line with the principles we have previously talked about—especially with Fullness and Character. Pray about the best way to develop and improve your relationships. Then, take a chance; ask some of your closest friends and family members and listen to them without giving them the *but, but, but*. You need to realize that this is paramount if your relationship skills are to improve and grow, and for your life to be filled with more contentment and love. What is in the way of your developing and exercising a good attitude? What about what God calls us to in regard to your outlook, spiritual development, and personality?

Attitude—a good one that is—can be tough for some people. Perhaps, you have been hurt and have recessed into a pit of anger and self-pity. Maybe you feel justified in holding onto the resentment because of what you have been through in life. The rejections from people, past failures, abandonment, exclusions, betrayal, and hurts have moved you away from the path that God intended. But, consider this: the bitterness will fester, and then tenaciously impact your decisions and relationships. Do you honestly believe you can develop good relationships if your attitude is skewed? Can you truly be happy and content if you are holding onto anger and bitterness? Do you realize the Holy Spirit gives you power to overcome this regardless of what you have been through in life? But, for Him to work effectively and completely, you have to let go of that bitterness and embrace Christ as Lord over all, including your hurts and fears.

For you were once darkness, but now you are light in the Lord. Live as children of light (for the fruit of the light consists in all goodness, righteousness and truth) and find out what pleases the Lord. Ephesians 5:8-10

Discovering how important and essential a good attitude is must occur before you can get out of the dark jungle of relationship confusion and get on the right path of Light and of good, effective relationships. We have to wake up from our bitterness to be in His Light. When we refuse to have a good attitude, all we do and say becomes corrupt and skewed; relationships will fall apart, people will be repulsed, and despair and further hurt will impound us deeper in that pit of despair! When we *arise,* as the Scripture calls us to, we will find our attitude refocused on the Light rather than the darkness.

Most, if not all, people love to be cared for. From the cradle of the infant to preparation for the grave in geriatrics, we start off our lives needing care, then end it needing care. During all those in-between times, we still need and like being cared for. In this need for care, we sometimes become experts on the receiving of care, of expecting others to treat us in a certain way. In addition, if they do not, we become dejected and callous toward them. So, we display the attitude that everyone owes us, or that we deserve better. With this mindset, we don't do a very good job of giving out quality care to others. If you are a Christian and mature in the faith, you will probably say, *no way! I'm not that way!* But, do you live your life that way? Do others see you in that poor light? Perhaps, unconsciously, you have a *me first* identity, always placing the emphasis on the *I* and the *me. If only I...if it could go this way for me...then I could....*so that the ownership of your life is completely self-focused and centered only on your needs, desires, and aspirations. All of your goals and attitudes are solely about you. The ownership of your life is yours and yours alone! Nevertheless, as a Christian, you know that is not the way your life should be carried out.

Consider this: Christ calls us to Him and out of ourselves. Our ownership has been transferred; our pink slip has been signed over from our sinful selves to grace in Christ——if you claim Christ as your Lord. What effect are you having on those around you? What effect is your attitude having on your relationships with family, friends, co-workers, acquaintances at school, or in dating, courtship, or marriage? When we relinquish ourselves to Christ, then the proper attitude of life will take over. Our minds and attitudes will become renewed, and our behaviors will become centered on His precepts. Our relationships will become focused on Christ and His work, not just centered upon ourselves.

To turn ourselves around from being mainly self-centered and producing a poor attitude, let us look at what we should be like if we would have a good attitude. The vision of our lives and the result of what we have will be based on a positive outlook—a positive attitude based solely on knowing, believing, and accepting what Christ has done for us. So, regardless of our external circumstances, we are to be totally focused on our Lord. This is what faith is all about! We then are to allow our attitudes to be Christ-centered. We can allow our circumstances to take the lead, or allow Christ to take the lead; the choice is given to us. The effects of our relationships—from keeping friends and a job to choosing a mate and holding onto a successful marriage—are pivoted upon our attitude. Our attitude is pivoted upon our growth and maturity in our faith, the acceptance of God's forgiveness, and seeking forgiveness from others so we can practice that Light.

Your attitude should be the same as that of Christ Jesus: Who, being in very nature God, did not consider equality with God something to be grasped. Philippians 2:5-6

If we are receivers, or *me first* oriented and not Christ-centered, then all of those circumstances and relationships will be squeezed, and bitterness and resentment will flow out of them. But, is that what we want out of life? Or, perhaps we can be Christ-centered and the oils of sweetness will pour out instead. Which do you want? What pours out from you? Is love and care modeled to those around you, or do bitterness and hostility flow from you? Your attitude will determine the health and prosperity of your relationships. Your attitude will be squeezed and formed from how you handle your circumstances and put godly character into practice. If your attitude is only the result of your circumstances, it will become chaotic and cause strife.

The way others—especially your spouse—will see you is from how Christ is exhibited in you. This will be from your focus and attitude, and *not* your circumstances. Your direction in life, your joy and happiness, your cares and concerns, and your willingness to reach beyond yourself will grow from your attitude and maturity, all stemming from who you are in Christ! This will fuel the positive outlook and growth of your relationships, all a result of your growing connection with Christ as Lord over all.

Consider it pure joy, my brothers, whenever you face trials of many kinds, because you know that the testing of your faith develops perseverance. Perseverance must finish its work so that you may be mature and complete, not lacking anything. James 1:2-4

Once you realize the error of the *me first* mentality, it will die, and the Christ-centered life will be birthed and take its place. Then, when your circumstances change, and life gets bumpy, you can count it as joy because Christ is still working in you. This is the way we are made, the reason we endure suffering, the way a fallen, sinful, and unjust world is turned from the glory of Satan into the glory of our Lord. We allow Christ to reach out to us and conform us to His image and character, regardless of what we are going through, regardless of our circumstances. This will be the glue that bonds a good marriage together and keeps it on course.

Your attitude is the impact that will strike at the issues of life; it affects all that you do, and determines how others see you. Your attitude can separate you from hurt and pain as you see the work of the Holy Spirit, recognizing the absorption of grace and the acceptance of Christ. We cannot trust in our education, wealth, success, failures, people, appearances, skill, giftedness, or circumstances. The trust must be laid at the foot of the cross and nowhere else. Our attitude must be Christ-driven and not appearances-driven. We must embrace the day with joy, knowing Christ is at work, both in us and in those around us. How will we be able to weather the storms of life and the arguments and stresses of marriage unless we count it all as joy and keep our attitude in line with Christ?

DEVELOPING A GOOD ATTITUDE

You were taught, with regard to your former way of life, to put off your old self, which is being corrupted by its deceitful desires; to be made new in the attitude of your minds; and to put on the new self, created to be like God in true righteousness and holiness. Ephesians 4:22-24

This statement has been said a lot by many people over the years: *life is 10 percent what happens to us, and 90 percent how we react to it.* I firmly believe this is very true. As Christians saved by grace, it is still up to us to work out of what Christ gives us; this is what Philippians, chapter two, is all about. Maturity will make the difference between a life of distinction and purpose, and a life governed by discord and disarray. So, what is your response; what is your attitude; where does your maturity lie?

Having a negative attitude cuts you off from the blessings and wonders that God has in store for you. You may not be rich or famous, but that is not important; it is the positive attitude of life and the receiving of His redemption and blessings that will give you meaning and true happiness. No car, job, house, spouse, or anything else could ever bring you that! Negative attitudes prevent us from experiencing life, joy, forgiveness, fulfillment, peace, love, and happiness, as does refusing to give up our will for our Lord and Savior!

Go through the next week being fully aware of your attitudes; keep a journal of them. Keep track of your negative attitudes and positive attitudes. Then, notice your feelings and responses in those situations. See what you find and see what happens!

There are times when I journal; that is, I keep a diary of what is going on in my life. I sometimes look back on it and gain new insight into what I was going through back then. I have become more adept at interpreting God's leading and plan for me as I experience life and receive what He has done. By looking back on what we have been through and seeing the hand of God there, we will be greatly comforted and encouraged for what we are going through now, as well as for what may lie ahead. As I gain new insight into my personality and the Lord's working through my issues and problems, I realize what mere shadows they are compared to His Lordship, holiness, and greatness!

By concentrating on Christ and what He has done, we will be lifted up and become more complete than through anything else we could ever do. Thus, the thrust of prayer and becoming more mature in Christ along with journaling has taught me to look beyond myself and keep focused on Christ. The other end of journaling is a problem for some people, including Christians. In their zeal to keep faithful to their journals, they become self-absorbed and only see themselves and their problems, but not the Lord. So, be careful if you do this exercise of journaling; keep focused on why you are doing it—which is to grow closer to the Lord—and not just for yourself. Yes, we are to do all we can to learn about and improve ourselves, but, we are not to be the god of our life. Always keep the focus on His Word and be in prayer. Use the journal to add what you have learned. When you are down, look at the journal and see how far you have come! It will help give you with the initiative to keep pursuing Him regardless of any situation in which you find yourself.

We are called to keep focused on Christ and not ourselves; so, we are looking at God's Word as a mirror to ourselves, to our soul—not to see us, but to see God working in us. When we only see ourselves, we see sin and brokenness, failure, self-seeking inclinations, and wrong attitudes, but we do not recognize it! This will translate into how we relate and how far we can develop healthy and good relationships. We must see God's interests and not our own; then, the journey of maturing in the faith will become more real. Our problems will become less as He becomes more.

The same thing can happen when we read the Word. We can become so consumed with our interests that we do not see the calling and response we are to give. Thus, we grow bitter, thinking that this devotion stuff is not for us, and we turn it off. We replace it with so much activity that God is pushed out of our lives except on Sunday morning. But, even then we are rushed and stressed and do not feel the worship or hear the lesson; we only hear ourselves and our problems of getting the kids ready, the stress at work, or whatever is occupying our minds.

We need to respond to the people God brings us with a surrendered will and a mind cleared of anxious thoughts. When we focus on our fears, hopes, dreams, needs, and emotions, we will have no room left to learn what God has for us, nor will we be able to relate deeply enough to others, let alone to the love we want. When our attitude is bad, there is no transformation of our nature or will—what philosophers call our *existential core*. There can be no serious behavioral or personality changes unless the core of who we are is changed, so that our attitude is changed. Christ is the only one who does that correctly! Attitude is the proof text that a change has transpired as it exhibits the *Fruit of the Spirit*. This is the transformation found in Romans 12. This transformation cannot happen when self is in the way. God will do as He pleases; however, He usually does not over-ride our will. He waits for us to surrendered and be poured out to Him. So, do not take the chance and allow your stubbornness and bad attitude to get in the way of God working in you and developing your relationships!

THE MOST IMPORTANT AND ESSENTIAL ATTITUDE: HUMILITY

Humble yourselves, therefore, under God's mighty hand, that he may lift you up in due time. Cast all your anxiety on him because he cares for you. 1 Peter 5:6-7

The principle attitude for the Christian life is *humility*. If we commit to the precepts of His Word, then from us should flow this most precious attitude of humility. Being humble minimizes arrogance and removes pride. It is our fallen nature and weaknesses that cause us to think we are better than we are, and that causes us to strive to lift ourselves above others and God. Humility recognizes our indebtedness to God. It is admitting that others, and most importantly God, are responsible for our achievements. Humbleness will enable us to be teachable people who are willing to have a good attitude of submission and servant hood, people who confess sin and remember how Christ served us!

Do not be wise in your own eyes; fear the LORD and shun evil. Proverbs 3:7

Being humble is being able to share with one another beyond our own agenda and needs. Being willing to cooperate creates an environment of trust and encouragement in relationships. In a church, people are drawn to join and belong where there is no pride or arrogance. When we are selfish and stingy with our sharing, an atmosphere of distrust is created. Who wants to be a part of that? How we react to the non-Christian environment will distinguish us as Christ-like or hypocrites; whom do you think our God desires?

Humble yourself in the sight of the Lord, and he shall lift you up. James 4:10

Humility is not self-hatred, spinelessness, or having a *poor me* attitude. It is not having hypocritical agreements with the opinions of others or accepting the fads of our time. Humility does not diminish you; rather, it lifts up God. Seeing others as important encourages them. Humility only takes away your bad characteristics; the power of God will then be released in your behalf.

When we refuse to embrace this attitude and apply it to our relationships, the result is not good. Arrogance and pride will overrun our relationships and cause destruction to people. These are the attitudes that say one is superior to another, even to the extent of regarding others with contempt, as if they were unworthy of any relationship or interaction with us! When we have contempt even for a friend, let alone a spouse, the relationship will not survive. There is nothing you can do to rescue it unless you repent of your disorder and dysfunction before it becomes malignant. If you think, *oh, no big deal; I have to have a healthy self-esteem.* Well, you are right; but, when your *self* becomes the center stage, you lift your self-interests and your self-sufficiencies over others—even over God. This may seem necessary by some who think, *hey, I am number one!* However, as number one, you are in a category all by yourself—alone and disconnected from life or effective relationships. That kind of thinking will cause you to end up in misery. Doesn't sound so good now, does it? Just think how it is for the other people in your life now. This rotten, dysfunctional attitude will convince you that you are self-sufficient; however, it will break down, further blinding you from seeing your need for redemption. It will also blind you from seeing your need for growth in spiritual matters. Therefore, self becomes the god, and any work of the One True God is muted and put aside. Any relationship that would be healthy will quickly die.

When humility is functioning in your relationships, you will be able to accept your human limitations and be dependent on Christ as LORD. This will transfer to how you relate with others because you will be able to recognize the other person's strengths, weaknesses, worth, and relevance in your relationship. You will know that you do indeed need them in your life. How you treat people and how you are treated comes directly from our real humbleness. You will able to produce one of the quintessential helps to create a successful relationship—COMMUNICATION! You cannot communicate effectively unless you are open, and you cannot be open if you are full of pride. Pride closes the door to everything!

If you still do not think you need to be humble, then consider Christ. As LORD, God, and Creator of the universe, He humbled Himself. He is God! He gave up His lofty position in Heaven to become human—one of us. He lived in our place in perfection, something we could not do; then He died, absorbing God's justified wrath on our behalf. So you, a mere person who feels that, *hey, I do not need to be humble*, will cause eternal consequences and even block your salvation. How can you accept God if you think you are a god? We can never say to Him, *but Lord, you do not understand*, because He does. Do you? When you do understand, you will begin to be much better at developing and maintaining relationships that will last a lifetime!

Having a good attitude will contribute greatly to your relationships, your marriage, and to finding the one who is right for you—if you are still looking. You will be able to work on yourself, and see your place in Christ. You will be able to communicate more effectively, especially in learning how to listen, which will build a stronger relationship with God, and which will affect all you do in life. Then, it helps in earning His favor and blessing, as we can see so clearly from Scripture. (With the exception of His grace and love; we cannot earn that.)

How do I develop a good attitude?

I want to know Christ and the power of his resurrection and the fellowship of sharing in his sufferings, becoming like him in his death. Philippians 3:10

Know what Christ has done for you! You have to be willing to empty your self will, so His will can take over. God has authority over you; so, accept it and embrace Him as LORD. This does not cheapen or take away *who you are*, but adds His grace and love so you can be your best for His glory. You do not become mindless automatons or robots, but mature Christians of distinction with virtue, character, and people who are poured out to Him. Because we desire to do so, it is the best way and plan for us. This is fun, exciting, and adventurous. Your source is His precepts from His Word, which you discover through the disciplines of the Christian faith such as Bible reading, study, devotions, prayer, fasting, and fellowship with mature Christians who can challenge you and hold you accountable.

Do not see life as a competition, but rather, a journey. Save the competition for sports; embrace relationships through what you can contribute and commit to. Be willing to take a risk, and go for it in making friends. A good attitude will see others as valued and of worth, and how one can complement the other. God does not see us or judge us on what we achieve, but how we are!

In Christ, we are all equal, whether you are Billy Graham or Joe Blow down the street. We all have different roles and calls in church and in society; who you are always means who you are in Christ, not what you do or have done. Do not be too proud to learn the routine aspects of life, whether it be your job or learning the life story of a new friend. Be willing to put in the extra listening prowess. If you do not, you will be too self-centered to appreciate the precious kindnesses of human relationships that make life special, satisfying, and more enjoyable. Character is precious and must be the prime principle for living.

Love must be sincere. Hate what is evil; cling to what is good. Be devoted to one another in brotherly love. Honor one another above yourselves. Romans 12:9-10

Never give in to negative emotions because they will produce a negative attitude. This negative attitude will cause others to be negative back to you and it will continue to escalate. Be in control, and know that negative emotions and the attitude that goes with them come from our own insecurities. Do not be afraid to express emotions. We have been created to express emotions; we all have them and use them. We have to realize just how powerful they are, and what they do to others in our wake when we misuse them. When we are hurt by the unkind words or actions of others, how do we react? Do we retaliate in kind, or in kindness? Are you a person who is known by your temper or your temperance? As Christians, we must resist the temptation to let our emotions control us. Yes, we will make mistakes and even fail, but our goal is not the success; rather it is in doing our best for His Highest.

Be a person who is committed to improve not only your attitude but that of others, as well! *How do I do that,* you say? With encouragement and nourishing words that lift others up. This will do wonders for people, just as we discussed in the last chapter. Showing others an uplifting attitude it will be infectious not only helping them but also helping us in return, as it is reciprocal. Therefore, we all must think about what we will say before our mouths start to move.

It is easy to look down on others; yet, to really take a look at ourselves can be quite a challenge. It is easy to let the wrongs that have been done to us consume us and even become our identity. But, remember, how we react will either tear us down or allow us to forgive. We should always search out the best in others, and not escalate the bad or even dwell on it. So, be willing to put good attitude forward! Enjoy life and all that is thrown at you. Accept what you have been given before you ask for more. Then, He will lift you up, and all that you do will be more bearable, more fun, more exciting, and more uplifting to others.

"I have been crucified with Christ; it is no longer I who live, but Christ lives in me; and the life which I now live in the flesh I live by faith in the Son of God, who loved me and gave Himself for me." (Galatians 2:20 NKJV)

Chapter VII
THE CHARACTER OF FRIENDSHIP

My command is this: Love each other as I have loved you. Greater love has no one than this, that he lay down his life for his friends. You are my friends if you do what I command. John 15:12-14

Have you ever wondered why certain people have all the friends, while others—perhaps even you—seem to have few to none? Have you wondered why some people succeed in business and finance even though they seem to have no skills or abilities to contribute effectively to their profession? I have struggled with this most of my life. The common factors most people look for are in the *wealth* and *looks* department; but, if you take an honest look at successful people, rarely do looks or wealth come into play. Even intelligence, education, and who their parents are do not seem to be major factors. Yes, these factors will help you, as a degree from Harvard is far better than one from the local community college; or, being from the Hamptons is a leg up from being from the inner-city. However, even those things will not sustain you. They may open a door, but they will not keep it open. There is something else lurking under their surface that pushed them up the food chain of relationship success.

What is the key that makes one person successful in life and another not, even though both have the same level of intelligence, education, and upbringing? The key is their ability to make friends! Networking relationships will move a person over the top as compared to the person who does not make friends well!

Friendship is the springboard to success, both in the business world and in the church. It is what invites evangelism and what propels success in general. It will build intimacy in the bedroom of marriage, and create vision and harmony in the boardroom of business. It is the quintessential element in relationship building as it encompasses all that we have talked about thus far, and puts into application what we will be talking about in the coming chapters. It will keep the relationship alive and headed in a positive direction for the parent and the child, the coworkers (with one another as well as with the boss), the husband and the wife, the police and the community—even the government and the people. It puts love into action and the church into the community. The question we all have to ask ourselves is whether or not the character of friendship is working in us. It is my prayer we can work through these issues and become *friend-builders* together.

You may be thinking, *I am an introvert,* or, *I do not like to go up to people and initiate conversations, let alone friendships;* do not be dismayed. Some people are just wired differently. You may not be inclined to do so; we all have various gifts and abilities as well as different personalities. Even if you are extremely shy, there are a few things you can do to improve your friendship factor. Some of the most successful people in business and politics either have been or are shy—including Bill Gates and Abraham Lincoln. I, myself, tend to be naturally shy and an introvert, even though I always test as an extrovert on personality tests. Why? Because, I was *forced* in my profession as a pastor to learn how to make friends and initiate conversations even when I did not want to, nor was naturally equipped to do so. You can learn, as I had to, some basic relational skills. But, that does not mean you can change who you are. We are not to be someone or something that we are not. I wanted to grow from being shy to being more outgoing. So, I set out in search of how to do that. After pretending to be someone other than who I really was around others, I learned a valuable lesson; I needed to be real. The best gift we can give another person is the honesty of who we are. That is, we are not to be pretentious or fake in any way. I also learned some skills, which I will pass on to you, that helped me be more of a "go-getter," one who would lift others up, even though I would rather be home reading a book or watching TV. As a result, I learned that relationships are far more fun than books *or* watching TV!

I no longer call you servants, because a servant does not know his master's business. Instead, I have called you friends, for everything that I learned from my Father I have made known to you. John 15:15

A lot of people think, *I do not need to know how to communicate or relate because I already know naturally.* So, when the pastor or counselor suggests to someone that he or she could use some communication skills, many people—including Christians—are turned off by the request. Yet, the fact is, few people really do know how to communicate! Still not sure? Then, take a look at all the relationships you have had throughout your life. How many of those have grown and lasted ? If you say *two* or *three*, you are far, far ahead of most people! The sad fact is that few people, even pastors, have close, lasting friends. Even fewer of us are influencers in the community. Why? Because few of us know how, and we are too prideful to admit it.

Instead of developing good communicating and relational skills, we develop bad habits, then rationalize them as good and OK. All too often, we insert what we think instead of what we can learn from God's Word. Thus, we remain in our predicaments, wondering why nobody likes us—why everybody hates us. So, we go into our rooms and shut the door on the world. We have to be willing to see how valuable and important a friendship is. Friends are essential in all that we do—in school, at work, in the church, (especially in evangelism), and in building a relationship with a spouse. Building relationships is like sharing the Gospel; it is not about what you say, it is about who you are. It is letting people read you as a person rather than just hearing what you say. John 13:34-35 and 15:13-17 gives us a template on the importance and value of friendships. Jesus, Himself, gives it the greatest validation by calling us His *friends*!

Friendship is operated on the principle of love. If you are not realizing it yet, all that we have talked about thus far converges here. This is where the rubber of character meets the road of life! Each aspect of love, character, and attitude combine to build us in His image. The bricks, made of godly character, are laid with the mortar of the Spirit, and used to build His house and church of love. These characteristics are what makes us friendly, and how we are to be known—by what Christ does with us, and calls us to. Character indeed counts, and it is the loudest broadcaster of what we are! So, what is your character proclaiming of you?

While in college, I had the great opportunity to be a teaching assistant in an elementary school in San Jose, California. This school was doing a pilot program on bussing. Various races were brought in, so an ethnically rounded school could be the test bed of some new ideas on race relations and learning theory. As a psychology major, I jumped at being a part of this. Soon, I was the acting assistant school psychologist, testing and evaluating the students, and watching all these new ideas we thought would work fail. Parents bickered and fought. Kids came in abused and hurt. Teachers were frustrated because the hope of a new system soon turned into despair. What we thought we could do through new ideas and in legislation and mandates, did not work. Why? Because people are naturally inclined to hate and *not* get along rather than to love and get along. I saw kids tear at each other like animals, parents get into fistfights—and, those were the good days! What we hoped for—that we could form an atmosphere of peace and togetherness—did not transpire.

In that school, I also volunteered as a teaching assistant in the kindergarten. We taught those kids how to use the scissors and glue, to not eat the glue, to sit in a chair, to learn their colors and how to behave, relate, have good manners, etc. No child came to us naturally equipped, able to interact in a good and pleasant way. We, as humans, did not come into this world equipped to be good. We had to learn how and keep learning. Just as we had to teach those kindergarteners how to behave and to not eat the glue, we have to learn the skills necessary to making friends. Some people get this training early in life, and learn those skills. They are the ones who tend to be successful and well-liked. The ability to learn and grow in this area is an essential foundation for making and building friendships.

Dear friend, I pray that you may enjoy good health and that all may go well with you, even as your soul is getting along well. It gave me great joy to have some brothers come and tell about your faithfulness to the truth and how you continue to walk in the truth. I have no greater joy than to hear that my children are walking in the truth. 3 John 1:2-4

The uniqueness of our humanity is that we do not need to learn how to be bad at stuff. We are naturally good at hate and evil. Those kindergarteners came to us unable to behave, while their parents fought and used colorful four-letter metaphors to express themselves. It is all part of our sinful nature. Thus, to grow beyond this filth of *works* (Galatians 5: 19-21), we have to be willing to learn to apply the Fruit of the Spirit (Galatians 5: 22-23). We offered the parents effectiveness training, yet few of them took advantage of this or any of our other programs designed to turn them from the harshness of their situations to a better direction. These parents lived in a pattern of life using what they knew and had experienced, and were not interested in growing from those experiences to better ones. They did not want to take advantage of getting better jobs, better living situations, or to get off drugs and alcohol. Even the immigrants, who were here illegally, could get citizenship under amnesty programs; yet, most did not want to. Many of them were on drugs, alcohol, welfare, and, were inundated with anger and bitterness, choosing to remain in that harsh attitude. They had the opportunity to change; the resources and money were there to help them, but few wanted it.

Wake up, O sleeper, rise from the dead, and Christ will shine on you. Ephesians 5:14b

I learned a valuable lesson on human behavior. We have to want something to get something. Work and effort are required. Even if it is dropped in our lap, we still have to be willing to pick it up. In that same college, I lived in the dorm and was amazed at the contrast between students whose parents paid for everything versus the students who had to work their way through school. Most of the students who had college and all they could possible need dropped in their laps, partied their way through school. Few respected their parents and even fewer made anything of themselves with careers, relationships, or character after graduation. They did not learn to *stretch*; all they had was ingratitude and no appreciation of what they were given. They squandered it all away. Conversely, the students who had to work generally became more successful in their careers, more appreciative, and had more character. *Stretch out your hand,* in Matthew 12: 13, implies that there is a connection between our faith and Jesus' healing power. The healing was given, but it also had to be received! The initiative needed to be taken. We have to *wake up,* and get moving (Ephesians. 5:14). Although grace is given, we still have to act on our faith to receive it. The same is true with relationships; we have to *want* to be good at them to be good at them!

We have to learn what love is, how to relate, and, how to make friends. We have to want to! We have to learn how to love, and keep learning how to love. We have to learn about character, put it into practice, and keep learning and practicing. There is no end to this cycle until we are called home. Once we stop, we stop relating, and our relationships stop. We need to see friendships as enjoyment—given to us to use. People are precious and are brought to us to enjoy. If we get this backwards, we will fail with life's precious gift. We are to seek the fun and the excitement of something special, because each friendship is special.

The secret to making friends is so simple.

Now the tax collectors and "sinners" were all gathering around to hear him. But the Pharisees and the teachers of the law muttered, "This man welcomes sinners and eats with them." Luke 15:1-2

Friendship is defined throughout Scripture as the companionship and closeness we are to have with one another. It is a commitment to build relationships by getting to know others while modeling and helping them learn the characters and precepts of God's Word. In turn, it helps us. Relationships are essential to life and is the Christian's number *two* priority in life. Number *one* is our growth in Christ! Friendship is not to be feared; rather it is to be embraced, even when it hurts!

The secret to making friends (beyond what we have talked about so far) is to be *friendly*! This is the key; if you want friends, you have to be a friend. If you want people to like you, you have to be likable. This may sound so simple that *why say it?* Well, most people are just not friendly! This goes along with the other fruit and characters found in Scripture as well. If you want to be loved, then you must love; if you want to be cared for, you must care, and so forth. In the churches where I have been on staff over the years, most people put on the pretentious, friendly façade on Sundays; then, on Mondays, the friendliness factor is absent. As the stresses of life become rooted in them, so the Sunday smiles turn upside down on Monday. Then, they wonder why others are not friendly with them. Not only are others not friendly with them, they gossip against them because most of them are being obtuse. However, they rationalize that it is the other person's problem. Well, it may be the other person, but that is not the issue. *They* are the issue. How is your friendliness factor? You are not responsible for how others treat you; you are only responsible for how you treat others—period! When we finally understand this, we will see some big changes in how others treat us in return!

Friendship is necessary, but not necessarily natural.

If it is possible, as far as it depends on you, live at peace with everyone. Romans 12:18

The Christian must realize that people are not naturally inclined to build friendships, but to destroy them; so, our friendships must be worked out. In doing so, we are never to take any of our relationships lightly or for granted. We need to see the power, eminence, and call that we have, so we can take what we have learned about character and love and put it into action. When this happens, we will seek to be friendly to everyone, even people who are mean and rude to us. We will be able to take the principles of the Sermon on the Mount (Matthew 5-7) and put them into practice, becoming peacemakers and forgivers.

He came to that which was his own, but his own did not receive him. John 1:11

Scripture also tells us what the opposite of friendship is and what happens when we fail at this vital call. Animosity and bitterness will replace the vacuum of good relationships. These rotten fruits will cause apprehension and discontentment in society as well as the church. Instead of the friendship and cooperation we could have had, we will be left with strife, gossip, backstabbing and such, causing all kinds of social breakdowns and destruction! This becomes an endless cycle that we pass on to all those around us, our children, and our children's children. That is what it means in Exodus 20:5 when it says, "the sins of the father will pass to three generations." We pass on our behaviors, habits, and mindsets, both good and bad! We have to get beyond our selfish inclinations, and focus on what God calls us to, as we discussed in the first chapter with the "four primary attitudes that lay the foundation for building effective relationships."

Friendship is a Priority

Share with God's people who are in need. Practice hospitality. Romans 12:13

Remember; friendship is an essential quality for a Christian to give and take, and is so important and needed in life! If you have ever wondered what the meaning of life is, or what your purpose is, or what is needed in your life, it is *building relationships*; first, with Christ, then with family, and finally, with others. When we ignore this, and become cut-off and distant, we are ignoring our call and responsibility in life. Yes, others will take advantage of and hurt you. What happens to you or how people may treat you is not your responsibility. You are only responsible for how you treat others! So, be willing to extend a loving hand, and also be willing to receive one. Friendship is risky, and it is critical. So, let us be individuals who apply the characters of Christ in our everyday experiences and encounters—to the best of our abilities!

With all this being said, the bottom line is—our friendships are a priority! Love is a priority, character is a priority, and our attitude is a priority. They all converge to work in the room of life. It is not enough to just believe that they are priorities; we must show to others that it is a priority. We are to consider people over our schedules. We need to take the time to see people as more important than our "stuff" and what we do. If you are so preoccupied with other stuff in your life—even what you think is important, such as your personal goals, needs, wants, desires, school, earning money, or building your career—your relationships will erode and you may even find yourself totally alone and bitter. This does not mean we should live our lives in a coffee house; we are not to forfeit our responsibility and call in society, as school and work—as we will see in a coming chapter—is important. Work, finding that career that we best fit in is important, but it is not the *only* important thing nor is it the *most* important thing. You are to strive to seek a balance while keeping your call, spiritual gifts, and relationships going in a biblical direction.

Sometimes, people can so over-extend themselves with so many relationships, they never develop close-knit friends. It has been my experience and observation that most people stay in groups, not in closeness, because they do not put the effort in it. They substitute the safety of the group for friendships rather than the intimacy of closeness. Perhaps, they find comfort in groups. Perhaps, they only want to divulge the superficial side of themselves, and fear the depths of intimacy and vulnerability. Maybe it is the discovery of people that it fun, but not the long-term pursuit. There is nothing wrong with large groups; in fact, it is a great way to find, develop, and practice relational skills. But, it is not a place to hide from others or yourself. We need to remember that being close to a few is far more valuable than being popular to many. This is a danger to pastors as most of us are popular to many and have few, if any, close friendships. Yes, we need to be popular to many to be effective, but we cannot forget the value of closeness.

Self-disclosure

Is any one of you in trouble? He should pray. Is anyone happy? Let him sing songs of praise. Is any one of you sick? He should call the elders of the church to pray over him and anoint him with oil in the name of the Lord. And the prayer offered in faith will make the sick person well; the Lord will raise him up. If he has sinned, he will be forgiven. Therefore confess your sins to each other and pray for each other so that you may be healed. The prayer of a righteous man is powerful and effective. James 5: 13-16

So, what is the key to getting out of the locked room at the shallow end of relationships? Well, it is the scary, dark place where most of us fear to go. It is the willingness to venture into the world of *self-disclosure*. Whether you are very shy or are the life of a party, one of the principle venues to having deep, meaningful relationships is the willingness to share and to listen beyond the surface *white noise* of life. People need to be heard; and, to be heard, you have to listen. You have to share your life. This does not mean you monopolize people's ears, nor do you let all of your problems hang out all of the time. The main issues of closeness are honesty, openness, and transparency, without being overly needy of others all of the time. We also have to remember that to make this work, we have to be accepting of others as persons—not their behavior—especially if they do something wrong.

Many of us hold back from this self-disclosure because it is perceived as a dark place where our fear of being rejected is the only thing we see. We may think, *if they knew the real me, they would not be interested in me*! But, that is not true. The most boring people I have known have had some of the best and closest relationships. The "Forest Gumps" and "James Bonds" of the world, to whom everything seems to happen, tend to be distant from those close relationships that the "boring" people have. There is no need to make stuff up, wear masks, or hide your true self. People are naturally drawn to others who are real. This is true whether you are living the life of James Bond or Joe the Mole. You are special and unique. The key to making friends is being open, honest, respectful of the other person, and letting people know the real you. God made you special and unique, so do not be afraid of who you are!

Take a Chance

You did not choose me, but I chose you and appointed you to go and bear fruit—fruit that will last. Then the Father will give you whatever you ask in my name. This is my command: Love each other. John 15:16-17

Have you ever realized that Jesus took a chance with you? Relationships require a chance and vulnerability. Once you realize what is holding you back and see God's comfort and grace, then you can start to take chances. The first change is being the first person to open up. In pastoral counseling, the secret way to get people to trust you—to share—is for the pastor to be willing to open up first. Usually, because they get to know you through the pulpit and life of the church, they are all ready to be open. If it is someone from the community, the counselor often needs to be first in divulging something about himself. This can be a mistake he made that is similar to their situation, or a story—something personal—so you earn the right for them to hear you. It is extremely important to be open and honest. When this happens, trust is established and listening begins. As you go into deeper areas, the relationship grows. It is the same with friendships.

Sometimes, you have to be the one to open up first, even if you are not naturally inclined to do so. Be willing to share first. Yes, it can be hard for some, but the payback is stronger relationships. If this is hard for you to grasp, then consider the life of our Lord when He walked this earth. God Incarnate was very real and transparent, totally lacking of pride and self, totally focused on God the Father and His mission as our example. Jesus did this in a culture where Rabbis were aloof and distant from the people. That is why the people were so astonished with Him. Besides His miracles, He showed He cared! They were shocked that He did this, and it attracted more people than did His miracles!

Remember, honesty must operate in the parameters of character. The *real you* must also have godly character. So, if you have a *beef* with someone, being argumentative is not the way to self-disclosure! Nor, are we to reveal feelings and/or information that will put others down; that is gossip and God hates that!

What about people we just do not like? I do not believe that God calls us to hang with people we do not get along with, although we should ponder why we feel this way. It has been my experience that what we hate in others is what we harbor in ourselves!

Affection

For God so loved the world that he gave his one and only Son, that whoever believes in him shall not perish but have eternal life. For God did not send his Son into the world to condemn the world, but to save the world through him. John 3:16-17

Another key aspect of friendliness that is attractive to others is how we use warmth and affection. When we are warm towards others, it makes them feel special, and people like to feel special! This, like other characteristics, must be real! If it is pretentious, most people will see right through it, especially kids. This is accomplished best by affirming others and letting them know they are special. There are various levels to this, however. How you express this to your spouse versus to a coworker are two completely different things; if not, you are in sin and in trouble!

We need to be accepting of others. That does not mean we must approve of their bad behaviors or sin. But, we acknowledge them as children of God who were created as we were created, and who are loved as we are loved. Jesus loves all the children of the world! Some will accept His love; others will reject it. We are called to spread it!

Friendships Evolve

Dear friends, let us love one another, for love comes from God. Everyone who loves has been born of God and knows God. Whoever does not love does not know God, because God is love. This is how God showed his love among us: He sent his one and only Son into the world that we might live through him. 1 John 4:7-9

Another thing to be aware of in relationships is that they are a *life form* that grows, evolves, and changes. Just as children grow and develop, we too all are always in a state of change as are our relationships. Two people may start at a particular level, then that level changes as they mature, endure experiences, experience growth, and so forth. So, the relationship evolves, and either grows closer or further apart. So, realize that where you are now is not where you will be a few months from now, and certainly not in a few years from now. We all go through various seasons of life affected by our environment, temperament, and spiritual growth. We need to know when to create space and boundaries and when to be there. The situation and temperament will be the clue, and listening will give you the directions. Life is about growth and change. You know this if you work with children or in a garden, as all life from plants, animals, and even humans are constantly in a state of change. So, expect, anticipate, and prepare yourself. Build roots that will stay and wings to take you around, as we need both roots and wings in life. The roots are your virtue and character and the wings are your ability to move and grow.

Even the best of relationships will become strained and may even end. Sometimes, that is the cycle, because it was just meant for a season and then is over; other times it was ended too soon. There is a lot that we can do to keep relationships. The key here is the willingness to forgive (which I will talk about in an upcoming chapter), even if you are not at fault. The other big issue is relinquishing your pride and honoring the relationship as more important than your self-importance. Forgiveness and eliminating pride are crucial in sustaining relationships!

If you see your relationships becoming stagnant, look over what we have discussed and use it as a check-up. This may be the time to check how you are coming across to others. How is your character and friendship factor? Are you evolving with the other person and his/her needs? Are you listening? Then see how others are with you in these areas. Be open and willing to discuss this with the other person in a loving, understanding, and tactful way. In my counseling experiences, most relationships end because one did not keep up or listen closely to the other's needs. One allowed pride to get the best of him/her, taking pride as the trophy and not the relationship. Thus, the relationship killers of withdrawal, defensiveness, criticism, anger, and contempt took over. Relationships are far more important than pride. This does not mean that we are to be doormats or allow ourselves to be taken advantage of, but, most of the time it is the little things that build up and eventually destroy relationships—like tiny termites taking down a large house. The termites do not eat the house all at once; it happens over a long period of time during which you have ample time to get rid of the bugs and fix the problem. If not, your house will eventually be eaten to near nothing and will become inhabitable. In the same way, your relationship *house* will fall down by neglect.

Loyalty

This is love: not that we loved God, but that he loved us and sent his Son as an atoning sacrifice for our sins. Dear friends, since God so loved us, we also ought to love one another. No one has ever seen God; but if we love one another, God lives in us and his love is made complete in us. 1 John 4:10-12

Another aspect in making good and lasting friends is *loyalty*. Loyalty means putting into practice listening, character, and the ability to keep a confidence. Confidence is not just for professionals such as doctors, lawyers, or pastors; I believe it is for everyone. Counselors and pastors must keep it even more rigidly, but the average Christian must keep his/her relationships important. You show your loyalty by not gossiping. This earns respect and trust from others so they will share, and feel comfortable in doing so because they know they can trust you. Even though we discussed the importance of a growing and evolving relationship, your loyalty and consistency must remain as part of the roots. This creates the stability and longevity factors of your relationships, especially in a marriage! Others admire your commitment to stay with it for the long run. That is something that can be held on too. If you are the one who gives up too easily, then that trust cannot be built. However, loyalty is not always 100 percent. You cannot expect the other person to be 100 percent loyal to you because, as a fallen creature, you will fail; others will disappoint you and you will disappoint them. We will all make mistakes; we are not perfect. This is where forgiveness comes into play. When you go through these tough times, reach out and experience forgiveness; your relationship will actually become stronger! And, like I said, the only way this will happen is for you to remove your pride.

Listening

We know that we live in him and he in us, because he has given us of his Spirit. And we have seen and testify that the Father has sent his Son to be the Savior of the world. If anyone acknowledges that Jesus is the Son of God, God lives in him and he in God. And so we know and rely on the love God has for us. 1 John 4:13-16

What else can I do to make friends? *Listen*! Someone told me a few years ago why he does not listen. He said, "I do not have the spiritual gift of listening, so I do not have to listen." I wish I had been able to respond to him, but I just stood there with my mouth open, dumbfounded. Listening is not a spiritual gift that some people have and some people do not have. Listening is something we all can do and are called to do, even if we are deaf. Listening is a natural ability and a skill that can be improved on; all it takes is the will to turn it on and let it work. We can also learn techniques to improve our abilities. To be an effectual friend, you must know how to listen.

I like to joke with my wife Mary. When she tells me that I'm not listening, I respond by saying, "I'm listening; I just don't remember what you said!" From birth to death, we have the need for someone to listen to us. One of the main problems facing youth today is that no one cares for or listens to them; that is a major reason why events like school shootings (such as the one at Columbine) happen. It can be a casual conversation or a deep therapy session; if you feel that the other person is not listening, then you feel they do not care. Being listened to is a lot like being loved; so, we must take this matter seriously and grow in this skill. And, as I have learned, listening is not just hearing, it is actively participating in the conversation with your full attention—putting your response on hold.

I can do several things at once naturally. I can watch TV, read a newspaper, and carry on a conversation simultaneously. My grandfather had a leg up on me; he could do all this and listen to the radio, too. Then he could recite everything that was going on—and he did not even finish the ninth grade! That is too much for me. However, both of us learned that our spouses feel much better when those distractions are not present. They like to be the only recipient of our attention, even though both of us could repeat every word *verbatim*. The other person needs to feel your presence, see your eyes, and know you care. They have to be the most important thing/one in the room or in the world at that time. This is what makes a magnificent counselor and one who is sought after in his job; it is also what causes a marriage to succeed. There is an old story about a student who comes to the great philosopher Socrates to be discipled by him. When this young student came to Socrates, he kept talking and talking and talking, so that Socrates could not get a word in edgewise. Socrates had to put his hand over the student's mouth and say "I'm going to have to charge you twice." The student asked "why?" Socrates said, "In order to make you a great leader, I will have to teach you two disciplines. First, you need to learn how to hold your tongue before you can learn the second discipline. And secondly, you will need to learn how to use your tongue correctly."

Greek philosophers put a very high premium on elegant speech, and Socrates was the best of them all. But, he knew very well you could not speak until you could listen. The early Christian community, as it was facing persecution, knew that to be a support and a leader, it must listen and progress in spiritual growth. The Christian, especially the leader, must be willing to listen. As followers of the Lord and relationship builders, we have to listen to His Word and to the people in our world. How we listen shows where our interests are and what our capabilities are as a friend. Are we mirroring Christ's character and grace or just seeing to our personal needs? The fruit that flows from listening is growth and spiritual maturity which leads to godly actions and creates friendships and real fellowship.

Listening is the quintessence of effective relationships. Combined with love, kindness, and character, listening will be the synergy to your being a winner in relationships, being real and effectual, and being better used by God. Listening people are the girders that connect and strengthen those four pillars of relationship building found in the first chapter. If I have not made my point yet, here it is: *listening is the key integral aspect of being a friend; you cannot be a good friend unless you listen.* You can look upon it as a support structure on the foundation of the Lord, where all the friendship aspects are part of the building. Listening makes up the frame that the whole structure is built on. Without the frame—without a skeleton—our bodies and houses would become limp and fall to destruction. Without the support of listening and caring, a friend will fade and a leader will fail. They will fall limp and surely fail, even if they are following the rest of the characteristics we have discussed so far!

Relationships are built on listening, both to God's Word and to one another. The relationship between a husband and wife is as good as each one's ability to listen. The leader in the church is as good as his ability to listen. The words that we hear are not as important as the care and effort put into them; the effect of listening is that the words are not the only interpreter of the message. The primary focus in communication is the hearer, the receiver of the communication; in relationship to each other, it means that the care is usually more important than the words, especially for the Christian. The words are the wrapper and the listening is the chocolate.

Humpty Dumpty once said, "I know you think you understand what you thought I said, but I'm not sure you are aware that what you heard is what I meant." (*Alice in Wonderland*, by Lewis Carroll)

There are many good books on how to listen, so I will not take too much time here other than to say, LISTENING IS ESSENTIAL! Good friend-makers are good listeners. Be the person who listens (John 8:47; James 1:19-25)!

Can I do this?

God is love. Whoever lives in love lives in God, and God in him. In this way, love is made complete among us so that we will have confidence on the day of judgment, because in this world we are like him. There is no fear in love. But perfect love drives out fear, because fear has to do with punishment. The one who fears is not made perfect in love. 1 John 4:16-19

Yes you can! If you think that this friendship stuff is too much and say, *Hey, I can not do that; I will be embarrassed.* Perhaps you will, especially if you are not used to it, so take it slowly. Look at the importance of praising people; maybe you have never done this, or feel very awkward at it. Start off by praising people for the things they have done. Then, start to praise them for who they are. Then, start to praise them for being special in your life. The more you do it, the more you will be comfortable with it. It may take time because your habits and mindsets will have to readjust. Your hurts and resentments will have to be held back and risks be placed forward.

Yes, you may get hurt. If you have never been hurt, then you have never ventured far in a relationship. Remember, relationships are dangerous to our self-concept and feelings. The self-concept and feelings of others may collide with ours. As with any collision, anything could occur, from a dent to being *totaled*. Just remember, our Lord owns the *body and repair shop*! You have to take yourself in through prayer, devotions, fellowship, and service to Him to get your *dents* pulled out, so to speak. If you do not go to the Lord, the dents will remain, and rust will cause even more damage. Crashes can turn a *ding* into a breakdown!

Our natural tendency is to criticize and put others down. We normally do this to make us feel better about ourselves. Yes, there are times we are to correct someone, such as a parent to a child, a boss to a worker, or a pastor to a parishioner. We, as humans, like to put the dents in others; some of us make it a sport; *who, and how many can I hit today!* But, as a Christian, our call is higher. We may still hurt others by our convictions and opinions or our personality, and that is OK, as long as we are being and acting on good character. Many people just do not like to be liked; some do not know how to handle a compliment, and others may detest you because you represent Christ here on earth. The point is, we are not to be intentional aggressors, causing *dents* in people; we are rather to be the *detailers* of others. The *detailer* is the person who washes and waxes, who buffs the shine in others, who brings out the best in others by example and love. *They will know we are Christians by our...LOVE!*

He who belongs to God hears what God says. The reason you do not hear is that you do not belong to God. John 8:47

Now remember; no one likes a pretentious *praiser* like the Eddie Haskell types of the world (the "Leave it to Beaver" neighbor) who goes around praising everyone and everything to achieve his own goals. Nor, do you want to manipulate the feelings of others so you can hear praise or receive affection for yourself. Praise must be real and not overused or it will be taken wrongly, even if one is sincere. Otherwise, people will not take you seriously; they will be suspicious of your motives and disregard you. This will cause you to repel friends instead of gather them. So, you need to find the balance of character, your personality, and assess the situation to determine when and how to praise.

There is also the male/female factor; men and women give and respond differently in relationships, especially with praise and feelings. Unsure? Does this sound too complicated? It really is simple. Character, love, being open, affection, listening——it all comes back to you being you and continually operating in those godly characters. Be consistent; that's it! The rest will fall into place as long as you are able to grow and mature in the faith.

Relationships are simple on the surface, and the ingredients needed to keep them functioning are simple, too. Relationships are also tough-stuff, because, as they are places in which to love, they are also places in which to be hurt. You will not be perfect; you will fail at times and others will fail you. But, be willing and able to get back up! Keep your eyes on the most important relationship you have, which is with Christ as Lord. Allow your growth and maturity in Him to be the template to fuel your steadfastness, consistency, and character. We have to keep trying even when we get knocked down! It may not seem worth it at times, but it *is* worth it! It is what life is about, and it is what you will take with you into eternity!

How to Discover My Friendship Factor

A man of many companions may come to ruin, but there is a friend who sticks closer than a brother. Proverbs 18:24

Here is how you can find out if you are effective at building and making friends. Take a careful look at this character and fruit of *Friendship* from God's most precious Word by examining these passages. Now ask yourself:

How are my friendships?

1. How do I define being *friendly*? Does it line up with what God says?
2. Do I like to be friendly? Why, or why not?
3. How do I exhibit friendship in my daily life?
4. What causes me to want to be friendly with someone?
5. What causes me not to be friendly, or to be bitter with someone?
6. What are my motives in being friendly with someone——personal gain, to get something, or love for others?

7. How do my feelings, mood, my day, or my attitude affect how I treat others?
8. How does being bitter counteract friendship? What happens to my relationship with God and with others when I am bitter?
9. Have hurt and rejection in the past affected the way I am with others now?
10. Do I have at least one close friend whom I can call anytime I am in need, and who will be there for me?
11. Have I been friendly with someone when I should not have been?
12. What are the things I judge someone by to see if they are worthy to be my friend? How do my standards reflect God's standards? What needs to change in my outlook and standards?
13. Am I the kind of friend to someone who will be there for them, no matter what?
14. Do I have a circle of people with whom I share my life?
15. Do I socialize with a vast multitude of people, but have no real, close friendships?
16. When have I been filled with friendship the most? Why?
17. What can I do to develop a better attitude of friendship?
18. What blocks or inhibits friendship and relationship building from happening in my life?
19. In what situation did I fail to be friendly when I should have been? Why?
20. Do I allow God's hand on me to help me develop the skill and willingness to be a friendlier person? If not, why not?
21. Is there someone with whom God wants me to seek a friendship, and I have not done so?
22. What issue is in my life that would improve by my being friendlier?
23. What do I need to work on to be a friendlier person?
24. How can I make my friendships function better, stronger, and faster, even in times of uncertainty and stress?
25. Think through the steps needed to put friendship into action in a specific instance, such as, *how can I prevent bitterness from taking root in me? How do my moods affect my friendliness factor? How can I build more and stronger interpersonal relationships?*

My dear brothers, take note of this: Everyone should be quick to listen, slow to speak and slow to become angry, for man's anger does not bring about the righteous life that God desires. Therefore, get rid of all moral filth and the evil that is so prevalent and humbly accept the word planted in you, which can save you. Do not merely listen to the word, and so deceive yourselves. Do what it says. Anyone who listens to the word but does not do what it says is like a man who looks at his face in a mirror and, after looking at himself, goes away and immediately forgets what he looks like. But the man who looks intently into the perfect law that gives freedom, and continues to do this, not forgetting what he has heard, but doing it—he will be blessed in what he does. James 1:19-25

Chapter VIII
HOW TO BUILD A GOOD PERSONALITY

Why do you look at the speck of sawdust in your brother's eye and pay no attention to the plank in your own eye? How can you say to your brother, "Let me take the speck out of your eye," when all the time there is a plank in your own eye? You hypocrite, first take the plank out of your own eye, and then you will see clearly to remove the speck from your brother's eye. Matthew 7:3-5

Do you think you have a good personality? Are you sure? I have rarely met someone who says *my personality stinks*! Yet, to be honest with you, most people do not have good personalities or, at the very least, they need improving, including mine. So, we have to be willing and able to take a hard look at ourselves, and in so doing, improve our personality so that we can be better at acquiring and developing relationships. We all have issues and things that we can work on. Presenting ourselves to be persons who desire to learn and grow will show us approved further by God.

Just think this through a bit. Think of people who attract you by their personality, character, and disposition. How do they come across? Usually, they exhibit the characters we talked about in the previous chapters. It is these characters that form the person and make them who they are to the people around them. Now, think about this: who were the best teachers you ever had? Why were they the best? Again, it is not necessarily their knowledge and insights, although those are important; it is how they treated and listened to you. Now, think about how you are to people around you. To get at this you have to peel away your assumptions about yourself, and take an honest assessment by asking others, even those who do not like you. Be in prayer, be discerning, and be open to critique and change.

This requires us to take a close look at ourselves. Self-examination is not an easy task; few of us like critics, and it is our human tendency to see problems in others and not in ourselves. We have to listen to what our Lord told us, "Why do you look at the speck of sawdust in your brother's eye and pay no attention to the plank in your own eye?" (Matthew 7:3) This means we must correct our own faults by removing the *beam* from our eye; then, we will able to *see*, discern, and help others who are not dealing with their faults.

Do not judge, or you too will be judged. For in the same way you judge others, you will be judged, and with the measure you use, it will be measured to you. Matthew 7:1-2

It is characteristic of our fallen, human, sinful nature to see the faults in others; but, more often than not, those very faults we point out in others are those we have too! And, a lot of people find fun and sport in doing this. However, as Christians, we must realize it is only funny on a TV sitcom, never in real life! We have to be willing to look at ourselves, our flaws, and all of those things we need to improve, and place our focus there seeking God's empowering help. Our responsibility is to grow in character, not point out faults in others unless it is done through the relationship of a mentor and with the disposition of the Fruit of the Spirit.

For good relationships to be built, we have to be willing and able to treat others in the same manner we want to be treated. This means having a good personality, being a person to whom others respond, and having a personality that is framed and built upon a growing relationship with Christ as Lord. We are called to be persons who live our lives to the glory of God, not persons who judge and are condescending to others. If we are centered upon Christ and His precepts, then our personality will still have what makes us unique, but will also allow others to see the reflection of our Lord in us.

In my experience in pastoral counseling and church management, I have found that the judging of others is one of the biggest problems in the church. People think they are OK, so they pick on and complain about others. I find it almost amusing that the faults they pick at in others are the ones I see in them. So, what does this mean regarding personality? *Do not do this!* Jesus tells us in Matthew 7, simply put, *DO NOT JUDGE!* That means we are not to be critical or have a measuring stick with which we compare everyone else! A Christian who is critical and condescending is a terrible, destructive force to the Kingdom of God, as he/she exhibits the direct opposite behavior of what a Christian's should be. This will also display your uniqueness as gone extremely astray, and will become the rotten personality others seek to avoid.

As a prisoner for the Lord, then, I urge you to live a life worthy of the calling you have received. Be completely humble and gentle; be patient, bearing with one another in love. Make every effort to keep the unity of the Spirit through the bond of peace. Ephesians 4:1-3

As a pastor, I have seen all kinds of various personalities in action, both functional and dysfunctional. Once, I was with some fellow pastors at a restaurant, and a church member of one of the pastors there came up to him with a real nasty attitude, yelling at him. He did nothing to spur that on, as I later found out. He was gracious with that individual and afterward told us, "well, that is just the way that person is; she will never change." It made me wonder; are people simply the way they are made, as some behavioral psychologists attest to, or do they choose to be that way, unwilling to change? Is our personality fixed at birth? My wondering did not last long because Jesus tells us to *remove the plank*; therefore, we must have the ability to do so. To remove the plank means we can change our personality, we can grow, and we can strive to be better. That pastor was just frustrated, and thinking that a person could not change gave him comfort so he did not feel a need to do anything to help people change. I saw him as a very sad person, because, that is how he acted—sad.

The view that people do not change is a common one, and most pastors that I have worked with would tend to agree with it. It is because we face so much strife and argumentation in the church; sometimes it is easy to see it that way, as that pastor I had lunch with did. Our beliefs can bring comfort; but we have to make sure they are the correct beliefs. And, in these views is the view of sin. A lot of mainline pastors do not believe in the reality of sin. I guess they do not read the newspapers, pay attention to people, or take God's Word seriously. So, if you do not think sin is real or relative, and whatever people do is just fine, then there is no need to improve or help others to do so. We have to separate sin from personality. To create a good personality, you are still being the unique *you* that God made, but the sin that has infected you and skewed your personality is cleaned out. The flaws we are to seek and remove are the character flaws that happen when we are not growing in the Lord or adhering to His precepts. We are to replace what we think with what we are to learn. We need not come up with excuses for our personality, but rather, find ways to get rid of the sin so our personality shows up better and cleaner.

Personality is not just a single part of how you come across; it includes all of our physical (as in body language), mental, and spiritual characteristics that come together synergistically with our experiences. Each of us is unique and special, so we will all have very different personalities. Our differences make us special but can also cause chaos. It is way beyond my ability to explain it, as it is unique to each individual. Yet, even though we are different and our distinctions are OK, there are traits to which Christ has called all of us to adhere. Even in adhering to good character, we will each use them in unique and special ways. The important thing is that we do so with excellence and maturity. What God gives us at birth combines with what we learn and experience in life; so, as with any organism, we are in a state of growth and change. Our personality is no different. It will grow and change for the better if we are willing to put the effort into it.

So I tell you this, and insist on it in the Lord, that you must no longer live as the Gentiles do, in the futility of their thinking. Ephesians 4: 17

We do not have to stay in our *narcissism* or sin; we can move away from our faults and be better towards others. When we develop those so-called flaws and defects, or what psychologists call *disorders*, what is, in fact, happening is that our experiences come into direct opposition to what Christ has given us. These can be the temptations to which we have given in, so we rationalize them as OK. Or, they can be hurts that we have experienced, and we cloak them with extra protection so we are not hurt again. Sometimes, we make faulty choices by our lack of discernment, and then repeat the same patterns by refusing to learn and to grow.

What we need to be doing is observing how we are in our relationships, and thinking of Scriptural principles to help us improve. When we have a clear idea of what Christ has called us to in terms of character (as we previously discussed), we can then see where we are in those precepts. Then we can brainstorm on how to apply them so that our lives change and our relationships improve. All some people need are the previous three sentences, and, *wham*, they are on the right track. For the rest of us, we may need a kick in the rear, or have a trusted friend show us. We may need a good counselor to help us work through these issues, especially when there has been prior trauma and abuse. Do not be afraid to probe inside yourself or have someone else help you, as it is far better to go through the process and improve—even if it is painful—than remain in dysfunction or refuse to respond to His higher love and calling. As with anything good, it may take time to change the old you and build a new you!

Questions to Ask of Yourself (be honest):

Carry each other's burdens, and in this way you will fulfill the law of Christ. Galatians 6:2

- How do I come across to others?
- What are the positive aspects of my personality that make people like me?
- What are the positive aspects of my personality that correspond with the good character found in Scripture?
- What are the personality traits that I may emulate that turn people away?
- What are the personality traits that I may emulate that correspond to he bad character found in Scripture?
- Why do certain people not like me? Is it their fault, or does it have something to do with how I come across to them?
- Do others see me as an attractive person (appealing personality, not looks), so they want to be around me, or do they seek to avoid me?
- Has there been significant trauma and/or dysfunction in my life that has contributed, in a dysfunctional way, to my personality?
- What can I do about it?

Keep in mind that there are no perfect people—including Christians! If you think you are totally OK, then you have a bigger problem than you will admit to. We all need improvement; we all need to strive to be better so we can glorify our Lord better and have better, lasting relationships.

You can take personality assessment tests—from the classic Myers-Briggs to the ones administered by professional counselors. You can also find some on the Web from www.eharmony.com and www.assess-yourself.org.

Keep this in mind, too; if you refuse to change, it will adversely affect your witness as a Christian to your family, friends, and your church. Why, why, *why* would you want to do that? A real, committed Christian is one who *acts out* his/her faith in the Lord and obeys His instructions. Therefore, we will be willing to repent and change, freely and gladly; if not, there is something amiss in our spiritual life. And, this process of self-examination, seeking the Lord, and striving to improve who and how we are is a continual one; it does not stop.

Did you know that after five years out of medical school, the things doctors learned there are mostly obsolete? There are scores of new treatments and dozens of new drugs that come out every year, so they have to be continually learning more about their craft. Hence, the word *practice* is really what a doctor does. If a doctor decided to stop learning about new treatments and procedures or the latest drugs, he/she would soon be ineffective as a physician and unable to effectively treat people, even placing them in danger. God gives the Christian a similar call as that of a doctor; *heal, and do no harm.* We, too, are to seek the healing of relationships and do no harm. As the doctor who refuses to learn, we could soon be causing harm, creating hurt and dysfunction instead of healing and harmony. We have to be willing to move ourselves from being sin-centered to being Christ-centered!

Matthew 15: 1-20

Don't you see that whatever enters the mouth goes into the stomach and then out of the body? But the things that come out of the mouth come from the heart, and these make a man "unclean.""" For out of the heart come evil thoughts, murder, adultery, sexual immorality, theft, false testimony, slander. These are what make a man "unclean"; but eating with unwashed hands does not make him "unclean." Matthew 15: 17-20

Jesus confronted the Pharisees, telling them that defilement—as in our words and deeds—comes from within, and that the show of pretence we make to cover them up does us no good. Our words are eternally important because what corrupts us are the lies, gossip, and slander we give out to one another; the traditions and pretences we put up as a shroud only hide them. We are to separate what our culture says is OK and what God calls us to, and follow God and His ways, as His are the best ways.

Some key ways to improve our personality:

The tongue also is a fire, a world of evil among the parts of the body. It corrupts the whole person, sets the whole course of his life on fire, and is itself set on fire by hell. James 3:6

- We are to commit ourselves to Jesus, who gives us wholeness and character!
- We are to keep our personality and traditions so that they match up with Scripture!
- We are to get rid of our personality and traditions that conflict with Scripture!
- We become increasingly aware that our goal in life is to glorify our Lord!
- We commit to honor our Lord in all that we do—and that means our actions as well as our words!

Perhaps, you may think that some of these passages for this chapter are harsh and do not apply to you. But, to improve our relationships, we have to start with how we honor and respond to our Lord and Savior! We are to respond to His precepts with our personal holiness! Because we received His grace that sanctified our heart and covered our sin, that should strike a chord within us to respond. Out of our gratitude for what He has done for us, we should be willing to strive to seek righteousness in all that we do. This is the sweetness that spills onto others; this is the honor and trustworthiness we earn in the hearts and minds of the people God brings into our lives. What builds a good personality? Our growing relationship with Christ! He is the one who changes us and forms our character. All we do is adoringly respond by faith and commit to His precepts.

When we are doing the above:

- We will realize that His grace is sufficient!
- We will have a thirst for righteousness!
- We will be speaking words that edify others, and bringing Christ glory because those words are attuned to Christian commitment!
- We will be using the resources that our Lord has given us with which to live a triumphant life!
- We will be taking the love and compassion He has given us to help others in need!

Here are some ways we can improve our personality by understanding the role of the church.

As Jesus was walking beside the Sea of Galilee, he saw two brothers, Simon called Peter and his brother Andrew. They were casting a net into the lake, for they were fishermen. "Come, follow me," Jesus said, "and I will make you fishers of men." At once they left their nets and followed him. Matthew 4:18-20

Why the church? As a Christian, you are the church. It is not a building; rather, it is people. We live in a fallen world, and we are all filled with sin. Sin affects our relationships by the way we treat people and the way they treat us. Yet, even in sin, we have the choice to make a difference and build His body, the church, effectively. One of the best ways to do this is to effectively understand the call of the church, as our personality and how we come across to others is a part of it. This is not *stuff* just for pastors and elders; it involves the precepts we all are to know and follow. It is about who He is and what He calls us to. So, are you building His church? Or, are you tearing it down? Knowing what Christ has called you to and how the church is supposed to work will greatly help you to empower your personality for the better!

The effectiveness in doing *church* is more about how the members relate to one another and the people whom God brings to them more than any other factor besides good, sound teaching. The Bible is clear on our responsibility; we are to look at those responsibilities and make them work in both our context of life and the needs of the community.

In the passage of Matthew 4:18-20, the veracity of the mission of who we are and what we are to do is summarized in a couple of sentences. Jesus is the voice; He is the Power; He is the reason; we are the receptors to Him! This passage gives us a picture of the male role in the church. First, Jesus calls us to Him! It is a simple call; *come follow me*. God calls us to know Him better and to grow in our faith, maturity, character, and attitude! Then Jesus calls us to others! It is a simple mission: to *make fishers of men*. We are to take our new life in Him and be willing and able to share it with others! And, in this simple formula for "doing" church lays an imperative precept on how we are to treat one another.

The question is not *do we hear the call?* For I believe we all do as Christians. Rather, the question is *will we obey and follow Him?* All too often in my experiences as a pastor, I have found that few will actually follow Him. Jesus is still there calling us! What we do instead is jam His call with all of what we think is important in life, mainly the noise of our will. We block His call with our ways and plans, so that the things done in our churches are the works of the flesh—the deeds of our sinful nature, as the work and call He gives goes unmet and un-followed! Then, we wonder why our lives are empty and our churches vacant!

When we take careful view of Scripture, from Genesis to Revelation, we see three areas of responsibility to which we are called. John, chapter 15, expresses these three priorities together beautifully. Turn to a concordance or to the back of the book to our Scriptural references and see for yourself passages that support these essential priorities. Out of these priorities, we can take God's Word and contextualize it to motivate us to be better people, so we can take it to the streets and to the direct needs of people, causing them to come to the knowledge of our Lord.

We see from Scripture the importance and mandate of relationship and intimacy from our Creator. The only way we can remain in that relationship and share His intimacy is to do just that—to *remain*. We remain in Him by His nourishment—not of ourselves, not of our thinking and sense, and not just emotional devotion (I am not saying we can lose our salvation; I do not believe that is possible or biblical). No, we need rational commitment that will have emotion *with* it, but not driven *by* it. Our nourishment will be determined by the time and effort we put in it, just as with anything else. The calls and priorities the Lord has for us will be greeted with anticipation and eagerness, and will build our personality and relational skills so we can do a better job at building His Kingdom.

PRIORITY ONE: OUR COMMITMENT TO CHRIST!

I am the vine; you are the branches. If a man remains in me and I in him, he will bear much fruit; apart from me you can do nothing. If anyone does not remain in me, he is like a branch that is thrown away and withers; such branches are picked up, thrown into the fire and burned. If you remain in me and my words remain in you, ask whatever you wish, and it will be given you. This is to my Father's glory, that you bear much fruit, showing yourselves to be my disciples. "As the Father has loved me, so have I loved you. Now remain in my love. If you obey my commands, you will remain in my love, just as I have obeyed my Father's commands and remain in his love. I have

told you this so that my joy may be in you and that your joy may be complete.
John 15:5-11

To *love, worship, and praise God* is to be our prime commitment and call from our Lord. Look over the scriptures testifying to this first priority in the "Scriptural References" in the *Appendix.*

The magnitude of this passage and that of many more Scriptures are almost overwhelming to our efforts and His call, but are still clearly there for us to understand and obey.

Remain, in the John passage, means to abide, to be steadfast and sure of our Lord and who He is, as well as who we are in Him. The imagery is perfect, as a vine needs nourishment throughout its whole system, from roots to leaves; and without any one of the main parts, the whole vine will die. It is also true with us; when we are not in Christ, we will wither and die. Only when we are rooted in Christ and are receiving our nutrients from Him can we grow and thrive! These nutrients will grow us into who and what we are!

We are the church, the people of His pasture in the care of His majesty. We are joined to Christ, and this is the true church. Thus, He is our Lord, our Purifier, Overseer, Boss, and Savior. If we remain in Him, then we fulfill the call He gives us, and the nourishment that flows from Him to us will then flow to those around us. As we remain in Him with surrendered wills, we will grow and receive purification. We must realize the gravity of our situation when we are not in Christ, or when we turn our will away from Him. When we are the fruitless branches, we will be subject to pruning that could mean suffering and trials brought on by our stubborn nature. He must purify, for He is holy and calls us to holiness. Let us not be the branch that is thrown away, the dead wood that sits in a pew and does nothing except receive salvation then is not willing to improve or heed to Christ as Lord, His call, or giving Him glory.

We cannot be saved by our own efforts. Nor can we receive or exercise the gifts for His purpose; this is nothing of our doing. When we bow to our own will over our Lord's, then, we will receive our self-inflicted damnation—strong language for a strong opposition and will. Our call is to seek holiness, not ourselves. Yet, at the same time, we need to be improving ourselves—not to uplift us, but to be better for His usage.

The principle priority of our life and work must be to abide in Christ. This will be one of the primary factors in our improvement. Without this sense of purpose, we will fail, as our schemes and worst laid plans will derail us from His holiness and will. Without our Lord's presence and leading, we cannot do anything; we could not have been created, we could not live, and we could not work and serve. *Nothing!* The only truly good thing we can ever do in life is to remain in Christ. Then the *fruit* will flow; however, it cannot do so unless we are in Him. No work can be good unless it is flowing from our Savior. If we start off good and grow in Christ, then forsake Him with our busyness and distractions, we will dry up and wither away. Let us stop, fall to our knees in prayer, and repent! With a surrendered purpose, we then can abide in His majesty to stop the action of the fire.

For us to have good working personalities, we must abide and remain in Him. A life of prayer will sustain the connection and the abiding. Our obedience comes from the worship, the Bible learning, and the prayer life that lays the pipes through which His nourishment can flow. We need to see it this way; when we are obedient, we will succeed and prosper, no matter what we face! So, let us embrace His friendship and directive. His incredible self-sacrifice should empower us to obey with power, conviction, and joy flowing from us to others.

We must be committed to Christ in our worship, devotions, service, and in our surrendered will. We are modeling His character and the relationship He gave us back to Him, being thankful for our grace. We must, and can do this by our loving response of worship, truly desiring to be poured out and surrendered to Him in fervent Bible study, learning His character and purpose, and through in-depth prayer and two-way communication with our Lord.

The model for us to follow is whom Christ is, how He abides in the Father, and how the Father loves His Son without any limits, measure, or boundaries. Before we were born and beyond our death, His love IS. So, what is our response to this first priority? Are we worshipping out of obligation, for social reasons, out of habit? Or, do we worship out of a response to His deep love for us? Is our worship so formal that we never see His presence, or is our worship so bare that we are as dry as the efforts we put in? Spurgeon says we ought to be "prevalent pleaders, and not formal worshipers." (*Morning and Evening*) The same, of course, goes in our personality development and temperament.

Give careful notice to this; you cannot worship God with a heart filled with yourself. You cannot worship God with a heart that is occupied by greed, slander, arrogance, pride, envy, or malice. Neither can you worship when you are filled with worry, because these things take up all the room in our worship and then no room is left for God! When we are not worshiping or not worshiping effectively, all we are and do suffers from our misdeeds, as do those around us.

Worship equals closeness to God and then motivates an improvement in our ability to be real and effective so we can become a person to whom others will be attracted. The best way is to spend our growth time joyfully, to be our best for His glory. We can do that by making sure that His call is released in us, and that His choice and election is fueling our response. Then, we will bear His Fruit.

Priority Two: Commitment to the Body of Christ!

My command is this: Love each other as I have loved you. Greater love has no one than this, that he lay down his life for his friends. You are my friends if you do what I command. I no longer call you servants, because a servant does not know his master's business. Instead, I have called you friends, for everything that I learned from my Father I have made known to you. John 15:12-15

Our second commitment and call from our Lord is *to love and care for one another in the body of Christ.* What flows out of the first priority is the response of gratitude passed it on to those around us!
Love comes from the self-sacrifice of our Lord who paved the way for our relationships (especially to God). We must respond gratefully to our fellow believers with the fruit called from us. It starts off as a commandment! Love is an imperative response of the will, a choice we make in order to follow His directive and will. Love is life and a response, and love is a reward for our obedience. Love comes before obedience, and love is the result of obedience; yet, this is non-contradicting. Love is the elixir of life and the reward for all that remains on the vine.

This was a core Jewish belief as stated in Leviticus 19:18, and is quoted by our Lord when He was asked what the greatest commandment was, found in Mark: 12:30-31. Since the Lord loves us, then we should respond in love to one another! Since Christ is our Lord and model, we should follow His example. Christ will walk with us. The question is, will we walk with Him and allow *priority one* to be our rule, so *priority two* can function and love can flow both ways? Remember how the first few chapters were about our mindset of fullness and love? This is what flows from these priorities.

Remember, the love that Christ showed us was sacrificial, not superficial, so our love should not have any strings attached and should be real and flowing.

Why talk more on love? Because, it is so essential. What flows from love is obedience, another response we are to give our Creator. This too will greatly fuel our personality. Just as our Lord was obedient to His call, so must we be to His call to us. Real friendship is trust and obedience—not too common today, but required in the body of Christ for it to function correctly. We place strings and conditions on our relationships (yes we need boundaries, to protect others and ourselves, but not chains), and then wonder why our families and churches are so dysfunctional. It has materialized and arisen from our refusal to obey our Lord!

The basic theme is for us to model the first priority, then extend our relationship with Christ to those around us. If we cannot do it, then our relationships with one another will be dysfunctional, just as with the daytime talk show crowd. Thus, when we are in a good healthy relationship with the Lord, good relationships with people around us should naturally surge from it.

Just as God the Father models to Christ the Son (Matthew 11:25-30), and a good earthly father will model to his son, we are to model to our siblings, that is, all those in the body of Christ. We are to be in growing and encouraging relationships which are based on His redemption and our loving response and heart for His people. All those in the body of Christ are our brothers and sisters. The more we grow in priority one, the more we will grow in priority two. This is progressive, just as in any growth. God asks us to sit at His feast and eat from His table. Do we do the same with those around us? If our relationships are not growing progressively, then we have something blocking us; usually it is sin and our selfish will getting in the way of our relationship with Christ!

Let us heed that great call that He first chose us! It is God's choice and not ours. What great comfort it is that He took the first step in our reconciliation. But, God did not choose us so we could be bitter and sculpt an ineffective personality, or let our dysfunctions and bad experiences compile to take over whom we are. He chose us for a reason and a plan. His plan is for us to bear fruit. Not to just do it when it is convenient or when we feel like it, but continually, whenever we are, so that time does not constrain us, whatever we are, so that culture does not hold us back, and wherever we are, so that our place or location brings no limits! The call for a good, productive church that builds the kingdom of God is for it to be encouraging of one another. If not, all we do is build a kingdom of disease and dysfunction; then, the blame is on us for refusing to play ball God's way, which is the best way.

PRIORITY THREE: COMMITMENT TO THE MISSION OF CHRIST!

If the world hates you, keep in mind that it hated me first. If you belonged to the world, it would love you as its own. As it is, you do not belong to the world, but I have chosen you out of the world. That is why the world hates you. Remember the words I spoke to you: "No servant is greater than his master." If they persecuted me, they will persecute you also. If they obeyed my teaching, they will obey yours also. They will treat you this way because of my name, for they do not know the One who sent me. If I had not come and spoken to them, they would not be guilty of sin. Now, however, they have no excuse for their sin. He who hates me hates my Father as well. If I had not done among them what no one else did, they would not be guilty of sin. But now they have seen these miracles, and yet they have hated both me and my Father. But this is to fulfill what is written in their Law: "They hated me without reason." When the Counselor comes, whom I will send to you from the Father, the Spirit of truth who goes out from the Father, he will testify about me. And you also must testify, for you have been with me from the beginning. John 15:18-27

To *love and care for one another in the community and world* is our third commitment and call from our Lord. What flows out of the first and second priorities is the response to pass it on to those around us in gratitude for what Christ has done for us!

Reaching out to the community and world is one of the prime purposes for the church. To build an effective and attractive personality, we need to be willing and able to reach others. We need to have the loved-based, character-infused personality that understands fullness and produces affection. This is what flows from our devotion and worship on to healthy relationships with Christ and one another. In a nutshell, these are our fruits! If we are not reaching out, then we become a dead sea, just like the Dead Sea in Israel. It has a fresh flow into it, but no flow out of it; thus, it is stagnate and lifeless. If we refuse to follow the Great Commission, we too will be a dead persona, stagnate and lifeless, existing only for our selfish purposes, not God's call. This selfishness makes us an ineffective personality and church; this is not what Christ has called us to do! We cannot just be a church for our own whims and agenda; we are to follow Him! Neither can we stay in our Christian subculture with no effect or love going to others around us. If we develop and mold our personality to His precepts, then do nothing with it, what good was it? This third priority is the reason we develop ourselves further!

When we receive insults and are rejected for living out our faith or for being kind and modeling Christ-like character, we are to rejoice, as our Lord is working in others, and us. Should we be expecting to receive such a positive response? Should we expect more? *No!* We are to respond to a need with a grateful will and with joy that flows from the first two priorities. In my experience, when we are good, more good usually boomerangs back to us! As Christians, we will receive the Lord's love and acceptance which is the greatest treat and gift conceivable. Thus, when we do not receive the world's devotion, we are not to retreat or fall back from our responsibility and call. We are secure in Christ and we do not need the security of society, even though we may feel it is necessary for our self-esteem. We are to rely on Christ's esteem, not our self-esteem!

We cannot go through life just eating junk food and sweets, just as we cannot expect to go through life just receiving praise. We should expect tension as we go against the flow of our society and even sometimes people in the body of Christ. Christ was crowned with thorns; should we expect to be crowned with anything better? We know better! If we grew up in the church or spent any time reading His Word, then we know better, even if we are fairly new to the faith.

John 15:22 tells us of the seriousness of our call. It is not a *maybe* or an *option*; it is clearly an imperative, that is, a straightforward command, such as a superior officer would give a direct order to his troops! God is our Lord, which means He is our commander and chief; no direction should cross our path that is not given from Him! When we refuse the command, we should expect punishment. This may not be a very "churchy" or "politically correct" idea in a *Jesus loves you, and will give you what you want* church. However, this is the truth from God's Word!

Although I hope to come to you soon, I am writing you these instructions so that, if I am delayed, you will know how people ought to conduct themselves in God's household, which is the church of the living God, the pillar and foundation of the truth. Beyond all question, the mystery of godliness is great.
1 Timothy 3:14-16

How can we worship and praise God, yet hate our neighbor? How can we kneel down in prayer, but not take time for people around us? If we sit and hear the teachings of our Lord and then do nothing with them, we are, in fact, practicing atheism and not Christianity! The philosophy of people who reject God is to reject His teaching. Thus, we are no better than they who claim themselves as their god!

The wonderful news of our directive is, we are not at it alone, and I do not mean our fellow believers. We have the Creator and Equipper of all things to empower us and come alongside to help! We are not alone! God first comes to us, and then desires us to love and worship Him and to allow that testimony to spill onto and fill those around us! The Holy Spirit is our power agent for the task (Ephesians 5:18). Now we have no excuse but to be poured out as He pours out His Spirit on us!

It is the role of the Holy Spirit to give a critique, and He will work with you *way* before using you to work with someone else! Every wrong personality flaw that you may observe in others already exists in you. If you are unwilling to deal with it while pointing it out in others, you are, as Proverbs so eloquently puts it, a fool! The chief characteristic of a Christian should be *humility*! Remember, if God judged you correctly and righteously, you would go straight to Hell, as we deserve neither grace nor His love. But, because of His grace, we have heaven—and Him—for eternity! So, we need to learn how to replicate that gospel of grace in human relational terms to help us to have that good personality. This will further help us build those good, loving, and content relationships.

You are probably thinking *so far, what he has been saying to me is good, but it is academic; give me some real help!* OK, here we go!

Ask yourself this: What does it mean to be a mature Christian? What are you willing to do about it?

The tongue also is a fire, a world of evil among the parts of the body. It corrupts the whole person, sets the whole course of his life on fire, and is itself set on fire by hell. James 3:6

- The key aspect in helping you improve yourself and your person-ality will be *how much time you spend in improving your spiritual life!* This is what builds the fullness, character, and love we have

been talking about! For a *how to* on this, see the Appendix on, "How to Build Your Faith"!
- Understand who Christ is and what He did for you!
- Understand that God loves you and wants your life to have purpose and meaning. God so loved_____, that he gave his only Son that when _____believes in Him, he/she should not perish, but have everlasting life *(Insert your name in the blanks)*. You may ask, If this is true, why is it that not everyone has a happy and meaningful *life?* It is because most people do not put it into practice!
- Understand that this does not *just happen*. You have to work at it; you have to grow in your faith and maturity. You cannot do this alone. Allow the Spirit to work in you, and allow others to sharpen you!

Unfortunately, strife, dysfunction, gossip, and slander are normal occurrences in our churches because our pride gets in the way of His call. Unless this filters into all of our relationships, the gifts will be neutralized or turned into weapons of dysfunction. Instead of reaching out and discipling, we fight among ourselves or develop false doctrines. The Body cannot do things well nor function when we are puffed-up with ourselves. We cannot function by pretending or out of hate. For us to be used by Christ effectively and build quality relationships, we must be infused with love, doing our part with joy. Unity is the responsibility of the believer to the church body. We have both unity and diversity; these are necessary in order to function together. We cannot all be the same. We are to acknowledge our differences, and be willing to fill in the gaps and deficiencies of one another. We are never to pretend with spiritual gifts or in ministry in general. Rather, we are to use them to encourage and build up, never tear down; authenticity is extremely important. God does not need us to wear masks and pretend. Kindness is the proof text to authenticity, and authenticity is crucial in building effective relationships!

When we have a healthy grasp of our redemption and the ways and means of the Gospel working in us, then our self-esteem should be spilling over with Christ-esteem. **Who we are to Christ is the most significant thing in the universe for the Christian!** We should never feel insecure or have the "poor me" attitude when we have Christ in our lives (Galatians 6: 3-5, 10). We need to be over-comers; this is a tough task, but we can do it with our Lord in control! We are never to go beyond our self-image at the expense of others, especially the Lord's. Remember this important fact: a *condescending Christian* is an "oxymoron" (with the emphasis on being a *moron*!). Like *jumbo* and *shrimp*, they just do not go together.

Are you wondering what this means for your daily life? Ask yourself, *Do people treat me unfairly? Do I treat others with dignity and respect?* Have you ever wondered why? Perhaps the way you treat others is not in line with what we have talked about thus far!

Here are some practical and important "dos" and "don'ts" that I have learned over the years which can help you see if you are on the right path with *how you are with others*!

For this very reason, make every effort to add to your faith goodness; and to goodness, knowledge; and to knowledge, self-control; and to self-control, perseverance; and to perseverance, godliness; and to godliness, brotherly kindness; and to brotherly kindness, love. 2 Peter 1:5-7

Hopefully, these suggestions will help you see what we have talked about by a simple application that you can easily do to help the process of improving who and how you are. Perhaps you will see something you have not thought of or have previously considered unimportant. Then, you can identify any flaw in your spiritual walk.

- DO smile; it costs nothing and is always appreciated!
- DON'T ignore people even when you do not want to talk; be friendly when someone says "Hello!" It is not about how you feel; it is about how you are supposed to be.
- DO make people feel important. Make each person feel that he/she is special and he/she is the most important person around!
- DON'T brag! No one likes a person who is full of self! Be an honest and humble person! It is far better that people find out about your achievements and abilities from sources other than you.
- DO have a sense of humor! Laugh and people will laugh with you;if all you do is cry, you will cry alone!
- DON'T always have problems, troubles, or need help; you will soon find yourself alone! We all have problems and need help; be discerning about knowing when to ask and when you are being a pest. The decision is based on whether you are seeking attention or relation.

- DO encourage people! Tell others what you like about them or when they are doing well. Encouragement is the fuel that moves the engine of the church.
- DON'T criticize or cut people down—including yourself! There is a difference between humbleness and a self-demeaning attitude.
- DO have an interest in many things. Be an interesting person, and people will be interested in you!
- DON'T grab the best, biggest, and most for yourself; give others a break! (unless you are a five-year-old!)
- DO meet strangers, although it may be difficult. You can make a great friend by being friendly to someone you do not know! We have to be willing to take risks as well as be discerning.
- DON'T make fun of others when they make a mistake or do something dumb! Be the one who goes to them first with encouragement.
- DO help others when they have a problem and share what you have with others! We are to be the people who give attention, not try to take it all of the time.
- DON'T have a bad temper or be an angry person looking for an argument or fight! Temperance is far better than temper!
- DO look good, clean, neat, and well groomed! It was Benjamin
- Franklin who said, *cleanliness is next to godliness.* The theology is off but the practice will be true.
- DON'T blame others for their mistakes, or worse, for yours! Be a person who takes responsibility, even if it is not your fault.
- DO keep a confidence. If someone tells you something, keep it to yourself; be trustworthy! You will never develop the essential quality of trust if you are a gossiper. There is only one thing that God hates more than gossip, and that is pride, so be on your guard against such actions.
- DON'T be too cool! Cool people are never popular people; they are too cool!
- DO listen and be an encourager! Listening is a sweet fruit that is needed by all. It says that you care, that others are important.
- DON'T over-correct people! Remember to first take the plank out of your own eye.

- DO take a joke and be a good sport! People who are teased a lot usually get that way because they have not learned how to take a joke and they overreact, spurring on the teasing.
- DO remember names! It shows others that they are important. The sweetest sound to some is their own name.
- DON'T be loud and obnoxious!
- DO thank people!

Make a tree good and its fruit will be good, or make a tree bad and its fruit will be bad, for a tree is recognized by its fruit. You brood of vipers, how can you who are evil say anything good? For out of the overflow of the heart the mouth speaks. The good man brings good things out of the good stored up in him, and the evil man brings evil things out of the evil stored up in him. But I tell you that men will have to give account on the day of judgment for every careless word they have spoken. For by your words you will be acquitted, and by your words you will be condemned. Matthew 12:33-37

Consider how you would like to be treated. You are a friendly person when you can be yourself in the unique and special way that God created you. Be authentic and real; at the same time, be tempered by godly character so the Fruit of the Spirit is real and flowing through you! Taking your cue from Galatians 5:22-25, make sure verses 19-21 do not happen to you!!!

Here is a simple, insightful exercise I used to do with both youth and adults. Perhaps you too may find it insightful.

Sit back, close your eyes, and visualize your spiritual and relational pilgrimage, which is your growth—all that you have been through in life. Include what you have learned and how you have applied the opportunities and experiences that God has given you.

- What is your first memory of God?
- What are some of the highest and closest times in your relationship with God?
- What are some of the lowest times?
- How has your spiritual sojourn/journey affected your relationships?

Now, on a piece of paper, draw a graph of years since you were born until today, and mark your ups and downs. Do another graph, using the same years and chart, on how you treated people—your family, your friends, people at church, and strangers. What were the results? Most of the time you can lay the graphs on top of each other in perfect correlation! Our *up* times with God coincide with our better treatment of others, and others' better treatment of us. Usually, when we treat others well, they reciprocate and treat us well, too. When we are growing in the Lord, regardless of our circumstances, we are more content and happy. When we are stressed, this flows into our attitude and how we treat others, then is replicated, bringing us down further. When we are centered upon our Lord, we will have more *up* time than *down* time! If you need further help in this area, seek a qualified and trusted pastor or Christian counselor. Also, seek someone to whom you can be accountable. In the Appendices are accountability questions; make use of them in your Bible study or small group!

Have you been thinking all along that we have been defending ourselves to you? We have been speaking in the sight of God as those in Christ; and everything we do, dear friends, is for your strengthening. For I am afraid that when I come I may not find you as I want you to be, and you may not find me as you want me to be. I fear that there may be quarreling, jealousy, outbursts of anger, factions, slander, gossip, arrogance and disorder. I am afraid that when I come again my God will humble me before you, and I will be grieved over many who have sinned earlier and have not repented of the impurity, sexual sin and debauchery in which they have indulged. 2 Corinthians 12:19-21

CHAPTER IX
COURTSHIP ANYONE?

But among you there must not be even a hint of sexual immorality, or of any kind of impurity, or of greed, because these are improper for God's holy people. Nor should there be obscenity, foolish talk or coarse joking, which are out of place, but rather thanksgiving. For of this you can be sure: No immoral, impure or greedy person—such a man is an idolater—has any inheritance in the kingdom of Christ and of God. Ephesians 5: 3-5

So, what should single Christians do instead of dating? Courting!

Most people in the United States have a very specific, shared idea on how to find a mate, and that is through dating! Did you know this is a relatively new phenomenon in history, having its beginnings in the 1950s? Did you know that a lot of high school and college young people today are rethinking dating, looking for alternatives? Let us explore some better ways!

Now that we have seen how important it is to get our attitudes and mindset aligned with God, and produce the character He calls us to, we can start to consider how this applies to the real world. Most Christians have no problem understanding why it is important to apply Biblical precepts to our marriages and friendships; but, what about dating? Can God's ideas help the dazed and confused Christian, as I once was, go about finding the love of a lifetime? The answer is a resounding, *yes!*

During the reign of all those reality shows on TV, most centered on finding the perfect mate, such as, *The Bachelor, The Bachelorette, Joe Millionaire,* and *Mr. Personality,* to name a few. My wife, Mary, got hooked and by default, I was forced to endure these silly shows which I had said were *nonsense.* However, my wife saw things that were appealing in them that I did not see. After all, there were no car chases, spaceships, or explosions to hold my attention. However, I did get some interesting insights. Each of these shows portrayed groups of people seeking and giving their all to win the prize—a lifetime relationship with the star of the show. After all of the manipulations, pretentious showmanship, games, and catfights, the Bachelor or the Bachelorette chose their winner, and off they went to commitment, engagement, and/or marriage. What I found so interesting was that after all of the intense role playing and manipulating to be the one chosen, most of the relationships did not work; some ended up so badly, it was quite pathetic and sad. And, I would bet big money that after a year, none of them would work; and, I was right!

The typical dating scene is very similar to those TV shows. Someone goes out on a hunt—whether a young man or a woman—out on the prowl, looking for the prey of fun, relationship, and perhaps marriage. Thus, they view the dating game as a game where they hide behind masks like one of those shows, *Mr. Personality*. With false pretences, they are looking for someone who is doing just as they are, hiding their real persona. Then, after winning their mate through all of the dating, the engagement, and marriage, the masks come off and the real person emerges. Both find themselves shocked, confused, hurt, and angry. It is no wonder most marriages do not last beyond five years. It was all a sham, leading up to a lifetime commitment! It may make good, entertaining TV, but not good reality!

Let no one deceive you with empty words, for because of such things God's wrath comes on those who are disobedient. Therefore do not be partners with them. Ephesians 5:6-7

Surely, there must be a better way to go about selecting our love-to-be, which will last through a lifetime. There must be a way we can seek the real person without the pretences, games, and *slight-of-hand*, so we will end up with who is best for us and not the consolation prize of the game "fruit basket upset." (pun intended)! That way is courtship! Courtship? Yes, courtship! This is a word our society sees as a joke from a long ago era that they presume is about oppression and doldrums. This word conjures up fears that we are not in control of the one with whom we settle down, that we will get ourselves into a bad and unloving marriage, while our true love will go to someone else as in the story of *Romeo and Juliet*. However, courtship, from biblical times through the Victorian period to the end of WW I, is a model of the best method of finding the right mate. No, this does not agree with our common thinking; but, stay with me and think this through. In courting, you lay aside the games and looking for the right person for you! In the past, the parents were the principle players, as they knew their children the best, and had the best in mind for them (This might scare you, as it did with me, but keep reading; most of the time this worked out great—of course, there were power plays and abuses). Thus, the parents were actively involved in the marriage process.

This may cause you great concerns, filling your mind with images of oppressive cultures who force their children into prearranged marriages. You may think of the Middle East or India and the recent news stories of how one young woman was murdered by her parents for refusing to marry the sixty-year-old man they picked out for her, but, instead, married someone else whom the parents considered to be the wrong man. However, these cultures and stories are of extreme beliefs and do not adhere to what the Bible has to say about courtship. We have to cast off our fears of what we think courtship is and take a careful look in history and Scripture to see the real benefits it may have.

Contrary to popular belief, most families did not arrange the marriage without the consent of the child. Sometimes, the parents found perspective mates, and the child was consulted for his or her opinion. Forcing two together then did not work any better than it does now, because, human behavior has not changed. Other times, the son would approach the daughter's father, and arrange the marriage with him. Today, a significant cultural rearmament in society would have to take place to make this model work. However, we can look at some of the precepts, and consider how they can apply today.

Of course, I went to a wedding of an arranged marriage in India not too long ago while I was writing this chapter, and the only people there who were happy were the mothers-in-law! The bride and groom were in a state of both shock and disgust, as both of their would-be suitors were also there, lurking and looking in from outside. It would have made a good story for a movie. But, again, this is rare even in countries where marriages are still arranged. This couple was thrown into it at the last moment and did not take the usual courtship steps. How did this couple do? Well, they got to know each other after the ceremony and discovered they had a lot in common, and that they liked each other. It looks like they will be quite happy. And, those two would-be suitors got together—with each other! (Yes, a good movie plot indeed!)

For centuries (when divorce was almost nonexistent), people were friends first; then, when one or both were interested, they "courted." There is nothing wrong with dating. The problem is how you go about it. If it is done in the tradition of the media, or what you think, or what you may have seen on an old TV game show or the latest radical TV show, you will get yourself in trouble. If it is done from biblical values, it will be a pleasurable adventure toward making the right decision for the love of your life! You will be building a lasting and enduring relationship versus one that will be miserable, and might end up in divorce court in a few years!

What's wrong with dating?

For you were once darkness, but now you are light in the Lord. Live as children of light (for the fruit of the light consists in all goodness, righteousness and truth) and find out what pleases the Lord. Ephesians 5:8-10

Just as there are many types of people, there are many ways to pursue dating. Perhaps this is the main problem. Since everyone has a different view of what is right and wrong, there are no standards, no rules, no values, and no "right" way. I am not saying *do not ever date*, because, there is nothing wrong with it as long as both people set boundaries and remain pure. Then, if standards of excellence are applied, and each one seeks to become acquainted without pretentious games or trying to hide the "real you," it will be OK. However, that is not the usual date, is it?

The main thing wrong with dating is that we tend to hide from each other. Traditional dating in the U.S. is based on lust, playing games, wearing masks, hiding one's true self, and seeking what friends and society say is right. In doing this, faults are hidden, and a false impression about oneself is given. In so doing, you are attempting to keep your date, then girl/boy friend, then fiancé, liking you. Recreational dating is even worse, as it is about self-gratification-seeking fulfillment in someone, or in multiple "someones," who cannot possibly meet that need in you; or, it is to satisfy your own sinful desires and needs.

Therefore, you will never develop a real, deep, meaningful, or impacting relationship with the person you are dating. So, when you do get married, you will not even know that person. You will only know the perception and idea that you have created for yourself. Then one day you ask, *who is that?* And—*wham!* You are disillusioned, hurt, and confused because that person is not who you thought he/she was. You married an idea, not the man or woman who was best for you. Thus, you begin a quest to change them into your idea of what they should be; and, of course, that never works. Consequently, you get frustrated, fed up, and end up in a shallow, distant relationship, or even worse, in divorce court—hurt, broken, confused, disillusioned, and missing out on God's wonderful plan for you!

Consider how dating is a *double standard*. In dating, you go from person to person, sometimes several at once, engaging in different forms of intimacy. Yet, when people get married, even in secular society, those various forms of intimacy such as co-habitation, kissing, hugging, sharing emotions, intimate relations, sex, and even bringing up children, are recognized as sacred between the man and wife. In addition, when that trust is betrayed by acting the way we do in dating, the other is appalled and deeply hurt. The problem is that we learn and practice one way, then all of a sudden we are expected to conform to an entirely different set of criteria. For most people, including Christians, this is too difficult to do.

Have nothing to do with the fruitless deeds of darkness, but rather expose them. For it is shameful even to mention what the disobedient do in secret. But everything exposed by the light becomes visible, for it is light that makes everything visible. This is why it is said: "Wake up, O sleeper, rise from the dead, and Christ will shine on you." Ephesians 5:11-14

In dating, we assume we are free to participate in the privileges of marriage with different partners. This sets up behavioral patterns that most people cannot break. Then, we are surprised if a married man or women has an affair, while it is quite acceptable for singles to have a different partner every week, each to whom they are physically and emotionally attached. Think about this: If you are giving away pieces of your heart to every Tom, Dick, and Harry/Debbie, Jane, and Kate, what will be left for that love of your life? Rampant emotional and sexual promiscuity will eat away at you and even remain in you, continually eating away! When we give ourselves away, the worst consequence is that it may not come back. Even at best, it will diminish us. Dating causes us to be too vulnerable. Most people date like they are married. They first live together, or act like they are in a marriage, but without the protection of commitment or of truly knowing each other! Think this through: you go out, date a stranger you never really get to know, spend a lot of time together, and give your hearts to each another—all with no life-long commitment or covenant!

If you are a child of God, saved by His grace, you have to realize how special you are, as is the person you will marry. You are His special property! So, until you say, "I do," and give your heart to another, be aware of who you are in Christ. Because you are God's child, you rob God and your future spouse when you engage in inappropriate sexual behaviors, even flirting and kissing. This is very dangerous and the reason most people are so hurt after breakups. It becomes an invitation to lose a part of yourself, and steal from both God and your spouse-to-be. Consider flirting; you are actually inviting someone else to be attracted to you and to lust after you when you do not yet belong to each other! You are causing someone else to sin and to desire something that neither you nor he/she can have—something holy, set apart to God!

In dating, there are no biblical values or precepts involved. Then you wonder why you get hurt! In courtship, you are preparing yourself and your future spouse for the covenant of marriage. This is the fortress, the castle that protects, because it is being built brick-by-brick. The bricks are made of material that builds a real relationship without the superficial mortar that causes the castle to collapse as soon as a rough patch comes along. Marriage is the boundary that protects your openness and vulnerability. Not convinced? Talk to anyone who just *broke up*. Sometimes the hurt stays for years; sometimes it never goes away! Then, they seek another person, only to end up breaking up with that one too. It becomes an endless cycle of emotional distress and confusion, as one seeks fulfillment in something that cannot fulfill.

Here are some more things wrong with dating:

Be very careful, then, how you live—not as unwise but as wise, making the most of every opportunity, because the days are evil. Ephesians 5:15-16

- Dating promotes lust and leads to sexual promiscuity.
- Dating promotes a self-centered model of love that is weak and un-biblical.
- Dating removes the vital friendship and getting-to-know-the-real-person stage of a relationship.
- Dating promotes a permanent bond between two people who are not meant for each other nor will spend their lives together.
- Dating devalues the real role of intimacy and sex for marriage.
- Dating teaches people to break relationships off when times are

difficult, an attitude which continues into marriage and initiates divorce.

- Dating promotes comparison to what the media says—un-biblical and unrealistic standards that few, if any, could ever meet. (Even the celebrities, with all of their money, power, and influence, virtually never meet the standards they promote!)
- Dating leads to false feelings of intimacy and ignores real commitment.
- Dating promotes an appetite for variety and change which will create discontentment and a desire for partner changing in marriage.
- Dating destroys friendships and even church fellowship, leaving Christians alienated from one another, and thus, ineffective for relational ministry.
- Dating confuses a *physical relationship* with *love*.
- Dating denies people who know you best to help you out—such as parents and mentors—so you will not make decisions based on lust, which will not last.
- Dating isolates a couple from other needed relationships, including church and parents.
- Dating distracts young adults from their education and preparing for their future.
- Dating creates an artificial environment for evaluating the character of another person.
- Dating will not prepare you for the realities of marriage as you hide things from each other, denying problems and potential problems until it is too late.
- Dating can cause a discontent and even a rejection of God's gift of singleness for those who have it.

Now you know what is wrong with dating. The main thing wrong with our culture's definition of love is that the definition often comes from song lyrics, poems, TV, and the movies, but rarely from real life or the Word of God!

What is Courting?

I will betroth you to me forever; I will betroth you in righteousness and justice, in love and compassion. I will betroth you in faithfulness, and you *will acknowledge the LORD. "In that day I will respond," declares the LORD— "I will respond to the skies, and they will respond to the earth; and the earth will respond to the grain, the new wine and oil, and they will respond to Jezreel. I will plant her for myself in the land; I will show my love to the one I called `Not my loved one.' I will say to those called `Not my people, ' `You are my people'; and they will say, `You are my God.' "* Hosea 2:19-23

Take a close look at Hosea chapter 2, verses 19-23. Notice the words *righteousness, justice, loving kindness, mercy* and *faithfulness* (NKJV), all in the context of being betrothed, which is the engagement—the final stage of courtship. Courtship is a framework for the goodness of what God has for each one to transfer to each other. It will help one to truly know the other, and to better see God working within the other, making it possible to trust and hold on to Him further.

Courting focuses first on building a friendship with the person in whom you are interested. It progresses slowly, develops deeper and stronger roots, and eliminates potentially dangerous, toxic, or wrong people for you. It looks to character and not just appearance. It seeks a real relationship without pretension or games. Courtship differs from dating in that it seeks closeness through friendship first, whereas dating seeks a contest and competition. Courting is an open and honest exploration of each other's lives, personalities, faults, desires, goals, and families, that builds and grows toward engagement and then marriage.

Courtship is about seeking a mate for marriage; so, you court in order to see if this is the right person for you *and* if there is any reason why you should not get married. The engagement is not just a time of planning the wedding; it is a time of seeing if you are truly compatible. If you are not, then break it off before it is too late! You cannot be afraid to break it off, even in the last days of the engagement. Otherwise, you will be walking into a life of misery at worst, and at best, requiring much more effort and patience to make it work. A late break-up would be very rare if you follow the precepts of the Word because you would have discovered early in the relationship if it was not going to work. This is the reason for the courting model.

In courting, you keep your pants and skirts on! You draw lines and barriers that both of you agree on of *no touch zones*. Personally, I believe that it is best not to even kiss until after you are engaged. There is no sexual interaction until after marriage. In addition, there should be no heavy, extended *make out* sessions before engagement, or, even before the commitment of marriage.

Courting seeks true intimacy and the building of a solid, lifelong relationship; dating pretends to be fun, but hides the most important process—that of getting to know the real person. You can compare dating to going to a cheap buffet of old, burnt, and watery food, unfit for a stray cat. You just *pick and choose*, trying different things in an attempt to satisfy your hunger, but never seriously looking for the right dish (pun intended). Courtship is like a fine restaurant filled with the best fare, seeking the finest, and savoring the meal. Courtship takes it slow and avoids the games and attitudes that lead to scores of heartbreaks and hurts.

Therefore do not be foolish, but understand what the Lord's will is. Do not get drunk on wine, which leads to debauchery. Instead, be filled with the Spirit. Speak to one another with psalms, hymns and spiritual songs. Sing and make music in your heart to the Lord, always giving thanks to God the Father for everything, in the name of our Lord Jesus Christ. Ephesians 5:17-20

Courtship allows realistic and healthy expectations to take place. You have to be comfortable as a single person in Christ. You cannot expect someone to fill a hole or a longing that exists because the health of your emotions and desires are not right. The goal of finding a mate is not to fill an empty hole of loneliness or something else that might be missing. If it is, you are seeking someone who cannot possibly do that, because only Christ can! You cannot expect even the best person for you to put meaning in your life. By doing that, you are diving into a shallow pool of codependency and strife. A life full of meaning and wholeness must be accomplished in Christ alone. You cannot expect your spouse to do that because that is the role of the Savior! Therefore, you need to be seeking a life-long covenant relationship. Real relationships are built on intimacy and based on trust, communication, and mutual benefit. Dating will not build a lasting relationship, because true intimacy will not be built, but rather subsisted for cheap sex and personal desires. A covenant relationship does not seek a way out nor easily gives up; it sticks it out with the goal of making it work, as God did with us!

When you become friends first, then you do not have to burn up a lot of time and energy developing a friendship with the person you are going out with. This will eliminate the games and the hiding we tend to do. If you skip the friendship, then your relationship building will be much tougher and a lot more complicated.

Common Objections to Courting

Submit to one another out of reverence for Christ. Ephesians 5:21

When I speak to single groups, I often get these objections to courtship: *There is nothing wrong with dating. It is part of our culture. "If I do not date, how can I learn how to relate with the opposite sex? Dating is the only way to meet men/women.* And, finally, *Courtship may have worked 100 years ago, but dating is the only way I can meet my potential partner in our modern society.*

The first objection centers on the assumption that we will not be able to know or relate to others without dating. This is not true. People seldom learn anything in the dating game because they are too busy putting on a show and playing games. When we are busy hiding our true self and trying to get the other person to like us, they are busy trying to hide themselves from us. So we become conformers and not learners. While we are so busy conforming our personality to theirs, we end up not changing anything of ourselves. In addition, we are placing the focus only on having fun, thus showing we are not interested in learning. It is usually the last thing considered. You could interview people who have maintained many relationships, and see if their behavior patterns change. You will find that they do not. In addition, if this *were* true, then we would have seen the divorce rate plummeting in the last 50 years, as dating has continually increased; yet, the opposite is true. We would also see marriages get better and stronger, when in fact, they have gone in the opposite direction. We would have also seen the rape percentages decrease, when in reality, they have exponentially increased over the population growth! Empirical evidence and personal experience will clearly show that we do not learn about the opposite sex through dating! We learn by becoming friends, listening, understanding, and discovering each another.

Okay, you think you have me now! How can we meet our partner without dating? Come on! Do you really think you will meet a good, quality person in a bar, in a nightclub, or in a dance hall? Maybe, if you are very lucky, but in over 20 years of counseling, I have never seen a good or successful marriage happen when the partner was found in such an establishment! I do not want to sound like a prude, as I liked dancing and nightclubs when I was younger; but, I would never would have considered the women there to be for me— nor should you. Yes, you may think, *hey, I might get lucky.* Maybe you will;

maybe you will win the lottery too, but the odds are not in your favor, and neither are they the values you should be seeking. You have to decide what the best environment and situation is in which to come to a decision about someone having the right qualities you desire in a mate. If you think it through, clubs are not it! Consider this thought: why are nightclubs and bars so dimly lit? You cannot even see what is being hid!

So, how do you meet someone? Churches, ministry outings, referrals from family, school, civic classes, study groups, clubs (school, community, hobby, or church based ones), friends, and friends of friends, etc. are excellent places. Look for places where there is no emotional involvement and no agenda where you would be forced to be someone other than yourself. Then, you can relax, be who you are, and get to know the person as a friend. That way, you will see his/her true personality, and the behaviors, likes, and dislikes of each other. You can evaluate how that person acts in a variety of circumstances—as they can about you. You can see if you *click*, and have things in common. When you do this before you commence the relationship, you will be miles ahead and far better off than you would have been in the dating game!

So, is dating—the way it is—OK because it is our culture? Consider that our culture also says it is OK to sleep around and live together first. So, are you going to follow a corrupt culture or God's truth? The Bible is clear on how we develop relationships. When we go against God's truth, we set ourselves up for a fall and for heartbreak, pain, needless suffering, and turmoil!

By following God's precepts, you will be able to prepare yourself and discern who is right for you!

...for we are members of his body. "For this reason a man will leave his father and mother and be united to his wife, and the two will become one flesh." Ephesians 5:30-31

CHAPTER X
PREPARING FOR A SUCCESSFUL AND HAPPY MARRIAGE

Now may our God and Father himself and our Lord Jesus clear the way for us to come to you. May the Lord make your love increase and overflow for each other and for everyone else, just as ours does for you. May he strengthen your hearts so that you will be blameless and holy in the presence of our God and Father when our Lord Jesus comes with all his holy ones. 1 Thessalonians 3: 11-13

A lot of young people these days do not want to learn about themselves or use sound reasoning in looking for who is right for them. They just want to go for it and let the chips fall as they may. They think they will be OK, and no harm or dire relationships will come their way. But, this thinking only serves to get them into trouble and into broken and hurtful relationships. That euphoria of finding someone and dating is quickly turned into chaos and strife when the wrong person is sought, and especially when the wrong person is brought home.

We must not be afraid to find out what God's plan is. Whether you have been emotionally involved with someone for a long time, or you have recently met your dream person, you may find out you are on the right track and you should get married to him or her. Perhaps, your worst fears will be realized, and you will discover that this person is wrong for you. You may feel the time you have spent has been wasted. But, consider this: building relationships is never a waste of time. It is far better to find out if someone or something is wrong and needs to be fixed before you are trapped in a marriage with a person who is not the right one for you. Yes, God can and will turn your mistakes into blessings, and He will work it out. You may have gotten yourself in with the wrong person, but He can make it right by making you right. However, why go through all the hardships, hassles, and disappointments when you can have someone better up front? Without having the right attitude and perspective on life, or, neglecting to glorify God and follow His will, you will not find the real love of your life!

Marriage is a wonderful and extraordinary relationship with a specific person that God has foreordained. A good relationship will bring glory to God by reflecting the relationship between Jesus and His bride, the church! Do not be afraid to make the right decision even if you have been in a relationship for years and are about to get married. If you know he/she are Mr. or Miss Wrong, get out; your time has not been wasted! Now is the time to move on! And, if you did get married to the wrong one, be willing to work on it; after all, a spark was there that got you together. In Christ, you will be able to turn your potential tragedy into a triumph. Even if you did not follow these precepts and married Mr. or Miss Wrong, he/she is the right person now. We have to be willing to connect and make it work.

Courtship can be the most excellent and paramount way to meet, and to know and grow in your relational development. You have to be willing to go against culture and take a stand for truth and virtue. Fortunately, this is not as hard today as it was a few years ago. The Postmodern generation is figuring out that what their parents and grandparents went through and tried did not work, so they are looking for alternatives.

Let us consider some simple steps that can help put these ideas into perspective and practice:

STEP I: FINDING AND GETTING TO KNOW EACH OTHER

Finally, brothers, we instructed you how to live in order to please God, as in fact you are living. Now we ask you and urge you in the Lord Jesus to do this more and more. For you know what instructions we gave you by the authority of the Lord Jesus. 1 Thessalonians 4:1-2

Consider first that the years of singleness are not wasted! Enjoy them! Use this time to work on yourself, your relationship, your growth in the Lord, and as a time of preparation for marriage. If you feel you do not want or need to get married, then don't! You may have the gift of *singleness*. The Bible calls us to be consecrated and holy before God. This means having His purpose and will in mind, seeking Christ and His Kingdom first, not our own desires.

You need to find out what your spiritual gifts and call are in life. Work on your education, and maybe a career. You must become comfortable with who you are before you seek someone else. How can you expect your future spouse's place in the church and world to be clear if you do not know what yours is? It is not a sin *not* to be married! Yes, a lot of churches look down on singles, but their view is not biblical. It is OK to be single, as a single person can contribute far more to a church than a person who is married and has a family!

Before you are engaged, you should hide some of your more expressive emotions and feelings in your heart. Expressions such as saying "I love you," kissing, and *making out* will move the relationship from a relational one to one that is emotionally based. You will be clouded from growing a deeper and better relationship. Such feelings need to be real and truly expressed with passion and conviction, not out of guilt or obligation. Most people use these words and touches to manipulate each other to get what they want, unconcerned with building a real relationship. This must not be your motivation! When you express too much emotion or do not set boundaries with physical contact before engagement, they will become rhetoric, losing their power and meaning. You will have built a foundation where you should not have, short-circuiting your real emotional expressions and love, and exchanging a quick and short lustful present for a life-long, love-covenant for the future. Remember, real love is patient!

Here are some ideas to pray about:

It is God's will that you should be sanctified: that you should avoid sexual immorality; that each of you should learn to control his own body in a way that is holy and honorable, not in passionate lust like the heathen, who do not know God; and that in this matter no one should wrong his brother or take advantage of him. The Lord will punish men for all such sins, as we have already told you and warned you. 1 Thessalonians 4:3-6

• Seek a potential mate from quality sources! Church is always the best place as are Christian single groups and clubs. But, you still have to be aware. Also, join a club or organization that interests you. Do you like to golf, build models, do community service, or? There you may find someone who has similar interests and you may already have major things in common. Do not try bars or nightclubs; good people with character and distinction will not be there!

- Look to be friends first. Build a friendship. This is your first priority and will lay the foundation for the entire relationship! That way, you will get to know each other more deeply and be more real!
- He or she must be a committed Christian, not just saved, but sharing the same theology and spiritual growth aspirations as you.
- You both need to be growing in the Lord, enjoy going to church, enjoy serving God and others, and be a faithful member of a church.
- You cannot enter in to a relationship or marriage in an attempt to fulfill your needs—or theirs!
- Be willing to address each other's faults and work them out with God in the theme of the fruit of the Spirit; seek a pastor or counselor if necessary.
- Do not rush or be too eager. Allow the relationship to build slowly over months and over years (at least two).
- Always be real and authentic, and allow the character and fruit of the Spirit to flow through you, being respectful and courteous to your date.
- If you are not naturally courteous and respectful, then do not fake it. Rather, allow the Lord to work on you before venturing out with others!
- Do not get into a long-term relationship too young! You have to learn about God and yourself first! Get some experience in building relationships with others before seeking marriage!
- Know your vulnerabilities and areas of past and potential hurts, and deal with them. If either of you are still suffering from childhood or adult traumas, you will be handicapped in effectively building a relationship. Get emotionally healthy first! Do not seek a relationship just to please your family, your friends, or anyone else!
- Be enthusiastic to know more about each other, and do not be shallow or superficial. Ask the penetrating questions, and do not have unrealistic expectations!
- Do not try to court more that one person at a time. In addition, put some time between relationships. Do not feel you have to be in a relationship to be whole!
- The potential mate does not have to be perfect, since no one is; but, you both need to be willing to grow and mature.
- You must know how to resolve conflict and differences *without* anger!
- Make sure both of you know how money works. Have a good biblical concept on how to deal with budgeting and debt. Most conflicts in marriage deal with finances!
- You cannot expect a future marriage partner to fulfill your needs, in any area, instead of God. Remember your commitment and covenant to God,

that as a Christian, you are holy and set apart for a higher purpose. Remain sexually pure until you get married! If you have committed your heart to God, then it becomes consecrated to Him!

- Know the type of person you are looking for in regard to intelligence, personality, goals, spiritual maturity, character, political outlook, future children (and how to raise them), chemistry (how you click and relate), and even appearance. Be realistic!
- Do not look for someone who is an opposite. They may attract you at first, but they will soon repel!
- Develop a healthy outlook of what real biblical love and intimacy are!
- Realize that the *dating game* is a dangerous game to play! It will rob you, your future spouse, and God! Whether you are the predator, or the prey, you will be hurt and diminished by the dating scene.
- Before you are engaged, you should hide some of your more expressive emotions (sexual) and feelings in your heart.
- Listen to your family and to the mature mentors whom you trust!
- God calls us to purity, so be pure! (1 Thessalonians 3: 11-13; 4:1-8) Please see our article in our Ministries Website www.intothyword.org on *Whatever happened to Virtue!*

Spend your energies on building a bountiful relationship, keeping in mind the precepts we have talked about in the preceding chapters.

STEP II: THE ENGAGEMENT PERIOD

Do not be yoked together with unbelievers. For what do righteousness and wickedness have in common? Or what fellowship can light have with darkness? What harmony is there between Christ and Belial? What does a believer have in common with an unbeliever? 2 Corinthians 6:14-15

When you think you have found the right person and have done the previous suggestions along with a lot of prayer, maybe it is time to *pop the question*! Enjoy your engagement! Save your more intimate emotions for this period. This is the time you will discover how well you work, solve problems, and plan a big event together. Plan your own wedding! If you hire this out, you will miss out on a big opportunity to see how you are working together. Only use a wedding planner as a consultant for ideas. The process of planning your wedding will either hone your relationship or show your true colors. If this is just a time of stress and chaos, then you need to stop, and go back to Step One. Things will NOT get better when you are married! This is the time when hidden personality problems, induced by stress, come out; and, if the two of you cannot work through them then, you definitely will not be able to do so in marriage! You will discover more about each other's relatives and how you relate to them. Therefore, you need to be willing to work even harder to continue building your relationship. Get into a good marriage-counseling program, and attend a marriage conference or retreat. Most people think once you are engaged, coupled with social and family pressures and expenditures, you *have* to get married. This idea is very WRONG! This period is *not* a guarantee that the two of you will get married; it is a time to make sure you are right for each other! If you force each other, or allow others to, you may end up in the wrong relationship. It is far better to have the heartbreak of a broken engagement and an empty checking account than a lifetime of a wrong marriage. Remember, God is in charge; He has a plan. Be in tune with His plan, and not yours!

What is the timeline for all of this? It totally depends on your maturity level, spiritual growth, and how deep you have gone on your journey of getting to know each other. Someone in his/her twenties may need at least two years to get to know the other and at least another year of engagement, while a person in his/her forties may just need half of that. It is always safe to say *longer is better*!

STEP III: A VERY HAPPY MARRIAGE! (SONG OF SOLOMON 3:4)

For God did not call us to be impure, but to live a holy life. Therefore, he who rejects this instruction does not reject man but God, who gives you his Holy Spirit. 1 Thessalonians 4:7-8

If one of you does not embrace any of those things we have talked about so far, you will have an extreme strain on your relationship, and the odds of success are a 50 percent divorce rate. Of the marriages that are left, from my experiences in counseling and research, most are miserable! So, consider how important it is to *get your act together* before you say, "I do!"
Make a covenant to choose to walk with surrendered, Lordship faith in Jesus Christ: "I choose to be filled with His Spirit. Since I choose to be filled with His Spirit, **I choose to love and honor my spouse!** "

The problems with Courtship:

Perseverance must finish its work so that you may be mature and complete, not lacking anything. If any of you lacks wisdom, he should ask God, who gives generously to all without finding fault, and it will be given to him. James 1: 4-5

This model is by far the best one that we can use to find the love of our life, because it is what the Bible teaches! That does not mean we will not have problems with it, as we live in a fallen sinful world, have a church that is not perfect, and are part of a community of Christians who do not always follow God's will or His precepts. And, there is also the problem of *you!* Yes, believe it or not, you are not perfect either; none of us are. Through my experiences in dating, going out, clubs, and even being engaged, only to have it broken, left me dazed and confused, I followed what society expected, and I got nowhere. I thought courtship was a silly, dysfunctional, social thing of the past, so I ignored biblical truth only to find myself chasing society's trends until I was lonely and confused. So, after a careful study in dating and courtship while I was in seminary, I saw the potential for courtship. I then taught what I had learned to many singles groups, and practiced it myself. In addition, after *getting my act together* and following the courtship/biblical precepts I have shared with you, God brought my wife Mary, the love of my life, into my life and we were married in 1995. If I had married the other women I was chasing (knowing them as I do today), and engaging in the world's ways of dating, I would have been in utter misery! God's precepts and plans were much better than mine! So, put your trust in Him and His ways!

What are the potential problems?

Now for the matters you wrote about: It is good for a man not to marry. But since there is so much immorality, each man should have his own wife, and each woman her own husband. The husband should fulfill his marital duty to his wife, and likewise the wife to her husband. The wife's body does not belong to her alone but also to her husband. In the same way, the husband's body does not belong to him alone but also to his wife. Do not deprive each other except by mutual consent and for a time, so that you may devote yourselves to prayer. Then come together again so that Satan will not tempt you because of your lack of self-control. 1 Corinthians 7:1-5

The first problem could be your parents! Good parents are able to filter out the trouble and problems you may get yourself into. Thus, in the courtship model, they are one of the primary participants in helping you with seeking and choosing your mate. When you are done screaming, "no, no, no," think it through. Who loves and knows you best? Because of social misgivings, busyness, not following Christ as Lord—even as a Christian—this vital role has been left empty for most single Christians. If your parents are deceased or refuse to think in light of biblical precepts, you will have to be more careful and discern for yourself. Seek a mentor, church leader, or pastor who is spiritually mature to help you weed out and protect you from *unqualified applicants*. Also, sometimes, even if your parents are not Christians, they still know you and can exercise great discernment on your behalf. Even if your parents do not want you to marry someone, and you feel they are not mature, or they are not Christians, still listen and heed their advice. They still have spiritual authority over you, and, in most cases, have your best interest in mind. In my experience, I have rarely known them to be wrong. Even if the parents are not in the ideal role, the only problem for you is being extra careful and discerning. Get a mentor!

His or Her Family: You have to know that when you marry someone, you marry his or her entire family, too just like in the popular movie a few years back, "My Big Fat Greek Wedding!" If his or her family does not like you, find out why, and what is wrong. Listen, and be discerning. Find out what you can do to make things better. Make sure you are in prayer and seeking what is best for the both of you and both families. Remember, God is sovereign and in control, even if the parents are unsaved! See their pastor for advice. If the family is not Christian, then consult the pastor of your potential mate. If you have his or her pastor's blessing, but not that of his or her parents, you may be on the right track. Seek counseling and remember; if his or her parents do not like you, and even if all the other signs point to *go for launch*, you will *still* have significant problems unless you can win them over.

One of you is divorced: Biblical marriage is an unbreakable, life-long covenant. Once you are married, even if you made a mistake, you still have to stick with it and make it work. The fact that you did get married to each other means there was and is a spark between the two of you, and you will have to figure out a way to make the fire flame again. There are tremendous amounts of good resources from *Focus on the Family* and *Family Life Today* that can help you (Matthew 5:32; 19:9; 1 Corinthians 7)!

As fallen human beings, we make mistakes and cater to our bad judgments. Fortunately for us, God is a God of forgiveness and healing. Sin is in the world, and Christians are not immune from making mistakes. However, this issue is in hot debate, as the Bible implies that if you did not get divorced for biblical reasons, such as unfaithfulness, abuse, or abandonment, you cannot be remarried. So, seek wise biblical counsel, and be in surrendered prayer to His will, and not your own. Then, if there is the factor that one or both of you have children, you have to consider their needs, the extra blessings, and the extra problems.

Not effectively communicating: If you work the courtship like our American style of dating, you will not build a solid, deep relationship. You must be able to ask questions, listen, and be vulnerable to reflect, challenge, and address each other's shortcomings, faults, and areas that need growth. Take it slow and develop your friendship first. If you do not do this, then you will be among the countless relationships in our culture filled with miscommunication, hurt, and misery!

Following God's plan is not easy. The world's way is! However, when we indulge in the world's way, the *easy* will quickly turn into *hurt* and *chaos*! So, the *easy* ends up being very difficult indeed! God, without a doubt, has a wonderful plan for you, but that plan will take effort, time, commitment, risk, and self surrender. It goes from what you may think is good and right to what really is good and right. Take to heart that these principles will work, and will enable you to find the love of your life, the one whom God gives you, and who is the best for you. It may happen quickly, or it may take years to find him or her.

Remember the characteristics of love from 1 Corinthians 13, and apply them to your search. Focus on the patience. At the same time, do not sit on the couch and wait. You have to get out there and take risks and endure rejection. You have to go where he or she is, work on yourself, and be open and vulnerable. If you are not willing to take a risk or work on yourself, you will be trading a little hurt from rejection and pride for the unwillingness to build your character, and that will result in a lifetime of hurt and loneliness. And, you will miss out on what God has for you.

Preparing and Building a Successful Marriage

Wives, submit to your husbands, as is fitting in the Lord. Husbands, love your wives and do not be harsh with them. Colossians 3:18-19

The world considers marriage to be an avenue of satisfaction for the self. This view seems to be from the standpoint of seeking fulfillment in pleasure, companionship, what "I" can get out of it, and how "I" can benefit from it. These are, of course, parts of a relationship, but not the main parts. People get confused, disillusioned, and eventually give up on marriage because the above aspects are not being fulfilled to their satisfaction and expectations. Thus, they are negating what is really important and meaningful in building a marriage!

It is my goal to start to put together the precepts we have been discussing so you will be prepared for marriage and/or better at your marriage. Let us take a look at the main viewpoints and directions that the Lord gives us from His Word so we can better prepare for the second most important thing we will ever do in life (the first being our salvation). Let us look at how to prepare for a successful marriage.

If you want to be successful in life and marriage, you need to get this point; the primary purpose of marriage is not to please ourselves (yeah, that surprised me too!), but to glorify and serve God. Our desires and pleasures are not God's number one priority! Yes, God wants us to be joyful, happy, and content, but being happy means being focused on Him and not on our circumstances. Thus, to have a successful marriage, you must be aware of what you are getting into and prepare for it. The most important guarantee for it to work is to follow His principles from His Word, not what you think, want, or have experienced. Remember, God designed marriage and us. He knows best!

This may not sound politically correct, but it is true. The Bible says that God created Eve as a *helpmate*. This means she was to help Adam perform his duties of working the garden and exercising dominion over the earth. It also means there was a co-relationship for a mutual benefit, so each could become a team, fulfilling their purpose together. Love, intimacy, and pleasure were certainly a part of it, but not the main part of their relationship and life. They did not just frolic around paradise in bliss, playing with and enjoying each other. They shared a common purpose as well as a common direction. So must we! We cannot just seek someone because they catch our eye, negating the process of knowing them and ourselves better. If we do that, as most people do, we will have a 50 percent failure rate. We would be very, very lucky to find happiness and contentment. If we just spend a little more time working on our relationship with each other, we will be miles ahead of the game of life and will enjoy a much happier and purposeful life that would please God, making us, and those around us, happier.

When we lose sight of the purpose of what God calls us to in life or in marriage, we will fall into a life of despair, not achieving desired fulfillment.

When we follow His precepts, we will find the right person, stay on the right path, and experience the ultimate pleasure and fun. The irony about society is that it seeks all these without including God. Therefore, people become disillusioned and angry with God when they do not get them. In addition, many Christians, for the most part, do the same!

Preparing for Marriage from the Perspective of Christ and the Church

Submit to one another out of reverence for Christ. Wives, submit to your husbands as to the Lord. For the husband is the head of the wife as Christ is the head of the church, his body, of which he is the Savior. Now as the church submits to Christ, so also wives should submit to their husbands in everything. *Husbands, love your wives, just as Christ loved the church and gave himself up for her to make her holy, cleansing her by the washing with water through the word, and to present her to himself as a radiant church, without stain or wrinkle or any other blemish, but holy and blameless.* Ephesians 5:21-27

Remember what we talked about in the chapter of "Building a Good Personality," especially the three priorities of the church and how they translate into whom and what we are. Understanding godly precepts in community as we do in church and in personality will be the key to any relationship, especially a marriage. The theme of these passages is submission, a far cry from the American ideals of personal freedom and choice. However, consider this; submission is not the tyrannical concept most of us harbor in our minds. Rather, it is freedom! It is a form of mutual respect. It allows us to be free, and to have the best flowing in and out of us. It is a safe harbor of smooth waters keeping us protected from the storms of wrong actions. It frees us from bad thinking that leads to bad choices which, in turn, leads to a life of misery and trouble! For a wife to respect her husband shows him unconditional love that helps fuel his desire to return love. He receives his value and honor that is so important to a man. The wife responds because she knows she is cared for and cherished. Love is often reciprocal, the husband loves and the wife responds with respect and honor and so conversely. And when things are not going well, the wife should and must still respect him (unless there is abuse), as should the husband who must still love, regardless of how the other is being with you. Then your relationship will vastly improve!

The Ephesians passage (Ephesians 5:1-2) starts off telling us to be *imitators of God*. For us to be imitators, we have to know God and His precepts for us, and we do this through reading the Word, and following our Lord's examples, and putting them into practice with our faith. This means we imitate His love and character in our relationships, especially with our spouse. So, in our relationships, we become *imitators* of God by walking in His love and allowing it to spill upon others. We do this because we honor and reverence our Lord Jesus Christ! As we grow in our faith and maturity, we will desire Him over the ways of the world. If we think we can do what we want while claiming Christ as Lord, we delude ourselves. How can we honor our Lord when we do not honor what He has taught us (John 14:15)? If we did this with our country, we would be considered traitors or terrorists! If we did this with our relationships, we would be considered flakes and hypocrites! If we did this with our work, we would be fired for insubordination or theft! Why would we do this with the LORD, who loves us and gives us grace? We have to remember that submission and biblical precepts are not meant to bring us down or *lord* it over us as a tyrannical dictator; rather, it is His love in action. God knows what is best, what works, and what creates good and lasting relationships. So, we should strive to live as *imitators* of Him in all we do! Wives are asked to submit, as to give respect to their husbands. Husbands are asked to love their wives. *Submit* translates from a military term (Ephesians 5:22 Greek: *hupotasso*), which means "to place under" or "to subordinate" as a line relationship (1 Peter 3:1). This is not because of weakness or inferiority, or that one is better than the other, but because God has placed, in the order of creation, the husband as head of the home, just as Christ is the head of the church. They have different roles, yet each one is equal in the sight of God! Thus, the husband loves and respects his wife and earns her devotion; the result is a continual, mutual respect that builds an effective, strong marriage relationship.

In ancient times, marriage contracts would advocate that the husband should make his wife submit with absolute obedience. Paul's asserting to his churches and readers to love, and because of love to submit, was very radical. To Paul, love was a duty (1 Corinthians 13). It was even considered weak by the *macho* mindsets of the times as well as with many people today. But, this is not weak; it is building the strength of a relationship and the bond of a family by creating a mutual partnership!

Do two walk together unless they have agreed to do so? Amos 3:3

Submission is respect, and thus is not to exceed the parameters of the will of God or of love and righteousness. To prove this, submission is not an excuse to batter or put wives down in any way. The directive to husbands is even more daunting than what has been given to the wives! Husbands are called to *love*, which is much greater in importance and prominence than submission! Love is what sets the tone and standard for the relationship. Submission is also a response! Because the husband is loving, because the husband is caring, because the husband is putting his wife's best interests forward, the wife submits, and he earns her devotion. It is the husband's responsibility to set the tone of love and care! Keep in mind; this was called for in a time and culture that considered women lower than farm animals! It was taught in a culture where the "alpha" male (i.e. the lead man of the family), ruled in absolute dominance for order, organization, structure, protection, and community. The mandate to love (1 Corinthians 13:4-7) was, and still is to some, an extreme wakeup call that commands the husband to thoroughly exhibit all of the qualities of biblical character in his relationship with his wife.

The verb for love (Greek: *agapete*) designates a continuous routine of action all of the time, not just when we feel like it. Christ loved the church *not because it was holy, but in order to make it holy*! Thus, we are not only called to find the person who is best for us, but to work at keeping the relationship within the parameters of love, submission, and commitment. Even if you made that wrong choice through impatience, wrong thinking, lust, and/or sin, you still have the call and opportunity to make it right, to make it work with the mate you have! Remember, that something special that got you together in the first place can be rekindled into a roaring fire. The wife is in submission as a response to the husband's love for her and his providing, as well as for having her best interest and care at heart. It is like when we respond to Christ with love and service because of His free gift of grace. We do not earn salvation for service; rather, it is a fruit of our gratitude. In the same way, this is how submission works. It is not to be forced, but offered freely in response to love. It is something we replicate as in responding in kindness so our response to each other is fueling the other's response, and so forth. In this way, we will be escalating love and kindness instead of repression and dysfunction.

Christ and the church are the prime models for us in a lifelong commitment of monogamous marriage. He did not give up on us when things went from bad to worse; His grace, forgiveness, and perseverance came through. It is the model relationship for the home, for the love of children, and the fellowships and relationships we are to have. The church is the bride of

Christ, and He loves her. Your spouse, or spouse to be, is your bride or groom where righteousness, love, commitment, and holiness are to be practiced and exercised in the best and fullest way possible for you (Revelation 21:1-2)!

Building Your Future Relationship with Love

However, each one of you also must love his wife as he loves himself, and the wife must respect her husband. Ephesians 5:33

Here are some important things to consider which may go against your conventional thinking, experience, and practice. Yet, these characteristics are very important and biblical; so, be willing to think them through as you read His Word, pray, and apply them to your relationships—both now and to come.

In your marriage or your search for the love of your life, you have to be willing to work on yourself. You are not perfect. Only Christ is! You have a whole host of faults and quirks that are unsuitable for public viewing or private relationships. We all do. Therefore, you have to be willing to put off arrogance and pride, address your faults, and work them out with God and a pastor or counselor, if necessary. Your spouse or potential mate has to be willing to do the same. If not, you will keep your bad patterns of behavior and they will just get worse as your denial gets stronger, then both of you will clash to the point you will not be able to make it work. Now, neither you nor your love to be has to be perfect; you just have to be willing and open to grow and develop into a spiritually and emotionally mature Christian.
You cannot expect a marriage partner to fulfill your needs in any area instead of, or in place of God!

Because we are seeking God's standards, we need to be looking for someone who has a growing relationship with God. You both need to be seeking to please, and growing in Christ. Both of you must have, at the foundation of your life, Jesus as your LORD, not just your Savior. This means you are ruled by His standards and precepts, not your own selfish inclinations and motives. Both of you need to be enthusiastic about growing closer to God, enjoy going to church, enjoy serving God and others, and about being a faithful and diligent member of a Bible-based church. Given this, both of you should be of the same theological thinking. The combination of a Catholic and a Protestant never, ever works. One will have to give up his/her faith (or both), and when the children come, then all hell will break loose! Even courting/dating across denominational lines can be sticky, as one will eventually have to leave and go to the other's church. Be aware and wise about this and be willing to brainstorm options without compromising biblical faith. You both have to be willing to endure this, and, of course, be on your knees during such decisions.

One of you may even have more passion for the LORD than the other, because experience, growth, and personality come into play. As you get to know each other, these things come out, and you will need to work through them. You do not have to agree with every point of doctrine. If both of you agree completely, then one of you is not thinking! Just be sure you can agree to disagree, and the disagreements are not about essential doctrine. You should also have similar views of society and of the world (Amos 3:3).

Be careful in a relationship with a person of different economic, social, or ethnic background. This relationship has more hurdles to get over and requires more work and maturity, not only with the two of you, but also with the families of both. I am definitely not saying to stay away, or that these are wrong. My wife Mary and I are different on each category. I am a white mutt with a great grandfather who was black; she is Hispanic. I grew up upper middle class; she grew up poor. My family rubs shoulders with the rich and famous of American society; hers with people from the streets of East LA— and the list goes on. Thus, we had to jump over many more problems with our families and social stigmas than in a normal (whatever that is) relationship. I leaned to appreciate her family and background, and I am very comfortable with them. This took time, patience, and the willingness to work at it.

Another thing you need to do in order to build a good marriage is to be accountable to someone, perhaps those in a small group. You will grow and change better and faster by having someone who knows you to push, encourage, and challenge you in the right direction and in the Word.

Make sure both of you know how money works. Have a good, biblical concept of how to deal with budgeting and debt. Most conflicts in marriage deal with finances. If one or both of you have a lot of dept, either credit cards or student loans, you must have a plan to pay them off, and preferably before marriage, if possible. Make sure you have solved any spending problems and money management issues. If just one of you cannot do this, you will have an immense amount of unnecessary problems in your marriage. A well-planned budget will help you greatly. Just read any book from Larry Burkett, Ron Blue, or go to crown.org for good resources on how to do a budget.

You must deal with any potential problems involving character, bitterness, unrepentant sin, absence of forgiveness, abuse, lust, past struggles, and emotional problems. If you do not address these issues before marriage, the probability of the relationship working is extremely low. But, it is not necessary to seek perfection. No one can do that, except Christ. You just need to be on the right track, and have a strong willingness and commitment to change. Moreover, allow Christ to work in you! Be willing, in your marriage, to check yourself out in the mirror of God's most precious Word; observe how God and others see you, and be willing to work on yourself for the better!

When you are going out with someone in courting, get feedback from mature friends, people who are older and wiser, and most importantly from your parents. You may think, *OH NO!* Nevertheless, consider this; they know you better than you know yourself. They have been there. You will probably not realize this until after you have kids. Do not make the mistake that Rehoboam, the son of King Solomon, made. He felt he did not need to listen to his father's advisers; instead, he listened to His friends, and in so doing, lost the most of the kingdom through his arrogance and refusal to listen (1 Kings 12). Do not lose out because you think you know it all; no one does. Even the President of the United States has a cabinet and advisors; so does every great and godly leader. Do not look to just one source of feedback. Consider all the possibilities and be unwilling to let your emotions and lust cloud your thinking.

If one of you does not embrace any of the points we have talked about so far, there *will be* an extreme strain on your relationship. The odds of success are a 50 percent divorce rate, and of the marriages that are left, mostly are miserable! I keep repeating this, because it is so true! So, consider how important it is to *get your act together* before you say, "I do!" And after you have said "I do," keep working at it; keep the love and respect going and you will see marvelous improvement!

Finally, all of you, live in harmony with one another; be sympathetic, love as brothers, be compassionate and humble. Do not repay evil with evil or insult with insult, but with blessing, because to this you were called so that you may inherit a blessing. 1 Peter 3:8-9

CHAPTER XI
HOW TO SET BOUNDARIES

Now we ask you, brothers, to respect those who work hard among you, who are over you in the LORD and who admonish you. Hold them in the highest regard in love because of their work. Live in peace with each other. And we urge you, brothers, warn those who are idle, encourage the timid, help the weak, be patient with everyone. Make sure that nobody pays back wrong for wrong, but always try to be kind to each other and to everyone else. 1 Thessalonians 5:12-15

We have already talked about why we should set boundaries when it comes to dating. We also need to know how to apply boundaries to the rest of our Christian life and relationships. Remember, we are called to be a people who act and respond to others with kindness and altruism. However, when you do this, people will sometimes take advantage of you. You need to be able to discern when to respond, how long to continue, and when you should stop. This goes into relationships and commitment. The key to this will be effective communication and listening.

Now, let us consider how we can be the person God called us to be while at the same time model Christ-like character (Hebrews 13:4), and balance between self-sacrifice and not being taken advantage of. A lot has been written on the subject of boundaries in the *pop-psychology* world, so what I have to say may not correspond because I am coming from the worldview of biblical precepts, which contradict some modern views. The world sees boundaries as fences to keep your will and self in tact, and ascertains that you are the center of your own universe. As Christians, we embrace God as our center and His character as our goal. So, we need to think of boundaries in a term from one part of the Fruit of the Spirit—*self-control.*

Self-Control is allowing God to be in control of your will and heart and seeking the Spirit to enable that. Then we will know what *not* to do, and guard the areas in which we are weak. This will allow us to have discipline and restraint with obedience to God and others. It is not letting distractions derail or remove us from His will and plan so we are not held back from what Christ calls us to do. This will also allow us to build and control relationships in light of what is healthy and best, based on the function of the rest of the fruit.

If we refuse to allow self-control to be a part of our personality and how we respond to others—especially our spouse—it will quickly be replaced by self-indulgence and/or codependency. We can experience self-indulgence from eating a pound of chocolate all at one time or partying our way to oblivion. Too much excess will leave us empty and alone. It will, at best, cause us to gain a lot of weight and/or lose friends. At worst, it will cause us to lose our life and miss out on our heavenly reward! Self-indulgence seeks what is fleeting, when we, as Christians, are made for eternity.

The night is nearly over; the day is almost here. So let us put aside the deeds of darkness and put on the armor of light. Let us behave decently, as in the daytime, not in orgies and drunkenness, not in sexual immorality and debauchery, not in dissension and jealousy. Rather, clothe yourselves with the LORD Jesus Christ, and do not think about how to gratify the desires of the sinful nature. Romans 13:12-14

Codependency basically is a kidnapping of your self-will away from your self and God, so you become identified and infused with another person. This other person becomes your identity, individuality, distinctiveness, and even your god. You become preoccupied beyond your call and mandate of Scripture, so you are dependent on them like a bad habit or drug. This can also escalate when you lock yourself into a bad relationship, and your real needs of love and security are not being met. You are either the person who is controlling, or, you are being controlled; either way, this is not how God designed healthy relationships. Anger, guilt, and loneliness will billow out of you, while real character will become stagnate. This will cause dysfunction in your relationship, and neuter your relationship with God.
Self-control is not a subject of the media. You may, perhaps, never see a movie with this as the premise because it is anti-climatic and even boring. The world wants us to *grab all of the gusto* that we can, go for that brass ring, regardless of the consequences or who we step on to get it, avoiding responsibility for our actions. Yet, Christ is calling us, by His example and

Word, to seek in eternity that which is permanent and lasting—not what is fleeting and empty. Christ was our greatest example, from the humbleness of the incarnation through Gethsemane and to the cross. He was the perfect model of self-control! Self-control is the key to inner strength that will help deliver us from fear, depression, harm, and the pain of life by our focusing on Christ and not our circumstances. It is your fence, guarding you from danger and preventing you from inflicting problems into relationships.

Self-control is Christ's strength in us, and something that we cannot do on our own! The key to receiving this strength is our surrender to His Lordship over *all* aspects of our lives! Remember, God wants us to have fun, enjoy life, and take risks to build relationships. We are not to be prudes; yet, at the same time, we are not to seek sin or be taken advantage of, either!

Keep in mind this important point; we produce the fruit by taking His yoke, so it will create the blossom. When we keep His yoke (our growth in our faith and the practice of being a disciple) we will grow and then bear fruit. It is what we are to Christ, not so much what we do in His name. It is cultivated from our obedience and maturity (Matthew 11:28-30).

Boundaries in Dating and Sex

Marriage should be honored by all, and the marriage bed kept pure, for God will judge the adulterer and all the sexually immoral. Keep your lives free from the love of money and be content with what you have, because God has said, "Never will I leave you; never will I forsake you." Hebrews 13:4-5

Now, *how* do we do it? One teenager once told me that staying a virgin involved *cold showers and lots of ice.* I think he was kidding, but, a better method would be discussing how far would be too far, then both of you agreeing to stick to it. Yes, this is hard. However, with an agreement in place, it is much, much easier.

The main areas of physical contact, in order of their usual occurrence, are holding hands, hugging, kissing (standard, then French), making out, oral stuff, and then intercourse. Some go even further with multiple partners and other extreme fetishes. (Christians must never practice these last two, married or not!) We have to realize that one sin or wrong action begets the other; the perceiving event will spur on the next, so each of these *contacts* leads to the next. If you kiss, you will end up making out, and so forth, unless you draw a line and make it your stand so you do not keep spiraling forward until you realize, *OH! NO!* afterwards!

Therefore, you need to make a line of demarcation. That is, draw your line one step away from the absolute *no go line*. My wife Mary and I drew the line at hugging. Therefore, we hugged and held hands, but we did not kiss until we were engaged, and did not go further until we got married. This worked great for us, and I highly recommend keeping kissing off-limits until after the engagement! But, this may not be for you. As a pastor, I felt I needed to set a higher standard; you may draw your line at kissing, but never go past making out. Know this for making your line; making out will lead to intercourse. Maybe not the first or second time, but after 20-plus years of counseling teens and singles, I have never known it not lead to sex at some point! It just gets too tempting, too heated. Then, if both of you lose control…. So, choose with Godly principles in mind, as if Jesus is there, because…well, He is!

God designed sex and the other various forms of expressing intimacy. So, we are not to fear them, but honor them in their proper place——the marriage bed! He desires us to lead godly, virtuous lives, and not tempt our friends, date, or even ourselves in any way——from wrong thinking to pornography. Even if you are definitely going to be married, do not cross that line. The line will be used to develop trust and lasting intimacy. Remember that real, true love is patient! If you are not patient, then you may not be in love—just in lust! In addition, if you are not sure, then you must not cross that line because that may not be your future wife or husband; they belong to someone else. You will be sinning against God by robbing Him of glory and stealing someone else's future spouse! How would you like someone making out with your spouse when you are married? You would be incensed, extremely angry, and hurt (Proverbs 6:32-35)! Well, that is what you are doing! In God's eyes, timing is irrelevant!

Here are some more helps:

But a man who commits adultery lacks judgment; whoever does so destroys himself. Blows and disgrace are his lot, and his shame will never be wiped away; for jealousy arouses a husband's fury, and he will show no mercy when he takes revenge. Proverbs 6:32-35

- Make a commitment to each other and God before the emotions start!
- Perhaps when you start getting serious, or even after the third time you go out, you can start to talk about it, so it clears the air and the

expectations. Something such as, *I do not believe in kissing until after I am engaged* will eliminate the pressure and expectations!

- Have the mindset of how you would expect someone else to treat your spouse. Then treat that person in the same way! Make sure it is biblical and not lustful or carefree!
- Stay in public places. If you are in a room, keep the door open!
- Have someone keep you accountable!
- Here is Billy Graham's rule that has kept him scandal free all the sixty plus years of his ministry; "Never be alone in a room with someone of the opposite sex (unless it is your wife)." He always takes a friend along with him when he travels. Why? To avoid any allegations of impropriety, and to protect him from seductive women!
- Avoid physically orientated, romantic relationships completely until you are ready to commit to marriage. Only engage in the romance after your commitment. You will have the pleasure of building a meaningful, lasting romance with the one person with whom you will spend the rest of your life!
- Ask yourself in dating, *is this all about honoring and glorifying God?*
- Do nothing you would not do in front of Christ! Are you trying to get as close as possible to God, or just trying to get in someone's skirt/ pants? And, what is that going to get you in eternity and in your future marriage?
- See the Accountability Questions in the Appendix for more insights.

A boundary is basically like a fence to ward off potential problems and to protect those in its guardianship. It sets a parameter to be a guide, as in computer programming parameters that keep the program in the right areas of operation. When we have those right areas of operation in our personal and ministerial lives, we will be more effective for His service. These principles are for all Christians, and will be much needed when you venture into a committed relationship, especially marriage.

You need to ask yourself:

Better a patient man than a warrior, a man who controls his temper than one who takes a city. Proverbs 16:32

- Are you willing to or do you spend adequate time with your family? Are you willing to or have a regular date night and separate family night with the kids at least once a week?
- Do you try to be too much to too many people? That is, do you spend too much time with friends so it will/does take away from your spouse? Do you spend so much time with your spouse you do not have or spend time with friends?
- Do you have unrealistic expectations, either going into a marriage or within your marriage, for yourself as well as others? We all need to have commitment, time, and passion in our relationships, but, also patience and temperament to allow God's timing. We are never to force ourselves onto others or allow them to do that to us.
- Do you say *no* with love and tact when others intrude too much in your personal time? Do you have realistic parameters with your time in light of Christ-like character? No one can do everything or be everywhere!
- Do you have a system of time management? Even Jesus took time off!
- Do you take regular time off from work and hobbies so you have time to build relationships?
- Do you take care of yourself physically by eating right, and exercising? Remember, your body is the temple of the Holy Spirit, so do not defile it!
- Do you have a good system to calendar and keep track of events and dates?
- Most important, do you spend adequate time with our LORD? At the very least, is it half an hour each day?

These questions will determine how you manage yourself, your expectations, and time. Remember, your time is the treasure that God has entrusted to you.

If any of the above areas are neglected, you are possibly headed for breakdown and sin! Your relationships will become stifled at best; or, at worst, they will break down altogether. You have to be willing to assess your time and commitments in light of biblical standards. Be encouraged that we are not expected to be perfect, but we need to be the best we can. Let these questions challenge and spur you on in the right direction. Set up the boundaries. Boundaries are not a fence to keep others out, but are to hang on to good, neighborly relationships. They will not eliminate all of the interruptions; we have to allow relationships to take priority, and interruptions come with the territory. We need to embrace and love our call and not be hermits to the people around us and whom God brings into our lives. Boundaries create a healthier atmosphere with balance. A marriage that has the foundation of love and care will not allow one person to be dictatorial or abusing of the other. Submission does not mean that the man is running the whole show. If it is, then he is not treating her in the light of the love he has been called to!

The boundaries we set will enable us to put limits on our over-working and ignoring of others, and at the same time, enable us to guard ourselves from others taking advantage of us—from physical, mental, and spiritual abuse to sexual sin. This will allow us to make our families the second priority in our life—Christ being the first. That means we will spend adequate time with them. Moreover, if we do not set limits, people will take advantage of us. Boundaries will also help us set priorities, so that we do not ignore problems because we are too busy. Problems rarely go away without help.

I cannot tell how many countless times I have started on my way home to my family and someone just shows up at the office to talk. Sometimes, it is a crisis, but most of the time, it is because of loneliness. Sometimes, someone shows up at my home, or I meet him or her, by chance, at the grocery store. I love people and it is natural for me to use my time and efforts to be with them. This is one of the main areas I love about pastoral ministry. That was OK when I was single; but now, as a married man, I have other priorities that need my attention. As ministers of God (all Christians are ministers), we need to be attentive to others as well as listeners and encouragers. However, we are not to neglect our own web of relationships and family. We cannot trade the fracture of the family for poor management of His people, thinking we are doing our best for ministry. I have leaned the hard way that poor ministry and misguided self-management will fracture your family and ministry.

Developing limits with your time and relationships will not happen overnight, as you have trained your friends and yourself in patterns that are very much ingrained. Yet, it is a *must* to reform, before it is too late. So, what can we do?

Healthy Biblical Outlook

"Come to me, all you who are weary and burdened, and I will give you rest. Take my yoke upon you and learn from me, for I am gentle and humble in heart, and you will find rest for your souls. For my yoke is easy and my burden is light." Matthew 11:28-30

First, have a healthy biblical outlook on what self-control is and how it relates with the rest of the Fruit of the Spirit. Be familiar with Galatians, chapter five, and Ephesians, chapter four. Involve other people in your life who complement both your gifts and shortcomings. In a family, one person cannot be the only caregiver because it will create an over dependence on one person; we are all ministers together. This will take the one person's time away from his/her family and call. Misguided management philosophy has destroyed major corporations as well as countless families; do not let it happen to you and your family. There are way too many good, Christian resources and helps available for any Christian to fail in this area.

Keep Track of Your Time

To the elders among you, I appeal as a fellow elder, a witness of Christ's sufferings and one who also will share in the glory to be revealed: Be shepherds of God's flock that is under your care, serving as overseers—not because you must, but because you are willing, as God wants you to be; not greedy for money, but eager to serve; not lording it over those entrusted to you, but being examples to the flock. 1 Peter 5:1-3

The second imperative thing to have is a good system of time management. This is the ability to keep track of appointments and events with some form of guideline to keep your time secure within a right sense of priorities. That way, you do not neglect your job, church commitments, or your family. This is not just for a CEO or a pastor; it is for anyone who desires to have his or her life run more efficiently and orderly. When you have a calendar or date book with all of your time scheduled out, you can see the big picture. Where are you spending your time? How is your time being used? What are areas where you have over-committed? What areas are being neglected? As you can see, a calendar system is very important. It does not have to be complicated; the simpler the better. I just use a month-at-a-glance appointment book. I like to see my whole month at once; others like to see a week or a day at a time.

You can improve your life by using a calendar. You can make sure you have time planned with family before you schedule hobbies, work, or outings with friends. If you have a demanding job that takes a lot of time and/or travel, make sure you keep your days off guarded as much as possible. If you are self-employed, set office hours; let your co-workers/clients know your schedule, so they know when and how to get in touch with you. Also, make sure you have good ways to relax each day, to take your mind off the stress of life—but not just TV.

Be aware of burnout

Very early in the morning, while it was still dark, Jesus got up, left the house and went off to a solitary place, where he prayed. Simon and his companions went to look for him, and when they found him, they exclaimed: "Everyone is looking for you!" Mark 1:35-37

The stress of life and the hassles of family will get you down and test the limits of even the best-run family. So, how can you tell if you are just tired or really burnt? First, you need to ask yourself the questions from the previous section about setting boundaries. If you are doing it correctly, it is probably just expressing exhaustion. However, if you find yourself being apathetic and detached from your family, you have a problem. You have to be on guard with that most destructive force, *pride*! Pride and arrogance will produce a superiority complex. So, when you become careless towards others, you lose your perspective and what God has called you to do. You will hurt your family, your friends, and, if you are married, you can cause intense harm to your spouse. In addition, either the pride or the refusal to set boundaries—even a combination of the two—will cause you to fall into burnout, and lead you into sexual sin. You have to be willing to determine if you need an overhaul or just a good night's sleep. A mentor or accountability partner can also help you see warning signs.

Here are some other ways you can do to prevent burnout:

1. Pray, and pray a lot. Have others pray for you! Let God in on what you are feeling; release your frustration to Him. You cannot tell God anything new; He already knows.
2. Learn to delegate; remember the boundaries and dangers we have previously discussed.
3. Keep your attitude in check.
4. Stay healthy, get regular checkups, and make sure you and your family eat right, rest, and exercise. We are of little use to God or others if we are always sick and tired. I repeat this because it is so overlooked, yet so important!
5. Guard your free time. We are on this earth for such a short bit of time, so keep your focus and your health in check.
6. Have a support base to keep you accountable, people that you can go to and who will listen to you. Small groups, Bible study groups, mentors, pastors, and trusted friends are great resources.
7. Engage in other interests outside of job and family, such as biking, hiking, civic events, or a hobby. Make sure they do not consume you, either!
8. Make sure you have the right focus and call in your life. A lot of people are in the wrong vocation; they are not utilizing their gifts, talents, or abilities. (Pastors can also be in the wrong profession.)
9. Realize that you are not God; He does not need you. He only chooses to use you out of grace. Therefore, we are not the Savior to our family or to the church; we are just the people He uses.
10. Be a learner; read; go to marriage and men's/women's conferences and retreats where you can learn and be refreshed.
11. Most importantly, be immersed in the Word.

Burnout means that our spiritual energies are totally exhausted, that we have no will or vitality either to make relationships work or to do whatever our task is. We are completely worn-out and spent. Thus, if we stay in our position without being refueled, we will just be throwing a monkey wrench into vital components, causing them to break. If you are a leader, burnout can be especially devastating to others when you become the monkey wrench that sabotages the machine of ministry. We may not desire or be willing to do so, but because of our lack of availability and due to the fact there is nothing left of us, we are of no service; we are, in fact, endangering the vitality and ministry of others.

Stress

But I call to God, and the LORD saves me. Evening, morning and noon I cry out in distress, and he hears my voice. Psalm 55:16

You can expect that people at home, church, work, your loved ones, friends, pets, and acquaintances will ask you for favors, such as your time, resources, talents, or attention. This is good, and you should do what you can; but, there will be times when they will deplete you and be the cause of your stress. You cannot be everywhere or do everything! So, you have to learn how to build a fence that says, *I love you, but can you leave me alone for now?* The most important aspect in setting boundaries is saying *NO* in a kind way. So, say it now … *NO!* Now start to practice saying it in a firm, yet kind way, with an explanation of why. That way, you can be better prepared. People deserve a reason, so do not just say, *no!* Be honest, even if you just need time alone. Do not feel guilty; you have to take care of yourself before you can take care of others!

Be aware of stress at family outings and projects, especially during holidays. They are stressful for many people. Take a look at why it is that way with you. Why does something produce stress in you? Is it your time? Fear…? Remember, you are not indispensable; if you think that, you need help from a good counselor or pastor! To help prevent many of the stresses of life, learn to plan ahead! For big events, make sure you plan them out ahead of time and delegate! Do not try to do too many things or take on too many projects, especially if they are new to you. If you are a procrastinator, like I am, do it early; force yourself. Once you figure out that life is easier and less stressful when you do things early, you will make it a habit of it.

You need to be willing and able to recognize what you will and can do. Then, pick the activities best suited for your time, abilities, and resources. If someone gives you a hard time (even your conscience), expecting you to do something you are not able to do, when you see yourself becoming overextended, just say *no* in a loving way!

During holidays, you need to place your focus on the religious aspects of the holiday, which is why we Christians have them. Christmas is not about trees and gifts; it is about Jesus coming down to earth to be identified as one of us. Easter is not about bunnies and chocolate (although I have pet bunnies and love chocolate); it is about Christ paying our penalty of sin on the cross so we can have grace and eternal life. Veterans Day and Memorial Day are about honoring our soldiers who have served and died for our country; it is not about BBQ! Birthdays are about celebrating someone's life and making them feel special; it is not about pleasing everyone else! Place the focus on the reason, not on pleasing.

Remember, the key to this is to be willing to say *no* in a loving and caring way. Do not allow people to force things on you just because you have done them before; they need to respect you and your time. Assertiveness is biblical when it is operated within the parameters of biblical character and the Fruit of the Spirit!

For further help, take breaks away from people for a time and just spend time with God. Take a drive, a walk, read a book, go somewhere where you feel comfortable, visit a friend or relative, or find something else or something new to do to take your mind off the stress. This will recharge your spiritual batteries as well as your physical energy. Prayer is your big ally to help set boundaries and prevent stress amongst the spiritual and maturity implications! Do not feel guilty! Try to simplify your life a bit. Remember the calendar; use it to check what you are up to—too much, too little...?

Also be aware of anxiety, phobias, and mental disorders that contribute to stress; they can keep us from our relationships and functions with family and church. Seek help from a good counselor or pastor!

Setting Boundaries with Obnoxious and Toxic people

"A wicked and adulterous generation looks for a miraculous sign, but none will be given it except the sign of Jonah." Jesus then left them and went away. Matthew 16:4

I am a person who is often taken advantage of, according to my loving wife. I tend to go the extra mile in relationships and in ministry, and people will tend to take advantage of that. I usually do not mind; but, I noticed that it bothered her, so I had to learn how to set boundaries. Perhaps you need to do so too.

Are you tired of people snapping at you? Then, do something about it. I had to. First, make sure you are not the cause of the trouble! Be willing to take an honest look at yourself, and do not *assume*! There is no biblical reason to take abuse from a rude or toxic person, unless you are called to as a missionary or in a ministry situation; but, again, it should be short. An exception would be if you are in a dire situation, such as a prison, where you have no control over your environment.

People who are rude and cause negativity all of the time may not be worth having in your life, even if they are close relatives. Pray about this hard and long! Do not be afraid to temporarily remove them from your life by staying away from them. I have sometimes seen, in pastoral counseling, that a person was in a toxic family situation and was being manipulated and controlled by people of bad character. After trying all sorts of relationship resolving methods, I had to recommend they cut ties with the person and move away. Each time, this was a person who had to leave the state to get away from a very bad family member—even a mother. Usually, after a time, the toxic person got the hint, and the relationship was healed; sometimes, people are so steeped in their pride, there is no help for them.

In most situations, you will not need to move out of your state; however, you do need to take some action. In a loving and caring way, you need to have a talk with the person, and give examples of how they are treating you. For example, if someone says something or has done something to you that has hurt you, just say, "I love you, but I can not accept your behavior." Then walk into another room and take a break, or talk to someone else. If the person follows you (I hate that!), then try to tell them again, still with a loving, but firm way, that their behavior is not acceptable, nor can you allow it. If they continue, then just say "goodbye," and leave without making a scene. At another time, go to see them and explain why you said and did that. If they refuse to listen, just say, "I will have to stay away from you for a while until you are willing to listen." Do not be afraid to do this; you will trade a small amount of stress from the confrontation for a lot of stress from their continual toxicity towards you and your family. If you are uncomfortable in doing this, then take a trusted friend or pastor with you. Make sure you keep them in prayer.

In John 21:15-19 Jesus asks Peter to *"feed My sheep."* We, through the power of the Holy Spirit, are the feeder; and as feeders, we need to be fed (1 Peter 5:1-2). People will depend on us to feed them, and they may drain us of our feed, personally and spiritually. Thus, we have to be careful to replenish ourselves with the right feed, that of growing in the faith through spiritual disciplines. If we do not, we endanger ourselves and the family entrusted to us.

If one falls down, his friend can help him up. But pity the man who falls and has no one to help him up! Ecclesiastes 4:10

It is a very good idea, before venturing into a long-term relationship, to self-evaluate with a few simple questions:

- What are the things that lure you to be self-indulgent?
- How do the excesses of life and other things counteract or block self-control?
- What happens to your relationship with God and others when you relinquish self-control?
- When have you been filled with self-control the most?
- In what situation did you fail to have self-control when you should have?
- How would your relationships improve with more self-control?
- Think through the steps you need to take to put self-control into action in a specific instance. For example, how can you place safeguards against the areas in your life where you are weak? What about premarital sex and boundaries to prevent it? Or, how can you make sure you act with kindness, but do not allow others to take advantage of you too much? Or, how can you avoid situations, things, certain people, and places that may cause you to lose control? Or, how can you balance having joy and fun, but not allowing them to become excesses that lead to sin?

When they had finished eating, Jesus said to Simon Peter, "Simon son of John, do you truly love me more than these?" "Yes, LORD," he said, "you know that I love you." Jesus said, "Feed my lambs." John 21:15

CHAPTER XII
WHAT THE BIBLE SAYS ABOUT SEX AND ROMANCE

Submit to one another out of reverence for Christ. Ephesians 5:21

The Bible is not a book on sex. However, it does contain a complete theology of sexuality. Its purpose, intent, warnings against its misuse, as well as a beautiful picture of true love and intimacy are given to us. The Bible also gives us the ideal picture of a physical relationship, which is set forth in the stunning poetry of the book the Song of Solomon. Some of its power does not come through in English or into an American culture with statements like "your teeth are like a flock of sheep" or "your hair is like a flock of goats;" nevertheless, the values and motivations are still alive for us to grasp and apply. So, yes, the Bible does tell us about sex, and it is not information that is out of touch, archaic, or irrelevant. The Bible is timeless because relationships are timeless! The same frustrations and struggles have existed since Adam and Eve bit into the apple. What the people in the Bible went through, we go through. And, since God is the Creator and Sustainer, perhaps He has a better way for us, even on the subject of sex. This way can be found from the precepts of His Word!

Sex is a Bond

But because of his great love for us, God, who is rich in mercy, made us alive with Christ even when we were dead in transgressions—it is by grace you have been saved. And God raised us up with Christ and seated us with him in the heavenly realms in Christ Jesus, in order that in the coming ages he might show the incomparable riches of his grace, expressed in his kindness to us in Christ Jesus. Ephesians 2:4-7

We have talked about Ephesians 5:21-32 a lot in the preceding chapters, because this passage is God's call for fullness in marriage. We even talked about submission and how it is tied to love in the chapter on "Preparing for a Successful Marriage." This passage also gives us a depiction of fullness with sex that is sacred and meant for a specific unity and purpose. That submission is important and meant for one person in the context of a unity that equals the sex life God meant for us, which is the best for us. A symbiotic love relationship is taught so that as a man loves a woman, she submits because of his love. This submission is a love in itself that becomes as *one flesh*. Literally it means our souls are tied together. This means the union of sex is to be between a man and a woman who are committed to each other for life in the covenant of marriage. This becomes a union from the Greek syntax, a union that should not be broken. So, our union with our spouse is meant to be a permanent as well as an intimate bond.

The illustration is given to us about the church, as it, too, is a union. In the case for the church, it is a union of believers that are bonded to one another by what Christ has done for them. Thus, the church is a permanent and intimate bond for those in a committed, relational connection with one another. These institutions of church and marriage are sacred, and we must work to keep it this way. When we acknowledge this sacredness, we develop a more vigorous respect for, and a response to motivate, encourage, and foster its development and care. When we view it as archaic, we demean the real value, power, and importance of sex, thus creating all kinds of problems down the line.

As you can see through the above passages, God considers this as exceptionally sacred and important, so we need to take this subject seriously. It is something that we are not to mess around with! Yet, the majority of young Christians do not take this seriously; when they get older, they are full of regret, guilt, and remorse for the actions they caused and inflicted upon others. They wonder why their sex life with their spouse is not like when they were first messing around. The reason is because the messing around messed them up! Sex forms a bond with another being, and if that person is not your spouse, that bond is formed anyway and stays with you for life! You formed a bond with someone or multiple some ones who were not meant for you. To make matters even more serious, messing around with sex steals the sacredness from the person it was meant for! The reverse is the case, too, when your spouse-to-be has not been chaste; they stole what was meant for you. Others have that bond that was meant for you! What about forgiveness and healing? Yes, it is there, as is God's grace; but, the consequences of messing around may remain, including the possibility of disease and brokenness that takes a significant amount of work to overcome—if it can be overcome. And, the disease may even take your life—not a good way to go.

Sex causes a bond meant for a sacred occasion; when it is misused, it is devastating to all involved. This is also the reason why sexual abuse is so devastating for people! The victim is bonded to his or her attacker in a perverse way, so it stays in the mind as he or she keeps living it out. So, in the case of abuse or mistakes, we have to be diligent to seek professional counseling to overcome, through God's grace, love, and forgiveness, these transgressions either we did or that were done to us. In a marriage where one or more of the spouses were not previously faithful, extra work and care needs to go into the relationship to seek the healing and forgiveness of that broken bond.

Knowing That God Made Me

The LORD God formed the man from the dust of the ground and breathed into his nostrils the breath of life, and the man became a living being. Genesis 2:7

We must realize, accept, and even be grateful that God made us as sexual beings. We are born with organs, physical features, and ways of thinking that are specifically male or female. In this are our personality traits and His perfect plan. In Matthew 19:4, Jesus says, "Haven't you read...that at the beginning the Creator made them male and female?" In other words, He is saying, *How come you do not understand? God made you as male and female, God made sex.* God brought Eve to Adam, and Adam's response was not, *I bet she has a wonderful personality.* Remember what Adam said? "This is now bone of my bones and flesh of my flesh." This translates in the modern vernacular as, *Yea, God!* Be grateful for God's gift and the way He made you. We need to get to the point where we can honestly say, *Thanks, God, that you made me with a body. Thanks for giving me the capacity for oneness within the covenant of marriage.* However, this does not mean we get to do what we want with our goodies! God has chosen that sexual relationships be reserved for the covenant of marriage! If you have been a victim of incest, abuse, or trauma of any kind, you must seek outside help from a qualified Christian pastor or counselor. If not, it will remain, and you will take that baggage into your marriage!

Because God made me, He is not against sex; He created it! What He is against is its misuse! In the Sermon on the Mount, Jesus delivered some strong words about what it means to be sexually righteous. This must be in the front of our minds whenever we seek God's plan and the right mate. If we do not, we will venture onto a path of potholes, strife, and contention, ending up in a relationship that is a result of sin. God can, of course, provide healing and forgiveness and even work it all out. However, the right road would have been so much better and more pleasant without the strife and hurt that not only affects you, but also all those around you for generations to come! This comes again from the first chapter where we talked about "Preparing for Relationships with the Right Mindset." The point is, if we do not have the right mindsets and parameters for our beliefs and actions, we will not be able to build relationships effectively. This is very true with sex!

Knowing Jesus' teachings will lead us to righteousness in sexual purity, and that will enable us to be in the right mindset to make the right choices. Because we are keeping the foundations of the attitudes of fullness and confession, along with the topics, "Be Willing To Learn About Yourself" and "Understanding the Kingdom of God" that we talked about in the first chapter and the knowledge that God made us, we can recognize that we belong to Him. This will enable us to prepare ourselves with biblical character and the ability to choose and to live right. This will translate into building a growing relationship as we have been called to do.

Not sure? Let's say you are still single and feel you have found the right person, the love of your life. What now? If you think you will live happily ever after with just finding the right person, you will wake up one day with a big surprise, *oh, my gosh! What did I do? Or, who is this messed up person next to me?* You will just be right there with most marriages—unhappy, already drifting apart, doing your own thing, or divorced instead of growing together, mutually benefiting and serving, and living a happy, content life. Yes, you will have ups and downs, but those foundational attitudes will help carry you though those tough times and make you stronger and better. Not the attitudes, so to speak, but the realization they bring to us—seeing, and allowing God's work in you! And, in marriage, when these attitudes are put into action, even if they were never practiced before, your relationships will vastly improve!

You have to be mature enough, as well as willing and able to engage in that relationship with the right attitudes and mindset. Choosing is only one aspect of your search in dating. You must get yourself—your attitudes—right, or you will just be a statistic on the divorce (or miserable) list! It is the same with marriage; be willing to put those attitudes in your marriage for its betterment, as you are upgrading with more "memory" and "CPU power."

The end result is a happier and stronger marriage because your computer-like mind has a better operating system—God's! When you lay your foundation with fullness, confession, and realize God made you, you can put into practice these other quintessential, paramount attitudes such as biblical love and character to further help you.

A Look at the Book of Love, the *Song of Solomon*

Scarcely had I passed them when I found the one my heart loves. I held him and would not let him go till I had brought him to my mother's house, to the room of the one who conceived me. Song of Solomon 3:4

We can learn a lot from the book of the *Song of Solomon*, sometimes called the *Song of Songs* (superlative referring to the greater song) or *Canticles* (Latin, for "song"). Unfortunately, it is rarely used as sermon material. It comes right after Ecclesiastes, and before Isaiah. It has the language of a love song or poetry. You may not fully understand the language, as your mind may fixate on *how beautiful can a flock of goats be*!? Just remember, in the Hellenistic culture, these images were beautiful.

Many scholars see this book as a collection of various love poetry, either written by, and/or collected by Solomon. This poetry expresses an intimate expression of true love to one's love of his life—Solomon to his love, an humble maiden, a Shulamite girl. It chronicles his adventure of love, through all of the joys and tribulations of courtship, to marriage. Jewish tradition sees this book as God's love for Israel, while Christians, through the centuries, saw this as God's love for the church.

This book shows us the importance and wonder of a commitment of love that lasts. As God's love lasts for us, our love must last for our spouse in the sanctity of marital love. This book does not shy away from the difficulties and realities of love and commitment, which makes for us a wondrous example from which to learn.

The Song of Solomon has six main precepts for us:

"Whoever has my commands and obeys them, he is the one who loves me. He who loves me will be loved by my Father, and I too will love him and show myself to him." John 14:21

1 Respect and honor the divine institution of marriage. It is not to be taken lightly or for granted. It is not something that is temporary until something or someone better comes along. It is the uniting of one man and one woman in love, a romance that lasts, even through the difficult times. Solomon started out in this mindset and practice, but eventually succumbed to hundreds of wives and concubines. All he could think of was this one woman, and the regret for all of the mistakes he made!

2 This is the model of God's love for Israel and the Church. We follow this model in both the preparation for marriage and in marriage. It has the core elements of redemption, forgiveness, reconciliation, and grace, all of which are what Christ did for us. It tells us how the relationship between a husband and wife should be! Remember, God sees marriage and the church as sacred initiations!

3 This book translates to us a model for dating. It is an example on how we can be better at dating. We need to look at the person for whom they really are, and seek them because of that, rather than for lusting or for physical pleasures, which will only hide the real person. This entire book is written in the precepts of the Song of Solomon!

4 This book translates to us a model for marriage. The stable love for one person is far superior to the lust and love of a thousand! Thus, the willingness and commitment to make it work, regardless of the ups and downs of life, are worth it. No lust, or satisfaction of that lust, is better than the love from the person God brings you! We gain the insight of the importance of marriage's staying power and sacredness.

5 Sex is designed for a proper place and time. God made sex. In and of itself, it is not evil or bad. However, it has the potential for great destruction. Outside of God's design, it becomes evil, brutal, distorts real love, and causes conflict-ridden relationships, disillusionment, and hurt.

6 Sex is not evil. Sex is not just for the promulgation of our gene pool, nor is it to be feared when it is in the confines of a husband and wife. A lot of misguided Christians, especially in the Victorian period, saw the abuses of sex, and they overreacted to say it is always evil unless you use it just to have children. This stance is not based in Scripture, but is rooted in ignorance and apprehension. Sex is to be embraced and exercised. We are called to romance our spouse, and to surprise him or her. This book is about the deep affection and romance written in poetry, further cementing this theme.

Daughters of Jerusalem, I charge you: Do not arouse or awaken love until it so desires. Song of Solomon 8:4

The Song of Solomon gives us a good model for dating and marriage with the attitude of romance, in addition to getting to know the real person without the pretensions and games most people play—including Christians! The games we play in relationships and sex create an atmosphere of distrust. We imagine an ideal person, and then project that fantasy onto the date. This continues through the process of going steady, becoming engaged, then into marriage. Thus, reality and truth are either absent, or hidden behind what we want and desire. We have to be willing to see what is best for us and what God has for us—not what our lust seeks.

In the dating world, even with long-term relationships, our games cause us to hide the *real* us from the other person. Because we are in an exclusive relationship does not mean we are getting to know that person. As a pastor in counseling, I run across many, countless people who have been married for years and they do not know each other very well! We have to think it through; *do I really know that person; if not, will I be willing to? If not, why? And, what is in my way?* In biblical times (and what is still practiced in many eastern cultures today), a couple gets to know the other person by friendship or through family connections where the person is already known—his or her personality, behaviors, likes, dislikes, and such. Therefore, there are no pretensions or hidden agendas. Then, if the couple likes each other and the families agree, they are betrothed (engaged).

The only physical things they can do together are communicating and getting to know each other better. By keeping away from the physical, the emphasis is on the building of a real relationship. This is still romantic, perhaps even more so, as wonder, excitement, and anticipation take the place of physical lust, which is what we have in our western culture.

Once the future marriage is defiled, it sets us up for all kinds of future problems. Communication, trust, and the building of a good relationship become very difficult or even lost. As the Word tells us, *marriage must be honored by all, and the marriage bed kept pure*, for *God will judge the adulterer and all the sexually immoral.* This is not because God has unattainable standards, but because He knows what works, what is best, and what we should avoid (Hebrews 13:4).

The Bible calls us to purity within marriage. When we get too physical and do not set up standards for ourselves, we allow ourselves to be tricked into false intimacy. Thus, the real romance becomes skewed and lost, and our wonder, our real excitement, and what is best becomes defiled. That is why God wants us to be righteous with our current and future relationships, so when we are married, we will have a solid marriage that will last, grow, and be much happier and joyful for us. Remember, God is the author of sexuality. In addition, He desires the expression of exclusive intimacy to be between a husband and wife. Adultery and premarital sex will ruin our current and future relationships.

What the Song of Solomon Translates to in Dating and Marriage

Drink water from your own cistern, running water from your own well. Proverbs 5:15

Dating can serve two roles in our American culture—a fun outing, or to seek a mate. This can involve fun and enjoyment with friends. In your dating and courting ventures for seeking a mate, your goal is to look for the right person. You must not over-emphasize what the media communicates to us, exaggerating the lust and flesh, and denying the real relationship, which also denies the spiritual.

The context is of a Jewish wedding ceremony and its sacred institution. God's plan for Christian marriage brings together both the spirit and the flesh, as in the *one flesh* of the marriage ceremony. Real intimacy is the total uniting of two people, each one seeking to meet the needs of the other. This cannot happen when sins of the misuse of sex and not getting to know each other properly gets in the way.

Allow the precepts of this neglected book from God's Word to motivate you on the importance of romance, commitment, and the value of a lasting growing relationship. Allow this book to warn you of the mistake and regret that Solomon made by not following his own wise advice. Do not be the person who looks back at his or her life with shame and regret. Yes, God will forgive; but, why put yourself in that situation? Be committed, be romantic, and be the Christian who loves and is loved!

A look at the book of Ruth

So Boaz took Ruth and she became his wife. Then he went to her, and the LORD enabled her to conceive, and she gave birth to a son. Ruth 4:13

The book of Ruth is set in the time of the Judges. Some scholars say it was during the time of the prophet Samuel and Saul and the early rein of David (1 Samuel; Ruth 4:7) around 1050 BC. This may be plausible due to the portrayal of good relationships between Moabites and the Israelites that was not there during the Judges. The term *during the Judges* in the first chapter possibly refers to the instability of the late period of Saul's rein. However, the main problem is that Ruth is also the great grandma to King David. History and textual criticism/debate aside, this book shows us the character of our God as the Redeemer.

This story follows the adventures of three principle characters, Ruth, Naomi, and Boaz. Ruth has just lost her husband and is in a state of loss and confusion. She felt helpless and hopeless, but turned from her false gods to pursue the One True God. Even though she was not a Jew, she remained faithful to God. Naomi was Ruth's mother-in-law, a Jewess, who was compelled by family remembrances to go back to her homeland, thereby exercising faith. Naomi trusted God even though she sinned against God by leaving her homeland in the first place and marring a Gentile. God looked beyond her sin and worked it out for good as He does with us. God protected her and Ruth, who was an alien, through many harsh trials and tribulations. God blessed Ruth's faithfulness and brought to her a new and better husband, Boaz. God even allowed her to be in the genealogy of Jesus. Naomi, at first, was bitter and did not want to take Ruth back with her, but learned about faith and also received blessings for her faithfulness. Boaz was a relative of Naomi, and culturally, held the position to redeem her, which meant to take care of her, which he did. In the process, both he and Ruth remained faithful to God, and took their time to get to know each other before falling in love. This book shows us the importance of faith and commitment.

Boaz was a man of integrity who had the opportunity to take advantage of a young, pretty widow. Instead, he chose righteousness as he protected Ruth and looked after her needs. He made an extremely difficult situation for her easier by not seeking his comfort or lust, and eventually enjoyed a beautiful marriage. If he had chosen the way of the world, he could never have had a good, enduring relationship with Ruth. Ruth, who remained faithful, would also have missed out on the relationship (Ruth 2:20; 3:10-11).

Boaz was the *Kinsman-Redeemer* for Ruth's family. This meant he was a close relative whose call and obligation was to come to the aid of a family member in distress. According to Levitical Law, he could redeem property, family members sold into slavery, assets such as farm animals, and he could care for a widow or orphans (Leviticus 25:25-34; 27:9-33). However, in practice, this rarely occurred because greed usually took over and people took advantage of the weak and helpless. This is one of the main reasons God judged the Israelites and sent then into captivity, as found in the book of Jeremiah.

In the New Testament, Christ is our ultimate *Kinsman-Redeemer*, as He represents humanity and our bloodline (Matthew. 1:1-17; Galatians 4:4; Heb. 2:16-17). He represents our need (John 10: 15-18; 1 John 3:16), and He has the resources (1 Corinthians 6:20; 1 Peter 1:18-19).

Be willing to keep God's standards

Why be captivated, my son, by an adulteress? Why embrace the bosom of another man's wife? Proverbs 5:20

Ruth took a great leap of faith and turned from her near hopeless situation to a wonderful, prosperous life filled with blessings and a lasting legacy. Ruth lost her husband; her sister-in-law lost hers, too. But, Ruth put her faith in God, and she was not even a Jew! So, she, with her mother-in-law Naomi's leading, left Moab and went to Israel. She committed herself to integrity and caught the eye of a godly man who redeemed her and later became her husband. Ruth was willing and able to yield to God's standards and keep them. As a result, her life was for the better as yours will be too!
Keeping God's standards enables us to receive His best for us because we will avoid the pitfalls and traps that lead us to become lost in sin. This is also so true in our sexuality! 1 Thessalonians 4:3 says, *It is God's will that you should be sanctified: that you should avoid sexual immorality.* This means we must reserve the sexual relationship for the permanent commitment of marriage. God intended sex to be for a husband and wife who have committed to each other permanently; only in the context of a permanent commitment can intimacy be truthfully, faithfully, and safely expressed. When there is physical intimacy without a permanent commitment, the hurt will extend to God, to you, and to your future spouse!!!

Thus, you need to know the Scriptures, so you can know God's will and what is best. By knowing God's best for you, you can make a commitment to it because it is in your best interest. This must be done before you get too far into a situation. If you do not, you will have waited too long and you will be tempted to break those standards. And, more often than not, you will break those standards and cause the harm we will talk about next under "lust!" If you wait until you are in the heat of temptation, you will fail fast. Unless you hold onto God's values and precepts, you are not going to make it. The pressure to go the opposite way from God's standards is very intense in our society, so you must decide ahead of time what you will do. If you are married and have not kept God's standards, then make the commitment to do so, even if you are the only one willing to do it! He will honor and bless you for it! It will be tough at first, but hang on and stay committed. Remember, it was rough for a while for Ruth, too.

What the Book of Ruth Translates Into Dating and Marriage

"I have also acquired Ruth the Moabitess, Mahlon's widow, as my wife, in order to maintain the name of the dead with his property, so that his name will not disappear from among his family or from the town records. Today you are witnesses!" Ruth 4:10

Christ is our Redeemer, and He does not take advantage of us or let us rot, as we deserve. Thus, in our dating and marriage relationships, we should also look to Boaz's example, who was a righteous gentleman. And, we can look at Ruth's example, who was a woman of faithfulness and patience. Boaz took it slowly, got to know Ruth, and did not take advantage of her. This led to a better, stronger relationship, with romance and love entering at its proper time and place. In addition, Ruth did not fall to immorality and prostitution, nor take advantage of Boaz. Ruth and Naomi were attracted to the kindness and integrity of Boaz as he treated them both well. Boaz was attracted to Ruth's humility and nobility. Thus, we are to be kind, listen, learn, not take advantage, care, share, and take care of one another! Although both were physically attractive, their attractiveness is not what caught each other's eye; nor should it be with us. We need to see the importance of nobility and authenticity, as it will pay off much better and greater than the ways of the fast world would. We are to be attracted to goodness and integrity, not looks, power, wealth, or position.

Be on Guard Against Lust

I made a covenant with my eyes not to look lustfully at a girl. Job 31:1

Sin is destructive, and sexual sin keeps destroying long after the initial deed is over! Jesus' purpose in Matthew is to warn us that lust and sin destroy! These additional Scriptures further speak to us about the importance of being on guard, confessing to and repenting for it so it does not happen, or, does not happen again. If you think you are sexually perfect and need no repentance because you have avoided committing physical adultery, think again. Lust runs much deeper than you may think, as it starts with wrong thinking, which leads us into wrong actions. This can involve reading a bad magazine or walking into a hotel room with someone you should not be with! There have been many great Christian leaders over the years who have failed due to sexual improprieties. Each one said they did not think it could ever happen to them, but it did. Each one failed to guard himself or apply God's standards, even though they taught others to do so.

Never forget God's call to holiness. Jesus cuts right to the root, the heart of the problem in Matthew, chapter five, on how we lose sight of holiness with lust, and cause extreme destruction to marriages. Instead of coming out and saying divorce is sin and wrong (which He does later in v. 31), He tells us to be watchful for what leads up to it, trying to save us the strife, confusion, the broken relationship, and the hurt before it is too late. He ties together the seventh and the tenth Commandments (Exodus 20: 14; 17) which are further honored by following the precepts of Ephesians 5:22-33. This means that to keep holiness is to prevent the seventh; in so doing, we have to safeguard the tenth. This means guarding ourselves from lust and modeling good character. Coupling this with real love will result in keeping a healthy marriage alive. Otherwise, lust will be the factor that leads to broken relationships and then to divorce. Then, Jesus suggests surgery, to cut the cancer of lust and sin out of the heart, as an illustration to the importance and urgency of this matter.

The words "lust," "lustfully," or "desire" in the Bible (Matthew 5:27-28) are translated from *"epiphemaho,"* which means *mismanaged sexual desire or fantasy or intent.* Imagine how offended the pious, fraud religious leaders were when Jesus told them they had personal problems with their view of their sexuality and righteousness! How would you react if Jesus directly challenged you with your lust, sexual motives, and un-confessed, unresolved sin? Well, He is doing just that! Jesus is not saying that since you have lusted/

committed adultery in your heart, you might as well go all the way because one sin is just as bad as the other. He says for you to *stop!* Lusting paves the road to adultery, as lust includes everything that is wrong within our heart.

Then, this lust we harbor migrates into deceit and betrayal, which breaks the promise and commitment we made with our spouse. This, in turn, causes so much damage to the family. If you think, *hey, I'm still single; this does not apply to me,* you are very wrong. First Thessalonians 4:6 tells us that sexual immorality defrauds, just as your sexual misadventures will rob your future spouse, literally swindling away what belongs to him or her. It will take away what is best for you, as well as further corrupting many other lives. Lust does not stop in your heart; adultery does not stay private, or remain in singles; it migrates with you in the long term with all of your relationships, and into your future marriage. Many others become affected, such as the future spouse of the person you were with, who gets robbed of what belongs to him or her, and so on, and so on. The entire family, friends, and the rest of the Christian community will share in your shame.

Lust still does not stop there. After all of that destruction in your family, future family, the families of others, the next generations, and so on, the sin keeps going! *What is left,* you wonder? Well, remember that bond? A bond is formed in you that will never be broken when you have sex with someone who was not meant for you. And, anyone who is not your spouse is not meant for you! It is not something you just forget; it stays, and no amount of therapy or costly psychological sessions will cure it. Just ask any competent Christian psychologist. When you have sex, you form a bond, and that person is living in your brain all of your life! Can you imagine an "ex" girlfriend or boyfriend living in your mind after you have broken up, and you hate each other? That is why so many relationships are messed up these days! That is why God hates this; it is not just a private matter; it is a community matter!

Be Willing to See Ahead so You can Maximize your Marriage

The husband should fulfill his marital duty to his wife, and likewise the wife to her husband. 1 Corinthians 7: 3

During the fun times and the busyness of the post-modern life, we forget that what we do now has lasting consequences. When we just live for the moment of fun now, we give up so much in the future that God had for us. We have to be willing to see ahead and how our actions and thoughts today will affect tomorrow and our spouse or future spouse. We have to be willing to see that God, indeed, has a plan for us, and commit to find and honor His plan. That plan is simple; it means, *keep His standards*. That does not mean you have to lock yourself away somewhere if you are still single; it is still OK to have fun and go out as long as you do not violate God's standard and character. Dating is a time for you to learn about yourself, and how to relate to the other sex. You need to be willing to learn why relationships do not work out, so you do not repeat bad patterns. When you date, the odds of that person being for you are very low, so you have to be willing to honor their future as well as yours. The best way to do this is to remember God's plan and keep it in your *sights* at all times. If you are already married, be willing to realize your past patterns will affect your marriage; so, do not allow the bad ones to continue to influence you, and do not repeat them.

By keeping God's standards in your sights, you will be honoring your spouse or future spouse. Why would you not want to do that? Even if it may be years before you are married, what you do now will affect him or her down the road regarding the quality of your relationship. Even if you have not met him or her yet, you can serve, pray for, and love your future spouse in your whole relationship, including your physical relationship and standards. *The husband should fulfill his marital duty to his wife, and likewise the wife to her husband. The wife's body does not belong to her alone but also to her husband. In the same way, the husband's body does not belong to him alone but also to his wife* (1 Corinthians 7:3-4). These are awesome words, which are not just for the future when you are married; they are for now, as they transcend time and place. Sexual fulfillment is within marriage only. God designed it this way and it is so important to God that He actually calls it your *duty*.

Remember, if you just live for the now, and party yourself away, you will bring yourself into a very sad situation and life. Yes, grace will heal you, but why mess yourself up in the first place, and live with the consequences of your bad choices? Your marital duty does not start when you say, "I do." It starts as soon as your hormones set in; it starts when you acknowledge Christ as your LORD! Make a commitment to maximize your current or future marriage!!! If you do not, you will be betraying your spouse, and the best of the plans God has for you!

If you follow these principles of acknowledging your sinful nature, living in accountability, and daily confession, being grateful for God's amazing gift of sexuality, you will be able to persevere with your resolve to keep

God's standards. This is especially true when it comes to sexual behavior. By keeping God's standards, you will be maximizing your marriage even if you are not married yet. We Christians who acknowledge Christ as LORD need to see Him and conduct ourselves as if He is LORD, as best you can. We can also do this by being willing to listen and learn; and as parents or future parents, we must be willing to train and equip our children to honor and follow God. That way, your offspring will not repeat the same bad patterns as you may have. That way, you will be in the right parameters to make right decisions, and grow to be the person God wants you to be. With God's standards, your marriage will be magnificent. As a single person, your future marriage will be magnificent! And with God's standards, you will find the right person, the love of your life! By applying God's standards in the body of Christ, you will find an island of sanity and wholeness in a sea of sexual chaos and pain.

Remember—this is so important from God's Word—when we have sex with someone, a bond is formed that will never be broken. This is why sexual abuse is so painful for decades afterwards! It is not just a one-time event; it keeps recurring in your mind, building and growing in pain and magnitude. When you have sex, you form a bond and that person is living in your brain, even past your retirement years!!! That is why so many relationships are messed up these days!!! Sex bonds us! Misplaced sex bonds us to the wrong person. This idea of a bond is a running theme throughout the Son of Solomon; the bond is never broken and lasts throughout your life (Ephesians 5: 8-33). We must keep God's standards or face God's judgment; *Do not arouse love or awaken love until its proper time* (Song 3:4-5). Most of the time His judgment is to let our actions run their course.

Therefore, brothers, we have an obligation—but it is not to the sinful nature, to live according to it. For if you live according to the sinful nature, you will die; but if by the Spirit you put to death the misdeeds of the body, you will live, because those who are led by the Spirit of God are sons of God.
Romans 8:12-14

Chapter XIII
LEARNING TO SEE IN RELATIONSHIPS

Every day they continued to meet together in the temple courts. They broke bread in their homes and ate together with glad and sincere hearts. Acts 2:46

I did not wake up one day and find myself happily married. There was a process that led up to it. I spent most of my adult life single, unhappy, and feeling that only a wife would fill that gap. So, I ventured into that jungle of confusing choices for many years, seeking the world's standards, while straddling it with God's. All that did was get me lost, confused, and lonely. It was not until I learned to trust in His precepts and work on my relationship with Him and on myself that He brought to me Mary, the love of my life. I had a lot to learn, even as an educated pastor and speaker; I had to own up to what I was saying to others. So, after years of getting it wrong myself, years of getting lost in that conflicting jungle of dating despair, I finally got it right! I finally learned that I had to change my presumptions from the world's standards to God's. I had to let go of what I wanted, and seek His principles. The ironic thing is that I knew this stuff. I just did not fully trust it, I was not sure, and I did not want to commit or be challenged away from my way and ideas. All the while, I was teaching other singles how to do it right. I came to realize that I had to put my faith into practice and do as I was teaching others to do. You see, I started teaching these principles in this book in back in 1983; yet I, myself, only took it seriously half of the time, until 1994. Yes, it took ten years to soak into my hard head so that I could open my eyes and see! I had to let go of my ideas and surrender to Christ's. Then, in 1995, I was married to the love of my life. Thus, I have some wisdom to impart to you. Wisdom from the Word and from timeless values and precepts that will work if you put your faith and trust in the One who leads—Christ, as LORD!

In this chapter, I am seeking to challenge single Christians to seek biblical principles in love and dating. Although this is geared to singles, the principles will be not only for all Christian singles, but also for those who are married as well as all those who are either dazed and confused, or think they have it right. Even if you have been married for years, you still need to know this stuff as you may influence children, friends, or relatives. Or, perhaps you will find principles that you either did not take care of before or ignored, and still need to work on. So, dig in and see how you may develop and build a lasting and godly relationship.

In building a genuine, God-centered relationship, you have to be real and be focused, that is, if you truly desire to follow God's precepts and not those of society. You have to be willing and able to cast off the games that people play in relationships. That means no hiding behind made-up masks and false identities. Get rid of your fixation on pleasure and the viewpoints from glamour magazines and TV shows. Rather, you must seek honesty, communication, and biblical precepts in order to be real and authentic. This translates into a real relationship that is flowing from a life that has been transformed by grace, and renewed by Christ as LORD of your life.

They devoted themselves to the apostles' teaching and to the fellowship, to the breaking of bread and to prayer. Acts 2:42

In order to accomplish this task, you must seek to know yourself as well as know the other person. If you are not honest about yourself, how can you expect to have a good relationship? The same applies in seeking honesty from the person you are courting. You have to be honest about who you are; that is, know your personality, aspirations, and desires, and be working on your relationship with Christ. You also have to be honest about what you plan to do and be in life. Then, you can seek that in others, and honestly assess how you feel about them and about what they do and say. The way to do this is to have open, honest communication, and be willing and able to ask the tough questions of yourself and your date. The hiding is then eliminated, and a real relationship is built! Open communication is a vital foundation for every relationship, from the workplace to friends, and especially in marriage, and is necessary in order to understand and help each other. Without it, you cannot see what is truly motivating the other, or what their ideas and intentions are. When you have differing points of view—and you will have—be willing to talk and listen. Simply by listening, 99 percent of the problems will be resolved. When you have this down before marriage, you will be light-years ahead of the game. If you are already married, then you can figure out what you have to work on in yourself and in your relationship with God and others.

We can be honest even in our Western dating culture. Yes, most people—Christians included—tend to stick to the shallow end of the communication pool. We spend time asking about favorite movies, hobbies, weather, and such, so the most important questions, such as our struggles, vulnerabilities, and insecurities, are not sought. Once you are honest, then you can explore love. If you do not take care of honesty, your love will not be honest. You will be in love with an idea and not a person. You will be building a false relationship, not a real one!

We will not be perfect, and we will make mistakes, but we have the Grace of God who makes up for our shortfalls. So, let God work in you. Be honest with Christ as your LORD, and be willing to learn, giving Him your fears and insecurities. Be willing to improve yourself before going out and trying to find someone. Be willing to improve yourself before trying to improve your spouse! You are not trying to seek someone to fill a hole that they cannot fill. Be accountable to and ask questions of someone who will always listen to you. By following these precepts from the Word, you will better prepare yourself for God's best, which is in your best interest, too!

Do not be yoked together with unbelievers. For what do righteousness and wickedness have in common? Or what fellowship can light have with darkness? 2 Corinthians 6:14

Oh, by the way, do not even think, consider, or attempt to do missionary dating (date someone who does not share the same faith and theology as you). After over 20 years of being a pastor to singles, I have *never* seen this work out! It only leads to distress and strife, especially when children come in to the picture!

Here are two attitudes that are essential if you are serious about following God's precepts in relationships:

And they did not do as we expected, but they gave themselves first to the LORD and then to us in keeping with God's will. 2 Corinthians 8:5

1 An attitude of Fellowship: Fellowship, (*koinonia*) is the Christian catchphrase for *getting together*. Perhaps it is over-used and under-used. We over-use it to describe anything from hanging out to having communion. Then we under-use it by not taking the reality and depth of its meaning to heart! Biblical fellowship is a partnership of relationships and resources that contains good communication, cooperation, and mutual benefit that is deeper and more gratifying than any mere secular idea of love. The Holy Spirit is our true partner in the church. This is true because of what Christ has done for us.

2 An attitude of real intimacy: As we talked about in the last chapter, for centuries the church has taught that sex was for procreation only, and there are still Christian groups proclaiming this. However, this is not what the Bible teaches. Sex was created by God to populate, to express unity, to know your mate, to express love, to meet each other's needs, to play, and to prevent sin. Intimacy also includes our being available to our spouse and showing him or her our undivided interest as an expression of love.

How do you know if you are "In Love?"

Charm is deceptive, and beauty is fleeting; but a woman who fears the LORD is to be praised. Give her the reward she has earned, and let her works bring her praise at the city gate. Proverbs 31: 30-31

According to the world's standards, and that of many Christians, being attracted to one another is our first consideration in dating or courting. However, is this right? or biblical? No! Yet, we often judge another person by our attraction to him or her, or the attraction of him or her to us, before we venture into a relationship. However, remember Proverbs 31: 30: Good looks, magnetism, beauty, being pretty, even charm are all vain, ineffective in building a relationship, and do not last. Love finds its roots in the deeper end of the pool where maturity in our relationship with Christ dwells, where He is LORD, and from where our trust and the model of all of our relations originate.

Now, I am not saying to only court people who you do not like or are not attracted to. That would not work well either! What we need to do is not let attraction be the only locomotive moving the train of the relationship, the only engine driving how we pick and choose with whom we want to be. That will not work out. Look for real beauty and the character within. If you find someone you like, and to whom you are attracted, make sure other qualities are there also. Keep in mind that there may be someone you may not have thought of who may be right for you! I am always amazed in single groups in churches at how so many of them do not even look at each other as their ideal mate because desire is blinding their search. Thus, the only thing fueling their search is vanity, and the perfect one may be sitting right next to them. So, look up, and look around beyond your limited set of parameters!

Love begins—real love, that is—when you have a firm grasp on what we have talked about so far. It happens when the presumptions and games are out of the way, when open communication is happening, and when both of you are growing in the faith. If you are meant for each other, *then* love will come. Love cannot be forced, manipulated, conjured up, or pretended to be real. You can try to force love for a while, but it would be like teaching a dog to walk on its two hind legs. It will be able to do it for a little while, but not very long, and not very well! You have to let love happen as stipulated in 1 Corinthians 13. Love is a choice, a decision, and a response; it is not merely a feeling!

For the lips of an adulteress drip honey, and her speech is smoother than oil. Proverbs 5:3

What does it mean to love someone? How do I know if I am *in love*? How do I really know if my potential mate loves me? It has often been said in Christian circles that *love is a choice*, but what kind of choice is it? When do we make that choice, and what if it is the wrong choice?

One of the first signs that your eyes are open in regard to love is your desire will be what is best for the other person, not for what you want! You begin to have his or her best interests in mind; with passion and/or conviction along side, his or her feelings and needs are of greater importance to you than your own. When you read 1 Corinthians 13, and see your mate and yourself in those words, then you may have real, authentic love. What love is *not* is when you place your needs and plans over his or hers and you project what you think his or her needs are or should be. When you become the one who chooses what the other wants, then you are on the path of self-gratification and manipulation, and not love.

There are times where you cannot meet all of the needs of another, nor should you. That has to be based on biblical values and precepts. That other person you love, or think you love, needs to be discipled and growing in the right direction, just as you do. He or she may need correction, you may need correction; he or she may need to change, and you may need to change. Therefore, your eyes need to be opened to the fact that a balance has to occur between fulfilling his or her needs and fulfilling the right needs. Nevertheless, the bottom line, the *litmus test*, is that you desire to put him or her before you. When you are not being selfish, manipulative, or having a hidden agenda and neither are they, you are on the right track. Of course, there will be times we want to control or change the other, but we have to be willing to repeal those selfish desires in our heart in favor of the desires of each other.

A biblical relationship, one between us and God, and one with another, will take the focus off of us and put it on what can be empowered and/or invested in the other person. With God, the surrender of our will goes along side that, too. Therefore, you have to discern where the line is between your obligation of real friendship and love. In addition, that can be different for each person. The main factor in determining where that line is will be the degree of excitement, passion, and desire present. The emotional factor should not be there in such force in a fellowship-based friendship.

With courtship, your eyes are opened when you are seeking to keep in your mind and heart the best interests of not only the person you are going out with, but also your future spouse. You need to do this because you are preparing yourself for the real love of your life, and if this one is not it, you can ruin yourself and that person you are out with, as well as your future spouse. This multiplies further, when you consider the future spouse of the person whom you are dating. Therefore, one person's sin/mistake will affect scores of people. That is why God hates sexual promiscuity. It negatively effects and destroys not only you, but many others too! Sin is sin because it does not just affect you; it is cancerous and communal, affecting all those around you. Keeping the other person's best interests at heart will result in saving your sexual and emotional purity for your true love.

Listen! My lover! Look! Here he comes, leaping across the mountains, bounding over the hills. Song of Solomon 2:8

One of the main objections to courtship is people feel when you do not have sex or a lot of physical contact with each other, you will not develop intimacy or even an attraction to each other. Then, when you do get married, you will find out there are no sexual or romantic feelings one for the other. Thus, you will never develop true love for your spouse. This thought is completely ridiculous! I know this from my personal experience in courting my wife, studying dating history, my 20 years of counseling singles, and of course, the Word.

The main reason that engaging in several romances is dangerous, as I have said in the preceding chapters, is that it will develop a lot of emotional baggage. Those people will stay in your thoughts and rob you of your emotional commitment to your spouse. I am not saying you are to have no romance before marriage. On the contrary; getting to know your spouse to be is romance. Romance does not mean sex outside of the marriage bed. Sex does not build romance, commitment, trust, or knowledge of, or for each another. It only satisfies the sin of lust, and blocks the building of real intimacy and romance. The physical can get in the way of real heartfelt romance, because it clouds the issues in the building of a relationship. I have never heard of anyone who, after courting and marriage, had a problem with sex, unless there were physical problems or past abuse issues. God has wired you to engage in sex without any problems in doing so. The problem is that our sinful nature has heightened and corrupted it. To build a good relationship, you should consider all aspects of building that relationship before you consider romance as in physical touch.

Also, if you are serious about that person and in honoring God, your eyes will be opened when you are willing to draw a line that you both agree not to cross in your touching of each other. That way, your lust does not get the best of you. The best defense is a good offence, plan, and agreement. So, draw the line, agree, and commit to how far you will go physically. Keep in mind biblical values! For some, it will not go past kissing until after you are engaged; for others, it is never going past the bikini/swim suit areas (conservative swim suit, not a thong!)!

If, after working through all the relational building process and making a commitment to each another leading to marriage, no attraction or romance develops, then you need to consider carefully that perhaps this relationship is not meant to be. If this is the case, you will be hurt; but also consider this—you will be saved from a lifetime of being with the wrong person, which would cause each of you and others around you much greater grief and strife! So, praise God, you have a friend and move on. The biblical process has saved you! Keep the friendship alive, because any work in building relationships is never a waste of time in God's eyes, unless it is hurtful or damaging.

My lover is mine and I am his; he browses among the lilies. Song of Solomon 2:16

Another thing to consider is that romance and attraction build over time. Most Christian counselors, as well as surveys have shown that older couples in a growing relationship with Christ say their love has increased over the years—not decreased! So, if you are in your 20s and are planning to be married, and you are worried that you do not feel attracted enough to each other, yet you meet the rest of the relationship-building criteria, you could still be on the right track. That feeling will change and you will grow fonder of each other!

Many people wonder, and ask, *does love come first or commitment?* The Bible gives us an answer that surprises a lot of people. In Ephesians 5:22-33, the context of this passage indicates *love the one you marry* rather than *marry the one you love*. Thus, romance is often skewed in our society, with the emphasis on feelings and not on commitment. When the tough times come, romance will not keep you together—only your commitment will. This is another reason that love is also a choice. As a result, I believe commitment will supersede love, and be a good indicator that love is in the mix!

How to Know if There is Compatibility

How beautiful you are, my darling! Oh, how beautiful! Your eyes behind your veil are doves. Your hair is like a flock of goats descending from Mount Gilead. Song of Solomon 4:1

You may not be looking for a flock of goats, but it is essential that in building an effective relationship, the two of you discover the personality, character traits, likes, dislikes, moods, and ambitions about each other. The best way to do this is go to a qualified and trained pastoral counselor who can give you a personality test/inventory. My personal favorite test is called the *Myers-Briggs.* Or, use a similar inventory. Then a good, trained counselor can sit down with the two of you and go over the results and the possible conflicts that may develop. That way, you are prepared, and know ahead of time what to expect. This will solve many relational problems that may crop up in the future.

To get a taste of this there are two great places on the web to check out your compatibility to each other: www.eharmony.com, www.personalitypathways.com, and www.assess-yourself.org.

Here are some more things to consider in knowing yourself and your partner's personality traits.

How delightful is your love, my sister, my bride! How much more pleasing is your love than wine, and the fragrance of your perfume than any spice! Song of Solomon 4:10

Open your eyes so you can make sure you or your partner do not have:

• **Loneliness, Emotional or Spiritual Emptiness:** I have said this a lot, because in over 20 years of experience, I see this as one of the biggest problems with single Christians. They are looking for a mate because they feel empty and lonely! A relationship will not help you, as you will trade one set of problems for a whole other set—a bigger set! That void cannot be filled with anything except what Christ has done. So, what do you do when you feel you am right with God and still feel empty? Do something about it! Build your relationship with Christ. Make friends. Go out on group dates for friendship, get to know people, and pray. Only Jesus can truly fulfill you in every way. If you have an emotional dependency on anyone or anything other than God, you will live a very bitter and depressing life!

• **Unfinished emotional issues:** This includes child abuse, past broken relationships, and dysfunctional family. In addition, self esteem problems and psychological disorders such as depression need to be addressed. These do not necessarily disqualify someone, but you have to get your act together; be aware, and be willing to work things out in yourself! If you do not, you will carry problems into marriage, and they will continue to be a problem! Both of you have to be willing to be vulnerable, to communicate, trust, be willing to share your emotions, and be mature enough to make a long-term relationship work! Manipulative, prideful, and arrogant people are toxic. Stay away from them!

• **Problems with Anger:** Anger will be overwhelming and cannot be quenched in a relationship. He/she or you must seek professional or pastoral help to dig to the root of the issue and solve it before a relationship can take place. If not, it may lie in wait under the surface, and then spring up out of control to kill and destroy!

• **Victim-Blame mentality:** This is also a very dangerous mindset, as the person will not be able to take responsibility, and will always be blaming you and others for his/her circumstances. He/she considers he/she is a victim and is unable to rise above it, with blaming and lists of "if, If, if..." This happens a lot in alcoholic homes. Change will only be a temporary remedy, and soon the pattern will come back. You will not be able to seriously develop intimacy or a good relationship with him/her unless help is sought to eliminate this mindset!

• **Fear of intimacy:** If you come from a divorced family, have been abused, or perhaps, if your parents were sparing with love and affection or have passed away, you may fear getting close to someone else. You may associate intimacy with loss, trauma, abuse, or lack of affection.

• **Fear of leaving a relationship:** If you do not want to leave because you fear hurting each other, being devastated, or perhaps because of guilt, you may stay in a relationship that is not meant to be. Be willing to make hard decisions based on facts, God's Word, good advice, quality assessments, counseling, time, and communication. Just one area may be enough, or not enough, since each situation is different. Yes, you will hurt. If not, you would not be human. However, it is better to hurt a little that go into a bad relationship that may last for a long time.

• **Looking for a parent and not a spouse:** If you are looking for someone to take care of you, or to fill a need, remember only God can do that. Another person can never fill that hole! You need to be looking for a partner, not a parent!

• **Addictions:** If you or your potential partner suffers from any type of addiction (sexual, chemical, etc.), he/she or you will not be able to fully invest in this relationship because of the distraction of the addiction. Your investment will be mostly wasted. Get help!

• **Repeating bad patterns:** If you or your potential mate come from a home of abuse (sexual, drugs, alcohol, physical, emotional or verbal), even if there is physical freedom of it, the emotional scars will remain, and the likelihood or replication is high. Of course, God can heal; but you, too, must be aware of it, and work it out (Philippians 2)! Being from an abusive situation certainly does not disqualify someone, as there are no perfect homes! But, if the attitude remains, it will cause problems/harm. The refusal to acknowledge it, or to seek healing and counseling is extremely detrimental.

• **Pressure:** Too much pressure from family, loneliness, realization that you are getting older, looking for change, sexual desire, church, or friends who are getting married can cause you to make bad choices or force you into something that is not meant for you. These can cause you to skip important selection and relational building time. These issues can deceive you into looking where you should not, or selecting whom you should not! Ask, *how can I glorify God? What contributes to my spiritual growth, emotional health, and maturity?*

• **Seeking change:** Do not think you can change someone when you get married. It never works!

• **Seeking Stability:** Finding stability, or a certain lifestyle, is not bad in itself; but, if that is your prime motivation, it will cloud the relational knowing and building process! You will end up in a very shallow relationship!

• **Rebellious undertones:** Are you choosing someone just to be rebellious? Most people, if not all of us, have a rebellious nature (and we all have that in our sinful nature) and desire to get back at someone, such as anger with your parents. Make sure you are not using, or are being used, for such a purpose in courting and marriage! Also, do not just seek someone because they are different (to tick your parents off) in ways such as race, social status, from a different country, or just new to you, as that will wear off quickly. Differences are OK, as long as there is sufficient compatibility. Do not be so open minded that your brains fall out!

• **Putting the cart in front of the horse:** Are you seeking commitment before you learn that you are compatible? Are you rushing things, tired of the dating games, seeking change, or any other reason that will speed up the processes of building a relationship? This is fun to watch in movies such as *Fools Rush In.* However, in real life, it is extremely detrimental, and it rarely, if ever, works out! A good relationship will take a couple of years, at least, before a commitment should be sought!

• **Blinded by lust and desire:** Lust will hide compatibility issues, as it will blind you from seeing that it is built on a foundation of quicksand, and not on the rock of truth!

• **There is too much of an age difference:** The two of you will have too little in common! Maturity, likes, dislikes, energy, outlook, plans… ten years should be the limit.

• **Bad potential in-laws:** If you ever seen the classic TV show *Everybody Loves Raymond,* you will know how toxic some in-laws can be! It is funny on TV, but not in real life! One spouse may take sides, and drag the other into conflict. Boundaries must be established and kept. If not, in-laws with dysfunctional personalities will destroy your relationship. Also, make sure you do not repeat the bad patterns of your parents! How can you overcome this? Moving away is perhaps the only way, in some cases, if the parents refuse to honor boundaries.

• **What about long distance relationships?** Forget it. You cannot build intimacy long distance, and the relationship will stay superficial. Put it on hold until the two of you can be together. One exception would be if it were for a specific length of time, such as a short mission trip, school, or a temporary job assignment.

Most of these compatibility flaws can be worked out with a good counselor or a pastor who is trained and experienced. Rather than impossible barriers, they are *red flags,* warning of potential problems. No person will be perfect, but both of you have to be willing to work things out. Trust, share from the heart, be honest, and seek the truth about yourself and your potential spouse. If you do not, these potential problems will turn into war and cause bitterness and strife that will eventually destroy your relationship. Your only chance for a good relationship is to face facts, work them out, and build on the positive with each other and through prayer. Ignoring these will only allow them to fester and erupt in the future. You must be willing to conquer and eliminate them!

I slept but my heart was awake. Listen! My lover is knocking: "Open to me, my sister, my darling, my dove, my flawless one. My head is drenched with dew, my hair with the dampness of the night." Song of Solomon 5:2

Are your eyes open? Do you see where you are going? Then make sure that you are:

• **Asking Questions!** Ask the hard questions of yourself and your potential mate! We often try to avoid these because we are afraid to offend, to lose the other, or we are too involved in the romance. Remember, love is blind—false love, that is! Your call is to seek knowledge of each other, as this builds a real relationship. You do this by not holding back your natural curiosity. Passion is good as God designed it, but we will misuse it when we allow it to hide the truth and growth that comes from asking and learning all we can about each other. Be open and honest with feelings and questions, and do not be afraid to ask and to respond. This is fun, this is building, and this is exciting, as you are getting to know each other! If you do not ask and respond, you will not grow or learn. You will think that you are in a castle in a fairyland, but you may soon wake up and find yourself in a dungeon of despair.

- **Ask questions such as:** Does he or she have addictions (drugs, alcohol, smoking, food, sex, pornography, etc.), debt and spending problems, anger problems, emotional instability, control-freak tendencies, or obsessive/compulsiveness? Is he or she manipulative, selfish, uncaring, over compromising, or have any psychological issues, such as the stuff we listed above? What are his or her goals, aspirations, desires? What is his or her relationship with Christ, and where is it going and growing, etc? Do not say you like something when you do not, thinking you will please the other. This will, in fact, set you up for disappointment instead!

1. Do you care more about your potential mate than he or she does about you, or *vise versa*?
2. Are you in love with what your potential mate can be, or who they are?
3. Do you share common life purposes and goals?
4. Is one of you on a rescue mission to do a *make over* on the other? Are you trying to *fix* them? Do you have more sympathy than love?
5. Are you projecting your desires and needs, or are you being honest in your evaluations?
6. What have you learned from past relationships, and how have you changed?
7. Do you feel safe expressing your feelings and thoughts with this person?
8. What are your weakness and strengths? How do you plan to overcome your weaknesses and grow in your strengths?
9. Are you attracted to just a feature, such as eyes, or a body part? Remember, those things change quickly. Make sure your attraction is based on character, and not lust!
10. Are you being honest about yourself to your potential mate?
11. Remember love is blind—false love, that is—so make sure you open your eyes with the Scripture and good judgment!
12. How do you handle crisis and stress?
13. Does your potential mate enjoy giving to others, or is he/she so wrapped up in themselves and self-absorbed that they do not care?
14. What do you not like about yourself? How would you want to change it?
15. Is your partner a role model, so that you idolize him/her? Is your

confidence based on him or her, and not who you are in Christ? If so, this can be a problem in the future when reality sets in.

16. Do you have compatibility in more that one area? The more areas of likeness, the better the relationship will be. Yes, we need our potential mate to fill in some of our gaps and complement us; however, opposites that attract at first may, later on, intensely repel!

17. Is your relationship one-sided, where one of you is contributing more, and the other is just feeding off of it?

18. Does he/she gossip and speak badly about others? If so, he/she will probably do the same about you and your family.

19. What do you want to change about yourself in the next five to ten years, to grow in maturity and faith?

20. How does he/she treat other people, including strangers, and especially, family? How someone treats his or her mother is a sure sign of how they will treat a spouse!

21. Are prayer and spiritual growth driving forces in his/her life?

22. Does he/she have gratitude, respect, and appreciation for God and others?

23. Are you hoping to change anything about this person after you are married? If so, remember, you will not be able to!

Their love, their hate and their jealousy have long since vanished; never again will they have a part in anything that happens under the sun. Ecclesiastes 9:9

Here are more helpful things to consider:

1. **Not just infatuated:** Do not just be attracted to good looks or a personality. Seek character! The verse, Proverbs 31:30, applies to both men and women!

2. **Get good pre-marriage counseling!** Do this when you become engaged. Even professional marriage counselors and pastors have to do this! Also, find an older married couple to help mentor you.

3. **Seek to bring into the relationship, not take out!** Seek to nurture and care by *bringing* character to them, not just trying to *get* what you want from them!

4. **Do not be afraid to break it off.** Do not be afraid to invest the time or to risk being hurt. But, as you follow the precepts of courting, you will

learn much more, and faster, and be able to weed out the *riffraff* before too much emotional investment is made; thus, your hurt will be a lot less!

5. **Do not choose someone as a reaction to a breakup.**
   Rebound relationships will rarely work out, because all the selection criteria we may normally have will be thrown out the window. Guard against seeking someone just like the person with whom you broke up, as there were reasons for that breakup that may be repeated!

6. **Not looking for the opposite of you.**
   Yes, we need to find someone to complement, or complete us. However, we have to have more in common than in difference.

7. **Never consider a serious relationship with a non-Christian!**
   (2 Corinthians 6:14) It may work for a while, but when children come into the family, this becomes a major problem. These relationships never work out!

8. **Do not play games with each other's feelings and emotions or with truth!** Do I really need to explain this? Remember, Christian character must be your driving force!

9. **Do not try to seek someone else's potential mate.** Do not seek someone who is married or in another relationship. You can rationalize it all you want, but no matter how you may look at it, it is wrong. Wait until this person is available, or move on to someone else!

10. **Do not try to court more that one person at a time**. Yes, this may seem like fun, to be a *player*, as some say, but it is very distracting. People want to be treated as special. How can you do that by playing the field? In addition, put some time between relationships. Do not feel you have to be in a relationship to be whole!

11. **Do not get married for the wrong reasons**! Examples might be pregnancy (25 percent of marriages are in this category!! They rarely work out!), rebounding, guilt, pity, escape, social pressure…and so on.

12. **Bad personality flaws:** Besides what we have already discussed, control-oriented people can devastate a marriage or create a codependency atmosphere. People who are prideful, judgmental, arrogant, condescending, and always having to have their own way/be in control will not be able to build a healthy relationship or intimacy!

13. **Financial irresponsibility:** Most marriage conflicts center on money— not the lack of it, but how it is handled! Make sure you both have a budget and can stick to it. If not, you may be doomed! There are too

many good resources out there, especially from *Crown Financial*, crown.org, to experience a problem in this area!

14. **Differing backgrounds:** If the two of you come from different social and economic backgrounds, you have to be willing to understand each other, listen, and compromise. This is also true if you have different educational backgrounds. The higher educated will tend to be controlling and condescending. You have to be willing to stop yourself, and recognize the worth and value of each other.

15. **Sexual performance problems or barrenness:** A good marriage can be built when a man cannot perform or the women cannot give birth. However, these can be mountainous obstacles to overcome. Think it through—not how you feel and are now, but how you may feel in five or ten years!

16. **Be willing to share and create mutual expectations and boundaries.** This is essential to creating a healthy relationship. You can create them together in a way that is consistent with your shared Christian values. See the wonder and excitement of your relationships, and be excited and joyful; do not allow the *work* of the relationship to take away the joy! You have to see the work as building joy and future happiness!

17. **Have you recovered and learned from your past relationships?** If you have not learned and grown, you will repeat the same mistakes all over again! Let's not do this!

So, what do I need to be doing?

A loving doe, a graceful deer—may her breasts satisfy you always, may you ever be captivated by her love. Why be captivated, my son, by an adulteress? Why embrace the bosom of another man's wife? For a man's ways are in full view of the LORD, and he examines all his paths. Proverbs 5:19-21

In your search for the love of your life, or how to improve your marriage and relationships in general, you need to have the right mindset in the biblical precepts about which we have been talking. We must be in tune with God's call and will, and not just with our desires and needs. That does not mean we completely throw out what we want, but make sure that what we want complies with God's standards, which are best for us!

a. Look for good character traits and not just good personality. Personality is important, but character is essential! In your marriage and current relationships; place the focus on your character and maturity development!

b. Make sure you both are committed to personal and spiritual growth, to learn and better yourself by leaning on the Word and growing in the faith, and that you are a teachable person, willing to receive correction and to listen, even if it hurts your perceptions and pride!

c. Be sure you both have a positive outlook on life and God is at work in you!

d. Be aware of each other's character flaws, past failures, and past emotional baggage; be willing and able to fix them!

e. Be willing to be open and honest. Be willing to express feelings about each other, and the desires, aspirations, and plans you see for yourself and for your partner. This will build communication and trust! If you cannot express yourself, then get help. Otherwise, it will only escalate from bad to worse. You cannot gain anything by lying or playing games!

f. Make sure your self-esteem is based on who you are in Christ and in nothing else such as job, money, appearance, friends, power, or position!

g. Make sure you understand the thought processes of each other, as a male and as a female, and the differences between the sexes.

h. Make sure you both are responsible and mature enough to be in a long-term relationship leading into marriage. Do you keep promises and respect each other? Are you willing to share possessions and resources and allow for boundaries? Is the Fruit of the Spirit exhibited in the two of you? Can you live on your own, and manage a household on your own? Can you budget, manage money, and support yourself? Do not expect the other to be the adult!

i. Know where the areas of sensitivity are for each other with regard to feelings and "buttons."

j. Know the concept and practice of time for each other. Are you always on time, or always late? Be respectful and plan accordingly for the flaws in each other in this area; be willing to grow to understand and respect each other.

k. Know the areas of irresponsibility in each other, such as with finances, health, returning phone calls, or not feeding the cat. Then, be willing to grow by becoming more responsible.

l. Be understanding and aware of spiritual warfare. Satan desires you to fail; so protect yourself with prayer and accountability.

It is my sincere prayer that you are in a solid, growing, Christ-centered relationship! Too many Christians have given up on godly values and caved in to desperation and desire when it comes to dating and even marriage. They are just seeking their way through life, hurt and confused. In dating, this can mean you have given up or are just seeking someone—anyone. Thus, many do not care who they get as long as it is a warm body. In marriage, perhaps you have given up and may be seeking to end it or are seeking gratification in sin. I have seen these cycles over and over for years and years, and people just do not learn or just do not want to *get it*. Then, they end up in dysfunctional relationships and pass those dysfunctions on to their children, and so on, and so on! Marriage can be so wonderful, so romantic and solid, if only God's values and precepts are brought into it. Do not let yourself become a statistic, imprisoned in a world of strife and chaos, when God has such a better plan for you.

Seek Him, and He will provide. Seek yourself and you will be sad and lonely in so many ways! He will die for lack of discipline, led astray by his own great folly. Proverbs 5:23

CHAPTER XIV
THE CALL OF FORGIVENESS

Then Peter came to Jesus and asked, "LORD, how many times shall I forgive my brother when he sins against me? Up to seven times?" Jesus answered, "I tell you, not seven times, but seventy-seven times. Matthew 18:21-22

The call of forgiveness is just that; it is a direct call from our LORD. It is something extremely special which we are given, and something precious we are to replicate to others. It is not easy. It requires the practice of maturity, the patience to allow the process to unfold, and the tact to endure it. Forgiveness is also a mandate from our LORD. We can take great comfort in knowing that He is working while we are waiting, and even suffering. We can best practice forgiveness by realizing how much we have been forgiven. We can then be imitators of that forgiveness when others willfully or unknowingly cause us setback or harm. The magnitude of forgiveness from our LORD for what we have done can never measure up to anything others could do to us. When we put forgiveness into practice, we will be free from the bondage of bitterness and pain that imprisons us, disconnecting us from life and its wonders, which God has provided for us.

I was watching one of those reality shows recently where a bunch of young people were put into a nice beach house to live and work together. The show is about the drama and strife each one causes the other, and how they *do not* work it out. After all, if they were a big, happy family, it would not make good TV, so I am told by a friend in that business. One young woman, in her early twenties, kept making the statement, "I refuse to forgive anyone for anything." So, in the episode I watched, the attention was centered on how she was alienating everyone in the house. The result was that she ended up alone, hated by the others. She would make a big deal if someone took her cookie, or gave her an objectionable look. She was a very sad and pathetic person, whose self-imposed code of conduct, created out of pride, made it impossible for her to make friends or cooperate with anyone in her life. She could not see that she was the problem; she reused to take any responsibility. In her interviews, she blamed everyone else for her problems. The sad fact is that this is typical behavior among many people today, even Christians in the church!

As human beings, we are prone to make mistakes, either intentionally or unintentionally. We all have hurt people, and we have all been hurt; we are all in the same boat of doing life together. So, when we refuse to forgive one another, it is like escaping the disaster of the sinking of the *Titanic* in a lifeboat, only to poke holes in the very lifeboat that saved us. Yet, that is what so many of us do; we sabotage the very vessel that will help bring us healthy relationships. Why do we do that? Because, as hurting people, we hurt others; we become so hurt that we intentionally or unintentionally seek to inflict that hurt upon friends and family. We need to understand that in Christ, our escape from the sinking ship is our redemption, which we do not deserve. Christ gives us the vessel of *forgiveness* to make us free. Since everyone else in the lifeboat needs the cross too, why try to sink one another? All you will accomplish is to sink yourself. To stop the replicable cycle of hurt, we have to step out of the sinking boat and be willing to forgive! We may get wet, but at least we will not drown!

So few of us will actually step out and forgive. So, out of the mistakes we make, or those others cause us, comes our pain, hurt, and resentment. This resentment escalates into animosity and builds into bitterness, until it destroys relationships and causes us isolation, just as it did with that young woman on TV. She refused to forgive, and built an impenetrable wall that caused bitterness and isolation as she wallowed in her troubles, blaming everyone else for them. She would not allow forgiveness to break down the wall that would permit the building of life and relationships. Forgiveness is the only human force that can stop the disintegration of relationships. This is why it is so essential. This is why our LORD calls us to forgive. If you have been hurt, or you have hurt others—as we all have—open your eyes and realize that it is the call of the Christian to dispel these conflicts. It is our call and mandate to forgive! It is also in our best interest and one of our main avenues to relationship contentment. Without forgiveness, our growth and maturity with Christ and our integrity with others cannot be built!

We may suffer betrayal from friends, family, coworkers, and even church members. However, we are called to forgive, anyway! Why? Because, *we* need to, and because we are imperfect, fallen, and full of sin. Even the Christian who is saved by grace is still in process of growth and sanctification. We are yet imperfect, no matter what our level of maturity. If you are thinking, *I refuse to forgive others,* just as that young woman did, consider this reason to forgive. *We forgive because God has forgiven us.* If we do not, the resentment will build and build—like battery acid that slowly eats away a car—until, unless we fix it, it will destroy. Even secular psychologists tell us that resentment is the most powerful, self-destructive emotion in our arsenal. Will you allow forgiveness to build, or bitterness to destroy your relationships and life?

God made him who had no sin to be sin for us, so that in him we might become the righteousness of God. 2 Corinthians 5:21

God desires that we seek forgiveness because God is a God of relationships, and is committed to relationships. God knows our human weaknesses and our self-destructive nature, and that our relationships tend to be fragile. Broken relationships come out of our sinful nature and our fallen world, which seeks its own gain. God's desire is to show the world our potential. Because of what Christ has done for us, we should not take pleasure in destructive situations—those that divide and draw relationships apart. Relationships are what life is all about! Satan seeks to destroy relationships. His first attempt was in the Garden of Eden, nearly defeating our relationship with God and with one another. God's plan is to prove Satan wrong, and our call is to build one another up, not destroy one another.

When we have been wronged, we experience feelings of betrayal and consider retaliation to be justified. God calls us out of retaliation and into reconciliation. When we fail to forgive, we are the ones who suffer the most. Anger, resentment, shame, bitterness, contempt, and defensiveness all synergistically build on top of one another, so every segment within us is held hostage with these emotions that stifle us. We are chained like a dog on a leash, unable to reach the destination we desire—what Christ has for us. Do not allow the bitterness to continue so that it festers, corrupting your whole being. The bitterness must not take hold in your life or it will block the flow of the Holy Spirit and self-controlling love, and the festering will continue to the point that as Christ is crying out to us in the wilderness, we cannot hear Him.

Our LORD is alerting us to the perils of being unforgiving, just as the call of battle stations on a naval vessel or the call of *red alert* in the TV show,

Star Trek, warns its crew of impending danger. If we do not heed the warning, our emotions will run wild, and we will no longer have control or composure, and be unable to recognize who we are in Christ. Thus, the anger and the uncontrolled emotions will become controlled by Satan. The *red alert* has been ignored, and our ship has been destroyed! Your relationship(s) have been destroyed!

This passage in Matthew, chapter eighteen, is a story of a forgiving king and a wicked servant. The king forgave this servant's enormous debt, which is a parallel to our enormous debt of sin that we held until Christ forgave us. This servant represents the Believer, who, after experiencing the forgiveness of God, harbored bitterness to another, and then refused to forgive his fellow Christian (or a non-Christian) for a much, much smaller debt. The king became furious, and handed the servant over to be tortured. The Bible is telling us that if we refuse to forgive one another, and continue to harbor bitterness, we will be tortured, too. My personal experience is when I have refused to forgive people in the past, I have become consumed with feelings of guilt and shame, and this is a torture I can do without. I feel much better, and sleep much better with an attitude of forgiveness; I cannot think well or sleep well with an attitude of bitterness. Why would a Christian want to go through life with feelings of bitterness, which consume him with misery and unrest, instead of giving it to the LORD, receiving forgiveness and be able to rest?

How can we go through our Christian life and experience, rationalizing our actions and deeds, only to face our LORD later at the judgment? What point are we to make, what feeling are we to base on, and what hope do we have? When we have the knowledge of God's mercy, then we have the responsibility of acting with mercy toward one another.

God calls Christians to operate in the parameters of forgiveness, love, and mercy. When we have not been forgiving, we will have a heart filled with suffering and torment. How can we receive Christ's forgiveness and claim Christ as our Savior when we are unable to forgive one another? When we have a forgiving attitude, then we will have a heart at rest and in peace!

What Forgiveness Looks Like

Do not let any unwholesome talk come out of your mouths, but only what is helpful for building others up according to their needs, that it may benefit those who listen. And do not grieve the Holy Spirit of God, with whom you were sealed for the day of redemption. Get rid of all bitterness, rage and anger, brawling and slander, along with every form of malice. Be kind and compassionate to one another, forgiving each other, just as in Christ God forgave you. Ephesians 4:29-32

Taking our primary lead from Matthew, chapter 18, and looking at various other Scriptures, we can see what God requires of us, and our appropriate response regarding the different categories of forgiveness. We, as Christians, must extend ourselves to other people with love, and that which flows out of love—forgiveness!

A new command I give you: Love one another. As I have loved you, so you must love one another. By this all men will know that you are my disciples, if you love one another. John 13:34-35

We are to love one another—period! No strings attached! This is the model we are to use to show God's love to the world! When we do not, our un-forgiveness becomes malice and actually grieves the Holy Spirit!
We should be clear on this. A healthy Christian is one who puts aside the malicious traits of an evil, sinful nature, and embraces others in love. What comes out of love is the release of our feelings of betrayal and hurt. The Christian is called to model kindness, love, empathy, and compassion; out of these, forgiveness will flow. God wants us to get with it, to wake up, and seize the wonders and opportunities He gives us. Why is God's Spirit grieved? An unforgiving attitude and its ugly rotten fruits, will choke us off from His wonders!

Ask yourself this question: *How do I handle forgiveness?* How do you respond when others forgive you? What do you do with opportunities that our LORD has for you? We must realize the generosity of grace and being in Christ, which we do not deserve. Our LORD does not want us to forgive begrudgingly, because He did not forgive us with conditions or with strings attached. A Christian that does not forgive is like a small child who refuses to share a game ball that he/she received as a gift. Thus, the child will not be able to play with that ball as it was designed to be used. That child will not be using it to its full potential. Unable to play a game because he refuses to share the ball, the child cries that he is alone and nobody will play with him, or he cries because he is not having any fun. When the Christian does not forgive, he/she distorts the relationships he enjoys. Without forgiveness, we forfeit relationships with others, and we are unable to play our games. We just end up cheating ourselves out of our potential, and the best plan that Christ has for us.

FIRST: FORGIVENESS IS HARD

"For my thoughts are not your thoughts, neither are your ways my ways," declares the LORD. "As the heavens are higher than the earth, so are my ways higher than your ways and my thoughts than your thoughts." Isaiah 55:8-9

True forgiveness is one of the hardest things to accomplish in the human experience, even for the mature Christian. Yet, this is our mandate and call. Forgiveness is hard because it demands a surrender of our right to *get even*. Forgiveness even causes suffering for the person who was wronged—the victim. The suffering, from our human perspective and reasoning, should belong to the instigator of the wrong. It is natural to consider this unfair. And, yes, it is unfair; it was unfair for our LORD to go through what He did to forgive us!

Forgiveness is also hard because we can easily avoid it; we can walk the other way, and execute revenge. And, it would be considered justified in the eyes of our friends, our relatives, and especially of society. We could even receive some kind of medal for coming up with a good scheme of revenge. As a youth, I loved the comic book, *The Punisher*, where the super hero was a victim of a severe crime, and his wife and kids were inadvertently killed by the mob. So, he makes it his life's crusade to bring about revenge on all criminals who evade the law. This is appealing; the criminals deserve the Punisher's revenge, especially since the law is unable to deal with them because of bribes, cut backs, and apathy. This pleases our human nature. However, God does not want us to rely on our human nature; rather, He desires for us to rely on Him.

"For my thoughts are not your thoughts, neither are your ways my ways..." This passage is telling us that our way of thinking is wrong. If God is the Creator of all things, including truth, and He is all knowing and all-powerful, then His ways are better than ours. We may not be able to recognize this because our perspective is limited, as is our knowledge and insight.

- God is governed by righteousness; whereas, desires and emotions drive us.
- God has a moral and virtuous purpose; our purpose is self-seeking.
- God's primary purpose in our lives is to bring us out of our self-destructive and self-seeking nature, and into the reclamation of redemption in Him; this is the work of Christ.
- God's thoughts are beyond our comprehension and imagination; therefore, we should rely on Him, and not on ourselves.

SECOND: FORGIVENESS IS COMPLETE

Therefore, as God's chosen people, holy and dearly loved, clothe yourselves with compassion, kindness, humility, gentleness and patience. Bear with each other and forgive whatever grievances you may have against one another. Forgive as the LORD forgave you. And over all these virtues put on love, which binds them all together in perfect unity. Colossians 3:12-14

Matthew 18:27 tells us, *The servant's master took pity on him, canceled the debt and let him go.* Forgiveness is actually canceling a debt. It is as if someone owes you one thousand dollars, and he or she cannot pay you back; you forgive the debt, never expecting to receive the money back. The amount owed to you is no longer owed or expected. You give up your right to seek the repayment of that debt. Forgiveness is bankruptcy; once filed, the creditor may not retrieve the debt, and it is wiped out. We need to see the cancellation of the debt as a *write-off*, and not some form of embezzlement. When we forgive, we forget; that is, we are no longer to even have the desire for restitution, pay back, or punishment.

There is a man at a church where I was once on staff, whom I admire greatly for exhibiting forgiveness in an instance that I do not think I could ever have done it; yet, with Christ, I should be able to, because all things are possible with Christ. His wife was murdered, indiscriminately, by a drive-by shooter in the Pasadena area a few years ago; she died in his arms. He realized that for him to go on with his life and faith, he needed to forgive that person. And, he did. Now, he did not tell the police to let the shooter go; forgiveness is not necessarily a release of the obligation, especially when a crime is committed. Rather, we, as Christians, are released from our personal desire for retribution. This form of forgiveness even prevents us from those *polite* sly remarks and glances; our revenge is repudiated…divorced from our desire to get even.

Forgiveness is so rare in our society. For it to become a powerful witnessing tool, it must be complete. Forgiveness does not make light of the wrong, nor should it give a license to others to take advantage of us, although they may. Yet, it is well worth it! Out of the completeness of forgiveness will come the forgetting. Then, out of the forgetting will come the healing. The healing we get from forgiveness will close the wounds we receive; it will allow us to go on with life. It will prevent our sufferings and setbacks from becoming our identity and obsession. For, without forgiveness, we give in to the bitterness that will consume and take us over, that will give us a purpose for existing but not for living. If we just try to forget, then agonize over it, we will get nowhere; but, through the process of surrender (Galatians 2:20-21) will come the forgetting. Forgetting is a process, and we cannot expect it to come right away. We must be patient, let the process unfold, and embrace the forgiveness that Christ has given us. It took that man many agonizing months to forgive his wife's killer. But, in the end, he and his remaining family were able to get on with their lives, honoring his wife's memory by living life. Had he remained in bitterness, not only would his kids have become dysfunctional, but a total breakdown of that family would have occurred, and his wife's memory would have been framed in bitterness, not in life! Forgiveness has to be complete; if not, it will not work, and you will not make it!

THIRD: FORGIVENESS IS COSTLY

But I tell you who hear me: Love your enemies, do good to those who hate you, bless those who curse you, pray for those who mistreat you. If someone strikes you on one cheek, turn to him the other also. If someone takes your cloak, do not stop him from taking your tunic. Give to everyone who asks you, and if anyone takes what belongs to you, do not demand it back. Do to others as you would have them do to you. Luke 6:27-31

When we forgive, it may incur a cost to us. We should realize this, and even welcome the cost. This goes against our inclination and will, but, remember, the *vengeance belongs to the LORD*. We are never to forget the cost our LORD paid on our behalf. No cost we could ever incur could compare with the cost He paid for us. When we forgive, we will be refocusing our plans for our pain into God's plan and God's ways. So, our pain is relieved, and our life can go on in a better direction!

We can live improved, quality lives when we forgive. Our relationships can grow, and we can become more useful to others, and especially to God.

When we understand that it does involve cost, we can gain the right mindset for forgiveness. We will realize from Scripture that we cannot base it on our feelings and desires, and we can focus on what forgiveness really is. We can see it as what Christ gave us, as He was our example. John 3:16 is the example of what forgiveness cost our LORD. His undeserved, painful death and separation from the Father was a substitution for what we deserved. This was our LORD's suffering and cost. In comparison, the cost for us will be very minimal and limited, and we need to keep this in view, using it as strength to get through it. Our cost is to live with the consequence of the evil that was brought on us. We then take the responsibility for the hurt brought on us. Understanding this is hard, even for the mature Christian, and virtually impossible for the non-Christian since it goes against the common sense of society. In the eyes of the world, the suffering should be put upon the one who did the wrong. Yet, the Scriptural view is a beacon, a witness to the supremacy of Christ.

We could normally avoid this form of suffering, but we are called to face it. We need to accept the consequences of the wrong, such as a parent forgiving a child for breaking a priceless object. The parent bears the cost to either replace it, or suffer without it, and the child gets off free (well, with some sort of punishment). This is the cost of suffering. In the case of the man who lost his wife to murder, his suffering is that he cannot be with his wife anymore. Forgiveness chooses to suffer. It is very hard to make that voluntary choice to take on the suffering, especially when we do not deserve it; yet, we must make it so we can grow in our walk with our LORD and toward our full potential.

Humanity owes a great deal to the Creator of the universe, and our willful disobedience to our Creator is a slap in His face. We owe a debt of which we could never conceive, much less pay for. Yet, most people live their lives as an insult to what Christ has done. And, Christ still pursues them with the ultimate love! Christ did not owe our debt, yet He paid it!

Christ was the substitute for our punishment, which we deserved. Forgiveness is a substitution too, since it requires a penalty to be paid, and the victim pays that penalty. It is a faint reflection of what Christ has done for us! We may not understand the mystery behind this, but we can trust in our LORD, who will carry us through it. The relation between what Christ went through so that we could be forgiven, and the call for us to take on the responsibility for a sin we did not commit will give us a deeper understanding into the character and nature of God. From this, we should mature to a deeper level, and be used in a greater way to further the cause of Christ. The result is that we take our response to evil and redirect it for good, and even to a point, taking the evil on ourselves. This way, Satan is defeated and prevented from receiving a prize, his reward that he craved to gain from our refusal to forgive. This is why the cost accepted by our LORD is the greatest cost of all. We need to realize this, and respond accordingly to one another.

Forgiveness is worth the agony we may go through, because it will heal the wounds and relieve the pain. Perhaps a scar will remain. But, take it to heart, and recognize that scar as a badge of honor to help you grow and mature, to redirect your wrong path onto the *right direction*. Be the person who forgives. Do not be the person who refuses to!

When we put forgiveness into practice in our relationships, whether with family, friends, church people, or our coworkers, we refocus our plans for our pain to God's plan and God's ways. So, our pain becomes relieved, and our life can go on in a better direction. We can live better quality lives by practicing forgiveness. Our relationships can grow. We can become more useful to others, and especially to God. Forgiveness is even worth the agony we may go through, because it will heal wounds and relieve pain. We need not fear forgiveness or its results, even if it scars us. We can take to heart and realize that scars can be badges of honor to help us grow and mature, and to redirect our wrong path onto the right direction. Now, we can see how forgiveness searches for, and actually goes in pursuit of us, and how we can put it into practical action in our relationships.

FOURTH: FORGIVENESS PURSUES

Therefore I am now going to allure her; I will lead her into the desert and speak tenderly to her. There I will give her back her vineyards, and will make the Valley of Achor a door of hope. There she will sing as in the days of her youth, as in the day she came up out of Egypt. Hosea 2:14-15

There is possibly nothing greater and more dramatic to us Christians, in regards to God's character, than His capacity to forgive! Most non-Christians cannot fathom this quality, and do not believe God can, or even should, forgive them. So, they blatantly reject His forgiveness. Other Christians only see a small facet of God's forgiveness, because they refuse to apply it in their lives, holding on, instead, to bitterness and strife as their identity. Or, perhaps they understand it a little, but think, *if someone wants my forgiveness, they have to come to me and seek it.* Or, *I do not have to do anything, because I am the person who was wronged.* But, these attitudes are wrong and unbiblical. The Bible tells us that the Christian has an obligation to actually pursue forgiveness. Even if we are the ones wronged, it is our duty to go after the person who wronged us—not to retaliate, but to forgive! We have to see why this is important, and from our human point of view, how forgiveness will help end the vicious cycle of revenge and payback even when we cannot or refuse to see His plan! We may think it is not worth it, but God says otherwise. We may think it is unfair, but was it fair for our LORD to go to the cross? This may go against our pride and our culture, but this is what we are called to do. God expects us to entice forgiveness from the person we offend, or the person who offends us.

I had a run-in with an Elder at a church where I was on staff a few years ago. I took his daughter, along with twenty other youth, to a winter camp. On the way home, the daughter realized she had forgotten her gloves. This Elder was furious with me because she had forgotten her gloves at camp. I apologized to the dad—the Elder—and took responsibility for the gloves. I told him I would contact the camp the first thing in the morning, and arrange to get the gloves back. But, this just seemed to infuriate him even more, and from then on he persisted in a very condescending and mean attitude toward me. Although I took responsibility, I asked him to forgive me, even while I felt I had done nothing wrong. After all, I was responsible for twenty kids, their safety and spiritual growth, and, according to that Elder, all of their articles of clothing, too.

This Elder just would not get it when it came to forgiveness. From his perspective, I did a great wrong toward him since his daughter did not bring back the expensive pair of gloves; therefore, as the leader, I was responsible. Even though we received the gloves in the mail a few days later, he would not forget the incident, and this tarnished not only our relationship, but also my reputation with him and with several other people in the church. He made it a point to let everyone know what a bad Youth Pastor I was, because his daughter's gloves were left at camp. Ten of those kids came to know the LORD, including his daughter, and this was one of the best camp experiences I have been a part of; but, the *gloves incident* is what everyone remembers.

Do not take revenge, my friends, but leave room for God's wrath, for it is written: "It is mine to avenge; I will repay," says the LORD. On the contrary: "If your enemy is hungry, feed him; if he is thirsty, give him something to drink. In doing this, you will heap burning coals on his head." And the LORD *will reward you.* Romans 12:19-20; Proverbs 25: 21-22

This experience gave me the chance to realize, firsthand, what the term, *burning coals,* was all about. The more I was nice and forgiving to this Elder, the more he was insolent and belligerent. In contrast, he had an issue with another pastor at this church, and this pastor decided not to follow Scriptural principles, but rather the ways of the world. They came to a mutual understanding and respect of one another. So, I wondered if forgiveness was worth it. Then I realized that probably neither of these men knew the LORD, or, at the very least, did not have a growing, effectual relationship with Christ. So, they did not know how to express themselves in a godly way. All they knew was Galatians 5:19-20. Verses 22-23 taught a foreign concept they did not want to pursue or acknowledge. So, I realized, that is why we are to offer forgiveness freely (as I tried to with that Elder I offended) even when we are not in the wrong. Forgiveness models Christ. People do not like Christ because He calls us from our complacency and comfort into conviction and growth where few are attracted or willing to go. So, we have to chase down forgiveness, because out of our pursuit of forgiveness, we will build better relationships and reconciliation A few years later, that Elder came around, and actually helped me when my car broke down. (Before that, he was more likely to run me over.)

The typical response from society is, *I could care less,* or forget *about it* (in a cynical tone). These are expressions of hurt, even though they verbally say otherwise. The *burning coals* will convict them or punish them. Because they do not see the cost that the LORD paid for them, they are unwilling to respond to the gift of grace. Christ pursues them, and all they have to do is respond to His call. The *world's* desire is to tell the person off and seek revenge. To observe this, watch the daytime talk shows. We, as Christians, are called to a higher standard—one that builds, edifies, and reconciles!

FIFTH: FORGIVENESS IS CONTINUAL

If your brother sins, rebuke him, and if he repents, forgive him. If he sins against you seven times in a day, and seven times comes back to you and says, "I repent," forgive him. Luke 17:3b-4

For the Hebrew, seventy-times-seven meant infinity, not just 490, because 490 has a limit. For Christ, there is no point beyond which our accumulation of sins becomes unforgivable. So, our response is to forgive others, as there is no cap, limit, or expiration to forgive. As followers of Christ, neither the intensity of nor the number of wrongs should have an impact on us. If we were to declare a limit, then our effect of building relationships would have a chain attached to it instead of having a chain reaction to grow. With a limit, you cannot grow. We must have the realization and capacity to understand how much we have been forgiven by Christ in order to forgive each other; this is crucial to the Christian experience. As our LORD continues to give us grace and forgiveness, are we not to do the same with each other? We show ourselves to be extremely selfish and prideful when we do not practice continual forgiveness!

God's forgiveness is not some cheap markdown or bargain; His cost was immeasurable. Paul, in Colossians 3:13, tells us to forgive freely as Christ has forgiven us. We must be willing to forgive as Christ has forgiven us. We must be willing to bear the cost, just as our LORD did. Forgiveness demands a substitution. So, how could we ever back away from forgiving each other? If we do, it is a bigger insult to our LORD than for the non-Christian to turn his or her back on His grace—*because we know better*. Remember, knowledge brings responsibility.

SIXTH: WHAT FORGIVENESS IS NOT

Alexander the metalworker did me a great deal of harm. The LORD will repay him for what he has done. You too should be on your guard against him, because he strongly opposed our message. 2 Timothy 4:14-15

We know *why* we must forgive. So, the question is, *what* must we forgive? I do not believe we need to forgive trivialities, because forgiveness is not trivial; its cost is high. So, things like bumping into someone, or typos and minor mistakes should not call us to forgive. Just a simple, polite apology is given, and then you move on. If a person was offended by an honest mistake, such as his or her name being misspelled in the church bulletin, he should not expect forgiveness because it was an honest, un-purposed mistake, with no malicious intent. There must be a reason for forgiveness, such as a hurt, where malice and forethought were at work.

Forgiveness does not minimize the offense. When we forgive, we are not saying, *hey, that was OK*. The offense does not need to be accepted; however, we are to embrace the person who committed the offense. It is like sin; we are to hate sin, but we are still called to love the sinner—unless it continues and they refuse to repent. Forgiveness is not the approval of the wrong; it only offers the grace of love, rather than vengeance. Forgiveness may not bring us to the level of trust that we had before. If a spouse cheats on you, you are called to forgive and reconcile. But, that trust will be eroded, and will take time to rebuild. Just forgiving the offender will not bring instant restitution of the relationship; perhaps the relationship will be severed completely. Perhaps a business partner embezzles and causes you to lose the business. You are to forgive that person, as we previously discussed, but this does not mean you would enter into a business relationship with that person again.

Forgiveness is directed to people, not causes or institutions. I, as a pastor, cannot forgive the victims of the Medieval Church for some of its notorieties, such as the Inquisition. If I worked for McDonalds, I could not forgive them for someone slipping on their floor unless I represented them in a legal capacity. Forgiveness will not erase the past. As for that man in who lost his wife, he will suffer greatly in her absence until they meet again in Heaven. She will not be brought back to life. We are to forget the past so the resentment will not build up; but, we also need to realize the event will not be undone.

"Not just human fairness, but excusing those things that could not be excused..." (C.S. Lewis)

When we do not forgive, we walk a path of self-destruction brought on by the build up of resentment and the unfulfilling nature of revenge. Nothing will wither our soul more than storing up this disease of *unforgiveness*. Pride and arrogance will take over, control, and ruin you. A Chinese proverb says, "First, before seeking revenge, you must dig two graves." The cost and pain of forgiveness—even though we may be the victims of it—will be far easier than the path of not seeking the forgiveness. We read in Job 5:2, *Resentment kills a fool, and envy slays the simple.* The goal of forgiveness is allowing Christ to transform us to our full potential. Because we may go through bad stuff in life, it is not meant to be a personal attack; rather, it is a strengthening of our character so we can be better used by our LORD. Consider this, Christ has defeated Satan, so the sins we incur can be turned around to His glory. Forgiveness will refocus God's plan, and make it our plan. Then, our sufferings will not be in vain, and can be turned around to further the Kingdom of God. The joy and happiness of who we are in Christ will bubble over, covering the pain and hurt.

And we know that in all things God works for the good of those who love him, who have been called according to his purpose. For those God foreknew he also predestined to be conformed to the likeness of his Son, that he might be the firstborn among many brothers. And those he predestined, he also called; those he called, he also justified; those he justified, he also glorified. What, then, shall we say in response to this? If God is for us, who can be against us? He who did not spare his own Son, but gave him up for us all—how will he not also, along with him, graciously give us all things? Who will bring any charge against those whom God has chosen? It is God who justifies. Who is he that condemns? Christ Jesus, who died—more than that, who was raised to life—is at the right hand of God and is also interceding for us. Who shall separate us from the love of Christ? Shall trouble or hardship or persecution or famine or nakedness or danger or sword? As it is written "For your sake we face death all day long; we are considered as sheep to be slaughtered." No, in all these things we are more than conquerors through him who loved us. For I am convinced that neither death nor life, neither angels nor demons, neither the present nor the future, nor any powers, neither height nor depth, nor anything else in all creation, will be able to separate us from the love of God that is in Christ Jesus our LORD. Romans 8:28-39

How do I know I have forgiven someone properly?

When you feel compassion toward the person who wronged you, then you can be assured you did truly forgive them. Let these scriptures impact and change you to the core of your being. Let the power of prayer be your focus, and the Scripture your heartbeat. Our standard is not that of the world, but that of God. We would not want to go through life in misery and bitterness, remembering those who wronged us, harboring grudges, and experiencing unhappiness. This is not the plan that Christ has for us! Bitter people have no impact for the kingdom of God except to cause division and distraction. They have the tenacity and drive to show everyone the hurts and wrongs they suffered. Do not let this happen to you, or to the people around you. Take your lead from this verse, not your inclinations.

When they hurled their insults at him, he did not retaliate; when he suffered, he made no threats. Instead, he entrusted himself to him who judges justly. He himself bore our sins in his body on the tree, so that we might die to sins and live for righteousness; by his wounds you have been healed. 1 Peter 2:23-24

God does not ask us to minimize the wrong, but He does call us to forgive the person. We are not to repay evil for evil, rather, evil for good, just as our LORD did for us.

THE BIBLICAL STEPS IN FORGIVING

Now that we have discussed the *why* and *what* of forgiveness, we need a practical way to apply it to our lives. Remember, we need to have the biblical mandates in mind and be willing to surrender our desires for revenge and the storage of wrongs for future bitterness.

First: Know what Christ did for you.

This righteousness from God comes through faith in Jesus Christ to all who believe. There is no difference, for all have sinned and fall short of the glory of God, and are justified freely by his grace through the redemption that came by Christ Jesus. Romans 3:22-24

For us to grasp the idea and call of forgiveness, we must have a deep sense of the price that Christ paid for us. Christ paid the ultimate price for us, and forgave us for acts deemed unpardonable. When we grasp what Christ has done for us, we should be motivated into overdrive, always seeking forgiveness. When we have the proper perspective of grace, what it cost and what it is, we then should be able to reciprocate to those around us. God forgave us for our failures, so why not forgive others? This realization must precede any of our efforts to reconcile, because with the knowledge of *what* and *why* we are forgiving, we will be able to follow the will of God and actually forgive with a willing and loving heart. We are not to let our emotions rule us or to over-react, making the situation worse.

With the understanding of what Christ did for us on behalf of forgiveness, we can put a bigger piece of trust and reliance onto our Lord. We must be able to fully trust, rely on, and surrender the control over to Christ. Thus, our dependence becomes who we are in Christ. When we then take the risk, we need not worry about the results or consequence of that action. We are to lean on and trust in our Lord, allowing His Grace to flow through us to those around us; this is the mark of a healthy Christian.

Second: We must be willing to take the risk.

Do not take revenge, my friends, but leave room for God's wrath, for it is written: "It is mine to avenge; I will repay," says the Lord. Romans 12:19

But a witless man can no more become wise than a wild donkey's colt can be born a man. Yet if you devote your heart to him and stretch out your hands to him, if you put away the sin that is in your hand and allow no evil to dwell in your tent, then you will lift up your face without shame; you will stand firm and without fear. Job 11:12-15

Forgiveness is a risky business. The person whom we choose to forgive may not realize or admit to the wrong. Nor, will they always accept our forgiveness. But, their response is not our responsibility; we are only to be obedient to our Lord, and give the forgiveness out of love, not expecting a warm response. That Elder who refused to forgive me for a perceived wrong I did to him is responsible for his actions to the Lord; I am not. I am responsible for my response. So, I sought the forgiveness, and he refused. That is a risk we all have to take. Also, the person whom we forgive may continue in the offense, such as that Elder who kept spreading rumors about me. He refused to stop; but, again, this is not my responsibility. We are to allow others the freedom to disappoint us and to fail our expectations. We must not disrupt our character from God's call, as our character will be the testimony to prove gossip and rumors wrong.

Godly sorrow brings repentance that leads to salvation and leaves no regret, but worldly sorrow brings death. See what this godly sorrow has produced in you: what earnestness, what eagerness to clear yourselves, what indignation, what alarm, what longing, what concern, what readiness to see justice done. At every point you have proved yourselves to be innocent in this matter. So even though I wrote to you, it was not on account of the one who did the wrong or of the injured party, but rather that before God you could see for yourselves how devoted to us you are. By all this we are encouraged. 2 Corinthians 7:10-13a

We need to be willing to put aside the concern that forgiveness will minimize the wrong brought against us. Sin is ugly. We should recognize that fact as well as the fact of its corrupting nature. Just forgiving someone does not make the sin go away. Forgiveness releases the guilt and stops the cycle of bitterness and dysfunction.

Third: We need to cancel the betrayal.

Hatred stirs up dissension, but love covers over all wrongs. Proverbs 10:12

He who covers over an offense promotes love, but whoever repeats the matter separates close friends. Proverbs 17:9

We have to give up our perceived right of revenge and retaliation. This can be a tough process, but one that we can accomplish through prayer and self-surrender. Try to look at it this way; the offense against you is actually an offense against God. As God's child, you are in His protection and care. When someone offends you, it also becomes an offense against God Himself. Thus, we are to surrender our rights to His, and cancel the debt—completely out of existence and out of our heart and mind. Give it over as if it never happened. You will be surprised that once you do this, you will feel the load lifted off you and you can rest in the comfort of the Lord.
When you pray to God, you need to be actually requesting that He would take the desire of revenge away; then, relinquish your desires of revenge!

Fourth: We need to offer personal forgiveness.

Do not be overcome by evil, but overcome evil with good. Romans 12:2

We must be willing to go to the person who offended us, and both verbally and non-verbally forgive them. Then, seek an appropriate reconciliation to that individual. Offer the love and acceptance to the *person*, not necessarily to *what they did*. God desires that we be involved in growing positive and healthy relationships. The primary purpose of our existence is relationships, relationships with God to us and then us to others. In relationships, we can model, grow in, make known, and glorify our Lord. This should be a driving force of who we are as Christians, saved by grace. It is the responsibility of the person who did the wrong to repent—not the person offended. You cannot force repentance from someone; you can only pray for him or her, and offer the forgiveness. The relationship can only positively continue when repentance and forgiveness are pursued.

If the offender refuses to repent or to accept the forgiveness, this means their nature is in denial. They feel no wrong was committed, and see you as trying to manipulate their will. They may be a *sociopath*, that is, have some form of mental disorder where they enjoy inflicting hurt and hardship on people. In any case, the reason is not your responsibility, nor are you responsible for their acceptance. Your responsibility is only to genuinely offer forgiveness. We need to accept this fact of human nature; some people just will not *play ball* God's way, especially some Christians. So, if this is the case with your forgiveness, then it still remains between you and Christ because you are God's child.

The end of all things is near. Therefore be clear-minded and self-controlled so that you can pray. Above all, love each other deeply, because love covers over a multitude of sins. 1 Peter 4:7-8

Fifth: We need to recognize the picture of forgiveness.

The result of forgiveness is letting go of the offense, and wishing blessings and compassion to the person who wronged you. Repentance simply means, biblically, to change one's perspective. In other words, you turn from your way of thinking to God's way. That is, you change your mind and heart from your desires to Christ's desires. When we do this, then we have truly forgiven that person. Leaving out any of the above steps, and only forcing your will into the situation means you are deluding yourself into thinking that you have forgiven; you have not. It is not about us; it is about God, and His desire for us is to live in peace and love.

We always need to keep reminding ourselves of our status in Christ, as we previously discussed, because this is paramount to continuing to go on in our lives without the hurt and bitterness. *But God demonstrates his own love for us in this: While we were still sinners, Christ died for us.* (Romans 5:8, NIV) This does not mean that we will not feel the pain, or perhaps suffer consequences from someone else's actions. What it means is, we are saved by grace, by what Christ has done. So, we need to reciprocate grace and peace to those around us, even though we may not want to.

This is what the Lord says "Let not the wise man boast of his wisdom or the strong man boast of his strength or the rich man boast of his riches, but let him who boasts boast about this: that he understands and knows me, that

I am the LORD, who exercises kindness, justice and righteousness on earth, for in these I delight," declares the LORD. Jeremiah 9:23-24

We need to keep ourselves tuned into God constantly and continually, and allow Him to carry us through.

If you are the offender:

If you are the person who hurt someone, and that person is unwilling to forgive you, it is up to you to make it right. You may not receive that person's forgiveness, but that is between them and God, and not you. You need to go through the steps of forgiveness, but with the emphasis on earnestly repenting and offering restitution. You need to confess, openly and publicly, before the person you offended. Then, you need to go to the person in private. Do not rationalize what you did or minimize it in anyway. Then, go to Christ, humbly and with a repentant attitude—which means you make a commitment to change your heart, mind, and actions!

If going to the person is impossible because of distance, death, or restraining order, then you will need to totally rely on God. Take your lead from 2 Corinthians 7:8-11. This allows Christ to be your Mediator. You are not off the hook for truly seeking repentance. Just because you may not be able to physically go to a person does not mean you do not have to forgive them. You can use a third party such as a pastor or a letter and definitely work through repentance and prayer.

When we refuse to forgive or refuse to repent, then we are holding ourselves back from God and His best for us. We rationalize the reality of the infection of sin and its destructive nature to our being, and to those around us. We create a wall to shut ourselves off from God and one another. Thus, we turn on ourselves with the consequence, without any reprieve or comfort. Because we become consumed with animosity and vengeance, we then suffer with the guilt and bitterness. Our personal lives dissolve, and our impact on the community, as Christians, becomes a hindrance instead of a blessing. Take a serious look at Psalm 32. Meditate over it carefully, and then surrender yourselves over to the love of Christ. Allow the sin to be forgiven and released. Be courageous. Seek out forgiveness, public confession, and reconciliation. Allow yourself to grow and mature to be the best, whole person Christ desires for you to be. There is simply no better way. This is liberation and true comfort:

Blessed is he whose transgressions are forgiven, whose sins are covered. Blessed is the man whose sin the Lord does not count against him and in whose spirit is no deceit. When I kept silent, my bones wasted away through my groaning all day long. For day and night your hand was heavy upon me; my strength was sapped as in the heat of summer. Then I acknowledged my sin to you and did not cover up my iniquity. I said, "I will confess my transgressions to the Lord"—and you forgave the guilt of my sin. Therefore let everyone who is godly pray to you while you may be found; surely when the mighty waters rise, they will not reach him. You are my hiding place; you will protect me from trouble and surround me with songs of deliverance. I will instruct you and teach you in the way you should go; I will counsel you and watch over you. Do not be like the horse or the mule, which have no understanding but must be controlled by bit and bridle or they will not come to you. Many are the woes of the wicked, but the Lord's unfailing love surrounds the man who trusts in him. Rejoice in the Lord and be glad, you righteous; sing, all you who are upright in heart! Psalm 32

Chapter XV
HOW TO UNDERSTAND, SOLVE, AND PREVENT CONFLICT

Do nothing out of selfish ambition or vain conceit, but in humility consider others better than yourselves. Each of you should look not only to your own interests, but also to the interests of others. Your attitude should be the same as that of Christ Jesus: Who, being in very nature God, did not consider equality with God something to be grasped. Philippians 2:3-6

A reality TV producer who goes to my church told me that *conflict makes good TV*. Then she said *conflict does not make good life*. Conflict is a part of life. Perhaps it is the least favorite part of life; nevertheless, we will all experience it if we experience other people in our lives. We will have run-ins with people and their ideas and wills that will come into conflict with our own ideas and wills. It is as if you are driving down a road that you thought you owned and are the only one on it going your way and exercising your will and self-determination when, *wham,* you hit another car. *Where did that car come from? Why is it on my road; how do I resolve this and move on? Do I keep hitting it so it goes away, or do I design a road so both of us can travel on it in opposite directions so we do not converge by accident again?* Dealing with this in a biblical way will be the hallmark of keeping and maintaining long-term relationships, a happier workplace, a kinder and more comfortable church, and solving some of life's most difficult problems.

We will come across various disagreements, misunderstandings, and distinctions with various views of moral and value stands with one another that will converge in our relationships. To illustrate this, we tend to see life as our own car on our own personal road, and then when we come in contact with another car, we wonder why that other car is on our road! Then the conflict emerges. You wonder why the other car is going in the wrong direction. The driver of the other car wonders the same about you! The car represents our ideas, assumptions, and experiences in life, and the road represents our plans, goals, and way. We will realize there are more and more cars on what we thought was our road. We will have disagreements concerning our values, our political understandings, and our aspirations, and these principles will not match up with those of others. Consequently, we have more opportunities for conflict today that would have been unheard of in years past. We now have a greater urgency to manage our relationships with care and veracity in order to deal with such convergences. If not, we will crash, and our relationships may not recover unless we are able to have a goal or some kind of a plan to drive that car safely on a road with directions and signs that can be shared with other cars .

Why we have Conflicts

What causes fights and quarrels among you? Don't they come from your desires that battle within you? You want something but don't get it. You kill and covet, but you cannot have what you want. You quarrel and fight. You do not have, because you do not ask God. When you ask, you do not receive, because you ask with wrong motives, that you may spend what you get on your pleasures. James 4:1-3

The Bible teaches us that conflict comes from the desires that battle within our heart. This is the result of our sinful nature. Sin is at the root as our securities are threatened, our happiness is at stake, our focus is misplaced, and our God is ignored. Sometimes, our good desires are escalated to sinful retaliation, truth becomes concealed and twisted, listening does not happen, we are not understood, and we do not understand the other person. Thus, a lot of conflicts, from blatant sin to simple misunderstandings, are rooted in our pride and willful refusal to acknowledge the other person or our responsibility.

Our inability to deal with conflict is primarily a spiritual problem. Our focus becomes skewed to only see ourselves, so we attack and blame others. We have to come to the point that we see Christ, and our worship of Him must affect all we do in our treatment of and listening to others. We will be wronged; others will wrong us, but this is the life we have been dealt due to sinful choices made over the millennias. To do anything about resolving conflict, we must be willing and able to remove the log from our own eye so we can see the splinter in another's.

Conflict is something we do not need to fear. It is a normal spice of life, and an outgrowth of our sinful nature, over which we are supposed to have dominion. God warned Cain that sin was "crouching at your door," and that he needed to master it or it would overtake and destroy him. Cain did not listen to God, but heeded only his anger and inclinations. Thus, the first interpersonal conflict resulted in the taking of the first life, Cain's own flesh and blood.

How can you say to your brother, "Let me take the speck out of your eye," when all the time there is a plank in your own eye? Matthew 7:4

We are all capable of causing conflict, and it is something we are called to master and eventually be able to end. As with any sin, we have the natural desire to do it, but we also have the natural ability not to. Even the non-Christian has the ability not to sin; but, as far as I know, no one in the entire history of humanity has ever gone without sinning—with the exception of Christ. Calvin taught that non-Christians have the civil ability to follow the law (civil), and this is the reason they do good works without being saved. Thus, as Christians, we should heed our responsibility to do what God calls us to do.

Conflict is not always something evil or bad. We must remember that God allows all things to work for good for His glory. Sometimes, relationships run their course, and He has someone better for you in friends and/or work (never in marriage unless there is irresolvable abuse or abandonment - 1 Corinthians:7). Sometimes, conflict draws people together for a cause and perspective, such as when I was involved with *Operation Rescue*. Conflict can open opportunities and communities and bring them together, but we are not to cause conflict for this effect. Well-managed conflict can be healthy and inspire growth and strength in relationships, helping to spur on our spiritual maturity. When a person sins and is disciplined, then comes out of it with repentance, he or she grows and becomes more effective for Christ.

Our first responsibility is to recognize the reasons we get into these conflicts (previously discussed), and their causes, and their cures. We also need to remember that love covers a multitude of sins. Love is the first fruit from whence all the other fruits derive, and sanctification is our growth in Christ. Our salvation is the result of love, paid for by the redemption of Christ. So, if you are a bitter person, and you discover love, the bitterness will be muted then erased by seeking the forgiveness of Christ. Then, the fruit is to go to others whom you have offended to seek their forgiveness. Conflict terminated. When we are full of pride (the polar opposite of love), we will be unable to manage conflict effectively, but only spread it out of our pride. We need to keep the focus on the love of Christ as our baseline for all that we do.

Talking your Way out of Conflict

Then you will win favor and a good name in the sight of God and man. Proverbs 3:4

As a pastor, I have been involved with every kind of conflict imaginable, from business disputes, personality clashes, monetary discord, land rights, probate, parent-teacher issues, to, of course, the most common-marital disputes. I learned over the years, not so much from my degrees in psychology, but rather my pastoral experience, how to talk my way out of problems. Being a person who hates conflict, I seek the easiest, most efficient way to put it down. I had to, for the sake of my survival and sanity, figure a way to focus people on the relationship more than the issue.

This worked great for many years in pastoral ministry until I came across domestic violence. These other issues were not life threatening, but then I came up against people in enraged situations trying to literally kill one another. For some strange reason, a person who hates conflict (me) had the opportunity to be a Chaplin for a Southern California Police Department for a couple years. My role was to ride along with and minister to the officers, and accompany them to the most dangerous police call there is—not bank robbery or dragnets—domestic violence. I spent a significant amount of time in training for this, and as a *man of the cloth,* so to speak, enraged, fighting couples were more agreeable to settle down without violence in my presence than for a uniformed officer. I had to learn fast—as my life and the officer's life depended on it—how to dissolve violent situations. These precepts, along with my pastoral training and experience, can be of help to you, too.

This is not the avoiding of problems (although I have been known to do that), but by carefully listening and coming to a solution to appease the person, the situation could be calmed down so the facts could be evaluated. Then, the concentration could be focused on the rebuilding of the relationship. Otherwise, the problem will continue and the relationship will suffer. The most important thing I had to learn is to not take problems at face value so that they overwhelmed me. I had to see the big picture—that God was still sovereign, and this, like any storm, would eventually pass and be forgotten.

Most problems seem complex; intertwined with so many people and so much hurt and communication ills, they seem overwhelming and hopeless. But, that is not the case; most problems have just a few simple components to them that can be isolated and dealt with. Even when I arrived on the scene with a man chasing his girlfriend with a knife, I was able to resolve the issue without shooting him. Of course you should never engage in a violent situation without significant training and someone at your side who is armed. But, you can resolve many issues in your life and the lives of others with a few simple hints. If you are not the one to do this, it is OK; most pastors should not. They should refer people with problems that they cannot handle to a good counselor or lawyer. And, with violence or potential violence, always, always call the police; do not take a chance. It is better to have a false arrest than a dead body!

Here is a roadmap to help you, your church, or a moderator through the biblical process of understanding and solving problems. This can be easily applied to church conflicts, business disputes, and martial clashes

Essential Points to Remember:

For out of the heart come evil thoughts, murder, adultery, sexual immorality, theft, false testimony, slander. Matthew 15:19

1. **You are Christ's loved one** (2 Corinthians 12:9-10)**:** Do not take the problem as a personal attack, even if it is. You may be a part of the conflict, or a third party trying to resolve it. You are Christ's child; He is your identity and defense! When you understand that, you can better see your role as a relationship builder—even when the other person is seeking to tear you down. This first point has saved me a lot of stress and disappointment!
2. **Conflict is an Opportunity** (1 Corinthians 6:1-8)**:** It is an opportunity to learn and give God honor. It is not necessarily bad or the end of a relationship. Know for certain that God can use conflict, whether it is sin, bad choices, a wrong turn, or a misunderstanding, and transform it into good if you let Him. God will be glorified, and you will grow in character, maturity, trust, love, obedience, and in faith.
3. **Listen** (Proverbs 28:13; James 1:19-25; 1 John 1:8-9)**:** The first job is listening, without opening your mouth. Effective listening and getting

each party to listen is essential! Until each one listens, nothing productive will happen. People need to be heard; the one who listens earns the right to be heard and resolve the issue. Make sure they know you are listening by giving eye contact, leaning forward, and being relaxed. Restate to clarify what you heard with as few words as possible, saying, *this is what I heard...* Be open and say, "I'm confused; let me try to restate what I think you said." Or, "You have said so much; let me see if I have heard it all."

4. **Understand Forgiveness** (Psalm 103:12; Isaiah 43:25; 1 Corinthians 13:5; Colossians 3:12-14)**:** Most Christians have a pale sense of the wonder that we have been forgiven, and often fail to show that forgiveness to others when wronged. Forgiveness is absolutely crucial for any relationship to continue, and critical to resolve any conflict! Remember how much you have been forgiven; do not fail to show it to others! Remember, God does not treat us the way we tend to treat others.

5. **Communicate** (Luke 15:11-24)**:** Seeking understanding is more important than resolving the issue. Most issues do not need to be resolved if all parties can understand one another's situation. Get them to talk and listen, and you are on the road to recovery*! Why is the person hurt? Why do they feel that way? What do they want? What can be done?*

How to do this—the ABCs of conflict communication:

If your brother sins against you, go and show him his fault, just between the two of you. If he listens to you, you have won your brother over. But if he will not listen, take one or two others along, so that every matter may be established by the testimony of two or three witnesses. If he refuses to listen to them, tell it to the church and if he refuses to listen even to the church, treat him as you would a pagan or a tax collector. Matthew 18:15-17

a. Pray for wisdom and discernment! Keep praying, gather all of the facts, and get second opinions and godly council without revealing confidences.

b. Be positive, have a win-win attitude, smile, and look the person in the eyes. Affirm each person; make him/her feel comfortable. Let him/her know you care and want to hear. Treat each person with utmost respect and kindness even if you feel they do not deserve it. Remember that they are God's child, too! Operate in the Fruit of the Spirit, not the works of the flesh!

c. Do not be afraid to give the moderating over to someone else if you cannot handle it. I have done this many times over the years, due to time, family, being out of my expertise, and personality clashes.

d. When you confront someone, ask yourself, *how would I want to be confronted?* Be humble and introspective so you can understand how you or (if you are the moderator) the participants have each contributed to the conflict.

e. Never compare your life and situations with that of others. God deals with everyone equally, yet differently. Think before you speak!

f. Write stuff down!

g. Validate each person as important.

h. Use humor only when it is appropriate, perhaps to diffuse a tense situation; never use it as an attack!

i. Identify the interests, concerns, desires, needs, limitations, and fears of each person involved.

j. Allow all the parties equal time to tell their side without interruption; then, get feedback from the others.

k. Do not be self-focused; focus on the issue, facts, feelings, and how this affects Christ's Kingdom and fullness.

l. If you are a part of the conflict, speak for yourself, not for the other person! As a moderator, make a ground rule that each person can only speak for themselves and not reword or restate the other's view. That way, the finger pointing is stopped and listening can begin.

m. Attack the issue, not the people; allow no condemnations, commands, threats, condescending attitudes, name calling, or disrespect!

n. Commit to understand one another and each side, and to refrain from interrupting.

o. Phrase the problem as questions and not attacks! Phrases such as, *you feel* (state the feeling) or *because* (state the content) are appropriate.

p. Do not blame! Have each party state how the issue affects him/her, and how they feel. For example, if a spouse is always gone and the other is angry about that, state, *When you are gone I feel... (Lonely),* rather than *You are never home.* This diffuses most arguments and refocuses blame by simply stating how he/she feels. When each one is aware of the other's feelings, especially in martial conflict, problem solving can begin.

q. Ask, *How is the problem dishonoring God? How is it hurting each person involved and how is it damaging the relationship?*

r. Be open and willing to listen to all solutions, no matter how ridiculous. Again, people need to be heard! This invites the willingness to cooperate and listen.

s. If people refuse to talk to one another, have them write their complaint on one page with a general description, their side of the dispute, what they think the other person did, and their solution. Then go over it, summarize it, and present it to both parties. Do not allow them to respond until it is fully read.

t. When sin is involved, it must be confessed and dealt with. The person whose attitude promoted the sin needs to be addressed and confronted.

u. Make sure you are listening and each person knows you are listening. If you are the moderator, you can restate each person's response. If it is a marriage situation with only the couple, restate your position in a positive way by saying, *this is what I heard.... * When you summarize, do not add new ideas or your agenda!

v. Keep to one issue at a time; do not allow other past conflicts to interrupt. When multiple problems are raised, the situation becomes too frustrating and overwhelming to solve. Solve one, or at least come to an understanding, before going to the next one.

w. Say, *What can we do to solve this problem together? What are the steps do you see that can resolve this issue?* If that does not work, place the issue on what the purpose of the Christian life is about, to worship and glorify Christ. *How can we develop a solution that glorifies our Lord?*

x. If the parties or you cannot calm down, take a break; if that does not work, reschedule for another time.

y. Start to work together by seeing each person on the same team and not opposing adversaries; we are all God's children, and in the same church family.

6. **Commit to a Positive Solution or Understanding** (James 4:1-12; Matthew 15:18-19): A lot of conflicts, especially marital, will continue as each person is constantly *pushing buttons*; they are on a merry-go-round without being merry. You have to make a decision that the pushing will stop, regardless of the hurt, for the sake of the relationship. Ask, *What can you both do differently to solve this problem so it does not continue?* Then resolution can begin. All parties must agree that the cycles of conflict must stop. Unless there is an agreement and a follow-through, no resolution will take place. Sometimes, problems cannot be

resolved, and that is OK if understanding is sought. If the person refuses to stop escalating the problem, they are obviously too steeped in pride and this problem will have to be referred to church elders and/or civil authorities. In the case of domestic violence, this is where I would *cuff and stuff* them into the patrol car. In the church, this is where they are asked to leave the fellowship until they get right with God.

Break down the issue in steps and then come to a solution that all can agree upon.

*Therefore, prepare your minds for action; be self-controlled; set your hope fully on the grace to be given you when Jesus Christ is revealed. As obedient children, do not conform to the evil desires you had when you lived in ignorance.*1 Peter 1:13-14

1. Gather all of the information you can. Write down the facts, feelings, possible outcomes if unresolved, and possible outcomes if resolved. Look for root issues; most problems are symptoms of deeper issues.
2. Write down the description(s) of the problem.
3. Write down what positive result each person would like to see.
4. Evaluate and summarize each person's statement so it describes the situation fairly.
5. Never discuss or try to resolve any conflict when either party is tired, hungry, or angry.
6. When you are dealing with substantive issues such as money, property, or human rights, you need to involve an attorney or professional in that field to help resolve the issue. If it is a theological issue, adhere to what is plainly taught in God's Word and your church confessions. But, even here, the goal is to be cooperative, not competitive.
7. Brainstorm possible solutions by thinking through ideas without critiquing them. Evaluate; do not argue! This is the *possibilities* stage; you do not need to jump to a conclusion. Take your time.
8. Look at all the ideas and then ask, *How might we come to a mutual solution? How can we create a new and better future?* Remember, all are on the same team!
9. If this is a conflict involving you, there is no moderator, and if things are not going smoothly, be humble; find a trusted, mutual friend, counselor, or pastor to moderate! Do not allow your pride to push others away and destroy relationships!

10. Now evaluate the ideas one by one. What are the advantages and disadvantages of the ideas? Which ones are acceptable to all parties? Which ones glorify our Lord the most? Remember to keep it positive; not everyone will be happy.
11. Create a schedule to implement the best possible solution.
12. Remember, when people are uncooperative, only God can change them and they need to have the willingness to allow Him to do so.
13. If you failed to come to an understanding, take this to heart; as long as you are obedient to Him, you did not fail—you succeeded immeasurably! Some situations cannot be resolved simply because of improper perspectives and pride.
14. Once an agreement is reached, commit to the fact that this incident does not need to be brought up again, especially in marriage. Then follow up on it in a couple of days, weeks, a month and six months later. *I will not complain about it, I will not dwell on it, I will not gossip about it; I will not use it against the other person. I will forgive and forget and move ahead in building our relationship!* If not, it will just start all over again!

APPLYING THESE ABCS TO A MARRIAGE PROBLEM

But we Christians have no veil over our faces; we can be mirrors that brightly reflect the glory of the Lord. 2 Corinthians 3:18

Each of these previous steps is a biblical way to deal with a marriage dispute through working with a qualified pastor or counselor. The principle issue is reconciliation with a *win/win* scenario. We can do this by realizing who we are in Christ, as we previously discussed, and that we are to mirror Christ-like character in our marriage even when it is tough! We have to lift the veil that blinds us to love, opportunities, and reconciliation; this veil blinds us to Christ as well! It is my experience, in countless marriage counseling sessions, that about 90 percent of the time, a misunderstanding is escalated by the pushing of each other's *buttons*, and by being blinded by the veil of pride and hurt. Both have to be willing to take a step back and work on themselves spiritually in maturity, and commit to stop the escalating of the matter. Also, keep to one issue at a time; do not allow the whole can of worms to be dumped. Work on one *worm* at a time, one problem or issue at a time! Then the steps can be effectively engaged. It will do wonders if a couple can act cordially to each other, if they can sit together, go through these steps one at a time, and spend a lot of time in prayer. But, it usually takes a pastor or counselor to make this process more effective and pleasant.

Each person brings his or her faults into any relationship. There are no perfect people. We all have personality dysfunctions and shortcomings which we have to be willing to work on. In the next chapter, we will be talking about relationship killers, such as being defensive, which greatly comes into play in resolving disagreements. Explain these *killers* to the couple if you are the counselor, to yourself if you are in the argument, and commit in the counseling session and at home not to engage in such destructible practices. You have to be willing to work on yourself first (Matthew 7:3-5). A married couple is on the same team; you are not each other's enemy! So, be willing to see your spouse as your teammate, and not your rival. In that way, you can avoid seeing the other as the problem, and focus on the issue and the solution!

Marital research has shown that 80 percent of problems do not even have to be solved when the couple talks through the issues and reaches mutual understanding (*Focus on the Family*). Most issues can just be talked out when both apply listening, understanding, and the Fruit of the Spirit over their will and hurt. Only the most difficult of problems will involve the use of Matthew 18 and intervention.

AGREEING TO DISAGREE WITHOUT DISUNITY

Do not repay anyone evil for evil. Be careful to do what is right in the eyes of everybody. If it is possible, as far as it depends on you, live at peace with everyone. Romans 12:17-18

The tone of Paul's letters, in resolving the various conflicts in the churches, centers on one crucial theme. Whatever the disagreement was, whether it was concerning the role of women, the spiritual gifts, the role of leadership, or the authority of the church, it centered on the issue of surrendering to the Lord and not to the flesh. Two thousand years later, we are dealing with those same issues. So, how do we respond? Just as Paul stated, led by the Spirit, we must allow ourselves to be taught by the Word and surrender to the Lordship of Christ-and not ourselves! Paul continues to remind us that we are to express our oneness in Christ by showing love and acceptance to others because Christ was, and is, accepting and loving of us.

True wisdom will solve any conflict, but our desires will keep us from seeing it. Our envy and selfish desires will always get in the way, but God's grace will eventually silence our reckoning and bring the peace. So, we must focus on the major issues and tenets of the faith, such as key theological issues, as Paul did. Paul took to task the issues of the physical resurrection of Christ, and that faith alone, by what Christ has done, saves us. Paul did not call us to be perfect, but we should be able to handle moral values as our Lord would. Thus, the minor issues should be *agree to disagree*, such as with the role of women in leadership. My denomination split over this issue a few years ago because the key areas of conflict management were not used. It is always best to be a listener of God so we can be in tune with Him and not ourselves! From our pettiness comes the conflict that ruins relationships and property. From our Lord comes the grace, mercy, and goodness that create the peacemaker. When we are in tune, then we will be that peacemaker. With our submissive hearts, minds, and souls, through which flow the good Fruit of the Spirit, we will be bearers of righteousness and not bearers of contemptible actions, bringing them into our relationships and His church! Remember James, chapters three and four, and the true causes of conflict.

Dealing with difficult people

For it is commendable if a man bears up under the pain of unjust suffering because he is conscious of God. 1 Peter 2:19

A lot of people are unreasonable—even Christians. We will run into people who will just not *get it*, listen, deal, resolve, or handle things God's way. They only want their way or the highway. Some people have hard hearts and are unwilling or unable, due to personality defects or chemical imbalances, to see another as God's child. They only see it for themselves. This is very sad and there is not much you can do with them. They are the ones who will be lonely and bitter because that is what they want. We are still called to pray and minister to them, but it is best not to take their attacks personally.

We have to remember that we all are difficult at times and we all have sinned and fallen way short of God standards. That is what the cross is about! That is why it is so important to prepare yourself spiritually and keep your focus on God—not people or situations—so His fruit can work in you.

Prayer is the most important act for us in any manner. Also, remember, your obedience is what counts, not how others respond to you. We are even called to bless these unreasonable people, and we do that by remaining true to His Lordship in our maturity. You cannot be responsible for how others respond and treat you when you are acting in godly character (Romans 12:14-21). Do not let the situation or the bad people get you down, or cause you to compromise biblical precepts or your character! Never close the Bible or neglect prayer; your spiritual journey and your trust and growth in Him will be your anchor to weather the storms. Do not allow yourself to suffer in your spiritual pilgrimage because of someone else. You are still God's special child (Colossians 3:1-4)! Do not let yourself fall to the world's way, regardless of what the other person does. Give them over to God; He is the one who dispenses justice and revenge, not you (Hebrews 12:6)!

These are the times you need to especially control your tongue and attitude. Focus on the Lord, not the situation. Do not allow yourself to get into a *pity party* so it is all about you; it is not; it is all about Him. You may not be able to do anything to resolve the problem in a relationship, but that does not mean you are to give up—especially in marriage. Your purpose is to take the focus off yourself and onto Christ as Lord. That way, the bitterness and resentment you got from others will not become a virus that affects you! Repentance and reconciliation may still come. Remember His timing; I have seen miracles of reconciliation long after I had given up hope. God is still at work, even when we do not see Him. God may use your character to speak to them down the road; no relationship or attempt at reconciliation is ever wasted in His Kingdom!

Satan thrives on conflict and he wants you in conflict

Submit yourselves, then, to God. Resist the devil, and he will flee from you. Come near to God and he will come near to you. James 4:7-8a

We need to realize we have an enemy who is nearly eternal, and fully desires to interfere with, steal, and destroy us. So, we are called to wage war on Satan and his onerous cohorts. We can do this through prayer and various techniques found in spiritual warfare resources available in most denominational resources centers and Christian bookstores.

This passage in James asks a crucial question—are we resisting God or resisting the devil? How we respond to life and others will be rooted in how we respond to God. Do we fight Him or do we glorify Him? How do we know? The answer lies in how we are in our attitudes and mindsets; are we humble or proud? If we are proud, we are serving the devil, even though we may think we are serving ourselves. If we are humble, then we are serving our Lord. This strikes at the root of our mindset and motivations in life.

We need to battle our sinful nature and the evil desires that come up from that nature. If we put no effort into self-discipline, then we will not last long in tough situations or grow to be fully used by our Lord.

How do I maintain my direction in life, so I am pleasing Him and seeking His purpose? The answer is found as we discover what course we are pursuing. When we draw to God, we are undertaking His precepts and applying them to life. *Draw near to God* means purification and developing your personal relationship with God through the disciplines of the faith. We are responsible for our spiritual growth; God provides the plan, Christ is the Way, and the Spirit is the guidance; however, we provide the will of our hearts exhibited by our hands and feet. The focus is on trust and obedience. God is consistent as when we seek Him, He has already sought us and will continue to reveal Himself and the depths of His love all of our days on earth and throughout eternity. The key to this is the willingness to confess our sin and move ahead to Him and away from false and deceitful ways. This directly applies to how we handle each other too.

Conflict is almost always necessary when the forces of darkness encroach upon the Christian life. It is necessary to stand up for the rights of the unborn. It is necessary to fight for morals and values in our schools and government. It is necessary not to yield to Satan and our evil desires. For, if we do not take a stand, our fall will be close at hand.

Preventing Conflict

My people have committed two sins: They have forsaken me, the spring of living water, and have dug their own cisterns, broken cisterns that cannot hold water. Jeremiah 2:13

Most of the conflict we experience in life comes from our selfish desires and our insistence on our own way over and against others. So, we are poised to pounce on one another to get our own way, while our Lord looks sadly at our pettiness and calls us to walk above it. But, do we listen? Desiring something is not necessarily wrong, but when we do not trust our Lord for it, then we have a problem. The Bible calls us to come before a Holy God by what Christ has done and resulting in a fountain of *Living Water,* which is our Lord. We are to rely on Him and not on our inclinations. When we do the latter, conflict is sure to erupt. When we walk in faith and realize our position before our Lord Jesus Christ, then we will bypass our self-will and yield to His.

Jesus answered her, if you knew the gift of God and who it is that asks you for a drink, you would have asked him and he would have given you living water. John 4:10

We need to understand how evil we are when we fight with one another because of our personal agendas and desires! It is God alone who provides us the *Living Waters.* So, why do we persist in digging our own wells, only to bring up dirt that is useless and worthless? Remember, Jesus IS the Living Water!

We can earn nothing on our own; our salvation is a gift from God, so our behaviors with one another must reflect this undeserved, free gift. The *free* does not mean we can engage in war with one another; rather, we are to pursue peace and love.

So, what do we do? How can we restrain our desires to manipulate, control, and to be aggressive, and rather repair relationships? Simply by realizing whom we are before a Holy God and our undeserving gift! Primary conflict is in us, so we need to control the sin that encroaches us, something Cain failed to do. We must discern between what we desire and what is provided to us. We need to discern between our goals and what the will of the Lord is. We need to discern between what we want and what God wants! Then, the conflicts and diseases of distraction that lead to relationship destruction will cease! Our Lord has already won the ultimate conflict of good vs. evil, of rebellion vs. sovereignty.

Remember, love covers a multitude of sins; so what shall we do? LOVE! Love with the love that Christ had for us when we did not deserve it, and with the response of the love we should have for each other. Jesus let go of His place with the Father—something of which we cannot conceive. He gave up a precious position for the mission of redeeming us. If we pursued the model that Christ laid before us, how much conflict would we have? Practically none! How could we fight with one another when we are focused on our Lord and the interests of others? How can we carry on conflicts with one another when we take a deep, introspective look into our desires and compare them to the Scriptures? Our focus must not be in our self-awareness, but on what Christ has done as a template for our behaviors and actions! By being a true example of our Lord, we will neutralize most conflicts. When self-desires are focused on our Lord, intrapersonal conflict will be dissolved; so, there will be no conflict with self-desires. Interpersonal conflict will cease because we will be a community of Believers on the *same page,* especially because we have the interests of others in mind and are willing to follow the biblical precepts to solving conflict. So, we are left with substantive conflicts between beliefs. When we are a community of Believers with a high view of the Scriptures, then we will eliminate most of those conflicts. So, the conflicts will be between Believers and aberrant and cult groups, and the minor theological distinctions can be on an *agree to disagree* venue. This may sound utopian and unattainable, but this is Christian community in its true, called action!

Problems do not have to ruin your life. They do not need to take you over or skew the purpose and direction of your call or your church. We all have the power to make the determination that we will not let the trivialities of life derail us from who we are in Christ and His purpose for us. Most conflict is trivial, but we are never to approach it as trivial. It is to be taken seriously so it can be resolved and the more important things in life can be pursued. Use this process to also learn more about the other person and yourself. Learn how to better your character and maturity and your relationship with God. See challenges as opportunities to learn and grow in His presence and His Fruit.

By following a few simple ideas from the precepts of His Word, we can save ourselves a lot of pain and hurt, and drastically improve our relationships. Just our understanding the other person will do wonders for relationships and our church! The focus is what we talked about in the first chapter with fullness and the Kingdom of God. The relationship is the priority, not the material goods or desires that may come up. When we are operating our lives in God's parameters, we are glorifying Him, building His Kingdom, and living in fullness. When we are steeped in our pride, we are destroying our relationships and bringing shame to His church. Why would we want to do that and take on all of the bitterness, resentment, hurt, and frustration in life, when we can have so much better?

Remember this very important fact; unresolved conflict costs much more than the cost to resolve it. In fact, to not manage conflict will enormously cost in your relationships, workplace, and church. It will cost you money, time, lost productivity, shattered relationships, lost children, dissolved marriages, bad decisions—and it can literally kill and destroy you and all that you know. It could have been turned around, but nobody wanted to bother with it! Do not let this happen to you, your family, your friends, your coworkers, or your church!

Remember, conflict may be a good plotline for TV or the movies, but not for your life! Be the person who wants to understand the love of God and allow His love to transform you and all of your relationships!

(More insights on how to resolve conflict are available on our Website www.intothyword.org in the "Church Leadership" Channel and the Sub Channel "Problem Solving.")

Therefore, brothers, we have an obligation—but it is not to the sinful nature, to live according to it. For if you live according to the sinful nature, you will die; but if by the Spirit you put to death the misdeeds of the body, you will live, because those who are led by the Spirit of God are sons of God. Romans 8:12-14

Chapter XVI
LONELINESS

I have not run away from being your shepherd; you know I have not desired the day of despair. What passes my lips is open before you. Do not be a terror to me; you are my refuge in the day of disaster. Jeremiah 17:16-17

I do not know about you, but I hate loneliness! I do not like to be alone for very long. Although I like to work alone, I like to play individual sports like skiing alone, and of course I like to read alone. However, I, for the most part, do not like to be alone—at least for very long. At some point in my day, I need to connect with people in authentic relationships. My life needs to be in touch with people and I have the call to touch others in the form of connections, interpersonal relationships, and in communication and sharing—that is, doing life together and tighter, as in harmony and close.

I found out long ago that I am not to be on this journey of life alone. Unlike skiing or reading, life is not an individual sport or activity. If I do not have friends and people with whom I can connect in my life, I fill with despair. I feel that a vital component of my life is missing and that it must be filled. There was a time I needed these relationships to fulfill me and give me purpose and meaning. I was empowered in life by what my friends thought of me. My direction and motivation came from the winds of my connections that were also my opportunities. But, as I grew in spiritual maturity as a Christian, I learned that my significance is in Christ alone. I do not need friends or people to tell me I am worthy or need them to make me feel fulfilled. Nor, do I need to heed their advice or influence.

But, I forsook many of my relationships by neglect, a side affect from working in ministry fulltime, going to school fulltime, and sometimes holding an extra job on the side. I had no time for relationships. I had to learn what God had for me, as well as how to balance a life of serving Him while still connecting with other people. I had to learn how to be an influencer without being negatively influenced, how to validate people, and to encourage and equip while also learning and growing from these experiences.

I did not always feel that way. I grew up in a dysfunctional home with an abusive stepfather, and then I had problems in school with my learning disabilities and stuttering. Thus, my home life was a wreck, and school, where the other kids teased me, was sometimes even worse. I consistently felt like I was going from the frying pan into the fire, but was not sure which was which. Thus, I came to an early conclusion in life that I did not need people. People were the ones who hurt me, and I did not want them in my life. I was at a place, in my early life, where the very thought of connecting with people was terrifying.

So, I decided that I could hang with my plants, books, and pets. I did gardening and rabbit care to the exclusion of human companionship, and to the point that it was becoming dysfunctional. I read everything I could, not just for my thirst for knowledge, but as a way to defend myself from others. Fortunately, as I grew older and went into high school, I discovered that I did have a few people in my life who cared and loved me, like my mom and grandparents, a few significant teachers, my tennis coach, my pastor, and then there was a girl or two. Thus, I started to venture into the world of relationships, leaving a neglected garden and a lonely bunny. I had to learn to conquer my fears and trust in my Lord. I found that I needed relationships; relationships are God's call for me. Other Christians are important. I needed to be in connection with people.

Keep your lives free from the love of money and be content with what you have, because God has said, "Never will I leave you; never will I forsake you." So we say with confidence, "The Lord is my helper; I will not be afraid. What can man do to me?" Hebrews 13:5-6

My graduation from withdrawing from others in fear and isolation coalesced when I realized that God is there; He is always there for me. Jeremiah, chapter 17, told me that God was my *shepherd* and *refuge* and I did not need to be in *despair*. Jesus said *I will never leave you. I will never forsake you.* Because He would never leave or forsake me, I can have more confidence in life, and I can engage in contact with others without the fear of being hurt.

Even when they do hurt, my comfort is in Christ and not in the words or deeds of other people. I learned that I can read, I can go to school, I can work, I can have my solitude, and I can connect with others. My life then started to come from the shadows of despair into the light of His precepts. I had friends, family, and He even brought my lovely wife, Mary. None of this could have happened if I had remained gripped by my fears in the despair of loneliness.

In this chapter, I am explaining how to deal with loneliness and how to be proactive in overcoming it. But, I need to state that there is a distinction between being alone and being lonely. We all need times to be alone for spiritual and emotional reasons. Our alone times will help prepare us spiritually and emotionally to know God more intimately and deal with life and others in a better way.

I learned that my solitude and devotional life were my pathways to knowing God. And, when my relationship with God improved and grew, I was prepared for my social life. There was a time to be alone for spiritual growth and education and a time to connect and play with others. I learned that in the Christian life, there is a time and place for both solitude and friendship. Solitude is essential, helping us focus on the Lord and His empowerment for us in life.

But, the alone time I am speaking of here is about when we are alone and we do not want to be and/or we should not be. We will know when the alone times have gotten out of control when we feel sad and misplaced by them. When we allow our fear of hurt, our anger, bitterness, self-pity, unforgiveness, addictions, conformity to bad thinking, being a workaholic, selfishness, blaming God or others, or whatever to hold us hostage from people we are having a problem with. Loneliness and all this other will block our relationships and the opportunities that God brings that are best for us.

THE SANDS OF LONELINESS

A man of many companions may come to ruin, but there is a friend who sticks closer than a brother. Proverbs 18:24

Loneliness is a form of passive aggression, a defense mechanism to protect us from what we may perceive as harm. We withdraw from others as an animal does who is hurt; they will scamper off to lick their wounds. But, the animal, once healed, will reengage in the hunt and pursuit of life. If they do not, they will die. We humans need times to be alone for various reasons, but, when we do not reengage in life, our relationships, as well as a part of us, will die.

Loneliness is a problem when we are not actively pursuing relationships and we put ourselves in a prison of self-isolation. When we embrace our solitude to the detriment of interpersonal relations so they are few to none, we have a problem and we need to deal with it. When we refuse to change and grow, but feel disconnected and trapped, this can and will lead us into depression and perhaps even the taking of our own life. We have to realize that there is hope and we can get through it! If you or people you know are trapped in this mindset, be proactive and get them some help, such as a trained pastor or counselor for intervention. You may save a life!

Loneliness is a yearning for relationships, one of the most feared and distasteful words we have in our English language. Even when we are face to face in crowds, loneliness can become even stronger and make us feel more isolated. We can come to a point in our thinking and feeling that we do not belong; we are not connected; we have no one to be at our side. This can range from a child whose parents are two aisles away in a market, to a single person finding him or herself in their late thirties or forties, wondering what happened. We can experience this in the mist of breakups, moves, the death of a loved one, job loss, a move, a new school, a new job, a new stage of life, or even new relationships.

Loneliness is not just being alone; it is being isolated from what is essential in life: God and/or others. It is not about who is around us; it is about feeling we are not connected. It is like a radio that is not plugged in so that no signals or sounds are received. We can be lonely from our situation through no fault of our own, or we can place ourselves there from our experiences and fears. Loneliness is an indicator light that something is wrong; we have a hole that needs to be filled and a predicament that needs to be renovated. Many of the people in the Bible struggled with this, including Joseph, Moses, David, Elijah, Job, Jeremiah, John the Baptist, Paul, and even Jesus! Loneliness is being disconnected from what is vital in life. It separates us from companions. We can be disconnected even in groups, such as the first few days at a new school, starting a new job, moving to a new city, or never learning to overcome the barriers preventing us from building companionships. There will be times in our journey of life we will be alone. We will become separated from others as friends move on, we move on, or the sufferings and trials of life take those connections away.

The reason we hate loneliness is because, as human beings, we are made to be social; it is hardwired into us. We are social beings and we are not made or meant to be alone much. When we forsake our relationship connections, either by our fault or by the fault of others, we become disconnected from what we were created and called to do—build relationships.

But, so much can crop up to thwart us in our relationships, cutting us off, and giving us hurts and bitterness so our fears prevent us from reengaging in life. We become entombed in our own prison of despair, a prison we detest, yet somehow, many of us do not know how to escape from it. The other countermeasure to healthy relationships that the Proverbs passage attests to is that we can also isolate ourselves by having so many acquaintances that we have no real friends, or we do not keep them very long. In either case we are isolated!

My command is this: Love each other as I have loved you. Greater love has no one than this, that he lay down his life for his friends. You are my friends if you do what I command. This is my command: Love each other. John 15:12-14, 17

Loneliness can turn into dysfunction and despair. We can experience depression, meaninglessness, guilt, distorted thinking, fantasy, and excess cares to the point that it leads to *codependency*. Any of these aspects can take us far off of God's path. Loneliness is a warning light that shows us we are empty and need to be filled up. It is universal; it goes cross culturally and cuts across race, creed, and status. It cannot be filled by money, possessions, sex, power, or fame. When it is filled with such things, the filling is straw and does not last very long. Nor can our aloneness be filled by a whole lot of just loose associations. All this does is take His *fullness* (which we talked about in the first chapter) and replace it with *fulfillment,* the wrong filler for our lives. This means we seek to be filled by what we think are assets and being in someone's company, usually the wrong company. However, our real fullness comes from His company and the company of others in healthy relationships which will complement us.

Even those who are rich and famous tend to be some of the loneliest people I have ever met. We all struggle with this; we all feel isolated at some point and at some time. The question is, *how much of that time is real loneliness and how much is solitude?* How many people do we have in our lives—too many or too few? We all need one another, and too many of us will not admit it or move with it. Life is meant for community and togetherness, not in a superficial way, but a deep yearning to connect and to share our lives and existence, our love and our life trek with another—several others.

But everyone who hears these words of mine and does not put them into practice is like a foolish man who built his house on sand. The rain came down, the streams rose, and the winds blew and beat against that house, and it fell with a great crash." Matthew 7: 26-27

Many Christians will not abide; they will not build their lives on His love or allow their love to touch others. These people build their lives on the sand, seeing only their ways and their assumptions. They may refuse to forgive, be filled with anxiety, refuse to trust in people because of past experiences, refuse to take risks in relationships, harbor bitterness, have a low self esteem, or turn out to be victims of bad parenting.

All of these will short-circuit their connections in life. The storms will come and the sand will shift, and the *building* of their lives will fail, leaving them alone with only sand in their hands. They may get mad at God, or blame others; perhaps, some will reboot their lives His Way and climb and rest on His Rock. The ones who do not will find life too harsh and be too hurt; they will be alone, even in a crowd. We have to recognize that this is not God's best for us. He does not want us in this life alone. He is there, and He wants others there with us and us with others. He wants our life on the Rock, not on the sand.

God will even carry us from the sand and place us on the rock. He cares for us in our loneliness. He solved Adam's problem and He will solve ours too, when we allow Him to do so. God cares for you and the others of "you" that are out there. He cares for me and the others of "me" out there. He wants all the others of "you" and "me" to be together in community, honoring His precepts, glorifying His Name, and building His community, His Kingdom. We are not made to be lonely; we are made to be a community! He wants us to go from being self-centered to being God—and others—centered.

There will be times when we will be alone, and that is OK. We will either make wrong decisions or our path will ferry us away from our previous friendships. We can be in the midst of a life change, in grief, a divorce, an empty nest, an illness, or a crisis. Becoming elderly will place us in God's waiting room, our life seemingly upside down and unplugged. In these times, we must seek healing in Him and seek Him for all we are and all that we are to do.

Maybe the people around us will not understand; perhaps they have not experienced what we have. When my wife Mary lost her dad not too long ago, her coworkers did not understand why she was so grieved and needed a few days off. They had never experienced such a loss, so they isolated her and treated her with contempt, due to no fault of my wife's. Her situation required decisive steps to reconcile, and when her younger, immature coworkers refused to do so, she decided to move on to another job. Sometimes, our loneliness means something needs to be done to get us back on track, perhaps time or opportunity.

Whether our loneliness is caused by unavoidable circumstances or deliberate self-isolation, we must not allow emotional hurts and fears to move us away from God and others. Others may isolate us, but we should not be the ones who isolate ourselves from others for very long. The wounds will heal unless we keep poking at them. (Then, they may not.) We need to make the determination to allow God to work in us so we start to get a grip on our life, even if it means making a new one. Our experiences can either move us into an isolated, bitter prison or they can hone us so we grow and become a help to others when they go through the journey of life. The choice is ours; short-term seclusion and isolation may not be a choice we undertake, but staying for the long term is!

Storms Cannot Buffet those in Christ

He replied, "You of little faith, why are you so afraid?" Then he got up and rebuked the winds and the waves, and it was completely calm. Matthew 8:26

This passage in Matthew is about relying on God's power to conquer our fears. To move on in our journey of life, we have to realize He is there and He will empower us. We can sojourn in Him! The Disciples believed and saw some incredible events. But, somehow, what they had observed and participated in firsthand did not create in them an ability to fully trust.

We will see this theme tested within ourselves when the storms of life buffet against us, too. This includes the tempests of frustration, the chaos of stress, the gossip from toxic people, the daily grind of life, wrong choices, people conflicts, and, of course, sin. How we deal with these is paramount to our ability to trust God. And, our trust in Christ is paramount for us as we develop healthy relationships. If we prepare to trust in Christ, we will be taken safely across the stormy seas we find ourselves in. If we do not, we may sink.

Yet, we will fight this notion of trust. We will think, *hey, I do not need anybody—not even God; I can do this on my own.* I held to this mantra for years. I did not have the power to overcome my loneliness, even as no human has control over the elements of matter in the universe, or even one another. We cannot say to the storm *be gone* and have it be gone. We also cannot say, *be gone all you dysfunctional and bad people,* because we may shoo ourselves away, too. We may think we are able to do things because we can, through technology, manipulate our environment and control people. Who knows; we may even one day be able to control the weather. But, ultimately, only God has real and total control, whether it is weather or people. In this passage, Jesus is defiantly demonstrating His Godhood by taking control of creation. We have to learn that He is indeed in control, and we can and must allow Him control over us.

In verse 23 Matthew tells us, *the disciples followed Him.* It is one thing to believe in something, and quite another to trust, and even more to obey an idea, plan, or cause. To follow Christ requires all three. We have to follow, we have to trust, and we have to obey. Each one follows the other and each one requires the other. We have to understand, put it into practice, and then trust in Him so we can continue. We need to receive His free gift of grace, for which we do nothing to obtain; at the same time, faith is required in order to receive it.

To help our faith and relationship with Christ and others to grow, and for Him to work in our lives, especially to touch others, we also have to be willing to trust and obey Christ as Lord over all things—including our lives and relationships. We see a common theme in the Gospels—that hearing the Word is not enough; we have to obey it. Mark records Jesus saying, *let us cross to the other side* (Mark 4:35-41). We have to allow Jesus to take us places in our faith we can never go or experience on our own. He helps make risks and trust happen, and this will help unlock the prison of seclusion in which we place ourselves.

Without warning, a furious storm came... as without warning, we, too, will face all kinds of troubles and opportunities. They always seem to come out of the blue without any advice, notice, or clue. The Sea of Galilee, where this passage takes place, is 13 miles long and eight miles wide, and is located in a basin 700 feet below sea level, making it one of the lowest points on earth. Mountains surround it, and at its southern end is a deep, cliff-lined valley.

Cool air from the Mediterranean is drawn down through the narrow mountain passes, and collides with the hot, humid air of Galilee lying over the lake. Thus, the size and shape of this area creates a vortex effect with weather patterns, so that sudden, violent storms come up without warning. A person in a boat would not see them coming until it was too late, because they are hidden behind the mountains. We usually do not see all the convergences to what lies ahead for us in life; we do not see the mountains or the climate conditions. Even if we do, we will still go through the storm. But, we can see our Lord leading us all the way through it safely!

Most first century fisherman stayed close to the shore at Capernaum. This was where it was safe, even though most of the fish were out further. For them, it was, perhaps, a good method for remaining safe. A small fishing boat and a typical fisherman who only stayed close to shore would be unprepared for such a storm. It would easily capsize the small boat, killing all aboard. This explains the fear the disciples had. But, in our faith and relationships, playing it safe will only leave us at the shallow end. If we just focus on our fear, we will not take the risks. You will not be able to develop the depth unless you go into the depth, *deep calls to deep* (Psalm 42:7). We have to be willing to take the risk and go out, even though the storms are lurking. The disciples showed some faith by being willing to go across the sea to the other side at Jesus' request.

One day Jesus said to his disciples, "Let's go over to the other side of the lake." So they got into a boat and set out. Luke 8:22

Let Jesus take you to the other side! Or else, you will stay close to the shore of your comfort in the Christian life, and never take risks or exercise real, impacting faith. To pursue the Christian life and make an impact, we may be required to venture where we may not want to go. But, we only do this by His leading, and only move by His empowerment. We merely trust and obey. This is also the pattern for life. We do not see what is ahead. We do not see how our choices, sin, and events may collide, causing sudden and violent storms of stress, chaos, strife, pain, and suffering. If real faith is shown when the storms come, what would your faith show now? Storms are a part of our lives in a fallen world. At any one moment, you are either in a storm, just got out of a storm, or are headed into a storm. So, are you prepared?

Realize that relationships take risks. People will hurt us. However, we can move on and grow deeper with one another when He is there, guiding. We can do this because our faith is in Christ, not our situations or in people. The key is to let Jesus take you to the other side. If not, you will remain in the shallow end of life and forsake your maturity and spiritual growth; this will cause isolation and loneliness that will only result in bitterness and lament. *Jesus was sleeping.* This gives us a picture of Jesus' humanity, as He must have been so totally exhausted from all of the crowds converging on Him, He fell asleep. Sometimes, we feel Jesus is asleep as life overwhelms us. But, rest assured; He is still there, caring for and carrying us. Even if He is asleep (He is not), and our troubles keep multiplying (and they will at times), we are still safe when we remain in the boat—in Him! Jesus was relaxed during the storm, a picture of faith for us to emulate. We can rest under His cover, and still be tranquil, composed, and free from stress.

I will lie down and sleep in peace, for you alone, O LORD, make me dwell in safety. Psalm 4:8

When the disciples awakened Jesus in a panic, He scolded them, saying, *you of little faith.* What a sting those words must have been to the worrisome disciples as they realized they had messed up again. They only saw the storm and not Who they were with. The secret to remaining joyful in the face of adversity is our faith, and our confidence and assurance that He is there in the boat with us. Jesus will not let the boat capsize. But, even if it did, He is still there. After He rebuked the disciples for their lack of faith, *He got up and rebuked the winds and the waves.* Only God has real and total power over His creation. Jesus demonstrated that He is God, because even the winds and sea obeyed Him.

Jesus is Lord over creation, but you have to exercise your will to move yourself out of the way so He can be Lord over your life. He will rarely bully His way over you; you have to reach out to Him by faith, even though He reached out first to save you. It is by faith alone we receive His grace that has been offered to us. Mark tells us, *peace be still* (Mark 4:39). In the Greek, this means to be muzzled, as in muzzle an ox. Jesus, being fully God, has power and authority over creation (Mark 1:27). He has authority in His teaching (Mark 1:22), the power to forgive our sins (Mark 2:10), and the power to save and empower us.

What kind of man is this? asked the disciples. They knew that Moses and Elijah were able to manipulate the weather; however, they did not do so on their own power, rather, by God working through them with His power! There were also stories told about angels coming who looked like men, but they could not manipulate the weather, either. There are numerous stories of Greek gods and pagan legends about manipulating the weather; these stories took place in the far distant past. In Hebrew tradition, only God has that power (Psalm 107:29; John 1:15). So, they were perplexed in trying to understand who Jesus was. Scripture and doctrine plainly tell us who Jesus is. The disciples had to discover it firsthand.

The fear of the LORD leads to life: Then one rests content, untouched by trouble. Proverbs 19:23

Who is this in your life? In all honesty, if you believe what Jesus had just done, the only answer to this rhetorical question is that He is God! God's presence and power were demonstrated as He controlled the weather. He has the power to mold you! At the very start of his gospel, Mark makes it clear that Jesus is God (Mark 1:1)! These miracles over nature helped the disciples to develop and increase their faith in Jesus. They testify to us not just His care, but His power to care.

There will be times when we are afraid. Sometimes we will be just a little nervous; sometimes we will be outright panic-stricken, as the disciples must have been. We will see the storms of life coming against us, setting us off to feel overwhelmed and frustrated, and causing us to withdraw in isolation and despair. Even those who have been through them before and have grown and matured will become tired and wearisome. The danger comes when our faith breaks down into fear so we do not venture out with it. We become stuck, and refuse to learn and grow.

Sometimes, Jesus may even take you through the storm to the very edge of your breaking point to get your attention. But, the only thing that will be broken will be what must be broken, and that is our will; the rest of us will become stronger. Just as most fisherman were unwilling to venture past the coastline (for good reason for them—not for us with faith), if you do the same with your walk in Christ you will sink in those shallow depths. You will not realize that Jesus is there to take you through it. All you will see is the storm and not the growth and fruit that it can bring you. You will not develop true confidence in our Lord nor will He be able to take you where you will learn the most and do the most good with your relationships.

God's care for us

But for Adam no suitable helper was found. Genesis 2:20b

Adam was in his perfect state of having all he needed, yet he still felt something was missing in his life; he was alone. Life is meant for community and togetherness, not in a superficial way, but a yearning to connect and to share. God cares for us in our loneliness just as He did with solving Adam's problem. He completed him by providing companionship, first by a relationship with Him, then with his wife Eve, then with a family. We can have this too; and, in addition to that, we have friends, acquaintances, church people, and co-workers. We can be confident that God cares about our relationships and our hurts. He knows where we are in life and where we are going. He will guide us to where we need to be, caring and carrying us through it!

And at the ninth hour Jesus cried out in a loud voice, "Eloi, Eloi, lama sabachthani?"—which means, "My God, my God, why have you forsaken me?" Mark 15:34

If you think that God does not care, think again! God knows the depths of loneliness; Jesus experienced this, firsthand, to an extreme we may never fathom. In Mark 15:34, Jesus Himself felt the most extreme cut-off of loneliness. He was cut off from who He was to take our sin upon Him. For a few moments, that seemed an eternity; the Trinity was severed, and the second Person bore our sin so the first Person, God, could remain pure. Christ took our penalty and God the Father had to turn away. We can never comprehend that isolation and pain. Jesus was abandoned not only by God the Father and His disciples; He gets abandoned by us, too. He lived a life and experienced all that we do. He knows our pain and He bore our pain.

To solve our loneliness, God asks us to *come to me, all you who are weary and burdened, and I will give you rest* (Matthew 11:28). This is a picture of Jesus offering Himself to us. He has the authority to invite and He is the author of our salvation. Jesus' load is heavy and requires our fullest trust and obedience for His Highest; yet, it is easy when our eyes and faith are on Him! This is a call to come to Him and He will give us rest! The ultimate loneliness is that our Lord gave Himself to us in relationship; we can now commune with God, the maker and sustainer of the universe. Take comfort that our Lord God is approachable; He is here for you! With this concept rooted in our hearts and minds, our fears will subside and we can connect with open arms and hearts flowing with love, even when others betray and hurt us.

Come unto me is a promise of wisdom and the offering of God's strength; and are, perhaps, the most endearing words uttered by our Lord! It is so simple for the humble to see and accept, yet so difficult for the mind preoccupied with pride, hurt, and distrust. To be embraced in His arms requires us to acknowledge Him and be humble. Without humbling ourselves, we cannot receive the Savior. Rather, we retain a need unmet and a soul that is empty, the ultimate loneliness.

But if we walk in the light, as he is in the light, we have fellowship with one another, and the blood of Jesus, his Son, purifies us from all sin. 1 John 1:7

God offers rest to the exhausted, tired, and weary; can you see yourself in His arms resting? Think how much your attitude and then your relationships could improve if you fully understood what this means for you and for others around you. But, as in any relationship, this can be tough stuff; it is not easy. *Yoke* refers to a crossbeam carried on the shoulders to pull a plow or a load. It is a symbol of work, of hardship. It is the image of subjection and strict obedience. God's Law was referred to as a *yoke* by many Jewish teachers. Following the law was impossible. Why is this important? Because, God offers His love in place of His wrath. He gives us grace that takes the Law off our shoulders. The catch? We turn to Him and away from all that is false. Until then, we will be lonely; perhaps this will even follow us into eternity, which is not a pleasant foresight for a *being* made for relationships. So, accept God's love and grace. Be complete in Him; see loneliness fall away and your relationships turn into prosperity and richness!

How can we do this? By knowing God is with us! In the depths of your despair and hurt He is there. He will bring you close to Himself and to the connections you need. The hand that is out to you is His, but you must reach for it. Do not allow your insecurities and fears rob you of His promise and presence. We must allow God to be God; that means He is Lord over our lives and relationships. When your peace and security are in Him, fears subside and connections flourish; loneliness will no longer be your prison.

God is more concerned with our obedience than with our knowledge. It is essential for us to understand and apply this! What we think we know pales in comparison to who Christ is and what He does for us. When we feel we are wise, we are like a four-year-old who thinks he knows more than his parents. How far can a four-year-old carry himself in life? How far can we carry ourselves in life without Christ? We may think we are doing well, but when we look back, our ways are revealed as very pathetic indeed! We need to allow God's truth to reign in us, and hold on to that reign with trust and obedience. When we do this without worry, but with trust, we grow, and real wisdom will flow to us and through us to those around us. Just be aware that God will not give you wisdom or gifts until you have mastered what He has already given you!

For we do not have a high priest who is unable to sympathize with our weaknesses, but we have one who has been tempted in every way, just as we are—yet was without sin. Let us then approach the throne of grace with confidence, so that we may receive mercy and find grace to help us in our time of need. Hebrews 4:15-16

We have a High Priest who knows us. He also can sympathize with us. That means that whatever we go through in life, He has already gone through as a man here on earth and as our High Priest. He cannot turn away from our plight or pain; He is there in our midst. What does this mean for our loneliness? It means we can have confidence in Him that will help give us confidence to pursue healthy relationships. We can place our confidence in Him so when others turn from us, hurt us, or betray us, our hurt is borne by Christ. At the same time, our true confidence and significance is in Him alone. We can have our cake and eat it too. We can have relationships and not be afraid of being hurt. We will have no reason to withdraw from others and isolate ourselves from His love or the love of others.

Jesus demonstrated to us how to overcome ultimate loneliness, and that is to understand that our Lord gave Himself to us in a relationship. We can commune with God, the maker and sustainer of the universe. God is approachable, gentle, and gives us rest. God's arms are open; yes, we have to give up ourselves and yield to Him as Lord, but what we give up is of no comparison to what we gain in return. Thus, if God is approachable to us, we can be so to others; we can take risks, set aside our past, and embrace the wonders of what may come.

The Christian life can be a difficult journey! We live in a fallen world corrupted by sin. Consequently, all we do is imperfect, and a struggle. We will make choices that affect the direction in which we proceed in life and in relationships. In so doing, we affect others around us in both positive and negative ways. Yet, when our efforts and motivations are centered upon being righteous, we will be doing as we are called to do, and even be blessed for it. As Christ's disciples, we must be willing to be led by the truth of His Word and by our faith and trust in Him. Everything that is worthy and excellent requires effort, from designing a building, painting a house, or preaching the Word. This journey of difficulty should not discourage us because it will build us up to be much better, stronger, and of better use to God as we put into practice what He puts in us.

So, enjoy it! See it as an adventure from which to learn and grow. Our character will improve and enable us to overcome obstacles and help others through them. Thus, we should make it a point to give Him our best for His glory because He first loved us, and respond to His grace with our gratitude. At the same time, we can take comfort in the fact that He will not give us anything we cannot handle (Philippians 2:10-13; Hebrews 2:10)! So, let us live with excellence and to our best for His glory!

The key to unlocking fear so it opens into contentment is our worship and prayer time. Remember, our solitude in Him builds our ability to connect with others. Our solitude in Him will help remove the doubts and fears that isolate us from others. Sometimes, all we can do is pray; but it is not a last resort. It is our front line and most important defense and is to be our preparation for the weathering of a storm. It will help us build our relationship with Christ so our faith, confidence, and courage will grow. Then, those storms and crises will make us stronger and allow us to help others through them, too. When we fully learn to trust, then we can obey; and that will build our confidence so we will sail across those storm tossed seas of life in confidence as Jesus Christ is there beside us, manning the helm!

How can I become reconnected?

Do your best to come to me quickly, for Demas, because he loved this world, has deserted me and has gone to Thessalonica. Crescens has gone to Galatia, and Titus to Dalmatia. 2 Timothy 4:9-10

We all have the natural tendency to push people away and become caught up in distractions and addictions that detour us from healthy relationships. So, we must see loneliness as a warning light that we need to get with the program of life. We have to be proactive! It all comes down the simple point of *what Christ has done for me*. So, make the determination to see the hope Christ has for you! Be the person who is thankful and humble regardless of the past or potential future. See His abundance, goodness, and love for you! How we respond to the love and grace we receive from Him will determine how we respond to others. How we receive mercy will determine how we dispense forgiveness; how we see His love for us will help us love others, and how we are grateful will help build intimacy with and fullness in Him and in our connections with others.

If we remain in bitterness and hurt, our fears will take over and all potential connections with others will be thwarted, leaving us disillusioned and even suicidal. Do not let this happen to you or others around you. Be the person who makes the call, does the visit, or sends the letter; be the one who extends the hand of friendship; be the one who says *I will be your friend!* Then, you can seek to be connected and pursue the avenues and ways to meet people. Yes, this can be difficult. The prison of loneliness can have the thickest and strongest bars we may ever face. But, remember, you made them and He can break them! When the bars are down, we see others more like Jesus sees them—their struggles and needs, and be more accepting and forgiving.

Keep in mind our prior discussions about unrealistic expectations and focusing on our circumstances and not God's. It comes down to our being willing and able to reach out beyond hurts and fears so we can engage others. Perhaps you are like I was and lack social skills. This is the time to learn and practice getting to know people and letting them know you. It may take time; be patient and continue your hope in Him.

Feel stuck? We need to be the one to initiate the relationship; remember the chapter on friendship! Paul was lonely and he made the determination to do something about it. He was able to stretch beyond his comfort zone and ask for help; he knew his mission, kept his focus on God and the Scriptures, and when his associates scampered off, he made new friends while also seeking out old ones. You, too, must be proactive to escape from the prison of self-seclusion. If you want to meet people, you need to talk to people. Put yourself in new situations where you can meet people, especially where you have an interest or skill and there will be others there the same interests. Seek out past relationships that were good but time and neglect have let go. People-centered activities and hobbies, clubs, associations, church, and small groups can be your best avenues for connection. See a pastor or counseling if you are unable to stretch beyond your circumstances.

As iron sharpens iron, so one man sharpens another. Proverbs 27:17

As a pastor, I have found that developing small groups in my church is essential in this area. Small groups can be the prime platform for establishing and instilling the Great Commandment and the Great Commission that Jesus gave us in Matthew 28:18-20 and Mark 12:29-31. The small group is also the vehicle by which to develop and experience authentic relationships and growing discipleship. This builds a church of authentic community, poured out to His precepts, and existing in relational intimacy and fullness in Him. This is what we are called to emulate from our Lord. Because people will be learning and growing, they will move from personal agendas and pride to growth and service to our Lord. This produces a supportive environment that has love and care, hospitality, and the Spirit impacting the people. This will then foster the engagement of the community and world for the Gospel.

"My people are destroyed for lack of knowledge" Hosea 4:6

Think about these points: *How do we live the Christian life? How do we apply His precepts?* In First Corinthians 11:1, Paul tells us to *follow my example, as I follow the example of Christ.* We are called to be people who learn of His Word and impart that knowledge to others. But, most of us live in a culture that fosters isolation, personal pride, loneliness, individualistic mindsets, hedonism, suspicion, distrust, and the fear of being vulnerable. Thus, we have to put forth an effort to live the Christian life! We have to step up and make the friendships, and not wait for them to come to us. In over 20 years of pastoral ministry, I have found no better way to take what we learn from the church and Word, work it out in our hearts and minds, and make an application with it than in small groups! small groups are essential and necessary in building supportive and meaningful relationships and Bible learning, and they must be a part of every church who seeks to know our Lord and make Him known. It takes an isolated church and a lonesome individual and helps revitalize them in Christ and in the community of interpersonal relationships and life. It helps create a church of real purpose—God's purpose—that is, one of dependence on God and the independence of one another. Without putting forth the effort personally and engaging in a small group, we will fall far short of learning and applying His precepts into our lives and community. We will have a church and a personal life that is fragmented, disconnected, isolated, and meaningless!

Small groups answer the question, *how do I grow in Christ and grow my church?* We grow by growing in Him! Small groups become the hub of learning, care, outreach, and discipleship, and lead in nurturing, encouraging, and in spiritual formation. We all need to have encouragement, connection, advice, and support from a community of Believers who are growing in Him. It should be a place to reflect on our life and situation, build community, encourage accountability, study the Bible and learn to apply it, pray for others, and reach out to the world around us. Thus learning to do life together, and receiving care, discipleship, and knowledge while learning about the ways of God through the Bible and prayer will build us up both as individuals and as a church. A good system of small groups are geared to provide all church members a rewarding benefit from their experiences in the church, and that benefit is their growth and maturity in Him that translates into character and reaching out as His witness!

Jesus Himself was in a small group of twelve. The church got its start in Acts from small groups. This is how our Lord chose to personally model ministry and to launch His church. The early church *devoted themselves* to Jesus' teaching and to one another. It was the small group where the Spirit impacted people and empowered them for ministry. It was the small groups where community and function were formed, even before the persecution came. The Lord blessed them and used them; we have no excuse not to. The church, your church, must have small groups at its core; not a few here and there, but all encompassing for all stages of life and ministry, from youth to the elderly. If you want to grow your church in spiritual maturity (which is far more important than growing numerically, but usually creates numerical growth, too), small groups are the way to go. If you want to personally grow in spiritual maturity, have a place to commune, feel safe, and to share your life by connecting with people, take this plunge and get yourself involved in a small group.

Let the peace of Christ rule in your hearts, since as members of one body you were called to peace. And be thankful. Let the word of Christ dwell in you richly as you teach and admonish one another with all wisdom, and as you sing psalms, hymns and spiritual songs with gratitude in your hearts to God. Colossians 3:15-16

You, and perhaps other people in your church, live in a disconnected and stress-filled world. Relationships are few and fragile and His Word is rarely applied. Without some kind of consistent connection, you cannot effectively grow personally or care for others. You just might stay lonely; and how sad it would be to have lonely people in your church or circle of influence. An opportunity to connect in depth, maturity, or community impact will go unmet. Then the caring, prayers, and support of one another are missed. Ministry and relationships form and accumulate best in small groups. When people are hurting, need direction, or can help others, it comes from the small group. Ministry and impacting the neighborhood comes from the small group. Your church will grow and be used by God through the small group. Small groups are not to replace the church's worship and teaching; rather, they are the participants and conventioneers of the church. Consider a church a convention of small groups united for prayer, worship, instruction, the proclamation of His Word, and synergistic ministry. If the people in your church are disconnected and lonely, then your church is called to make small groups (resources for this are available on our website www.intothyword.org)!

So, why aren't more people doing this to overcome their loneliness or to become more connected? The biggest reason is because they are fearful. Being vulnerable to people who may intentionally or unintentionally betray you is very scary. For some, it is scary to meet new people, go to a stranger's house, or take the time to make such a commitment. In addition, to share your life and woes with a stranger or to be afraid that you may not know the answers and look stupid in front of others is threatening. But, we have to get over our fears and embrace the community. When we share with others, we commune and grow tighter and together, building community and effectual relationships. Yes, people will hurt you; and, *guess what*, you will hurt others, too. But, we still need one another; we need forgiveness, to be willing to forgive others, and to be open and vulnerable. This is a *must* to growing in faith. The main hurdle is YOU and your willingness to more deeply pursue your faith and your relationships. We need one another to grow further in the faith!

So do not fear, for I am with you; do not be dismayed, for I am your God. I will strengthen you and help you; I will uphold you with my righteous right hand. Isaiah 41:10

Understand this as a season; sometimes, we need to be alone and *cocoon* in God's love, but this is just for a time. This state that you are in is temporary; it will not last. There is hope in Christ; His plan for you is still active, no matter how old you are. It only stops when we are called home to eternity. You are not to be on this journey of life alone, and you are not alone in your feelings and hurt! So, do not let despair take over or allow putdowns by negative and uncaring people trap you. Loneliness is a sign that we need something; it is not a sign of weakness or immaturity.

People, especially Christians, are created *from* community *for* community by a triune God. As Christians, we are called to know one another. Just look up *one another* in a concordance and see all of the passages listed. We are made for community; we need community. But, that does not mean it will just magically function. We all have to put in the effort and take the risks. Once we are willing to take the risks, then the time, commitment, and effort to press on will become easier as we see the benefits outweighing the fears. As Christians, we are doing life together. Thus, we need to learn and practice the sharing, learning, caring, and prayer with one another! The primary function is relational—*how do I deal with life? How do I grow by learning His Word and allowing others to help me encounter Christ and others?* The benefits are being able to share your life, learn from the experiences and encounters with God others have had, and to feel a part of God's family. Other benefits are being able to deal with life, stress, better being able to overcome extreme hardships such as the death of a loved one, and help in living a more stable life.

Remember, we are never truly alone when as Christians, we have the Creator and Lord of the universe dwelling within us! Our friends may scamper off, family and others may disown us or die, people may hurt and disappoint us, but our Lord will always be there and will never forsake us!

Heal me, O LORD, and I will be healed; save me and I will be saved, for you are the one I praise. Jeremiah 17:14

Chapter XVII
HOW TO DESTROY A RELATIONSHIP

People will be lovers of themselves, lovers of money, boastful, proud, abusive, disobedient to their parents, ungrateful, unholy, without love, unforgiving, slanderous, without self-control, brutal, not lovers of the good, treacherous, rash, conceited, lovers of pleasure rather than lovers of God—having a form of godliness but denying its power. Have nothing to do with them. 2 Timothy 3:2-5

"How to Destroy a Relationship!" Why would we want to talk about this? This may sound like it is *left field*. Why talk about how to destroy a relationship? Are we not already pretty good at this? Does this subject fit in to how to find and build a better relationship? The answer is, *yes*. Because, if we know what destroys our relationships, we can be on guard to prevent it, just as we need to know how Satan operates so we can buffet an attack and go through spiritual warfare unscarred. It is the same in relationships; we have to know what destroys them so we can guard ourselves and protect others. It is my experience, as a counseling pastor, that most people are very good at destroying relationships, including me. But, what we tend not to be good at is recognizing how and why we do it. We do not realize the subtle ploys that have become habits that imbed like a wedge into each other, thus, pushing others away. In fact, most of us are just too good at taking down good friendships and causing once—good marriages to end in irreconcilable differences. Once harmonious and reconciled, the knowledge of how and why this happens will be one of your great allies to building and keeping healthy relationships effective!

In the course of research that went into the Bible studies, articles, and sermons that preceded this book, and aside from having a degree in psychology, I also interviewed scores of psychologists and counseling pastors, asking them, *What are the main reasons people fight with one another? What are the tactics that keep those fights going? What are the main causes of marriage breakups?* I then looked at my own experiences and compared them to my exegetical research. All I seemed to find from the world of psychology were symptoms. Although these are important to know and deal with, they are not the root causes. After careful research and compiling, I found five key categories of symptoms that tear at the heart of relationships like a cancer. Each of these is rooted in a prime cause. Several years later I stumbled upon a major study that found similar results (Research compiled by Dr. John Gottman, Ph.D. www.gottman.com). Although his marital research has provided outstanding results, insights, and areas for pastors and counselors to be aware of and cover, his findings, I believe, are also just symptoms and not the root of the problem.

So what is the root? *Sin!* Sin is the elephant in the living room that very few people in psychology talk about, yet sin is in every aspect of our human endeavor. Each of these symptoms comes from our sinful nature and pride that are at the root of every conflict and problem we face. Our personal agendas take precedence over God and His precepts and call. This is sin! Thus, our sinful nature creates these symptoms as offensive attacks and defensive countermeasures. They are drummed up to protect us from hurt, isolate us from harm, and protect our fears; yet, all they do is escalate problems and conflict, bringing the very hurt and harm we may have wanted to avoid in the first place.

These five symptoms grow slowly and mutate, then spread to all areas of the relationship under attack until it becomes a pattern for a life and existence of hurt, bitterness, and anger. Yet, as powerful as these symptoms are, they are not the reason for the relationship breakdowns. They just are the wedge that the swinging sledgehammer of pride, anger, and our personal will finally hits. These symptoms are flowing from the cause that creates the hurt and bitterness, which triggers virtually all fights in friendships and marriages. These symptoms, which are so hard to contain and stop, are rooted at one source—our PRIDE. By the way, pride is the quintessential thing God hates the most; see the Scriptures in the back for your proof.

Relationship breakdown is festered by our response from others.

In his pride the wicked does not seek him; in all his thoughts there is no room for God. Psalm 10:4

There are five key aspects which we humans use as a defense mechanism when we come against one another in our relationships. These responses become our arsenal for attacking others so we are protected from their attack. We use them for self-protection by creating offensive measures while destroying others—from simple arguments to total war. These are the root issues from which our behaviors and responses stem. These five responses are:

1. Being Defensive!
2. Being Critical!
3. Being Condescending!
4. Withdrawing from others!
5. Uncontrolled Anger! (which we will tackle in the next chapter)

How often do these defense mechanisms take place in your relationships? How often do you personally engage in one or more of these? Defensiveness, being critical, showing contempt and withdrawal are all formed from our anger, disappointments, and hurt and all rooted in our *pride.* This is a cancer to the living body of relationships. In these negative, dysfunctional responses, we will push God aside and fuel them with our anger and betrayal, thus continuing the cycle of relationship breakdown!!!
When we become aware of these cancerous underpinnings that we all harbor, we can begin to bridle them. In this way, they can be controlled and steered away from harming our loved ones and friends. *How can I bridle these cancerous emotions and attacks?* By knowing who you are in Christ, and by the knowledge that God accepts you in spite of your failures and sin because of His delivered grace. This realization helps us in all aspects of relationship building, so we can choose to be deliverers of His grace to others. By being willing to stop the escalation of relationship breakdown through the exchange of our hurt and anger for love, grace, and forgiveness, our lives will be tremendously more content, joyful, and fulfilling.

But, before we get to the healing, we need to realize that all relationships involve emotions. We have a natural tendency to put up our guard to protect us from getting hurt. These guards have weapons of *relationship mass-destruction* available from the smallest offence to the biggest betrayal. We will launch a first strike with our weapons of *Defensiveness, Contempt, Criticism, and Withdrawal,* often unaware or callused to their effect. We have to understand that our emotional guards involve these weapons. When we start to see as Christ sees, we will realize these weapons are outmoded by His work and supremacy. We do not need them since all they do is cause destruction; they have no building or equipping power. They just indiscriminately destroy, when Christ calls us to build. Christ gives us care and affection; therefore, we have the call to show care and affection for others.

And he is the head of the body, the church; he is the beginning and the firstborn from among the dead, so that in everything he might have the supremacy. Colossians 1:18

God calls us to bear each other's burdens without letting those burdens break us. By understanding the role of restoring, we can pursue restoration rather than the defensiveness of our hurts. We have a tendency to protect our hurts, fears, and wounds from others by attacking them first. In military terms, this is a classic preemptive attack, which is the *attack-before-they-attack-us* approach. However, in relationships, we are not to be at war or in a combative mode; rather, we are to be in a reconciling mode.

THE ROOT OF PRIDE

Pride goes before destruction, a haughty spirit before a fall. Proverbs 16:18

Pride is defined as the attitude that one is superior to another, even to the extent of regarding others with contempt as if they were unworthy of any relation or interaction. Pride shows the basic thinking that *I am better than you are!* Other biblical synonyms for pride are arrogant, insolent, boastful, stiff-necked, and haughty. These aspects of pride clog us up and away from our loving Savior as they restrict the flow of His character into our lives and inhibit goodness from flowing to others through us. It keeps Jesus Christ from being the ultimate plumber and unplugging our spiritual drainpipes. So, all we can do is pour our waste all over the floor of life, and refuse to allow godly characteristics to flow in our relational pipes.

Pride is evil because it unveils and lifts our self-interests and our self-sufficiencies, which seem necessary and good. But, when we are self-sufficient, we will not only fail to see our need for redemption, but also fail to see our need for growth in spiritual matters. Therefore, self becomes the god, and any work of the One True God is muted and put aside. When this happens, all of our relationships—from family to work—will be distorted and eventually utterly destroyed. A person's pride comes between him and God and distorts the Word and work He has for him. It cancels out relationships, growth, and purpose in life. People who practice arrogance and condescension toward others will not surrender to God as Lord. They think of themselves as self-reliant, which is a slap in the face of God. Self-reliance is an *oxymoron* and has no place in healthy relationships!

We need to see the imperative God warns us of in regard to pride. Why? Because we are still in rebellion against His decrees and His best for us when pride rules our thoughts and actions. We cannot see the value nor get a grasp of the promises of God until we surrender our pride and will to His preeminence. Make the determination to be His; do not allow your self-will to be in His way! Allow Christ to take you beyond your hopes and dreams (John 3:5).

Pride creates defensive mechanisms.

A wicked man listens to evil lips; a liar pays attention to a malicious tongue. Proverbs 17:4

Pride combines with our hurt and fears to create our defense-mechanisms. Therefore, our hurts and fears motivate our words and deeds and as hurting people, we hurt other people. If you think this does not apply to you, consider this: do you cover up your frailties by attacking and criticizing others to throw the dogs off your scent? Are you grateful for what Christ has done or do you take it for granted? If you still think you are immune, then you have the problem of pride! As human beings, we get hurt, we have fears, and we all engage in defense mechanisms. The difference is that the mature person, the Christian who wants to please God, will do something about it. That something is the seeking of reconciliation and harmony.

What can I do? Pay attention to yourself and how others react to you. When we are focused on seeing the failings, disappointments, corruption, and deceit in others, usually it is because we are filled with it ourselves, and we do not take the Word of God seriously. What if God judged us as we do others? So, the answer is, *don't!* Don't play these games; relationships are too precious and valuable to destroy them with our whims or hurts. Yet, Christians can be some of the most critical and arrogant people on earth! As

Christians, we need to be an example for Him wherever we are. We must set ourselves above pettiness and let God remove our pride! Let us look at the first four big relationship killers:

Defensiveness

Starting a quarrel is like breaching a dam; so drop the matter before a dispute breaks out. Proverbs 17:14

Do you have a passion to always defend yourself or have an excuse for every occasion? Do you always use the phrase "I" or "me" to the point "we" and "us" never come up? Do you have an excuse for every possible occasion? Are you the type of person who rarely apologizes or admits any fault? Do you ward off people's attacks by attacking them first? Then, you may have a problem with defensiveness! Believe it or not, what you have to say is not more important than hearing what others have to say!

Defensiveness is a weapon that allows you to be negative to others. It fools you into not taking responsibility. This weapon comes into play in our communication by warding off of a question we do not want to answer, or a verbal attack from another person by attacking them first. It permits us to over-explain our position to the determent of the other person. We will not be able to listen, see facts, our see our role in the conflict. It is projecting blame on someone else, causing us to be skeptical of the motives and intentions of others. While the blame is on them, we are ducking out of it ourselves.

When we do this, we will not be able to see positive, alternate options or the hope Christ brings. We will then not allow trust to be built, and will defend ourselves so we will not have to be intimate. It appears to protect us from hurt, but all it does is bring more strife. When we are only seeking responsibility in the other person and commit them to the issue while we ignore them, then no resolution or healing can take place. All this does is pour gas on a fire. This also negates the personal responsibility which God calls us to have. We think we are being proactive and protective, when in fact, we are destroying relationships by using our personal WMD's (verbal Weapons of Mass Destruction).

Proverbs, chapter 17, has some very important instructions for us on how *not* to deal with problems. What are we *not* to do? We are not to be quarrelsome, or in other words, defensive. Being defensive is deliberately or unconsciously attacking another person. We do this by arguing needlessly, making up issues, covering up with pretext and pretense, distorting situations and escalating problems, overreacting, as in *making a mountain out of a molehill*, dominating the other person, being in denial, rationalizing that only we are right, making up situations, and rejecting any reconciliation or ideas from anyone else. Defensiveness can also include intimidation, one-sided conversations, not listening, being emotionally draining on another by only exposing our issues and not caring about theirs, being dictatorial, being in denial, and rationalizing that only we are right.

This basic *diverting-attention-from-ourselves-by-attacking-the-other-person-first* is to protect us from attack. This is a natural defense mechanism that psychologists tell us seeks to protect self from worry that turns into anxiety (which is worry out of control) and stress (the inability to control our life that turns into trauma). We escalate this by causing stress for others. You can see how this could easily spiral out of control; two people can start with a simple misunderstanding and escalate it into a murder. In marriage, this can build and build until the cap off the toothpaste escalates into divorce. I have seen this happen more than once. We keep up the attacks and never take a breather to think the issue through or pray, seeking forgiveness and reconciliation. Our only care is self- protection. Most people who do this may not even know they are doing it. This is why seeking a third party, such as a pastor or counselor to moderate a troubled relationship is essential in uncovering such tendencies.

Defensiveness is a form of selfishness as the concern is only on self and not the other person. We need to see the other person as a child of God, too! We need to see His love for us and them! Then, we can grasp the wonders He has for us. When we are only considering ourselves, we will not see the other person or Christ working in both of us. Seek the application of love and practice it on the other person—regardless of how they treat you. It takes two to tango; when you are the one to sit down, seeking God's promises and love, prayer, and love, then the other person is dancing alone, being the lone carrier of the argument or issue. Then, you can work on yourself and model for them that perhaps they need to do so, too. Remember, this defense mechanism is usually unconsciously done; that is, most people are not aware they are doing it. So, be open to hear instruction from God's Word and from godly people. Then, and only then, will you, by the Spirits leading, humble yourself and stop this malignancy to relationships!

Contempt

Flee the evil desires of youth, and pursue righteousness, faith, love and peace, along with those who call on the Lord out of a pure heart. Don't have anything to do with foolish and stupid arguments, because you know they produce quarrels. And the Lord's servant must not quarrel; instead, he must be kind to everyone, able to teach, not resentful. 2 Timothy 2:22-24

Do you like to consciously or unconsciously, deliberately or instinctively push people with your agenda and issues? Do you like to "rub it in?" Do you think you always know what other people's motives are, or that yours are always better? Do you feel you are entitled to special favor and response from others, even your spouse? Do you ignore the feelings and needs of others and insist on having your own needs fulfilled? Do you feel you have to put others down to make yourself look or feel good? Then, you may be a person who is steeped in condescension.

Contempt is a weapon that cancels out the other person's value, It declares that they are not worthy of you, so you treat them with arrogance and put them down. It is a defensive weapon to protect your insecurities by focusing on the insecurities of others. So, you put them down before they have an opportunity to put you down. This symptom tells you that the thoughts and feelings of the other person are worthless. That way, you are not forced to reach out or take risks. It is usually rooted in low self esteem and not realizing who you are in Christ. This devalues people!

Being condescending is saying that the other person is invalid. This creates frustration and sorrow in another that their thoughts, feelings, and experiences are unimportant. This is to cover-up effective communication with putdowns to elevate your self or protect your feelings. Being unfairly negative or having unfair expectations is extremely damaging to relationships, especially with children. You cannot live your life vicariously through your children or put too much burden on them. They must be loved and encouraged with realistic expectations tempered with the example of love and responsibility from you.

Because having contempt is the attitude of regarding someone else as inferior or worthless, it devalues God's work in them. It is a form of arrogance and pride that turns into your being condescending, showing your disapproval, and being judgmental in that you only see yourself and your personal needs, ignoring the worth that God has given the other person. With this attitude, you will harbor resentment and create divisions—not connections. Contempt is actually mocking another person, making fun of them and putting them down by words and deeds. Their feelings, contributions, and worth are negated by your disrespect and scorn. This is done by always correcting someone just to be superior to them, or treating another person as worthless. This trait can be used against people in authority and even in our view and treatment of God. It is taking our anger, fear or dislike and using this attitude of being condescending as a defense mechanism. Dr. Gottman calls contempt the *sulfuric acid of love*. And, I believe he is totally right; it will dissolve any relationship fast and furiously! In my counseling experiences, I never found this trait in a loving relationship, but only in dysfunctional situations, divorces, and lawsuits!

So, what does God have to say about our being contemptuous? It is not good! In Romans 2:1-16, we are told that those who judge others while disobeying God themselves are inexcusable and will not escape the judgment of God. Being judgmental will not work; it will only backfire on you. Our guilt and sin are personal and individual; thus, our evil desires to judge come from our being self-seeking as opposed to being Christ-seeking. God does not care about our deeds or pedigree, and no one is immune! It is ONLY by what Christ has done that we can be saved. Our sins have been neutered on the cross and covered by His righteousness. Thus, we have been judged by God's standards of holiness with Christ taking our place in judgment (John 5:24). Because of our sin and what Christ did for us, we have no right or basis to judge others.

We have to realize that even though these responses may come from us naturally and we see them as funny on TV, they are not OK in real life . They are disruptive to relationships and a deathblow to a marriage! When we are willing and able to see ourselves engaging in these behaviors, we can commit to prayer and self-discipline to start to get over them. In a healthy relationship, especially a marriage, there has to be a mindset of equality. There is not to be a dominance of one person over another unless it is in the military or a workplace between a boss and employee. Even in these situations, successful relations are keyed by encouragement and compliments. Bringing out the best in another is done with encouragement, not by subjugation.

A person who is contemptuous to others is being judgmental; this is extreme foolishness, because you are, in fact, throwing a boomerang of condemnation that comes back to hit you harder than you threw it. God judges according to truth; we judge according to personal agendas, greed, and misunderstanding. Do you value others in the same way you do yourself? Is the scale balanced?

Criticism

A man of knowledge uses words with restraint, and a man of understanding is even-tempered. Even a fool is thought wise if he keeps silent, and discerning if he holds his tongue. ... Without wood a fire goes out; without gossip a quarrel dies down. Proverbs 17:27-28; 26:20

Do you feel you have to be right, even when you do not have all the facts? Do you have the passion to interrupt? Do you refuse to listen to others? Are you good at finding and picking at the flaws of others? Then you may have a problem with criticism. Criticism is seeking the shortcomings and faults in others and then joyfully exposing them. This, too, comes naturally to fallen humanity. We attack the other person with putdowns, devious remarks, and sayings such as, *you are always*...or, *you never*... Perhaps, we are seeking to be verbally dominant for whatever personal agenda we may have. This is just the escalation of negativity. In a marriage, it can be *putting down* our spouse or not caring how his/her day was. It can also be exhibited by always talking about yourself and never caring or listening to another person. This is being *self-centered* and not *Christ-centered.*

Criticism is the best way to escalate any conflict. This rotten symptom is a weapon that helps create weapons for the other side. It builds *defensiveness* and *withdrawal* armaments in the other person. It is a weapon factory that makes other weapons for both sides! It creates a negative response that keeps escalating back and forth. It can take a minor disagreement all the way up the mountain to become a full-blown conflict. This weapon will not allow a ceasefire or solution, so the circumstances will get worse and worse. It hurts others before they can hurt or continue to hurt you.

Criticism in play is the action that comes from our feeling that the other person is wrong and we are right. This is not the same criticism as to examine something or someone; rather, it is deliberately putting others down. We pick and poke at others like chickens in a henhouse. This comes from our self-centered nature. We tend to criticize others without serious examination, engaging in verbal abuse, discouraging others, giving critical comments, making our disapproval well known, pointing out the faults in others like a joyful game and engaging in physical abuse. Instead of helping someone, we are tearing them down. We have to see that being critical by using our personal agendas to put others down can be very damaging. This leaves emotional scars and broken relationships. Yes, it is easier to critique others than encourage them. However, we are called to encourage and not to discourage. Consider how you feel when someone gives you that critical comment, a comment designed as a quip, or the start or parlay of gossip.

When criticism is in action, we are exercising condemnation. The Bible goes on to say that people who do this are also spreading gossip which means having malicious intentions. Even if you do not start it or do not do it as much as the people who start the gossip in the first place, you are still guilty when you spread it. This is a form of malice and leads to destruction of persons and property; it is just as bad as if a fire destroyed a home or even a church. We quickly rationalize that it is OK to gossip and do whatever it takes to put that person down, even a family member or spouse. It can escalate to the point that we give credence to every rumor, story, or criticism that springs up about them. It does not make any difference if it is true or not, because, since we do not like them, we rationalize that it is OK. When this happens we develop trust for falsehoods and become nonchalant with the truth. Gossip destroys and erodes trust to the point that we do not care if it is true or not because we feel no responsibility for its truthfulness. This is also a form of hatred.

Criticism creates strife and its only purpose is to treat people in a condescending and damaging manner. It hurts others and leaves us depleted and resentful. The result of this gossip being spread is an atmosphere of discontentment and distrust. We will miss the mark that Christ has for us. This is a lesson for all of us; we all have skills and issues that we need to work on in our spiritual walk with the Lord. I do not believe we, as Christians, will ever reach full perfection; actually, God does not call us to be totally perfect. However, God does call us to be our best and bring out the best in others. When we refuse to be encouraging, all we succeed in doing is criticizing and, in turn, hurting Christ, His people, and ourselves.

Good and positive communication is a powerful builder of relationships while criticism destroys relationships. (*Fake listening* or ignoring it yet saying nothing does nil to help you!) Be real and be sincere. Do not keep bringing up past hurts, rehashing and trying to manipulate others by guilt, toying with feelings, or attacking others personally as well as their families. If you keep bringing up the same arguments and flaws in others, you will never solve them. You will, however, be causing abuse, the reverse of God's call for the Christian.

Remember, people need to be listened to; this is a key, if not the most important component of healthy relationships. The old adage is so true; *people will not care what you say until they know that you care.* Showing criticism is showing that you do not care!

Withdraw

I have told you these things, so that in me you may have peace. In this world you will have trouble. But take heart! I have overcome the world. John 16:33

Do you hate to get into fights and conflict? That is good! What about hiding yourself from them so you never have to deal with them? What about having unexpressed feelings and distancing yourself from people? Then, perhaps you have a problem with *withdrawal*. When you remain isolated and show no signs that you care (even if you do), then you convince the other person that he/she is not important, and you have lost the relationship. Overly clinging to a person is the opposite of withdrawing which is also dysfunctional; it is called *codependency*. You need to give the other person some space.

Withdrawal is a form of avoidance and the unwillingness to solve issues and/or explain your feelings. It is not giving up; rather it is a first strike weapon that prevents and disrupts communication. We do this by not listening, not caring, or getting up and leaving the person. It is a way to not participate so you can "turn off" yourself during a disagreement.

This will keep the person who uses withdrawal from engaging in important discussions by physically and/or mentally turning the other person off. This is to prevent their involvement and to protect what they feel is more important than their feeling or fears. Withdrawal is a form of *passive/aggressive behavior*, to confront an attack or to initiate an attack oneself. It is a form of rejection that seeks peace but only brings further conflict. This is basically *stonewalling* another person so they are forced to chase us. People engage in withdrawal because of the fear of loss or of criticism, or to avoid the contempt and disapproval of another. To ignore someone is retreating from the fight as well as the reconciliation. This is one of the best ways to escalate a problem or argument. This is done by not talking, avoiding eye contact, and refusing to talk about the problem (hoping to bring resolution), or to seek opportunities to heal. Withdrawal focuses on the other person, and they become angry because they cannot draw us out. We attack by closing ourselves off from others. This creates isolation; we may feel protected, but in actuality, we hinder any relationship growth and even cause relationships to fail. Remember, it takes two to tango. If one refuses to, then the dance will not continue—a relationship will not continue.

"You are the salt of the earth. But if the salt loses its saltiness, how can it be made salty again? It is no longer good for anything, except to be thrown out and trampled by men. Matthew 5:13

Why do we withdraw? As in the other defensive mechanisms, this is a form of protection; here, however, it is mainly the act of protecting ourselves from disappointments while cutting our selves off from opportunities. We need to be willing and able to come out of our hiding, learn to deal with the conflict, and be willing to actively listen because the healing can only begin when we are in good communication. When we realize that Jesus overcame the world and paid our dept, we have no need to withdraw, for we are complete in Him.

Just think this through; what are the buttons people push that cause you the most alarm and harm? Usually it is when someone is being defensive toward you. They are not taking responsibility, nor are they listening to you. It is as if they are attacking you without cause or reason, or are overreacting and you have no opportunity to make the peace, explain it, or work it out. Now, look at what happens to you when a loved one treats you with contempt. How do you feel? He/she is actually treating you as though you are not worthy of his/her time or effort, or he/she sees self as superior. What happens when your best friend is always being critical towards you? You probably will not stay friends long, will you? What happens when your coworkers do not include you in their plans or conversations, they withdraw and have little or nothing to do with you, or they do not even respond. Now, place all this in a marriage situation where each one of these comes into play. Perhaps he/she is critical and you withdraw; he/she treats you with contempt so you retaliate by being defensive—and so on and so on. Then, the ammunition is replenished by each blow you receive until you see no hope for peace talks and suddenly you are in full-blown war, alone, lonely, bitter, or very glad they have gone, but you are left with your wounds. They hurt you so you hurt them back; you hurt them first because you do not want to be hurt and so on and so on. It does not have to be this way!

Getting over it

If anyone thinks he is something when he is nothing, he deceives himself. Each one should test his own actions. Then he can take pride in himself, without comparing himself to somebody else, for each one should carry his own load. Galatians 6:3-5

All of these defense mechanisms are rooted in our self-centeredness. Do you struggle with self-centeredness? If so, you should take careful note that this mindset is one of the best ways to find the wrath of God! This is something you may not want to experience! We have to know there is only one God and, guess what? You are not Him! A Christian must practice what he preaches. We cannot be *two-faced*, doing one thing and saying another. If you like to do this or find comfort in it, you need to know that this is a great way to bring up dysfunctional children! This is a great way to destroy the work of God in your church. It is also a great way to keep people away from you. But, of course, this should *not* be your goal. Self-centeredness only makes you lose out on life's precious opportunities. Now, we need to ask ourselves, *Do I do this? Am I self-centered? Do I condemn others for what I do in secret?* If so, what are you going to do about it?

Paul's point is this; everyone should know better than to sin! Healthy relationships cannot exist in the atmosphere of self-centeredness! When we engage in these behaviors, we are putting down the very people for whom God died on the cross. He gave His life, in agony and pain, to redeem, and yet we find it necessary to put down that same person. We have to see this as heinous. It is unproductive, destructive, and slaps our Lord in the face, saying, in essence, that we know better than He does!

What can you do to stop these defense mechanisms of pride and self-centeredness from ruining your relationships? Start to be aware of how you come across to others. Listen to positive feedback as well as negative. Ask a friend or pastor for advice, and be willing to listen without engaging in negative attitudes. Realizing that you are engaging in disruptive behaviors is half the battle; the other half is much easier.

Start to consciously replace your negative feedback with positive comments. Start to use compliments and be encouraging without faking it. See yourself as a diplomat for Christ and conform your attitude likewise. See others as Christ sees them—as His child and loved by Him. So, when you have a concern or a conflict, slow down, observe your attitude and behaviors, and start to listen to the other person. Then, repeat what they said and give them positive feedback. Seek the effective repair of your relationship and not the escalation of the hurt or anger. Then, deal with the concern in a loving way. Place the focus on the situation and not the person, validating them as a person for whom you care while seeking forgiveness and reconciliation. See the "replacement words" in Chapter V, *Understanding the Importance of Being Good.*

Consider how you use personal pronouns such as *you never, you always, you should, you cannot…* Simply replacing "you" with "I" and "we" will do wonders to your relationships. Such as, *I would, I like, I love, I feel, I hear, how might I …* And, *we should, we can, we could, we need, in what ways might we.* By taking the "you" away you place "yourself" into the conversation. Taking the "you" out brings you in! You will be able to remove blame so the focus is on reconciliation. You will be able to remove contempt because you have to bow yourself to the other person. You will be able to remove criticism as you cannot criticize with an "I". You will then be able to remove defensiveness because the wall made of the bricks of "you" has been torn down. Then you can be a builder and equipper, not a person who pushes others away!

Who can discern his errors? Forgive my hidden faults. Keep your servant also from willful sins; may they not rule over me. Then will I be blameless, innocent of great transgression. Psalm 19:12-13

We already all have way too much criticism in our lives from our coworkers, bosses, teachers, parents, siblings, friends, the media, and church members; there is no need to add to it. The key is to stay away from judgments, seeking fault in others, and putdowns, and focusing on goodness. Then we will be able to praise, encourage, and respect our spouse and the people around us, earning their trust because we make them feel safe and secure. We will be building our communication through being **respectful.** When we are being **r**esponsible, we are **e**volving our relationship, becoming more **s**incere, learning **p**atience, finding **e**njoyment and **c**ontentment, and building **t**enderness, **f**aithfulness, **u**nderstanding, and **l**istening skills. This all spells respectful! We can build this security by speaking the truth in love, encouraging, and listening.

When we do not put a stop to our avoidances and putdowns of others all this will do is boomerang back at us. Remember relationships are communal and continual.

Do I always have to do this? What about if the other person is pushing too much? If you are in an abusive relationship, get out of it, even if it is a marriage. Abuse is physical, mental, and spiritual. It is hitting, manipulating, and the refusal to stop and get help. Get out and get help; then, after the abuse is over and you are confident it will not recur, then reconcile. Make sure you have a trusted and trained counselor helping you in the process! Keep in mind the percepts we discussed in Chapter XI, "How to set Boundaries."

The bottom line in stopping relationship dysfunction is to know we do not need to always be defending and attacking others, whether it is a legitimate betrayal from a trusted friend or spouse, or a misunderstanding. Why? Because, our true security is in Christ; when we realize this, we can put up with the dysfunction and negativity of others, and reduce our fears so we can pursue relationships and their healing.

Don't allow disappointments to consume you.

Whatever happens, conduct yourselves in a manner worthy of the gospel of Christ. Then, whether I come and see you or only hear about you in my absence, I will know that you stand firm in one spirit, contending as one man for the faith of the gospel without being frightened in any way by those who oppose you. This is a sign to them that they will be destroyed, but that you will be saved—and that by God. Philippians 1:27-28

Disappointments can be defined as the collisions between our expectations and our experiences, ignoring the signposts of God's promises. Our expectations will collide with our experiences and then create a life wrecked by self-pity and resentment. Or, it can lead to a triumphant life. The choice is ours and the key is where we look to for our hope! This is about our circumstances and how we look at our Lord. How we see adversity and His sovereignty will totally affect how we learn from and deal with it.
Unanchored stress and disappointment, along with detachment from looking to God, will prevent us from seeing His signposts of precepts. We cannot just expect God to get us through without any effort on our part. To grow, we have to struggle and work it out. It is the struggle that helps us, that builds us, and that forms us. Without it, there is no growth, real impacting faith, honest character, genuine patience, or maturity—and thus, unhealthy relationships result.

We can grow beyond our natural tendency to put others down by focusing on what Christ did for us and realizing He did that for others too, even the one(s) we seek to *put down*. The antidote to criticism is the continual practice of encouragement. When we decide to bring comfort and consolation to others rather than condescending comments and retorts, we are actually putting courage into another person. Consider that when we put down a friend, a loved one, or a spouse, we are actually saying *you are not worthy, you are not loved, and you are not accepted or appreciated.* We are actually called to build up our friends, coworkers, and spouse. We are called to make them feel loved, accepted, and appreciated. We are to show Christ's love, not our disapproval.

The Bible gives us clear direction on how we are to keep our attitude and mouths under God's direction and not ours. The book of Proverbs gives us many verses that show us our human weaknesses and fallen state that seeks out the destruction of one another instead of building one another up as God desires us to do.

Turning from Destroying to Building Healthy Relationships

Blessed are you when people insult you, persecute you and falsely say all kinds of evil against you because of me. Rejoice and be glad, because great is your reward in heaven, for in the same way they persecuted the prophets who were before you. Matthew 5:11-12

Our behaviors are reflections of our motives, each one leading to another, as a chain reaction. By cutting the top of the link of the sin chain, we can remove most of the problems we cause, experience, and endure from others in our personal life, church, and even society at large. The inward choice to hold onto dysfunction and anger will lead to murder, maybe not literally, but as a destroyer of relationships. And, in God's eyes, relationships are the most important things in our lives—besides Him!

We have a call to keep our relations healthy by being people who are willing to relinquish pride and seek forgiveness and reconciliation. This is essential before we can go to God. We are to seek resolution to problems quickly, as they come up. When we do not, they fester, get worse, and *kill* the relationship. So, be a person who is willing to reconcile and to solve problems, not escalate them—one who will do all in your power to end them! Do not neglect your motives or the root causes of broken relationships, sin, and the murder of what God has given you.

You can stop the escalation of hurling verbal weapons that destroy relationships. You have the call and the power to stop the misunderstandings, depression, anger, hurt, frustration, and fears. How? By understanding that Christianity is about yielding—yielding to God—and placing Him and others first. Thus, there is no need to hold the high ground in an argument for attack purposes. Rather, surrender your ground for a common peace. This does not mean that you should be a doormat, letting people walk all over and manipulate you. Remember the section on boundaries. This does not mean you are being a coward, but rather a person of maturity! This is about placing Christ first as Lord over all. Life is not always about you; it is always about Him—Christ as Lord!

By being a person who seeks reconciliation, we will avoid needless strife and stress in our lives—especially in the church. How sad it is when secular courts have to go in and resolve deputes between brothers in the Lord! Having an unforgiving attitude is fatal to worship; we cannot truly worship God with a heart of anger, contempt, and/or bitterness! It is an extreme insult to Him when we seek to worship Him in that state. This attitude will have lasting consequences into judgment and eternity!

Don't you know that you yourselves are God's temple and that God's Spirit lives in you? If anyone destroys God's temple, God will destroy him; for God's temple is sacred, and you are that temple. 1 Corinthians 3:16-17

What can we do? We need to yield to the knowledge and trust of God's goodness as well as His supremacy and right of judgment. It is imperative that we live what we preach. Being a hypocrite is a disgusting obsession in the face of our loving and gracious Lord as well as in our witness to others! We need to receive the offering of His grace ourselves and be willing and able to give grace to others. We must commit to use His goodness as a guide on how to treat others. We need to feel sorrow for our miss-actions and compassion towards others for theirs within reason; there is no license to keep on sinning. God is generous with His grace, so we should be generous toward one another and be thankful. Finally, if we refuse to see His goodness and refuse to turn from sin, we are acting with ultimate contempt to our loving Lord! Thus, our relationships will not be healthy!

Remember the importance of integrity; keep your promises, especially to a spouse and children. Remember the place and purpose of humor; it is to lift others up, never to bring them down. It must not be used to cover feelings or as an instrument used to withdraw from others by using jokes instead of real words of communication.

Make the decision and then commit to making your relationships work, especially with a family member or in a marriage. Make sure you expose the positive! Tell someone when they have done something good, especially a child! Stop the escalation of "button pushing" and inciting the other. You have the power in Christ to stop this cascade of relational dysfunction. Remember, you are not responsible for how they treat you; however, you are responsible for how you treat them! You are the bearer of hope—His Hope. You are the temple of the Holy Spirit, so act accordingly! Of course, if the relationship is too dysfunctional, seek qualified help and do not place yourself in a compromising situation or in danger. Not all relationships will work, and that is OK! The exception is that if you are married, you are called to make it work unless there are biblical grounds not to. You also need to recognize there will be disappointments and setbacks in reconciliation. It takes patience, tact, and a lot of prayer to rebuild from the hurts and fears you may have experienced. Remember that others have had them, too!

Jesus knew that the Father had put all things under his power, and that he had come from God and was returning to God; so he got up from the meal, took off his outer clothing, and wrapped a towel around his waist. John 13:3-4

Chapter XVIII
HOW TO DEAL WITH ANGER

Brothers, if someone is caught in a sin, you who are spiritual should restore him gently. But watch yourself, or you also may be tempted. Carry each other's burdens, and in this way you will fulfill the law of Christ. Galatians 6:1-2

The problems we face in life will often lay the groundwork for how we mature and deal with life. In the midst of these will be our response to our circumstances which can either erupt into anger or be smoothed over by love. It is all about how we choose to deal with problems. Thus, we need to be aware that problems are coming toward us right now. We are either in a problem, going through multiple problems, and/or getting out of one problem just to be headed into another one. We have a choice of how to handle it and that choice will either benefit us and those around us, or tear those around us apart, leaving everyone helplessly hurt and destitute. The choice is ours; we can either be a destroyer or a builder!

The four symptoms discussed in the previous chapter will grow slowly and mutate if we do not become aware of and deal with them. When we neglect our weapons, they will build and spread to all areas of our relationships. Anger will be the catalyst that grows these defense-mechanism weapons. Anger will be synergized to arm and dispatch them. Then, these defense mechanisms will attack people until they become a pattern in our life and existence, a life of hurt, bitterness, and anger. When we are aware of these devastations our anger can cause—the anger all of us harbor—we can keep it under control. In this way, they can be controlled and steered away from harming loved ones and friends. As I have stated before, the key to control is in knowing who you are in Christ and the knowledge that God accepts you in spite of your failures and sin, because He delivered you. This realization helps in all aspects of relationship building so we can choose to be deliverers of His grace to others.

When you were dead in your sins and in the uncircumcision of your sinful nature, God made you alive with Christ. He forgave us all our sins. Colossians 2:13

We can take great comfort that He who overcame the world can help us overcome our issues, even our anger! God, end to end through His Word, gives us a roadmap of how these symptoms cause mass destruction to His church. Keep in mind that the church is not an institution or a building; it is His people. These endless cycles of abuse we do to one another has to stop at the foot of the cross. Ephesians tells us anger is at the root, and anger comes from our pride being hurt (Ephesians 1:7; 4:25-27). When we do not stop, we are actually grieving His Holy Spirit! This means we are causing God to be sorrowful and hurt. Our hurts hurt Him because we are hurting ourselves and His other people, too! He loves and cares for us and desires us not to hurt or be hurt. God knows we will be hurt by others; He knows we will become angry, as He has been angry with our sin. But, He is saying *do not sin in your anger*. That means, let it stop at the end of the day so it does not erode into defensiveness, contempt, criticism, or withdrawal as the hurt continues to fester. We can even use our anger as a warning.

Pride the Root of Anger

To fear the LORD is to hate evil; I hate pride and arrogance, evil behavior and perverse speech. Proverbs 8:13

The passage in Matthew 5:17-26 starts a series of applications for us to learn how to deal with the harshness of life. Why does Jesus lay down such stern pronouncements? Because God's law is a reflection of God's purity and holiness, and because He is a God of details. He gives us specific issues that are to show root causes of sin and unrighteousness. Jesus cuts right to the issue of pride and arrogance, the quintessential thing God hates most, and the root cause of all sin, including murder. Jesus uses the word *reca* which means, "empty-headed one." This is a Hebrew colloquialism for *contempt*; He is calling prideful people *stupid*. Is this harsh? Check out the Scripture references in the back for yourself.

Let us look at a few key phrases in the Matthew passage, as Jesus gives us pronouncements on how to handle ourselves in light of anger and pride. Look at the phrase "without a cause." This means a right or just cause where anger would be OK when there is unrepentant sin from the other party. God is just in being angry with us. But, it is not OK for us to escalate that anger so it harms others. Another phrase is, "you fool." This refers to verbal abuse and swearing. The Pharisees had very specific words and word usages that were considered wrong and to be avoided; thus, they would say it was OK to swear by or at the Temple but not at the offering, or at a particular person but not other Pharisees. Jesus countermands them by saying **all** foul and harmful language is wrong. This should cause us to take an inventory on how we use language and our mouth—to edify, or to put down—and what Christ expects of our words.

Our refusal to deal with sin through repentance will have lasting and dire consequences, both here on earth and for eternity to come! We must be aware of the serious, destructive nature of pride and anger! The inward choice to hold onto anger will destroy relationships. In God's eyes, relationships are the most important things in our lives besides Him! Do not ignore your motives and the root causes of broken relationships, sin, breakups, breakdowns— even of murder; it all results from our pride.

Jesus gives us a word picture—*agree with your adversary*—that gives us an image of God's Heavenly court and how He reconciled Himself to us. Therefore, when we refuse to reconcile, it is an extreme insult to Him. We have a call to keep our dealings with others healthy by being people who are willing to relinquish pride, and seek forgiveness and reconciliation. This is essential before we can go to God. This should cause us to ask ourselves, *what good is it to ask for forgiveness or help from Christ if we are unwilling to do such a small thing for someone else?*

Jesus is referring to a contrast from the minor debt imprisonment like small claims court of today (although you could be held until you repaid what you owed, and your family could be sold for it) to the Sanhedrim, which was like our Supreme Court. When we have a grip on how our pride functions and what causes us to be angry, creating those symptoms of contempt, criticism, defensiveness, and withdrawal, we will be willing and able to seek resolution to our problems and conflicts quickly, as they come up. When we do not, they fester, get worse, and kill the relationship. So, be a person who is willing to reconcile, and to solve problems, not escalate them, doing all in your power to end the conflict (Ephesians 4:26-27)!

Why does Jesus use such impacting and powerful language to make His point? Because, He calls us to distinction! By being a person who seeks reconciliation, we will avoid needless strife and stress in our lives—especially in our marriages and the church. How sad it is when secular courts have to go in and resolve deputes between brothers in the Lord! Jesus is also calling to our attention that having an unforgiving attitude is fatal to worship; we cannot truly worship God with a heart of pride, anger, contempt, or bitterness! When we seek to worship Him in that state, it too is an extreme insult to Him! This attitude will have lasting consequences into eternity and judgment! Jesus calls us to deal with our pride and the anger that so often leads to murder in various forms, from literally killing someone to destroying relationships and escalating small problems into big ones, simply because our pride is in the way. If we truly desire to be His disciples, we will be as committed to reconciling with others as He is with us (John 3:5; 1 Peter 1:22-23)!

Is anger controlling you or are you controlling it?

A patient man has great understanding, but a quick-tempered man displays folly. Proverbs 14:29

If you want to destroy a relationship fast and furiously, allow your anger to get the best of you and let it flow, unhindered. Your good relationships will disappear or become totally dysfunctional and you may even end up dead or in prison. This is not God's best plan for you! So, do you have your temper tempered? Is your anger controlled? Here is how you can find out. Take a careful look at Galatians 5: 22-23 as compared to Galatians 5:19-21. Now ask yourself:

1. How do I exhibit anger, in a righteous way, when I have to?
2. What can I do to develop a better control over my temper, so that I will value people rather than allowing them to annoy me?
3. What blocks the control of anger from working and being exhibited in me?
4. How can I control my anger so that *goodness* functions better, stronger, and faster, even in times of uncertainty and stress?

Righteous Anger

For by the grace given me I say to every one of you: Do not think of yourself more highly than you ought, but rather think of yourself with sober judgment, in accordance with the measure of faith God has given you. Romans 12:3

Can anger be a "good character?" Yes, when it is *constrained*! The Bible tells us that it is OK to be angry, but not to allow it to cause us to sin! Jesus saw His house of worship and prayer turned into a market, and modeled to us the correct way to channel our hostility in fervent action. Anger can either be a solution or a real problem, depending on how we handle it!
What happens when our anger goes un-tempered? We turn it into bitterness, resentment, and hostility. These become evil, rotten fruits when anger is unhitched from our temper and control. They will harden our hearts, and cause us to become people who do not forgive, filled with all of the various defense mechanisms, empowered further as resentfulness, contempt, defensiveness, bitterness, critical nature, and withdrawal become the dominating forces of our personality. They kill, they cause wars and hatred, they destroy relationships and society, and, they put an end to our effectiveness in being a reflection of Christ's character and call.

When we get angry, we have to ask if there is a just cause for it; if not, it becomes a possibly dangerous and volatile situation. It will soon become sin, as we lose our control and our temper. We are called to stay in control of our temper, which the Bible calls to *be sober,* and under *self-control!* Self-control is the governor to our anger, and these two characters must work in unison, lest we lose the soberness of our temper, as well as eventually losing the other characters such as joy and patience. When we have self-control, anger can give us the motivation to resolve problems, respond to injustice, get God's point across, or get our attention so we move in a better direction. Anger can convict us of sin and place us back on God's path.

When we experience disappointments, frustrations, and hurts, we come face to face with anger, because anger is a response to our circumstances. Thus, when we are *let down,* we get angry. We have to ask, *how do we handle disappointments?* If we don't, we will lose control of our temper, and become representatives of the ways of the world and the Devil, not Christ. We will cause destruction to His church, to His people, and to all those around us! We need to remember that people will always disappoint us, which will cause us frustration and hurt—period! We cannot expect others to always treat us justly. Where our expectations or hopes are not realized, when we do not get what we want, or fail to attain our goals, there will be anger. Pain and hurt that are inflicted upon us will cause anger. Disappointments create frustrations which lead to hurt. Each one of these is impacting to our emotions, and each one is codependent on the other, as each one will cause the other two to flare up. Each one can quickly tilt our temper into uncontrolled anger. When we are wise to our circumstances and have our eyes upon Him, we will have a better grip on our temper.

The key to handling anger is the ability to look past the annoyance, pain, and hurt we experience. Then, we can seek resolve to the issue in the framework of Galatians 5:22-23, and not Galatians 5:19-21. This is done by effective communication, understanding, and seeking reconciliation. We need to ask ourselves, *with God's help, how can I keep myself from being overcome with anger*—even *when family and friends push my buttons, or provoke me?* We can take an inventory of our life, and ask a mentor or pastor to help set up a system to warn us when our anger is starting to override our temper control. It is to be a time of prayer. When we keep those who "bug" us in prayer, we can have a better control and response in good, Christ-like character. If we do not handle our response to our circumstances in the right way and we allow the pain to overwhelm us to the point that it controls our emotions and character, then, we will be unable to embrace healing.

We can warn ourselves of when our anger starts to override our character by consciously being aware of our thoughts, motivations, and feelings before we say a word. Instead of escalating your anger, try explaining why you are hurt and deal with that. Seek out how the other person feels before you speak, then share your feelings and thoughts in a manner consistent with the Fruit of the Spirit. Self-control will help develop discipline so we can handle fear, antagonism, and even disillusionment. If not, we will betray relationships and the way we model our Lord. This will accumulate, increasing the anger, until it builds into bitterness and resentment, totally cutting us off from life, and even God! None of the other characters will be able to function.

Here are some tips for handling anger

"In your anger do not sin": Do not let the sun go down while you are still angry, and do not give the devil a foothold. Ephesians 4:26-27

When we allow anger to control us, it is like being blindfolded and stuffed into a car trunk by hoodlums; it is a kidnapping of our character and maturity. It takes us away to a distant place where pain rules. We are in control of those hoodlums; we can get ourselves of out the trunk of despair and into His Light so we do not create the distance and pain.

How can we stop anger from kidnapping us? By simply knowing what causes us to get angry. Why does such a situation or person anger us? Be aware of it. These symptoms cause the most anger, which are created by anger. It is an unending cycle unless you choose to end it. Defensiveness means *I must defend myself from attack*. It also means *I do not like it when others are being defensive with me because...* Contempt means *I will put this person down so they do not hurt me*. It also means *when someone is being contemptuous with me I hate that because...* Criticism means *I can cut others down so they do not hurt me. I hate people criticizing me because... I withdraw from a situation so I do not have to deal with the hurt. I am hurt by others/ withdraw because...* The classic question is *why do I feel this way?* Knowing why these symptoms hurt you and why you use these weapons will help you understand the bigger picture in the light of Scripture. Then you will be able to predict what you will do so you can deal with it. Being in prayer and understanding the precepts of these passages will be your biggest help.

1. Anger is a natural defense reaction we all have, so be sure you handle it as God calls you to. Resolve it quickly (Ecclesiastes 7:9; Ephesians 4:26)!
2. Anger can help you protect yourself, but make sure it is not your fuel to rationalize yourself out of your responsibility (1 Samuel 31:4)!
3. It is OK to be angry; it is how you handle it that matters. Try to spend time in prayer, and read the Psalms to calm you down! Go for a walk (do not take a drive!) or exercise to help release your stress. Make sure you are praying for those causing you frustrations (Acts 24:16).
4. Focus on Christ and His interests, not your own. Place your anger in His management (Philippians 2:4).
5. Focus on the root cause of the anger, not the person or situation (Proverbs 29:11)!
6. Ask yourself, *have I analyzed the circumstances correctly, or am I overreacting?* As a pastor, I would say that 95 percent of people overreact!

7. Ask for help from an impartial friend, counselor, or pastor to help you through it. Make sure you do not aim your anger at them (Matthew 5:23-24)!

8. Ask yourself, *why am I angry? Why do I feel this way? What I did I do to spur this on? Why am I threatened? What are my "hot buttons," the things that cause me to be excessively angry? Will my anger be a benefit or a hindrance? Am I focused on God or my expectations and comfort? How will my anger benefit my spiritual growth, my witness, and God's call in my life?* There is a bigger picture and reason to life than what you may be feeling (Proverbs 15:18; 29:22)!

9. Seek what your part is in it, and resolve it. Do not rationalize everything as a personal attack upon you. You will do far better to focus on the problem—not the people or yourself (Matthew 7:1-5).

10. Perhaps, God is using you to confront someone; if so, do it with tact (Proverbs 15:1; Ephesians 4:15-25).

11. Realize that sometimes there is no outlet for your anger because it could hurt someone more than help. However, you can always go to God with it. You can also try to write it down in a journal (Psalm 10:1-18; 1 Peter 5:6-7)!

12. Do you have unconfessed sin? We all do; so, repent! Unconfessed sin will quickly become rationalized and projected onto others, which will fuel your insecurity and anger (Matthew 7:11; 2 Corinthians 5:7)!

13. Anger can teach us about ourselves, our weaknesses, and areas we need to improve in, as well as how we treat events and people around us. Anger will show real love. The key is being able to look at yourself honestly, at what you need to "put off" and, to "put on." So, seek Christ, and improve by His precepts working in you (Proverbs 14:17; 29:11; Ephesians 4:22-24: 1 Peter 4:8)!

14. Anger can spur on forgiveness, the essential component to healing relationships (Matthew 5:43-46; 6:12; Ephesians 4:32-5:2).

15. Let Scripture guide you in how you handle yourself, not the waves of your emotions (Matthew 18:15; Romans 12:17-21; Colossians 3:16)!

16. You cannot change people; so, keep your focus on the power of Christ which can change lives and attitudes (Philippians 4:13).

17. Anger is no excuse to lose control of your emotions or to put others down. Learn how to react more slowly and see the situation from a bigger perspective (Proverbs 14:29; Ephesians 4:32; Psalm 4:4; 103: 11-12).

18. Never let anger turn into hatred or bitterness. If you do, you will find yourself far away from God's will (Proverbs 16:14; Zephaniah 3:8; James 1:19, 20)!

19. People will disappoint you, and at times be better than you! Be aware that jealousy, unforgiveness, and envy will incite your anger. Expect it, and have a plan to handle it (Proverbs 3:31; 6:32-35; 23:17; 27:4).

20. When a bomb is dropped on you, do not hang on to it; let it go, or it will explode! You have to come to a point where you let the anger go. If not, it may remain repressed until it explodes at a later, inopportune time, or, it will fester inside you, building up bitterness (Proverbs 10:18).

21. You may not be able to change your situation, but you can change yourself. Letting anger go can only happen from a growing and/or mature relationship with Christ. You cannot do it alone (Proverbs 29:11; Hebrews 4:12)!

22. How you handle anger is directly related to how you understand your relationship with Christ. This will shape your view of people and events and build the maturity to handle all that life throws at you. Thus, time spent in His Word and in prayer will shape you greatly and make you one who behaves as a wise person, and not the fool of Proverbs fame. If you want to change your feelings, then you need to change your thinking (Romans 12:2)!

23. A lot of times we become angry because we are selfish or have skewed ideas or expectations of God. His concern is for our growth and maturity, not our wealth or comfort. When we change our thinking, we will change our feelings (Romans 12; 2 Corinthians 5:16-19)!

24. Learn to trust and have confidence in God and not in your situation. Our security is in Christ and nothing else (Psalm 23:4; 27:1-14; Proverbs 1:7; 3:3-10; Hebrews 11:6; James 1:17)!

25. Remember this important point; God uses people and circumstances to improve your character. So, make the most of your harsh circumstances and surrender yourselves to Christ as Lord (Galatians 2:20-21; 5:16; 1 Peter 4:12-16)!

Jesus calls us to deal with our anger that so often leads to murder in various forms, from literally killing someone, to destroying relationships and escalating small problems into big ones, because our pride is in the way. If we truly desire to be His disciple, we will be as committed to reconciliation as He is!

When we find ourselves angry, we are to look to our Lord through His Word and in prayer. Think of the example of a red light on the dashboard of a car warning us of a potential breakdown. When the lights are ignored, a simple fix averted will soon become an expensive, exhausting problem. Do not allow your anger to get out of control and become an exhausting problem! We are not to let our pride be hurt or allow other people to threaten us with potential hurt. Because relationships sometimes hurt, people will hurt you and you will hurt others. We must know this and deal with it so we do not escalate the hurt. This is what it means to guard your heart (Proverbs 4:23). It is OK to feel hurt and anger; it is not OK to allow your hurt to hurt others. Do not let anger to be your anchor! When we allow anger to get out of control we create those weapons of defensiveness, contempt, criticism, and withdrawal. To learn how to forgive and move on is essential so these weapons will not be used!

"Anyone can become angry—that is easy. But to be angry with the right person, to the right degree, at the right time, for the right purpose, and in the right way—this is not easy (Aristotle)."

We have to beware that anger kills! It kills all relationships including marriages, partnerships, friendships, churches, and can literally become homicide. Our behaviors are reflections of our motives, each one leading to another, as a chain reaction. By cutting the top of the link of the sin chain, we can remove most of the problems we cause, experience, and endure from others in our personal life, church, and even society at large.
Consider this; murder just does not happen. Something leads up to it——and that *something* is the sin and uncontrolled anger we all have.

Let us look at what Scripture has to say about the symptoms that come from our pride and anger.

They pour out arrogant words; all the evildoers are full of boasting. Psalm 94:4

The root of defensiveness, contempt, criticism, and withdrawal, stemming from anger, is our arrogance and pride. We create these weapons of defensiveness, contempt, criticism, and withdrawal when we:

1. Desire to be humorous or sarcastic, not realizing how we are coming across to others (Proverbs 26:18, 2 Samuel 6:20).
2. Desire that we know better than others; even if we do, it is never an excuse to put others down (Proverbs 18:2).
3. Desire an argument or thrive on conflict; we should never seek attention through conflict or strife (2 Timothy 2:23-24; Proverbs 17: 14).
4. Desire our motivations and emotions instead of reason (Proverbs 29:9).
5. Desire to harass the other person (Proverbs 27:15).
6. Desire to be heard but do not listen (Proverbs 18:2).

When we do not get our own way from our desires, we harbor:

1. Complaining (Philippians 2:14-15).
2. Gossip (1 Timothy 5:13).
3. Bitterness (Hebrews 12:15; Ephesians 4:31-32).
4. Quarrelling (Genesis 13:7).
5. Division (2 Samuel 6).
6. Deceitfulness (2 Timothy 3:13).
7. Revenge (1 Peter 2:21-27).

When we are living in the ammo depot of our anger and pride, we will be applying our desires as:

1. always thinking we are right, even when we do not have all the facts!
2. always making assumptions and jumping to conclusions.
3. having an excuse for all occasions so we do not have to take responsibility!
4. never apologizing because we refuse to see that we can be wrong!
5. expecting others to respond to us first!
6. insisting on our way or no way!
7. pointing to the flaws of others yet never our own!
8. be putting the other person down further if we are proven right!
9. manipulating others with guilt or rewards to get our way!
10. never letting things go; keeping on bringing up past conflicts!
11. never yielding in an argument and refusing to look at mutually beneficial solutions!
12. never considering the other person's true motives!
13. ignoring the plight of and compassion for others!

14.making promises but never keeping them!
15.always having to be the person who commands attention or withdraws from others!
16.not admitting we need to change but insisting the other person has to!
17.using humor to hide the real you, so people never know how you really feel!
18.never really listening; putting your desires ahead of that of others!
19.turning to artificial substances as your comfort, such as drugs and alcohol!

The great news is that even when these weapons are being used at their maximum capacity and you have taken so much damage you cannot go on, the relationship can still be saved and be rebuilt better than ever! We can simply rid ourselves from self-destructive behaviors by seeing God's way of:

1. Grace (Colossians 4:6; Ephesians 4:32).
2. Truth (Proverbs 12; John 1:14).
3. Using language (Matthew 5:17-26)
4. Patience (Proverbs 25:15).
5. Humility (Philippians 2:3-8).
6. Respectfulness (1 Peter 2:17, 1 Peter 3: 7).
7. Reassurance (Proverbs 12:25-28).
8. Valuing others (The Book of Ruth; Ephesians 4:11-15).
9. Speaking the truth in love (Ephesians 4:15; 1 John 3:16, 1 Peter 1:22).

Simple from the concept, easy on the surface, yet tough in the practice! *Can I actually do this? Is it possible?* Yes, it is; or else we would not be called to do it! Just think this through; what would your life be like if you were actually putting into practice these "God's Way" attitudes? How would your friendships improve, your workplace, your marriage? We can take these Scriptures and make them real in our life. We cannot just apply it to our lives; rather, apply our lives to God's Word!

When we have His picture of how life is suppose to be, we can make the determination to follow His precepts. We can be committed to live at peace with others by putting the principles of the Fruit of the Spirit in the forefront. There will be times we cannot reconcile, but we can be determined to be peaceful.

We can take these preceding Scriptures and resolve to:

1. be committed to change our attitude, allowing it to change our behavior so we model God's ways.
2. give gentle answers and not hash attacks.
3. be instigators of reconciliation.
4. understand the other person's situation and point of view.
5. know that we are responsible and accountable for our behaviors.
6. be confessors of our sin and not allow sin to confess us.
7. understand the effect we are having on others.
8. be committed to forgiving and letting things go.
9. not allowing our behaviors to be justified to us so we rationalize them as OK.
10. own up to our misdeeds by seeking to give restitution.
11. know what causes us to be hurt and angry so we do not let it fester.
12. not denying the other person's value to God, so they can be of value to us.
13. see the hope He has for us so we see it in all situations.
14. be interested in others' interests and opinions.
15. be grateful for what Christ did for us, so we can respond in kind to others.
16. be a committed listener and understand the other person.
17. remember what love is all about!

Jesus knew that the Father had put all things under his power, and that he had come from God and was returning to God; so he got up from the meal, took off his outer clothing, and wrapped a towel around his waist. John 13:3-4

In the mist of a heated battle with a friend, business partner, or spouse, we concede to our emotions and allow our pride to create those symptoms. Even though we may know better, we forget and just go to our weapons. But, we can do a few simple things like change how we use some words, and make a big difference in our relationships. Perhaps, after a few minor changes, we can get the hint that God's ways are better than ours. I already covered some of this in the chapter on "Understanding the Importance of Being Good!" in the section on "replacement words." The emphasis is on encouraging and equipping communication to uplift instead of tear down. Remember, good words encourage and lift up while wrong words can tear a person down for years. The words, and how we use them, will either make us abusers or people who cherish others! A bad sentence can last decades and cause needless hurt and stress. In your relationships, Christ wants us to make others feel safe and secure and we cannot do that with unsafe and insecure language. This is especially true in a marriage; you need to make your spouse feel secure and safe with you in order to build intimacy and lasting endearment!

Do not be deceived: God cannot be mocked. A man reaps what he sows. Galatians 6:7

Compassion

Finally, all of you, live in harmony with one another; be sympathetic, love as brothers, be compassionate and humble. 1 Peter 3:8

Putting into practice the character of *compassion* will allow us to feel the pain and plight of others, and to see from their perspective and situation in life. It will enable us to convey a deep feeling of love and concern that moves us to meet their distresses, struggles, and needs. This all flows from our understanding of who God is, and our obedience, trust in, and gratitude for what He has done for us. When we have our lives motivated by who we are in Christ and nothing else, our anger will be under control and our relationships healthy!

Now, let us look at what happens when compassion is absent from us. We will exhibit a lack of sympathy; we will be cold and thoughtless. These are rotten characters that are the opposite of God's call and plan for us. *Unmerciful* or *malicious* in Scripture usually refers to those who are unmerciful to the poor (Proverbs 17:4-5). However, it also means people who are without compassion, who do not feel for the distresses of others, and even those who cause these distresses. These are all opposites of what God does with us, and how He calls us to respond to others. True compassion is a result of the poured out life that has been devoted to God and attached to His interests. The trials and tribulations we endure give us the strength and character to be of better use in the lives of others. Because we have been through it, we can help others through it, too. It will also make us more confident in our Lord and His working within and through us.

Compassion means not bringing our own needs, ideas, sympathies, or agendas—no matter how needed and good—to a situation. Rather, it is identifying with others, allowing God's ideas and interests to take us beyond ourselves to the situations of others, and helping to bring them closer to Christ. We are to seek His intervention, but not demand that God fulfill that need. We are to bring ourselves closer to Him and experience His presence and preeminence.

Compassion also gives us the ability to feel genuine empathy and concern for those who suffer distressing physical, mental, or emotional problems, to tolerate, and even serve them cheerfully. We are to reflect Christ's love, seeking to alleviate their sufferings as well as motivating others to help. This is a prime aspect of the Spiritual Gift of *Mercy*; however, not having that gift is no reason or excuse to not act on it.

A true test of our election is the amount of love and sympathy we have for one another and the lost. This is what leads us to intercessory prayer, even for those we do not like. So, how much time do you devote to intercession? If you feel stale and dry of love and companionship in your life, especially with God, you have a big problem! Those for whom we intercede in prayer are those with whom we rarely have anger issues. So, drop to your knees in surrendered prayer and seek His face! (Keep in mind emotional level differs with each person's personality. God does not care about our emotional level. Rather, He is interested in our faith, trust, and response for what He has done.) How do I know if I have compassion? Kindness is the proof text to authenticity that is a result of God working in us. Grace means an undeserving act of kindness. Compassion is exercising that kindness!

Or do you show contempt for the riches of his kindness, tolerance and patience, not realizing that God's kindness leads you toward repentance? Romans 2:4

In Romans 2:4, the word for *despise* (NKJV)/*contempt* (NIV) refers to the refusal to yield to the knowledge and trust of God's goodness and His right of judgment. That means we refuse to use His goodness as a guide so we can experience sorrow for our own miss-actions, and develop compassion towards others for theirs (within reason; this is no license to keep sinning). God is generous with His grace, so we should be generous toward one another, and be thankful. If we refuse to see His goodness and turn from sin, we will be exhibiting the ultimate contempt for our loving Lord!

Give thanks to the LORD, for he is good. His love endures forever. Psalm 136:1

What else can I do? See the other person in Christ by seeking to *walk in his/her shoes,* to empathize with his/her feelings and views. See yourself in Christ and the gratitude you have for the forgiveness you have received as a Christian. This will help your attitude and approach to others. Listen and repeat what the other person has said; sincerely and actively listen. Remember how important this is! Listening clears up miscommunications and misunderstandings! When we do not put a stop to our avoidances and putdowns of others, this will boomerang back at us. Remember, relationships are to be communal and continual. Perhaps you can start to see the affect you have on others and then be willing to work at overcoming your frailties. Remember to show the Fruit of the Spirit—show that love and care, and value each one as a person!

Speak softly and slowly, using encouraging words; become vulnerable by admitting where you have failed and seek to make sincere amends. Take responsibility for your actions and do not let your pride get the best of you. Do not focus on blaming another or on who is correct; rather, seek healing. This is the first step in a forgiveness that leads to relationship healing, as well as its growth and strength. Make sure you have read (and you may need to reread) the chapter on *forgiveness*! Do not make the mistake of saying that the other person is always at fault so they have to make the changes. You step up and make them, even if you are not in the wrong.

Learn to take your life and your surroundings as they are, then strive to build them into what they can be for His glory, not just how you want it. If our hearts and minds are divided between seeking God and seeking ourselves, we will become double-minded. We will become spiritually and emotionally unstable and thus sink in the waves of stress and life! We will literally be torn apart both spiritually and physically by our stress and worry because we have not yielded to Him. Let go and let God; allow your wholehearted devotion be toward Christ and not yourself. God will not make your decisions for you; you need to seek His precepts and distil what is best for the sake of values and character; then, He will enable you to form it and grow.

Perseverance must finish its work so that you may be mature and complete, not lacking anything. James 1:4

What do I do when I am overwhelmed? Ask God for help, for He is able! Trust in His control! He is the God who can keep you walking above the waves, and keep you alive and going when you are under them! Go through His Word, seek what you are to learn, how you can get through, and for wisdom. If we do not learn, all those *waves* (James 1:5-8) will just be a waste; perhaps we will keep going through them until we do learn. Do not escalate your situation by complaining or distort it by denial, bitterness, or isolation! Do not be dumb, trapped in your own anger and regret. Be smart; be a Christian who learns and grows and who is committed to obedience, spiritual growth, and maturity. Instead of moaning, seek His grace to solve the situation! Do not blame or seek fault in others; rather, get on with life and your commitment to Christ. Allow His amazing work to grow in you! Resistance to God, bad attitudes, and anger only cause us more harm, tossing us about in the seas of life without hope or purpose. Let Christ be your anchor or else you will drown; your life will be a series of wasted opportunities. When you could have and should have grown, you will have wasted His call and put your energies into complaints and your mindsets and attitudes into bitterness and anger. We need to come to the point that we trust in the Lord, regardless of how good or how bad life is; this life is temporary. What we learn will be eternal!

We may not understand our problems or ever get a reason, just as Job did not; however, we can still trust in Him who loves us and is "caring" us through! Do you accept His caring? It is sad how so few Christians, when faced with problems, will really seek and rely on God. They tend to only see their situation while they cower in bitterness and anger, even aiming that anger toward God. They do not see that He is, indeed, in control. Thus, many Christians withdraw into these defensive mechanisms, turning their lives into ones of isolation, bitterness, and denial, while avoiding His true love and plan for them. We have to have the mindset to learn; if we are not willing to grow and learn, we will not, and our relationships will suffer greatly. We have to grow before we can grow. If not, we become stagnate and our circumstances will sink us. We have already been given victory. That is what the Christian experience is all about—our victory over sin and despair by what Christ has done on our behalf. If we do not declare the victory, we will only see defeat. Even though we already have the victory, we will still be defeated!

Relationships require initiative. We have to take the initiative to reach out and accept His Hand and allow Him to lead us out of our disappointments and hurts. Do not try to swim by yourself, as the waters of life are too strong;

the currents and tides of desires and wrong opportunities will overwhelm you. Anticipate what may lie ahead and prepare; this is James' whole point! Unequivocally, we have to reach out for Christ and Him only! We can choose not to be bitter, and rather, be better!

We must be aware of the serious, destructive nature of the defense mechanisms in the previous chapter and how they are supercharged by our anger. Jesus calls us to deal with our anger that so often leads to murder in various forms, from literally killing someone, to destroying relationships, and escalating small problem into big ones, because our pride is in the way. If we truly desire to be His disciple, we will be as committed to reconciliation with others as He is with us!

So, step up to the place of responsibility in your relationships. Do not have an excuse; have a plan of healing, encouragement, and open ears. Excuses only push others away; people do not listen to them anyway, so at best, they are a waste of breath; at worst, they cover motives and reconciliation. This chapter makes the assumption you are physically and mentally healthy. If you still have problems and are overwhelmed, you need to take this seriously and seek professional help from a qualified therapist. Perhaps medical intervention is necessary. There is no shame in this! Not seeking help is a shame! Living in a sin-infested world, our bodies become corrupted; we get sick and get chemical imbalances. So, seek the proper treatment as well as seeking God!

Now we ask you, brothers, to respect those who work hard among you, who are over you in the Lord and who admonish you. Hold them in the highest regard in love because of their work. Live in peace with each other.
1 Thessalonians 5:12-13

CHAPTER XIX
RELATIONSHIPS IN THE WORKPLACE

God blessed them and said to them, "Be fruitful and increase in number; fill the earth and subdue it. Rule over the fish of the sea and the birds of the air and over every living creature that moves on the ground." Genesis 1:28

It has been said that employment, by definition, is "blood, sweat, and tears!" And Ecclesiastes 4: 8 tells us, "This too is meaningless—a miserable business!" The very word and idea of work has struck fear and avoidance, depression and stress to countless people over the millenniums. But, can work be more? We work and toil to earn a wage to live a life in a mutually dependent society. We are Christians, yet we are also human, so we come together to form functions for mutual goals of building a society that can provide substance to all of its members. We are material beings who need a livelihood to provide for the daily needed materials of life, from food and shelter to leisure and entertainment. Work becomes a necessary means for us to live and function in society, a society that is mutually dependent on one another. We cannot all be farmers. Who would process the food? Who would market the food? Who would inspect the food? Who would distribute the food? Who would sell the food? Each one's work is dependent on another's for substance and life. Work is a relationship, and we, as interdependent to one another, must consider how, as a relationship, work can model Christian principles and glorify our Lord.

In converse, most people see work as the necessary evil we must do in order to survive. We have to do it whether we want to or not. But, is this true? Actually, when you read the creation narrative in Genesis, chapters one to four, you will see that our God is a God who works. After He created humanity, and before the Fall, He gave them the privilege to work, too. The privilege? Yes, because God said it is a *blessing*! He gave us work so we can be stewards of and for His creation. That means to manage His stuff. This is an incredible and powerful opportunity and responsibility. Thus, God trusts us with the care of His creation and to be faithful and productive. Work has a purpose; it is to be a godly endeavor, not just a necessity for our livelihood.

Even though work is a necessity for survival in any culture, whether capitalistic, communist, or agrarian, our vocation can be more than that—better than that; it can be a blessing and a centrality to healthy relationships. Work combines the talents and abilities as well as the spiritual gifts He gives us and then calls us to work as a cooperative collective. This helps fuel a healthy society and spawns goodness. Relationships and life in general are made better by work. Work is a blessing, even when we do not feel like it is. Work is not a result of sin and the Fall. It is a result of God blessing us to be productive with one another and in the world. Thus, when we catch on to this crucial point, we will start to transform our attitudes, then our abilities, and to reclaim work, from being a hostage to wrong thinking, back to a healthy outlook.

HOW TO BE A CHRISTIAN IN THE WORKPLACE AND HOW TO DEAL WITH COWORKERS

The LORD God took the man and put him in the Garden of Eden to work it and take care of it. Genesis 2:15

A *call*, a *career*, a *vocation*, or a *job*, whatever you call what you do in between your days of worship and church, and whether it be a priest or a fry cook, it all has a purpose. We have to realize that our work can be a potential for so much more if we see it as a blessing and not a curse. Work has a purpose to it, and that is to glorify God and build relationships. We all have a job, or at least we need to have a job. Sometimes the purpose is the same, and sometimes not, as we may be in the wrong place and job. Nevertheless, we have a call to be employed, to function in society, and to behave in that call with distinction and Christian maturity. At the same time, we have to be careful that our work does not consume us and become our identity, taking us away from our primary purpose to know God and make Him known.

Ask yourself a few questions and see what your attitude is and how you feel about your work:

1. What is your attitude about work?
2. How is your attitude at work?
3. Are you functioning well there?
4. Do you have healthy relationships there?
5. Are you consumed by your work?
6. Is your identity in what you do?
7. Are you known by your occupation?
8. Does your self-worth come from what you do from 9 a.m. to 5 p.m.?
9. Is God using you there? If not, why not?

There is a balance between being a faithful worker and being a faithful Christian. They can go together harmoniously. Basically, we need to see that our work is a blessing and a call. We also need to see that our worth is in Christ and not in what we do. We are secure in Him by what He has done for us! We are not secure in what we do *for* Him or others. Thus, we are to do our best in our work, and be our best as His child, both in Him and in the world. A lot of Christians prefer to see these ideas as mutually exclusive, that they cannot go together. But, they do go together; they are the ice cream inside the cone!

What we do is important. We need to find that special *niche* where our unique gifts and calling can be used and pursue a vocation that best fits us. However, our career or job—whether we sling hash or sit in the Oval Office— is not our real identity. Our identity and self-worth should only come from Christ and what He has done for us. Unfortunately, this biblical mindset of worth as focused on Christ is not the popular notion in Western society. In fact, our job in American society tends to be our identity. Is someone blue collar or white collar, a tax accountant or a carpenter, a police officer or a lawyer, a pastor or an engineer, a mailroom attendant or a gardener, a cook or a CEO? We are measured and recognized by others by our worth, and are appreciated, hated, or ignored based on what we do during the week. As you speed down a freeway, what occupation would you rather pass by—a police officer or a cable person? When your car breaks down in the middle of nowhere, who would you rather see—that cable person or a police officer? We identify worth as to what people do because of what we need or what we want. Even Christians buy into this mindset. Just think, when you meet a new person, how long does it take, in terms of questions you ask, until you get to this question: *And what do you do during the week?* Usually it is our second question—right after we ask their name. Not convinced? Then, of what percentage are your social and personal conversations about work? Usually, they take up over 50 percent; sometimes they dominate every relationship encounter and conversation we have. Why is this so? An unhealthy outlook about work, whether we consider it unimportant, or to the other extreme, that it is our all in all, creates dysfunction. Why are we, as Christians, not focused on Christ as our absolute identity, as our name *Christian* implies? Our focuses become skewed away from what Christ calls and toward what we want.

Obviously, we have some sociological growth to do, so we can reorient our mindsets to fullness, character, and the Kingdom of God as our primary, all-encompassing identity (The prime precepts in the first chapter). But, that does not mean we are to ignore our work. We have to find the best possible way to spend our work hours, doing our best with excellence and integrity. We have to find a way to apply our purpose in life—as in our spiritual growth and maturity—so it influences and involves who we are and how we are at work and with the relationships we have there, all the while glorifying our Lord. But, work still consumes us. All kinds of emotions, from absolute frustration to ecstasy, consume us in our work environment.

The earth is the LORD'S, and everything in it, the world, and all who live in it. Psalm 24:1

How often do we hear or perhaps say these phrases:

I do not like my new boss!
My coworker is gossiping about me!
I do not feel fulfilled here!
I have to do whatever it takes to make it to the top!
I hate my job!
I love my job!
My job is my life!
My job is relocating; what am I going to do?
I am going to get laid off!
I got fired!
I hate to work!
I am always covering for this person and he/she just got promoted!
My office is too small!
I am overqualified for this job!

I do not understand what I am supposed to do!
My commute is too far!
I do not make enough money!
I will never be satisfied until I am at the top, so I will do whatever it takes and ruin whomever I have to, to make this so!
My work hours are changing and I do not like it!
I am overwhelmed!
I am bored!
I feel stagnate here!
I have to make a change!

These are actual quotes I collected when I asked Christians what they thought about their job! Perhaps Mel Brooks, the movie producer, said it best. *Life stinks*!

If you have spent any time in the workplace, you will have observed many different kinds of attitudes, personalities, and ways of approaching the job there. In this society of work, as Christians, we work with other Christians as well as non-Christians. We all have different personalities, habits, desires, experiences, and expectations, all converging and conflicting. The water cooler area or loading dock becomes a gathering place for hearing the latest gossip, and a hotbed of conflict and chaos. Somehow, in the midst of all this, we, as Christians, are called to distinction. We are called to put our identity as Christians toward the goal of glorifying our Lord Jesus Christ while at work. It is not necessary to preach the gospel, as that may not be appropriate or legal, but we are to be a person who models Christ-like character so that we become contagious with His love. This may rub us against the grain of our coworkers and employers who have conflicting ideas. The Christian who goes into the secular workplace (and we should), enters into a struggle of identity, values, attitudes, and feelings, all producing stress and fatigue. And, it will be how we are to people in the mist of these kingdoms in conflict that will bring God glory, and reduce our stress. Or else, these above quotes become our *mantra*. Then, what Mel Brooks said will become our reality instead of contentment in our Lord.

And God is able to make all grace abound to you, so that in all things at all times, having all that you need, you will abound in every good work.
2 Corinthians 9:8

Changing our mindsets may not happen overnight. As all of our experiences, expectations, aptitudes, and attitudes come together in the workplace, all of these distinctions converge into our mindset and attitudes at work, where we see ourselves as either the kingpin at work or just another monkey with a wrench. We are also social beings, not just tools or devices, slaves or machines; we are not just another device at work. Our work is relational and impacting, and our work relationships can become some of our most important relationships. These are the people we tend to spend the most time with, even more than with our own spouse. We are spiritual beings who have been saved by our God and Creator, and given the call to be virtuous and righteous. Because of that, these work relationships reflect our relationship with Christ. Thus, our work relationships can become meaningful or dysfunctional, depending on how we handle and view our place in their lives and in Him. So, what is the right attitude and approach with which to do our work? How do we get along with coworkers, bosses, and our God? How you answer and deal with these questions will help make your workplace either a place of contentment or dysfunction.

Work, occupation, job, or vocation are some of the words we use to describe what we do in life. *Vocation* has its root from the Latin verb "*to call.*" Our vocation, our job, is actually a call, similar to that of a minister. So, we need to understand its role and significance in our life, and how we are to act in our vocation as well as what it means in our walk with our Lord. Let us venture into God's Word and see what He has to say about what we do during the workweek. Why do we have *work?* What are we to do in that vocation, and how should we respond to others around us? The following sections are thoughts based on Scriptural insights. This is designed for you to pray about in order to nudge yourself into being a better person at work. You may discover this very important truth about life as a Christian: what we do is not as important as how we do it! (For more understanding and references, see the Scriptural References in the back of this book. They are arranged so you can spend some time in the Word in order to help you to develop a biblical attitude of work.)

GOD'S CALL FOR THE EMPLOYEE

Serve wholeheartedly, as if you were serving the Lord, not men, because you know that the Lord will reward everyone for whatever good he does, whether he is slave or free. Ephesians 6:7-8

The word *bondservant (slave)* is from the word *doulos* in the Greek. It means slave, as in a person who is indentured to another for service and work. Most of these bondservants were so involuntarily, from being taken captive during war, born into it, or captured and sold as Joseph was. Some became voluntary by selling themselves to pay a debt. Paul uses this term allegorically to convey a sense of subservience. This is a total obligation, and a *doulos* usually was a slave for life. The Bible is telling us that obedience through submission is a principle way to model Christ-like character and bring glory to God. We share our Lord's humiliation and suffering, which, as some have stated, is a good way to define our jobs. We are not slaves in a literal sense, although you may feel like a slave at work. Or, perhaps you treat others in that way, thinking, *I am in command. They work for me, and they have to do what I say!* But, the key to this passage is the attitude we are to have, that of looking to Christ as our employer so we do our work in Him and for Him——to be Christ-seeking and not self-seeking. Therefore, we are to be our best for His glory, regardless of our circumstances.

We may have a paycheck from McDonald's and a boss who needs some acne treatments, but our ultimate authority and manager is Christ Himself! We may be a CEO, a CFO, a vice president at a Fortune 500 company, or just starting out in the workplace. Whatever role we have, we all have one main role——to look to our Lord. The second word in this passage in Ephesians is *wholeheartedly.* As with the word *be obedient* in Philippians, this means for us to listen carefully and attentively so that we can conform to a command or authority and obey. We show our value—that Christ paid a price for us—so we in turn can respond with a good work ethic (1 Corinthians 7:23). We must adjust our mindset to see work as an opportunity to please Him, and in so doing, be a blessing to those around us.

As an employee, we are called to diligence! This allows us to operate with our best for Christ's highest and with excitement and passion in order to complete our work and call from the Lord. It means being a learner and a teacher, allowing others to make an impact on us and making an impact on others. It is practical obedience, which is the loving of our call and the pursuing of our work so we are doing our best for His glory. Thus, our call in the workplace is to seek Christ as Lord, and be obedient to His call so we are demonstrating Christ in our lives and we can be our best to our employer and coworkers. Then we can seek how we can be used to make a difference in our workplace and with our coworkers. Because we are developing our faith, we can integrate our faith so we can   have an effect on Christ's influence upon others. Work is where we are to serve, not just where we get paid. When we do this, we are more likely to be happy because we are in His will and not just because of our ambitions, which will lead to nothingness.

He who tends a fig tree will eat its fruit, and he who looks after his master will be honored. Proverbs 27:18

Here are some more Scriptures about being an employee:

1. Genesis 1:26-28: As God demonstrated for us, work can be a place for us to learn and exercise creativity.
2. Exodus 23:12; 35:2: Remember to rest and pace yourself so you do not burn out.
3. Proverbs 10:26: Being lazy affects everyone and causes others to do your work. This causes great harm to your reputation and relationships.
4. Proverbs 22:29: Work is a place where we can build our confidence and prepare ourselves for further opportunities that are ahead.
5. Proverbs 25:13: Being trustworthy causes your reputation to increase and greatly improves your work relationships.
6. Ecclesiastes 2:4: Be industrious and proactive in your work.
7. Ecclesiastes 5:12: Do not take more work or responsibility than you are able to deal with effectively.
8. Ecclesiastes 10:10: See your work as a place to learn and grow in your skills.
9. Matthew 18: 23-34: Work can be a place where we can exercise our abilities for stewardship.
10. Luke 16:10-12: Work can be a primary place to develop and practice your good character and values.
11. Ephesians 4:28: Work is a place to develop the skills and the resources to share at church and with those in need.
12. Colossians 3:17: Be thankful you are able to work; do it with gratitude and for the Lord.
13. Colossians 3: 22-25: Commit to build Christian values and principles that lead to quality and beneficial relationships in your work habits.
14. 2 Thessalonians 3:10: Work is important for the betterment of society; if you are able to but refuse to work, you should not take from others who do work.
15. 1 Timothy 6:2: Always show respect to your employer whether you feel he/she deserves it or not.

16. Titus 2:9-10: Seek to please and do your best regardless of how you are treated in return.
17. 1 Peter 2:18-20: Focus on God and not your circumstances. Obey your employer so you show him/her honor and respect. In so doing, you are honoring our Lord.

GOD'S CALL FOR THE EMPLOYER

Masters, provide your slaves with what is right and fair, because you know that you also have a Master in heaven. Devote yourselves to prayer, being watchful and thankful. Colossians 4:1-2

God's call to the employer is the same as it is to the employee. However, the employer has more responsibility. God honors *diligence* and *fairness;* and as an employer, you are called to uphold these two characteristics! These are the two characteristics that we are to have in the workplace, and are especially essential for the manager. God hates the exploitation of people and will judge with severity those who exploit others. So, why bother with the rotten characters of dishonesty and exploitation when you can have a much more efficient and happy workplace, one where the workers are cared for and encouraged to produce instead of being forced and made to condescend.

If you think having a happy, cooperative workplace is not efficient, consider that the managing elite in the former Soviet Union greatly abused, coerced, and forced its workers to produce its economy as they lived in poverty and despair, while those in power lived a life of comfort and splendor. After many decades of this mentality, the Soviet Union was a country in decline, had poor infrastructure, was hopeless, and abused and took advantage of other developing countries. In contrast, the United States, for the most part, has created an atmosphere of cooperation, industriousness, and ethic which has created a world power that helps other developing countries. The typical American worker has a home, a car, and a quality family life, while in the rest of the world only 10 percent own cars and less than 3 percent own a home. In addition, the average income for the rest of the world is less than $50 a month (Statistics from *World Vision*). Most of the larger countries, such as the former Soviet Union, Mexico, and India actually have more and better natural resources. So, why are they Third World countries and not the United States? Because of a work ethic brought on from the Bible and as expounded by the Reformer John Calvin and the Puritan faith. Honoring God, cohesion, cooperation, and character will build a better country and workplace than manipulation, coercion, and abusive control.

An example of an American business is on Madison Avenue in New York City where most of the big advertising agencies are based. In the eighties and nineties, there was fierce competition, and many agencies were either bought out or closed their doors. The ones that were successful treated their employees with empowerment, encouragement, and let them operate in their skills as teams. The other agencies used stagnating business paradigms of control and manipulation. Biblical principles work for your work. Opinionated desires do not!

Here are some Scriptural principles about being an employer:

1. Leviticus 19:13: Do not defraud your employer or employees.
2. Deuteronomy 24:4b: Do not bring sin into your land (workplace).
3. Deuteronomy 24:14-15: Do not take advantage of people; always treat people fairly. Always pay a person a just and fair wage.
4. Proverbs 27:18: Take your responsibility seriously and industriously.
5. Malachi 3:5: Be reasonable. Do not defraud people; care for your employees; they are God's children, too.
6. Luke 10:7: People deserve to be compensated and treated well.
7. 1 Corinthians 9:6-12: Allow cooperation and input from your boss and your workers. See the other person's job from his or her point of view.
8. Ephesians 6:8-9: We all work for God; He is the One from whom we are to seek a reward. God rewards honor. Never show favoritism.
9. Colossians 3:17: Do your job as if Christ is beside you, because He is.
10. Colossians 4:1: Seek how you can please God; in so doing, you will create a better workplace.
11. 1 Timothy 5:17-18: Leadership is about equipping and empowering people, never taking advantage or abusing people.
12. James 5:4: Do not allow yourself to take advantage of others or steer people in the wrong direction.

Are you a good employee or employer? Are you honoring godly precepts or are you so consumed with bitterness or ambition that the goal of glorifying our Lord has become too distant to see? Read His Word; look over these passages and ask, *am I doing this? How I can apply theses principles?*

After reading the above selected Scriptures, ask yourself these questions:

1. What attitudes, desires, and habits do you have that need to be changed?
2. How can you be encouraged by God's truths, and encourage those who are in the workplace?
3. What warning is God giving you?
4. How can you lead a distinctive lifestyle in the workplace?
5. Have you considered the eternal results of a healthy work attitude, even in the face of strife and chaos?

GOD'S CALL FOR THE WORKPLACE

Lazy hands make a man poor, but diligent hands bring wealth. He who gathers crops in summer is a wise son, but he who sleeps during harvest is a disgraceful son. Proverbs 10:4-5

God has a lot to say to us—workers as well as employers—regarding our virtue at work:

1. We are called to work with respect and honor to God and others!
2. We are called to work with integrity!
3. We are warned about laziness!
4. We are called to honor just remuneration!

Go to the ant, you sluggard; consider its ways and be wise! It has no commander, no overseer or ruler. Proverbs 6:6-7

Here are some thoughts for your consideration, and remember what God calls us to do:

Slaves, obey your earthly masters in everything; and do it, not only when their eye is on you and to win their favor, but with sincerity of heart and reverence for the Lord. Whatever you do, work at it with all your heart, as working for the Lord, not for men, since you know that you will receive an

inheritance from the Lord as a reward. It is the Lord Christ you are serving.
Colossians 3:22-24

Colossians 3:22-25 tells us that our work does not ultimately define us nor is it how God sees us. Our work will either mature or devalue us. But, in Him we always have real, eternal value! How we respond and model character will be the eternal value——showing our true selves is what is pleasing to God. Work can even be a means through which to worship our Lord! Our work is not to define us, regardless of what our society may imply. What we have in Christ is so much more! Even though this may be the first question we ask someone new to us, or is asked of us, our work is what we do, not who we are! Work is not our identity or our worth!

Work, in most societies, is center stage for our social classification and the search for identity, and can even be an addiction to fulfill our deeper needs! But, even though work is important, it is not what we do that matters; we can concentrate our work efforts to be better employees. How? Why? Because, what we are doing is for God and not human slave drivers or overseers. Work is to be how we are to others and to God! Our worth as a Christian is who we are in Christ, Not what we do for a living! Imagine how your relationships will be refocused and improve with this biblical precept implanted in you.

Ecclesiastes 2:4; 4:7-8 asks, *what benefit do we gain?* This passage gives us the impression that our toil and work are merely temporary. We may find work necessary in order to live, but it is not permanent or eternal. So, we can refocus on our character and behaviors in our work to be our best because that is pleasing to God. Work, then, is not just for a paycheck or a promotion, because we are contributing to the Kingdom of God. A much greater value is given to us than just what is on a paycheck stub or a yearly evaluation. The importance becomes how people will see Christ through us in the workplace—either as a God to come to, or, one from whom to be repelled. How do people at work see Christ through you?

The Dangers and Concerns in the Workplace

His divine power has given us everything we need for life and godliness through our knowledge of him who called us by his own glory and goodness. Through these he has given us his very great and precious promises, so that through them you may participate in the divine nature and escape the corruption in the world caused by evil desires. 2 Peter 1:3-4

Take to heart the previous chapter on how to destroy a relationship; each precept there has a direct application to work. If you have problems socially, get help! Ask yourself how you handle anger. Maybe you are fine at church or at home, but what about your work? Anger is one of the biggest enemies for the employee as well as the employer! We are to be known by our love; yet, it is anger that most often communicates who we are. Thus, we must beware of its vicious and destructive ways! Here are some additional thoughts to consider:

1. Our inner feelings of inadequacy can be the fuel for a negative reaction of anger toward a boss or coworker. Thus, we have to see ourselves as God sees us: redeemed, and as His child. Then, we can have a healthier self-image that gives us confidence but does not allow pride.
2. Do not try to just ignore your anger. Walking away from or stopping the anger will not solve the problem; it often even prolongs it. Put an end to the anger by seeking the root of the conflict. Let the anger give you the fuel to react quickly and confidently, but do not let it control you!
3. Gossiping, name-calling, and/or trying to get even will only escalate the problem and give others a very wrong impression of our Lord! Remember, our essential self worth is not our job; it is who we are in Him!
4. Do not take anger personally! View your work as a service to Christ, not a personal, esteem-building venture!
5. Do not be defensive. Rather, let integrity be your guide. Virtue will build actions, even if you are under attack by an angry employer or fellow-employee. Show Christ-like character, and in the long run, you will win out. If not, shake the dust off your feet and move on, because in God's eyes, you are the winner!
6. If the employer or fellow-employee is angry, do not let it influence you! Do not acknowledge the anger, and refuse to accept the tone, because that gives it more fuel and you will lose control.
7. Separate the emotion of the anger from the words and content of what a person is saying. Do not respond to their anger with your own! Let them vent; then, get to the root of the problem. Listen, and ask, *how do you want me to resolve this?* Find a solution, especially if it is your fault. And, if that be the case, take responsibility; do not blame others; deal and act!
8. Restate the content of their complaint in your own words without the emotion. Use phrases such as, *I didn't know you disagreed with that*

policy. Or, *I'm glad to know how you feel. Let us find a solution about that.*

9. Let the person know you are glad they came to you (even if they acted inappropriately, because, we all do so at some point). When you are positive and looking to help them, you will be able to defuse the anger faster than anything else you could do. Also, be in prayer, asking God to give you the strength and the appropriate words. Remember, He is there too!

10. Keep your cool! Do not allow the fever of your hurt to become anger that gets out of control. If so, you are tossing gasoline on yourself or on another person's fever and then you will create rage (That is why those workplace shootings happen!)!

11. Remember Christ-like attitude and the Fruit of the Spirit, as well as sensibleness, prudence, self-control, and cooperation. Seek to emulate His character and you will excel.

You may be asking, *How can I do this?* Take the Scriptures and precepts in this chapter seriously. Do a word-study on *excellence* by looking it up in a concordance, and see what you find. Notice how these principles affected not only the people in the Bible, but also how they can affect you. Then, take those precepts and attitudes and ask yourself, *how can I apply them in my workplace?*

KEYS TO BUILDING BETTER RELATIONSHIPS WITH CO-WORKERS

Whatever you do, work at it with all your heart, as working for the Lord, not for men, since you know that you will receive an inheritance from the Lord as a reward. It is the Lord Christ you are serving. Colossians 3:23-24

1. To be interesting and liked, you need to be interested in and like others!
2. Be open to others around you who can teach you more about your job!
3. Care about what you do, and show you care.
4. Know what your employer expects and what you are supposed to do; then do it with excellence.
5. Be a pleasing and warm person, not a gossiper, a conniver, or a schemer!
6. Find an expert from whom you could learn insights about your job, so you can seek how to be better in it. No matter how long you have been

there, you can always learn more, and ultimately become the best you can be for our Lord!

7. Avoid laziness and procrastination like the *plague*!
8. Remember, your work is an act of worship, since it is God you are serving!
9. Re-evaluate your attitude toward your employer and fellow employees as much as you can.
10. Notice others in your workplace, how you can learn from them, and how you can come along side and help them!
11. Focus on objectives, not obstacles, and make sure your objectives are clear!
12. Be totally honest with your time, expenses, and relationships!
13. Treat others with dignity and respect, even though they may not treat you back in kind!
14. Remember, your workplace is also your most effective outreach. You may not be able to verbally share the Gospel, nor should you on work time, but you can be a Christ-like example so others will seek you out and ask you what makes you different!

Fighting Emotional Stress in the Workplace

For I know the plans I have for you," declares the LORD, "plans to prosper you and not to harm you, plans to give you hope and a future. Jeremiah 29:11

I have held various jobs over the years besides being a pastor and a missionary. I was a grocery checker for several years, a salesman, a business development consultant, and a trainer for a bank, not to mention all the "temp jobs" I have held. I have noticed from myself and many coworkers over the years that the emotional onslaughts at work will either make us or break us; thus, we need to know them, and be on guard and in a learning mode.

What can you do? Make sure you have someone in your church you can talk to and vent to at times, such as a small group or a trusted friend. Be growing in your faith and study of the Word. That will make you stronger and will enable you to better weather the storms of life. Be aware of emotional onslaughts, especially depression, which is usually a sign of a deeper problem. Do not afraid to seek help. Even Moses, Elijah, and Jonah suffered from depression! The real problem is not so much on how you feel, but what the root cause(s) of those feelings are.

Here are three of the most common causes of emotional distress and depression—fear, fatigue, and frustration.

Fear: Elijah had this problem! Whenever you try to manage all of your worries and fears, they can get out of your control and your body will break down. Instead of focusing on your depression, ask yourself, *what is the worse case scenario? How can I get through it with help from God and others? Are my fears realistic? How can I let go of them?* Elijah had to recognize that God was indeed in control and then learn to trust Him to handle the situations in which he found himself (1 Kings 19: 1-18).

Fatigue: Moses had this problem! If you are a *control freak,* attempting to control everything and everyone around you, you will be riddled with anxiety. When you try to continue in a stressed out and hectic pace without delegating or having support, you will burn out. This will set you up for depression as well as many other problems! You cannot do it all! So, you need to be a team player, seeking out relationships and team building, not competition and antagonism. Moses' father-in-law had to teach him to delegate. (Numbers 11:10-17).

Frustration: Jonah had this problem! When you do not see a plan or purpose behind the trials and activities of your life, you will get confused, and even disillusioned! Eventually, hopelessness will come in and overpower you. We, as humans, need to feel significant and needed. Thus, when we feel our life has no meaning, we will become depressed. When we finally understand God's purpose for our life, or just trust Him for it, our depression will fade fast! Jonah also had to trust that God was in control and had a bigger plan that what he could envision (Jonah 1-4)!

Sometimes, life in the workplace can seem to be an endless cycle of dysfunction and hurt. You may feel you are in the mist of the "Running of the Bulls" in Pamplona, Spain! Stop and rethink your actions, your attitudes, and your options. Search out these Scriptures on how you can improve your situation, understanding that the best way we can do that is improve ourselves! Do not be afraid to leave your job for another career or job if that is what God is saying to you. Be flexible, go back to school, do some research. Ask yourself, *what is my dream job? What are my real gifts and abilities? Do they match up?* Then, be in more prayer and seek what God has for you; take the jump; take the risk (within reason—not negating your responsibilities to your life and family). Ask God to open your eyes and help you see His purpose and plan for your life. If you still feel disoriented and confused, focus on the character of Christ and the Fruit of the Spirit that we are to emulate, as this is the primary Will of God and what we are to heed! Remember, God made you. He loves you, and has something to say to you, so focus on Him and not your situation!

How to Get Excited For Work

Do you not know that your body is a temple of the Holy Spirit, who is in you, whom you have received from God? You are not your own; you were bought at a price. Therefore honor God with your body. 1 Corinthians 6:19-20

Getting excited to go to my dream job? Perhaps, but the one I have now? How can I, when I usually dread it? We can get excited when we are doing our best for His glory, wherever we are, whatever we are doing! The key is to realize that Christ is there with us! We are called to uphold Him to others. But, sometimes we do not feel like it, do we? Those emotional distresses get in the way. If the fatigue is there, and it is too much, we need to be willing to be proactive about it. We can see that our work has a purpose beyond just a way to earn money; more precisely, it is a means to honor our Lord. Work is not where our dignity is to come from, but is where it is to be put into practice. In this way, the rut of work becomes a plan and purpose for our Lord. Of course, we still have to determine if where we are in our employment is where we should be.

When we stay in a rut or a bad situation with continual weariness and fatigue, we will lose our primary focus, become ineffective, or a stumbling block to others, burn out, or go into a depression. We will miss out on other options and opportunities, start to disintegrate into a person with a bad attitude, and even become ill!

I am mainly speaking about physical and emotional fatigue, which can turn into spiritual fatigue. There is no normal order. Each one could be the one to start it off and the other two will soon follow! Thus, frustration, stress, worry, anger, guilt, indecision, unrealistic expectations, resentment, and many other negative emotions will accumulate to bring us down in our interpersonal relationships, family, and our relationship to God. We, therefore, will not be able to function as He called us, nor will we be able to worship, which is our primary reason for being and existing in life! Work, which is supposed to be a tool for living and an opportunity for outreach, becomes our focus and sole purpose, when it is not meant to be so.

You can visualize your personal and work life as a three legged stool of caring for yourself, the care of our attitude, and the care of our spiritual life. The first leg is a good diet of fresh vegetables, whole grains, lean meat, and lots of clean filtered water, with good vitamin supplements and exercise along with a lot of regular rest to help out the physical fatigue. The second leg is a concentration on attitude and outlook, which will help you with the emotional fatigue. The third leg is a good church, Bible study, daily prayer, and devotions that will help your spiritual life. Each one leans against the other. If you let one leg go, you will not be able to stand or work effectively! Remember, as human beings we are body, soul, and mind, and each one needs to be fed and cared for! Remember, your body is the temple for the Holy Spirit (1 Corinthians 3:16-17; 6:19)!

Are you thinking *I just need a vacation*? Just a little more rest will be some help to you, but it will not keep the stool from falling from beneath you. Neither would even a week of rest and fun. You must develop a plan including all three legs, and be consistent! God desires you to take good care of His temple, your body!

More Ways to Balance your *Stool* and Work

Command those who are rich in this present world not to be arrogant nor to put their hope in wealth, which is so uncertain, but to put their hope in God, who richly provides us with everything for our enjoyment. 1 Timothy 6:17

1. Be a person who forgives, who lets things roll off his/her back. If you let resentment build, it will break your back. If you let it go, you will be stronger and more effective (1 John 1: 9)!
2. Keep your focus on Christ. Look at your work as worship, and as serving Him, not just a labor or chore. Be open for opportunities, and take them as gaining insights and experience so as to be better for Him and others around you! If you get stuck, consider a new perspective. Try to look at your work from a different viewpoint. You cannot always

control your situation, but you can control your attitude and respond as our Lord has called you to do!

3. Anxiety and stress are often matters of outlook (Colossians 3:23).
4. Get yourself involved in a good church (Isaiah 40:31).
5. Surround yourself with people who will listen to you and give you godly advice (Hebrews 10:25).
6. See your work as a means to use the talents, creativity, and gifts that God has given you (Genesis 1: 26-28).
7. Let your work give you self-respect and self-confidence, but not be your identity (Proverbs 22:29).
8. Allow your work to develop your aptitude and confidence; with patience, forgiveness, values, loyalty, and integrity, let it be a place to build and develop character (Ecclesiastes 10: 10; Luke 16:10-12).
9. Set goals and keep focused (Philippians 3: 13-16).
10. Remember that what you do is not as important as how and why you do it (Ephesians 4:1-6)!

Allow your work to build you up, not tear you down. If it does tear you down, and you have tried all of these suggestions, perhaps you are not in the career for which you were designed. Be proactive, take a career assessment test. The classic *Strong-Campbell Interest Inventory* or the book, *What Color is your Parachute?* will help you greatly, as well as many good Christian organizations such as *Crown Ministries* (www.crown.org). Remember, we are not to be devoted to our work, but rather devoted to our Savior. At the same time, we are to be diligent and be the best we can be in our job. We should attempt to find the best job to fit the unique gifts and calling He has given us. The Christian should be the finest person at his or her job by means of integrity, godly character, and modeling Christ, regardless of the situation!

What would we have to gain if we put all of our selves and our time in our career, giving up all the other aspects of life? Nothing! When I visit rest homes with youth groups, I ask the youth to get life stories and perspectives from the elderly residents to catch sight of what they have learned in life, and what the youth can learn from them. This is very rewarding. With dozens upon dozens of visits over twenty years, we never had anyone say they regretted that they did not spend more time in their career. The regrets expressed, if any, were about losing time with family by being workaholics, forfeiting relationships, and such. All could have been avoided just by adhering to Jesus' simple words in Mark 8:36. Look it up and see for yourself!

Our work ethic will be the measure of how people see our true character, as well as that of our Lord! Our good work ethic will greatly empower our relationships!

This was sent to me from a supporter of our ministry (original author is unknown):

How do I pray for my coworkers or workplace? B-L-E-S-S them!

Praying for unsaved and hurting coworkers:

B. Body - health, protection, strength
L. Labor - work, income, security
E. Emotional - joy, peace, hope
S. Social - getting along at home, at work, and in the neighborhood
S. Spiritual - salvation, faith, grace

Praying for others at work:

B. Board of Directors
L. Lordship of the business
E. Employees
S. Senior management, Supervision
S. Stockholders

Praying for my company:

B. Bottom line, profitability, paying expenses
L. Lawful, longevity, lasting
E. Excellence, equality
S. Synergy - good relationships between management and employees
S. Satisfied customer/clients and employees

Brothers, I do not consider myself yet to have taken hold of it. But one thing I do: Forgetting what is behind and straining toward what is ahead, I press on toward the goal to win the prize for which God has called me heavenward in Christ Jesus. All of us who are mature should take such a view of things. And if on some point you think differently, that too God will make clear to you. Only let us live up to what we have already attained.
Philippians 3: 13-16

Chapter XX
PUTTING IT ALL TOGETHER

I desire to do Your will, O my God; Your law is within my heart. Psalm
40:8

The bottom line for us is to know that relationships are essential and vital
and what our life here on earth is all about. First, we need a personal
relationship with Christ as Savior and Lord; then, we get our relationship
with ourselves healthy, and then we will be able to commune with those
around us with His Fruit. When we realize how important relationships are
and take to heart that Jesus is there loving, equipping, and empowering us,
we will be able to see where we need to go with them. We can do this with
wonder and confidence, and without fear, even when we are not sure of the
way, because we have been given a map. God knows the way. With His map
in hand, we no longer see our relationships as mysterious or foreboding—if
we choose to use the map God gives us and not the one we make for ourselves,
or the cheap one with all the wrong directions we get from the world. The
map we are inclined to use in our jungle is the map we make for ourselves
from the ink of how we are treated by others. But, God wants us to use His
map from His truth.

Why is the map important? Because, every connection we experience in
life will either prosper or disappear, become loose associations or friendships
of real depth and meaning. They will either grow us or hurt us, build us up or
destroy us, and they will either make us content or bitter. The choice is ours
as to which "or" will be the direction we go in life. While in this journey of
life, we are pursuing and engaging, and the direction we tend to go is usually
determined by our reaction to life. The focus and call He has for us is in how
we are to treat others and learn from our experiences and setbacks.
Relationships are not just about "me" and how I feel or desire, although
these are prime factors; rather, it is more important how I am honoring God

and His principles to others. Then the joy and contentment will be louder and honoring to both us and others. When the call to reverence Jesus first is heeded, we will start to see what relationships are really about, our connection to Him, and how we bring Him with us to all those around us. It is not about how we are treated; it is about how we treat others!

Each of these preceding chapters builds upon the other. When we have the foundation of putting into practice the first chapter's theme of fullness, the Kingdom of God, confession, and being willing to learn, we will be able to put into practice the following chapters on love, friendship, and so forth. That way, we take our "or" (which direction I am to go) and proceed in the right direction, which takes us out of the jungle of confusion and chaos into His Light and Wonder. When we know who we are in Christ, our role in the Kingdom, and our purpose, all things in our life will be influenced and prosper for His glory. We will have His fullness in us, so His Fruit comes from us to create love and healthy relationships.

When we have learned love, we can create character and build good, lasting relationships all stemming from our growth and maturity in Christ. Then our "or" goes from despair to prosperity, from associations to friendships of depth. Then our friendships bloom, our dating becomes God focused, and our marriages improve. Our "or" goes from hurt to growth, from bitter to happy. Not because of magic words and ideas, but because we are growing and learning and applying our lives to His precepts. This is what fullness in Christ is all about—growth in Him! Your growth sponsors growth in others as His Spirit infuses and empowers us in community.

Yet, so much can encumber us. The "or" we choose can easily go in the opposite direction of God's call. We become focused on our past failures and hurts so we do not venture out. We become alone and bitter. All the attention becomes on "me;" only "you" are the focus of your existence. In life we are placing ourselves into another person's life; they are placing themselves in ours. We become the "you" to the other "yous" in life. As we all are the "me" and the "you" in life; you are a "me" to yourself and a "you" to someone else, someone else's "me" is your "you" and so forth. Confusing perhaps, but understand this; we are all connected in this life on this small globe at this time. As Christians, we are collective and connected in His one Church no matter what creed or denomination; we will be in eternity together, so we might as well get along—not because of obligation or coercion, but rather to be better ourselves and to please God because of who He is and what He has done for us!

Relationships are communal and essential, compacted, yet simple. All of life is about relationships—us to God, God to us, and us to those around us. Every aspect of life is relational, even the relationship you have with yourself. Relationships are communal because we need one another to have relationships. Relationships are complicated because we make them that way; they are simple because that is how God made them. How we choose to live and build our lives will determine the success and failures of how we relate to others and build lasting, quality relationships.

But God demonstrates his own love for us in this: While we were still sinners, Christ died for us. Romans 5:8

Remember, He loves us; He has our best in mind; His ways are truly best. All of our affairs in life come down to the point of who we are in Him and how we relate who we are to others. How we relate to our next-door neighbor, our teacher, boss, coworker, parent, friend, stranger, spouse, and even God all comes from how we learn and grow in life. If we are not learning and growing, we are not building and encouraging. Our success in life is determined from the map He gives us, and how we take and apply our lives to God's Word.

The choice is ours to make them simple or complicated, to be hurt or to be happy. By simply following 1 Corinthians 13 and Galatians 5:22-23, our relationships will vastly improve because we will be acting as God calls us to, and people normally respond in kind to how they are treated. The choice requires our faith in action and our growth in Him. It requires us all to recognize what Christ has done for us so our fears and letdowns do not become our gods and our focus in life. He is to be the focus; He is our God.

We Are Called To a Relationship

Now I rejoice in what was suffered for you, and I fill up in my flesh what is still lacking in regard to Christ's afflictions, for the sake of his body, which is the church. Colossians 1:24

John 15 is the most beautiful description of our relationship to our LORD. He wants us to be with Him! Just as Christ wanted the disciples alongside Him so He could train them, love them, and enjoy their companionship, He wants that of us. He wants love, closeness, and relationship so we can learn and be contagious. This is our primary call and the will of the LORD. Everything else falls from this prime directive: He loves me! He wants to be with me! Do we want to be with Him? Do we want that close, loving relationship? Do we want to walk as Abraham walked, building altars, placing God first and foremost? Do we want to build our life on the worship of God in response to His promise and His fulfilling of that promise?

Abide, or, *remains in me* are the key words in John 15. We are to *abide* which simply means we are to trust and depend on Him. This word, *abide*, is very powerful. It means *God is our dwelling place*. The early Israelites lived in tents in a community under God in the feast of the Tabernacles. It is about collective community, Christ's steadfastness and preeminence, and His love and lordship. He is the One who nourishes us. Because He is the One who gives us our nutrients through His vine, we can dwell in Him, grow in Him, flourish in Him, and then even put up with whatever comes our way in our dealings with one another. As a *branch* that is cut off from the vine is lifeless, if we choose to live our life the way we see fit, we, the Christians, will have no fruitfulness in our lives. In the same way, there can be no fulfillment or abundance when we are away from our union and fellowship with Christ.

Following Christ means that we give up our personal plans and the goals and ambitions we had for our future. Yes, it will be a difficult struggle to leave the plans of our family and friends—our needs—behind, and to humbly follow as a servant to give our LORD the glory with our obedience, doing what our LORD desires over our own ambitions. So, are you willing? Are you eager to do great things for Christ? Consider how important this is for your maturity, character development, and your relationships, which translates to our joy and contentment in life. Following His precepts gives Christ the glory. And, when we follow through with what Christ has done for us by letting it flow to others around us, we bring the results of love and obedience. The deeper the commitment we bring to our LORD, the deeper impact we have on the glory of His kingdom and people around us.

The key to the success of finding and building quality relationships is simple: obedience, willingness to serve God over our needs, and even before we know what the call may be, taking this mindset into life and to others! God's will for our lives is for us to totally surrender and trust in His power and authority. Abide in Him. He will shape our destiny if we allow Him. He will teach us His ways if we will walk in His ways. Trust yourself to our LORD and receive His call to build yourself and others up!

It always seems easier not to obey, but in the long run it only creates further hardships. If you are thinking that this is too much, remember God's supernatural power that He has for us to make it happen. He creates the impossible relationship. Let your relationship to God be as natural as taking a breath so your other relationships become natural. Remember, this takes work and obedience as well as our continual effort and consistence. But, the more we do, the easier it is to do. It becomes even easier when we stop dictating our demands to God and start to commune with Him.

At first, you may clearly see God's will, like in breaking off a bad relationship, or in changing a bad behavior or habit. But, in other areas, it may not be as clear. However, God will guide you by your faith. Relationships are work, but they are worth the work; they are worth the risk even when we fail and get hurt. Do not allow your stubborn nature to rule your will. *It is not just what God gives to us that make our relationships grow; it is Christ's redemption and who He is in us. Our call is to respond to Him.*

Living our Lives Worthy

If you have any encouragement from being united with Christ, if any comfort from his love, if any fellowship with the Spirit, if any tenderness and compassion, then make my joy complete by being like-minded, having the same love, being one in spirit and purpose. Philippians 2:1-2

Is your joy complete? Have you considered the power and impact the Holy Spirit has on you? Not the grand stances and the show some people put on, then claim it is the Spirit, but the way the Spirit works from the Word of God. There is another spirit the Bible talks about that is important and often overlooked—the spirit of community. As Believers, we are one in spirit and are to be in one Spirit. One in spirit means our connection to one another is to be as in one mind—to be in unity. In the context of Philippians, we are to conduct ourselves as being worthy of citizens of the Kingdom of God as representatives of Christ. One Spirit is the result of living in the Spirit and exhibiting the conduct and call of Christ.

"...stand fast in one spirit with one mind striving together for the faith of the gospel" Philippians 1:27

This *one in spirit* is the character of Christ living in us all year long. The point of the Christian life is not about self-realization, but in knowing Jesus Christ. It is my recognition of Him in me and not allowing anything to take

His place in my thinking, my emotions, and the daily experiences of life. The spiritual and mature Christian will never think his circumstances are merely haphazard, nor will he think of himself as the center of the universe. Rather, Christians are to be Christ-like in what this Philippians passage calls *attitude* and *form*. Usually, we just skip over such words and miss their depth and meaning. In the Greek, "attitude" in the NIV, or "mind" in the NKJV, (Philippians 2:5) means a mental state based on feeling rather than just thinking. It signifies a concern for others, whereas just *thinking* keeps the focus upon us. The opposite of this is *pride*, which is what Paul was confronting in these verses.

The characteristics of *nature* or *form* in the Greek mean an *inward character and goodness that is reflected from a primary source.* It does not mean a shape, but rather imitating; we are to imitate Christ's character! It comes from Plato's Philosophy of Imitation in which he used the illustration that as a fire reflects a shadow on a cave wall, life and all that we perceive as real is just a shadow on the wall. So, all that we see and experience in life is a shadow of the true reality that is hidden from us. Thus, Paul is drawing upon Plato's themes in pointing us to the ONE true reality, and that is Christ. We only see a mere shadow of Him until we are called home.

This *attitude* and *form* are key words for Paul and what the book of Philippians is all about—not to mention what *life* is all about! This is what helps produce our attitude and relationships. This is why Christ came. Yes, He came to save you from your sins, but then what? Are you to sit in a pew and complain, throw pity parties when things do not go your way? Are you free to push people away and live a life of discontentment? Are you to hate the relatives during the holidays or be a loner at work, *NO! NO!* The Holy Spirit is determined that we realize Jesus Christ in every aspect of our life. This means *all* aspects! There is to be no part of our lives cut off or off limits to His work. If so, He will bring us back to the same scenario repeatedly until we learn the lessons He has for us, and until we get it right.

Whether we do menial activities like raking leaves or tackle big projects for the church, the mature Christian will see everything as Christ does, even in those times when it seems He has *dumped* on him. Thus, our daily activities, as well as those bad circumstances such as stress, setbacks, and failures are a means of growth and learning and becoming more like Him. We are to see all that there is in life as a journey to further secure the knowledge of Jesus Christ in our lives, even to the point of being recklessly abandoned to Him.

After that, he poured water into a basin and began to wash his disciples' feet, drying them with the towel that was wrapped around him. John 13:5

When He walked this earth in human form, Christ realized His relationship to the Father even in his normal, day-to-day activities. Jesus knew that He was God, but as a man He "took a towel," the most lowly and menial task of His day. It would compare today to our washing a toilet. Can you imagine Bill Gates going down to the warehouse and washing the dockworkers feet? Or going to their homes and cleaning their toilets? Yet, Christ, who is God, Creator, and Sustainer of all things did this for us! So, if the Creator of the universe was able to be humble and guided by the seemingly small voice in a loud and large world, why can't we?

Self-realization is thinking that we are *all* that leads to the believing. We are the center of the universe. It is in thinking that if we are good we will go to heaven, or that we are good persons and we work hard, so we do not need Christ in our lives. It is saying that if He is there, we will keep Him on a *short leash*. This is total anti-biblical thinking. When we have this mindset, no growth will accrue. There will be no seizing the maturity of the Christian life, and no partaking in the real meaning of life. Instead, the focus in life will be on the trivialities, desires, pleasures, eating, drinking, or the chasing of the latest fun and not the example of our Lord as He demonstrated in the washing of the disciples' feet. We forsake each other for ourselves or use others as a means to gain status or whatever it is we desire. The Holy Spirit is there all along, trying to guide us in, calling us to relationships like an airport attendant with two flashlights guiding in a jumbo jet. The pilot must keep a careful eye on the person guiding him as well as the controls of the aircraft or else the multimillion dollar plane and the hundreds on board will be in dire jeopardy. We too, must keep watch on the Spirit and His guiding, a teaching that is clearly seen in these verses.

We must watch. We must give up the controls so He can steer our life His way, lest we crash, resulting in a consequence to all those around us. He is our Pilot, not a copilot, navigator, or traffic controller. How does one do this? By keeping our eyes on Him. It may come small, like a small man with an even smaller flashlight as compared to the monstrous 747 jet. However, the 747 cannot park in the dark, nor can the passengers go on their way without the guidance from two very small flashlights. We have to take the initiative and realize Jesus Christ in every phase of our daily life. If we don't, a counterfeit will invade in the place of Jesus.

...that at the name of Jesus every knee should bow, in heaven and on earth and under the earth, and every tongue confess that Jesus Christ is Lord, to the glory of God the Father. Philippians 2:10-11

The aim of the mature, spiritual Christian who desires to live the true Christian faith is to have this Christ-like theme imprinted upon his heart and mind. This theme will permeate every activity and aspect of his life from preaching a sermon to washing a toilet, from buying groceries to leading a person to the Lord, *that I may know Him* (Philippians 3:10). Do you know Him where you are today? If not, you are failing Him. This may seem harsh and un-Christ-like from what is popular in the pulpit today, but very biblically true. Let us not be confused in our culture, our desires, our needs and wants, or our ideas of what we think the Christian life is to be like, and let us surrender ourselves to what the Word is really calling us, to maturity and growth in Him!

We are not on this earth to just appreciate ourselves, but to know Jesus and to make Him known. In our evangelical Christian subculture, the trends in thinking are too often placed solely on the idea that *something needs to be fixed and I must be the one to do it.* Yes, something must be fixed, work must be done, and we must do it. Nevertheless, we do it, not just for the aspect of work, but because of whom we are and what we have been called to do— mature and grow. What usually needs to be fixed is us! We need to allow Him to fix us. When everyday Christians are pursuing the heart of Christ by following His character in *attitude* and *form*, then we will see our relationships change; then our churches will change and then society will change. It all begins with your saying, *I will abide in His work!*

That I may know Him. Do you know Him where you are today? If so, what can you do to implement the Christ-like character? If not, what is in the way? Takes this to heart; what we experience in life, what we go through, what we suffer through, what we give up is all just a mere shadow compared to the eternity to come. What we seem to lose is of no comparison to what we gain in Him! Christianity and suffering are the ultimate in *delayed gratification*!

Do you know Him so that your direction and source of inspiration comes only from Christ? Most of us will look to our creeds and confessions for that answer and for good reason. But, I want to challenge you to go deeper in your faith and personal responsibility. That is, *how can I take my faith so seriously that it becomes so personal, so real, that all my thoughts, ideas, directions, goals, and inspirations are in the direction of serving my Lord?* To take your faith to a deeper level is about *abiding*, so it is yours and personal; it is not just because this is what your family is and does, not just because you are part of a good church and school or work. That your faith is only because of what Christ has done for you and nothing else is solely the work of the Holy Spirit! But, we have a responsibility to respond, to grow, and to build on what we are given! It takes trust, faith, and surrender of your will, surrender of your dreams, and surrender of your ideas to the LORDSHIP of Christ. You must acknowledge that He is Lord over you by His love for you, and that His ways are better than yours. Christ is our King, so let us live our lives in response to what He did for us!

BUILDING YOUR LIFE ON THE ROCK OF THE WORD

Therefore everyone who hears these words of mine and puts them into practice is like a wise man who built his house on the rock. Matthew 7:24

In this Matthew passage, Jesus is closing the Sermon on the Mount with the importance of application (Matthew 5-7). This passage implies the contrast, found in Proverbs, of building a house of wisdom versus the folly that can destroy it. This discourse is His final message and is on the precepts for living our life to the *max* and building the Kingdom of God. He states that it is useless to call ourselves Christians unless we practice what He has taught us, which we are to believe and also teach. Some have stated this is an utopian approach to Christianity, one that none of us could ever achieve, while others have taken this stance further saying *why should we even bother with something we cannot possibly do?* But their error is that we can do it, or Jesus would not have called us to His precepts in the first place. We may fail, I know I have, but we are still to follow through to bring His utopia to the best of our abilities. If not, we are only building on sinking and shaky sand. We will just fall.

To achieve more intimacy with and function for our Lord, we must be willing to take a look at ourselves to see where we are and on what foundation our lives are built. This passage tells us where we lay the foundation for our lives. What is it that moves, stimulates, and inspires us? Will we be able to weather the storms of life, or will we be washed away? Is our life built on shifting sand, the ways of the world that distract us and lead us away from Him? Does everything we consider to be valuable and important just wash away from the stresses, chaos, misdirected deeds, and bad decisions of life—from SIN? Or, do we build on His foundation and from the precepts of His Word, where we remain steadfast and secure?

When we build on the Rock, we are securing a firm foundation with our obedience and trust in what Christ has done, as we put it in all aspects of our life. So, our motivation is based on who we are in Him. This is not done by our proclamations and speeches; it is manifested by taking the knowledge of our Lord and His work and the relationship we have with Him so it becomes the transforming force to motivate us in all other relationships. If all we have is knowledge, we have nothing. We are just fat sheep, perfect for the kill by our enemy, as a fat sheep cannot function well. If all we do are *works* in His name, without the knowledge of who Christ is, we have nothing. We must have the knowledge and put it to work, making it alive and relevant. Thus, doing the Christian life and building healthy relationships requires us to be totally bought by our Lord, transformed by His grace, and living out His precepts to the best of our ability, always striving and always willing!

To weather the storms of life and to please and glorify God, we must be real, authentic Christians, whose lives are transformed and built on His foundation as we will be tested in life in preparation for eternity. Being only a *fair-weathered* Christian who has never struggled or who has never taken his/her faith seriously may soon find out that he/she had neither faith nor a relationship with Christ as Lord! Do you?

But the one who received the seed that fell on good soil is the man who hears the word and understands it. He produces a crop, yielding a hundred, sixty or thirty times what was sown. Matthew 13:23

In Matthew 13:23 we have two key words that strike at the foundation of our compliancy, *hears* and *understands.* These two words tend to convict and challenge us where we may not like to go, as most of us do not like to listen, and especially, we do not like to carry it out. But, this journey takes us on the road of His will, His love, and His best for us and those around us. Jesus calls us to wake up and do something with our faith, not to just sit in a pew and complain, or lay on a couch as life drifts by. A call is pronounced. An action must take place to secure His precepts and be an impact. We cannot just hear; we have to obey. Obedience is not in words, but in deeds that demonstrate our words through practice and action. This is not about our salvation; it is about our worth and our impact. Our salvation by faith alone may secure us, but for what impact if we do nothing with it? As His elect, whenever we read and/or hear the Word of God, we will have the desire and heed the call to put it into action.

Yes, there will be times when we do not feel like it. Life is tough; it is full of setbacks and hurts that seem to cripple us. So, we go on permanent disability even while Christ is there with His healing power. We ignore Him and go on hurting; and, in turn, we hurt others. Yes, we will hurt and we will need times to recover, but we must make the determination to recover and not stay disabled from abiding in Him. Obedience will override our feelings so we do remain steadfast and secure. We can praise our Lord because He heals! He takes those of us who are broken hearted, and holds us, cares for us, and encourages us to keep going.

In Jesus' time, the teachers of the Law would debate on which was more important—hearing or doing the Law. Some taught that all you need to do is hear and memorize it, while others held to the fact that you had to do it, too. The argument that won out at the time was that if you did not hear it, you could not do it, so, hearing was more important. Jesus uses their words against them as He did in other themes of His sermon. As we know, from actually reading the Bible and not just debating it, both are necessary. You must first know it, then apply it, which applies to the Christian, his/her faith, and the Word of God.

We have to have more in our spiritual arsenal than just belief. We have to have more to grow in Him and make our relationships work. Our faith cannot just be academic, an idea, or even just a hope; it has to be real. Judas was an example of a person who knew *about* Christ. He had the knowledge and firsthand experience that we do not have; yet, he did not put it into practice. To him, Jesus was just an idea and a hope for his agenda and purpose. Judas was not willing, and thus was not able to *abide*. When his storm came, he failed; he betrayed his Lord, so his house fell away. His foundation was sand, made of the gains of false expectations, misplaced hopes, false ideas, and a skewed determination. He knew the will of God, but he did not obey the will of God.

In verse 24 of Matthew seven, we see the word *house*. It is not about a building or a residence or even a home. Yet it is something we build. *House* is the life we build, who we are, and how we respond. The *foundation* is the thinking, teaching, doctrine, or philosophy to which we subscribe. Life is what we make of it; He gives us the materials and it is up to us to build. We can build just about anywhere we want to, but will it be the right foundation and place? Jesus' point was to encourage people to get out and do what He was teaching by contrasting the difference between those who are just listeners and those who are doers. We have to ask ourselves, *what about us?* We are the *builders;* we all will build our lives and form our relationships! The question is whether we will be wise or foolish builders. Will our house stand up to the storms of life?

The *storms* are the tests and situations we will be faced with, from minor hurts to major illnesses, loss of friends, loss of loved ones, the mistakes we make, financial setbacks, what others do to us, and our sin, our decisions, and other principalities and people acting against us. God knows the storms are coming, but what do we do? The hearers of Jesus' parable knew they would need to prepare for storms. Palestine is basically a desert and storms are very infrequent. However, when they do occur, they come up fast, without warning, and are tremendous (Matthew 8:24-25). A few years ago in the city where I live, a housing development was built on a flood plain. The flood plain was clearly marked in the city records and the builder and investor knew about it; it was even near a canyon and a river. But, since there had been no flood in the past two decades, they surmised it was worth the risk, went ahead and built, and hoped there would be no flooding. Well, soon after people moved into those homes, the floods came, the damage and distress came, then the lawsuits, the media, and the blame shifting. Where we build is important; it does matter now, in life, and resonates in eternity to come.

The passage goes on to say that whoever *does not do them* is a fool. This does not mean just being stupid; it is a reference to judgment. We all will be ultimately judged, and when we hear and do not obey, there will be trouble. Our deeds will be as worthless as a love song with no love in it (Ezekiel 33:30-33). When we hear something from God, we have the responsibility to put it into action by changing our mindset so it affects our behavior, strengthens our faith, and motivates others as well. Our character development will be the quintessential test of how we weathered the storms and built our foundation, because our character becomes the essential building material that helps us weather those storms and even takes the storm's substance to build more perseverance! Unlike weather storms, the tempests we go through actually give us stronger and better materials to add on and remodel our house to be better and stronger. I say this out of love, not out of condemnation; it comes down to two choices, to *abide* or to *ignore*, sand or rock, *well done, good and faithful servant...* (Matthew 25:21) or *you wicked and lazy servant...* (Matthew 25:26). Which will it be for you?

When anyone hears the message about the kingdom and does not understand it, the evil one comes and snatches away what was sown in his heart. Matthew 13:19

In any population, people build wherever they can, looking to the moment and not to the long term. The city where I live in Southern California has building codes that help protect people from their shortsightedness. In many poor desert regions today, such as in India, there are few to no codes, so people build shanty homes in flood planes out of desperation or ignorance, thinking they are safe for a time, until the rains come down and their homes are washed away. Where the builder in my city did it out of greed, they tend to do it out of their perceived necessity. I have seen this firsthand too many times, as so many lives are literally washed away. We, too, wash away our own lives when we build in the wrong place and with the wrong materials. When we ignore the Word of the Lord, we will be left out in the storm. The storms come for the foolish, those who do as they please, without forethought or faith, and they will face the destruction of their houses. All they are and have can be totally annihilated because the ways of the world and its lies become their refuge, shanty homes built on shifting, foundationless sand in a flood plane. You can hide from God and do as you please for a time, but sooner or later the rains will come to you! We must allow God to be our shelter from the storm. Like an unscrupulous building contractor who builds on a flood plane, or with shoddy craftsmanship, the storm will reveal the real quality of character. Real goodness will outlive and outlast any worldly imitation.

Not as the Scribes

Woe to you, teachers of the law and Pharisees, you hypocrites! You shut the kingdom of heaven in men's faces. You yourselves do not enter, nor will you let those enter who are trying to. Matthew 23:23

In verse 29 of Matthew seven, *not as the Scribes* was a putdown to those who liked to just sit and talk and do nothing with it. The Jewish leaders placed their trust and faith in their knowledge, but did nothing with it. Their comfort was who they thought they were because of their position and acceptance in society, and the show they made with their works. They held onto the faith of their forefathers, but rarely, if ever, confessed that faith themselves. Rabbis would often go as far as to quote one another as their proof text to back up their arguments. Yet, they did nothing with it. The Pharisees had the Scribes transcribe their new laws called the *Mishnah*, a collection of commentaries and insights to the first five books of God's Word, going back to the time of Nehemiah in 400 B.C. and continuing through the third century. The *Mishnah* is reverenced, almost worshiped, yet not put into practice. The Jews still have this today as one of their main commentaries. The other main book the Jews use, besides the *Torah*, is the *Talmud*, which is made up of commentaries on the *Mishnah*. This is so sad, as it is so much commentary and great insights, and so little action to accommodate it.

We Christians do the same with our skewed focuses, traditions, and misdirected motivations, while our opportunities and relationships go distorted and slip away by the sands. For example, in the *Talmud*, there are 156 pages devoted just to the observing of the Sabbath as it applied to life! The Jews placed traditions and rules on top of traditions and rules, covering the original rules of God with their own roadblocks of reasoning and self-proclaimed devotion. Many Christians today do this, too. We can place so much emphasis on tradition that we forget what it is and who it is we are to worship and do church for. Then, we do this in our own life as our past experiences can become our personal traditions that form a pattern we keep repeating. If it is a bad pattern, the repetitions will be bad; if the pattern is good and based on God's precepts, then we do well.

We can see how serious the Pharisees were about keeping the Law. They wrote down all of the laws, such as the Ten Commandments, then applied layers and layers of duties and commentaries over them, so the original meaning eventually became lost. Thus, when a rabbi wanted to speak on a topic or give a sermon, he went to the *Talmud* as his first and sometimes only prime source and not into the actual Word of God. His authority was tradition and building more tradition. Jesus went straight to the Word with Himself/God as the authority, which astounded people. As a Christian, we are always to teach what the Word of God plainly says, adding none of our false presumptions or traditions. We have no teacher in Jewish history who taught with the authority that Jesus did. Authority was reserved for the Law itself, whereas Jesus came to fulfill the Law. Let us abide in His authority.

We have to produce relationships; they do not just happen.

...And he worked for Laban another seven years. Genesis 29:30b

Keeping in mind the precepts from God's Word we have looked at in this book, one resounding theme is that *relationships just do not magically happen.* Something happens to spur them on, to keep them going, and to modify them to continue. Jacob saw the woman he wanted to marry, and broke away from his culture and family to make it work. He was cheated by his father-in-law about his wages numerous times, he was deceived in what was supposed to be his and that he worked for, and subsequently was given the "wrong" wife, yet he committed to work another seven years for Rachel, whom he loved.

Perhaps, Jacob did not follow godly precepts in all he did in life, especially in how he cheated his brother Esau and then ran away from his responsibility and family; then there was the wrestling-with-God thing; but, he does give us a great picture of romance and commitment. He was willing to endure what was done wrongly to him to pursue love and be faithful. In his culture, he could have had a prearranged marriage or even bought a wife; but, he chose to go to the best source and seek the best person for him. Then, he had to make the determination to go through all the hoops to work for her and follow through. He had to produce in order to receive. The lesson for us today is that we, too, must pursue and produce our relationships. They have to be worked; they do not just happen. We have to get in there and be effectual.

Remember this: Whoever sows sparingly will also reap sparingly, and whoever sows generously will also reap generously. 2 Corinthians 9:6

When I was in grade school, my family moved to a new house in an unfamiliar neighborhood. My neighbor always saw me playing by myself. So, she walked me down the street to meet another boy my age who also usually played by himself. We both thought we were the only kids in the neighborhood and were surprised that each other existed; we became best friends for years. His name was J.P. I learned early on from J.P. I had to make an effort to just meet him, and as we grew to know each other more, I learned it took even more effort to keep our friendship going. But, somehow this lesson has not always stayed with me. When I grew older and discovered girls, I was thwarted in dating because I was terrified of rejection. And, sure enough, I was rejected by a girl I liked *right off the bat* in junior high. This paralyzed me in dating. As I gained the courage to ask a girl I liked out, I was turned down each time. Perhaps, I asked the wrong ones or in the wrong way, but whatever the case, I rarely asked girls out, even in high school and college. Those early experiences of rejection kept me from taking risks.

Risk is important in finding and building relationships. As I have said before, we will get hurt and we will hurt others. If we allow our fears to capture us and hold us back, we are not sowing; so, we end up not reaping. Yes, for some people, making friends and getting along with people seems easy. The cool kids, the popular people, and the extroverts seem to do this with ease while those of us who are shy and introverted have a tougher time. But, the difference I have seen between being *reserved* and being *out-going* is in how we handle rejection and fear. Regardless of our personality, we need to take a risk and at the same time guard our heart (Psalm 147:1-3; Proverbs 4:34). A balance must be struck to handle the tough stuff while venturing out in life so we make connections with the lives of others. We won't be touched much if we do not go out and make contact. If we venture not, we gain not.

I can do everything through him who gives me strength. Philippians 4:13

God's Word is the material for our growth and life. He hands it to us and we create even more building blocks by our trust and obedience. But, the key is we have to engage in and continue the practice. I cannot tell you how many times people have come to me and said their relationships were not working or they did not have any. After listening to them, I quickly discovered that they did little or nothing to work or pursue them, for which I also was once guilty. For some reason, they expected God to provide a wife or husband, give them a best friend, or provide the ideal co-workers by dropping from heaven, right in front of them. Now, I would not say that God would not work this way, because I have seen things dropped right in front of me and others, but the usual way this works is we have to pursue them.

Our relationships are a responsibility, not only to connect with others, but to do our best to persist in them. Building healthy relationships does not always come naturally; in fact, I have rarely seen them come naturally. It takes effort, determination, persistence, and the pursuit of God.

Take up the Cross

Whoever finds his life will lose it, and whoever loses his life for my sake will find it. Matthew 10: 39

Jesus, in the passage of Matthew 10: 34-42, calls us to take up the cross. This passage goes against the grain of most Christian mindsets, as it did when Jesus first gave it. Yet, it is essential for us to understand who we are in Christ and allow His empowerment to come into our relationships. *What does this mean and how does this affect my relationships?* It involves and influences all we are and all that we do. We must remember, life is not free or happenstance; it is work and it has a cost. Our grace is free, but our grace had an incredible cost we did not nor could not pay; He did it for us. We can sit on the *Christian couch* and do nothing with our faith if we choose. Our salvation is secured if it is real, but what kind of life is that? We must get out, and we do this by carrying the cross into the depths of who we are and then to all of our connections, opportunities, and daily life!

The call is *Jesus is Lord over all!* When Christ is Lord, He is God and Savior, and also our Guide and Governor, as well as Friend and Father to us. Jesus is demanding our allegiance and loyalty before anything else. Nothing must be in His way, the way of Christ working in us and using us. Taking up the cross means we need to be committed and tactful while modeling the Fruit of the Spirit. We must be as kind and as loving as possible so we can hold back as much inconsistency as possible. When Christ is first, it does not mean we are to ignore our family and friends or hate them; because He is Supreme, our relationship with them improves exponentially, as we are still called to build them up. Rather, this means we are not to put others before the Lord!

The *cross,* in this passage, refers to the crossbeam (not the entire cross) that a criminal would carry to his crucifixion and death (See my article on the crucifixion of Jesus at intothyword.org), penitently going to a shameful and painful end. He would endure a mob of people cheering for his death as well as his horrified family members. It is a picture of what some Christians go through in life with antagonistic people reveling in the prospect of their suffering, seeking to destroy them while they continue, undaunted, in Him. The cross shows us the importance of obedience and trust in Him. We are to be identified with Christ even if it means losing our life. This is not a burden that we pick up on His behalf or that God imposes upon us; rather, it is a joy to serve because of what He does for us.

Does this sound too hard and harsh? Is this too tough or scary a commitment, too much to handle? Yes, it is! The cost of surrendering ourselves to the Lordship of Christ is high! It was high for God, and it can be difficult and troublesome for us as well—troublesome as in how the ways of the world will come against us. But, remember, our faith is wonderful because our security is in Him. If we do not seize the peace, we will have trepidation in life and be disconnected from God. Take comfort, for the payoff for the cost is far more than we could ever conceive. We have the joy and wonder of trusting and obeying Him! Jesus tells us, *he who finds his life*; we find greater treasure for us here and now, and that resounds all through eternity. As His representatives and ambassadors, we model and embody Christ; thus, what is done to us is also done to Him!

This can cause fear and apprehension in the life of an unbeliever as he wonders if he should choose this way, and even to the Christian who fears what might happen if he surrenders his all. The good news is that when we surrender, we give up a losing and costly battle for a better plan of peace. It is allowing God to control the beachhead of our life, because He can do better with it. And, the clincher is, what we give up is in no comparison to what we receive in return. The deal is good for us, beyond our imaginations and plans.

He gives us the *cup of cold water* (Matthew 10:42). A *cup of cold water* was the most highly praised and most difficult gift to give then. Remember, there were no ice machines; they had to go climb a mountain and bring the ice back, taking weeks of incredible effort. It is also the best gift a poor person was able to give, since one did not buy it, but rather went out and got it. This is a gift of commitment that brings comfort, an illustration of what Christ does for us and what we can do for others. This reinforces the fact that we are precious and acceptable to God, and He has our best in His will. We do not need to fear; He will care for us and empower us no matter what we face or give up, impacting all we are and all those we touch. As Christians, we are bearing Christ and bring Him into the lives of others by His strength!

He must become greater; I must become less. John 3:30

This concept is hard to grasp for many modern day American Christians. Most naturally assume all will be well, as the plan for us is good and wonderful. And, this is true! But, what God sees is what is good—character, love, relationships, and spiritual growth. This competes with what we see as good-desires, possessions, positions, and power. Strife will result and our relationships may suffer, as convictions and assumptions clash with Truth. We have to make sure we are learning what is right and what Truth is. We need to screen out the world's wrongness and pay attention to the principles of God. Most Christians are getting bad theology from the airways and even the church, with the thinking that we do not need to put in the effort, that

God will not allow suffering or hardship if we have enough faith. But, when you read the Bible, you see that the opposite is true; hardship built character and maturity in the lives of the persons in the Bible. God is much more concerned with our spiritual growth, maturity, character, and how we are interacting with one another than anything else. Our focus tends to be on conveniences and on comfort; His focus is on how to sanctify and perfect us, not to please and pamper us!

The result of following this call is the enthusiasm, motivation, inspiration, strength, and passion to keep going in His direction with greater love. The only one who could demand greater love is God. This translates into our role in the world, our purpose, and our significance. Our significance is who we are in Christ, not what we have or want. Christ is our vindication; knowing this will prevent most of our quarrels, both within our selves and with others, as our eyes will be on Him and not on our desires. Jesus is saying this peace of physical comfort is some time in the future, and not to take our comfort in that. Our significance in Christ affects our ability to build effective relationships; not knowing who we are in Him fuels our wrongdoing. Thus, taking up the cross will cause us to come face to face with the ultimate conflict, our will versus His, as the nature of the conflict is the collision of presumptions and wills. It is His versus ours and ours versus others. When our eyes are on His will, and our presumptions are sequestered under His precepts, we will see only the strife caused by the Gospel!

He who receives you receives me, and he who receives me receives the one who sent me. Matthew 10:40

In this passage, a *righteous man* emphasizes the fact that we, as Christians, are in Christ, and when someone receives us, they receive Him. When they reject us (provided we are following His call and character), they also reject Him. Carrying the cross empowers us to be more hospitable and more loving. Imagine what your relationships will be like when this call takes root in you and overflows to others around you! When we are dependent on God, we are also being hospitable, assisting, helping, motivating, encouraging, and providing for others appreciably. These are not to be secondary after thoughts! All too often, we ignore the needs of others and only see to our own needs. How sad that is!

If we refuse this vital call, God just may allow those hardships to come our way, breaking us down so we will yield and grow as His child. Just as a good, loving parent will discipline his child, we too will receive discipline. But, this is not a personal attack; rather, it is a way we can grow and be better used by our Lord. We have to be willing to be identified with Him no matter what the cost, as the rewards will be far greater than we could ever imagine! So, are you willing to reduce yourself to the real you, as you are called by Jesus Christ to be so that He is greater in character and precepts in your trust and faith, and in your obedience and application of life? And, so you become less in your will, aspirations, lust, and sin? If not, what is in the way of God working in you?

What does this come down to?

For in Christ all the fullness of the Deity lives in bodily form, and you have been given fullness in Christ, who is the head over every power and authority. Colossians 2:9-10

Our relationship to God and our connections with others comes down to the fact that *I must die to my self-will and put on His will*. It is not just applying Scripture to my life, but applying my life to Scripture. When we do this, we are being the transformed Christian, impacting, loving, and encouraging.

1. Jesus authority is ultimate (Ephesians 1:20-22; 1 Timothy 6:14-15; 1 Peter 3:22)!
2. His authority is based on the fact that all things were made by Him and for Him (Psalm 2:8; John 1:1-3; Heb. 1:2, 6; Colossians 1:16).
3. He is worthy to be worshiped (Hebrews 1:6; Revelation 1:5; 5:11-12; 7:9-10).
4. He is our Redeemer, and we are purchased by His blood (Acts 20:28; Ephesians 1:7; 5:23; 1 Peter 1:18-19).
5. He is the supreme, the head of the body of all Christians, of His Church (Colossians 1:18).
6. Jesus sent His Spirit to guide us into the truth (John 16:12-13).
7. We are called to teach others to observe all that He commanded (Matthew 28:20; John 13:20).

When we are doing the above then we will realize:

1. I need to commit myself to Christ as LORD over all, and do this completely, repentantly, and without doubt.
2. I can take the *One Another* passages (see appendix or a concordance) seriously and reverently.
3. I can reflect on God's call and plan for me.
4. I can reflect and proceed with God's call for me in my relationships—past, present, and future.
5. I can see my marriage as God's plan and provision, that it needs my continual work, effort, and love, and that this is God's will—what He desires.
6. I can submit myself to my spouse with respect and love him/her with honor unconditionally, humbly, honestly, and completely.
7. I can commit to positive and active communication.
8. I can admit my sin and failures.
9. I can seek and ask forgiveness.
10. My relationships will be edified, equipped, and empowered by what Christ has done for me and is working in me.
11. I can renew my relationships through His empowering of me.
12. I will be modeling and representing Christ, His character, and His love in all that I do.
23. My relationships will become healthy, and setbacks will be overcome.

Heal me, O LORD, and I will be healed; save me and I will be saved, for you are the one I praise. Jeremiah 17:14

A biblical mindset lays a biblical foundation for a life transformed and triumphant! It is the realization that God loves us, He has a plan for us, and our relationships are important and foundational. Our lives are not happenstance; they are purposeful when we are in Him. The people in your life are the people God has brought to you. Your husband or wife in whatever choice or circumstance that brought you together is your spouse and your responsibility; even if you married the wrong person, he/she is the right person now. We have to be willing to connect and make it work. And, we need to persevere with our church members, coworkers, family, and friends.

By recognizing who He is, we can abide and build on His Rock. By our obedience in faith, we may suffer temptations, trouble, persecution, setbacks, and condemnation from the world, and even from other Christians. It may seem our foundation has shifted by that constant beating, but He will remain unconditionally steadfast in us and even more powerfully when we remain steadfast in our faith! Keep your faith real, valuable, and practical on His solid Rock. He will not leave you nor forsake you. So, let Him be the Rock-solid foundation of your life and your relationships!

There is so much more that I could never possibly cover it all, as it would take massive volumes of psychological research, examples, and outcomes. Then, I would be overly complicating what is really simple—if we focus on Christ as LORD and not ourselves.

Then he said to them all: "If anyone would come after me, he must deny himself and take up his cross daily and follow me. For whoever wants to save his life will lose it, but whoever loses his life for me will save it. What good is it for a man to gain the whole world, and yet lose or forfeit his very self? Luke 9:23-25

APPENDIX I
HOW TO BUILD YOUR FAITH

The man without the Spirit does not accept the things that come from the Spirit of God, for they are foolishness to him, and he cannot understand them, because they are spiritually discerned. The spiritual man makes judgments about all things, but he himself is not subject to any man's judgment.
1 Corinthians 2:14-15

HOW TO DEVELOP A DEVOTIONAL TIME

Draw closer to the heart of God by building a deeper relationship with God!

First Peter talks about humbleness (2 Peter 1:5-7) which is characterized by the willingness to grow in Christ, receive learning, and experience growth. Two of the best ways to do this is through personal devotional time and by being a part of a small group Bible study. Peter tells us we ought to be humble toward one another so that we can know the grace of God and not be in opposition to God. Secondly, he says we had better be humble, not only toward one another, but toward God. This is so straightforward. This is so essential to be a blessed Christian and church and to be a growing Christian and church, growing not necessarily in numbers, but in what is most important—discipleship, which is leaning on, learning from, and growing in Christ, leading to a lifestyle of worship!

How can I develop quality time with our Lord so I can become a deeper and more mature Christian?

Here are nine thoughts to get you pointed in the right direction:

1. **GOAL**: **See where you are spiritually (Acts 22:8-10; Philippians 2:13) and** determine where you need to go. Then, make a goal, and understand it. Your goal is to become complete, that is, to find fullness in Christ (Col. 1: 28). To say it another way, it is to become a mature Christian, a person whose attitudes and actions are like Christ's (Eph. 4: 13). Where are you spiritually and where do you need to go? Where is God calling you to go?

2. **PROCESS: Understand there is a process (Psalm 16:11; 73:28; Proverbs 16:9;** Hebrews 11:1-6) at work. It does not happen overnight, and you cannot get it in a bottle, off a shelf, or by sitting in a pew. The process is one of the main growth builders. It is about the journey as well as the destination. It is an essential step toward reaching your goal to spend personal, daily time with God. Thus, the journey is as important, if not more so, than the destination, because as you walk you are learning and growing! If we just arrived at the goal without the struggles of getting there, we would not have built any depth, strength, or maturity! Make sure your goals are a match to God's! We must never allow our presumptions and pride to cloud His way!

3. **PLAN: Plan ahead (Isaiah 26:3; Mark 1:35). This does not automatically** happen. You need to plan out your devotions to make them more effective. You can get many prepared devotional schedules at a Christian bookstore or sit down on Sunday and decide exactly what paragraphs or chapters you will be studying during each of the next seven days. Doing this will eliminate the problem of spending half of your devotional time trying to decide what you will study that day. You can use a Bible reading chart, quality devotional books, or a pre-written guide, but don't just dive in. You will get much more out of your experience by having a plan.

4. **CONTENT: Put into your devotional time variety and consistency (Psalm 16:8-**11) in what you study. One month, you might study an Epistle. Then, you might spend a month or two in a narrative passage such as 1 Samuel. Then, you might go back to the N.T. to study a doctrinal passage such as Romans. Then, switch again to a minor prophet such as Joel. Try to go through the entire Bible within a year, or two years at the most. Do not stay in just one section, such as the Epistles, and do not skip the O.T., as you cannot understand the N.T. without the O.T.! Do not use the same plan year after year. Break it up, and try new ones. Do the same with your devotional books. Mix them

up. If you have a good one such as *My Utmost for His Highest* by Oswald Chambers, stick with it for the entire year, go to another one, and then go back to Chambers in the following year. When we are too consistent, it may turn into rhetoric, and then you will have a habit, not time with Christ!

5. **FOCUS: Set aside time each day by focusing on the purpose for your** growth and maturity (Psalm 119:130; Isaiah 42:16; John 4: 23-24; 15), and then make it a priority. In doing so, you will be able to *go for it* with passion and vigor. Let Christ transform you through His Word. ATTITUDE is essential. You must start with the proper attitude! You are going before a Holy GOD!!! Usually, it is good to spend most of your devotional time closely examining a few verses, not rushing through multiple passages. This will help keep you focused. Some find it best to take notes, write down questions, and ask a mentor. In addition, you can set aside one day a week to switch from taking detailed notes on a few verses to reading a chapter or two from a different passage without taking any notes. Whatever way you choose , stay focused and do not bite off more than you can chew!

6. **MATERIALS: Get the best stuff you can get, and buy a good Bible** (Ephesians 4:1-3) in an easily understood translation such as the *New Living Translation.* Consider using a Study Bible. I prefer *The Reformation Study Bible*. For serious study use the NIV, the NASB, or the NKJV. The best devotional books are *My Utmost for His Highest* by Chambers, and *Evening by Evening* by Spurgeon. You can also get a notebook that can be used exclusively for things that pertain to your relationship to God and to other believers so you can write down what you learn and any questions you may have.

7. **PLACE OR LOCATION: Select a quiet place (Luke 5:16) to study where you** are free from distractions. Remove all distractions. Close the drapes, shut the door, turn off the TV and radio, clear all busy work from your desk, take the phone off the hook, and lock the cat in the bathroom—whatever it takes. You will then be better able to concentrate and have better quality time with Him. Be serious about meeting God!

8. **TIME: Select a quality time (Ephesians 2:18). Chose a time for your devotions** when you are at your best. Usually, early morning is best, because outside distractions are at a minimum during this time. If you are not a morning person, do it when you are most alert. Give God

your best! Set aside "x" number of minutes to study, and "y" number of minutes to pray. Be flexible to the Spirit's leading within this framework! If you have a short attention span as I do, then break it up throughout the day. Perhaps read from the OT in the morning, a passage from the NT at lunch, then read a devotion and practice intercessory prayer before bedtime. Remember, this time is holy, which means it is to be set apart, to and for God only. If you are just being devoted to your plan and time, then there will be little room for Christ. The plan is the tool for growth, not the growth itself.

9. **SHARE: What you have leaned (Psalm 55:14; Matthew 18:20; Romans 12; 2** Corinthians 12:18). We learn also by doing and sharing. What we have been given is usually not meant for us solely; it is a gift that keeps on giving as we, in turn, help others! A willing heart, a teachable spirit, and the willingness and availability to share are essential for a disciple of our Lord!

From these nine precepts, we realize that from the character of Christ comes the conduct of Christ, if we choose to follow Him. Then, those values of our daily walk that drive our behaviors will, in turn, influence others and build our character. You cannot lead where you have not been, or when you do not know the direction to go. This is why discipleship is so essential to the aspect of being a Christian. We are called, not to just visualize discipleship, but to do it; not to just talk about it, but to do it. One cannot just think about dinner and satisfy hunger. The ingredients need to be gathered, the meal has to be prepared. Then it is eaten! The Christian who wants to become deeper and more mature in Christ and the effective church will take Scripture and the call of our Lord seriously, and then implement it into the function of applying it into their lives!

APPLICATIONS

Here are some thoughts to consider about turning your devotional time into action:

1 You will never be able to fully experience the complete value of a devotional time until you discipline yourself to apply what you have learned. Study with the determination that God will give you an application. Then, be willing and able to put it into action without fear or trepidations. Allow your trust in Christ to be real and exercised!

2 Make your applications measurable. Think through the *who, what, where, when, how* and *why*, such as *I will begin showing more love to my neighbor by asking if there is anything I can pick up for them at the store next time I go shopping.*

3 Sometimes, you will see four or five specific ways the passage you have studied can be applied. It is better to select one you want to apply from the Word that day and do it. If you try to implement three or more ways, you will most likely get frustrated and fail. If you cannot decide, stick to the first one that pops up, or the area where you need the most help.

4 Make most of your applications short-range, such as things you will do within the next day or so, or within the week. Periodically, God will give you an application that you will need to work on for a longer time. When that happens, rejoice and praise God, for this will build you up. At the same time, continue to work on fresh, short-range applications. See them as baby steps that will eventually turn into a marathon. Let God do a new work in you each day, and be thankful He wants to work in you.

CONCLUSION

There are many ways we can do devotions and study the Bible effectively. There is no "best" way, only that we do it! Many Christians feel all they have to do for their spiritual growth is sit in a pew, turn on the television or radio, or receive their knowledge for being a Christian naturally. However, this is not the way to transform our lives. You can no more grow deeper in Christ without any effort than you can go to a grocery store, stand in the produce section, and become a cucumber. To be a mature and growing Christian, we must read and get into the Word of God ourselves. We do it through prayer, hard work, discipline, concentration, application, and even more **prayer!**
Take this to heart: Jesus never asked anyone to do anything without enabling them with the power to do it. Let this be your encouraging motive (Matt. 28:20)!

Remember, Christ loves you, and wants the best for you. His way is the best way, and we need to have Him and the perspective of eternity in mind, not our limited feelings and desires!

Some passages to consider on discipleship and mentoring which are not options, but commands: Proverbs 18:24; Matthew 7:18-24; 10:1-42; 19:28-30; 28:16-20; Mark 1:1-5; 1:35 -2:12; Luke 9:23-25; 48; Luke 14:26-27; John. 8:31; 12:20-26; John 14; 15; 1 John: 5:3; Romans 12; 1 Corinthians 3:5-11; 12; Galatians 6:1-10; 2 Timothy 2:7; 1 Peter 3:15.

More tools on Discipleship are available at www.intothyword.org and www.discipleshiptools.org

APPENDIX II
ACCOUNTABILITY QUESTIONS

Therefore confess your sins to each other and pray for each other so that you may be healed. The prayer of a righteous man is powerful and effective. James 5:15-16

Key passages: Proverbs 25:12; 27:17; Ecclesiastes 4:8-12; Romans 14: 13-23; 2 Corinthians 12:19-13:6; Galatians 6: 1-6; Colossians 3:16; Ephesians 4:9-13; 1 Thessalonians 5:14; James 5:15-16; Hebrews 3:13

Accountability allows us to be answerable to one another with the focus on improving our key relationships with people such as our spouse, close friends, colleagues, coworkers, a boss, small group members, or a pastor. Accountability will also enhance our integrity, maturity, character relationships in general, and our growth in Christ. Accountability is sharing, in confidence, our heartfelt Christian sojourn in an atmosphere of trust so we can give an answer for what we do, see where we need help, understand our struggles and where we are weak, be encouraged to stay on track, seek prayer, care, and support when we fail, and model guideposts for one another to keep us going.

Below are some key accountability questions you can ask yourself and/or have a mentor ask you. These are designed for small groups and mentoring for those from high school youth to seasoned adults. They are for men's groups, women's groups, or anything in between. Because of the number of questions, all you need to do is choose three or four questions for each week. If there is a particular struggle area, add that one, too. Also, incorporate one of the key passages above and spend significant time in prayer:

1. Did you spend significant time with God through His Word, prayer, quiet time, devotions, and other spiritual disciplines? How much; how constant? Is He your driving force?

2. What blocks your growth in Christ? What blocks growth in your other relationships from becoming more mature and effectual?

3. How has your time with God been? Did you pray for others? Are you satisfied with the time you spent with our Lord this week? How so? What can you do to improve it? Did you pray for the others in this group?

4. Have you faithfully served the Lord, His people, and the lost?

5. Did you go and participate in church activities and worship this week? How so? Why not?

6. Did you set spiritual goals this week? What were they? Did you achieve your spiritual goals?

7. Have you made your family a priority? What noteworthy activity or deed did you do for your spouse and/or family?

8. How have you struggled with sin? What are the sins that have weighted down your walk with God this week?

9. What did you do to enhance your relationship with your spouse/friends? What can you do to make that relationship better?

10. In what ways has God blessed you this week? How have you shared your blessings?

11. What disappointments did you face? Did they consume your thoughts? What did you do about it? What can you learn?

12. Have you filled the mandates of your call, work and school, practicing excellence, and being the best 100 percent as you can be for His glory?

13. Have you committed any sexual sin? Did you look at someone lustfully? Have you been alone in a compromising situation? Have you been flirtatious? Have you struggled with pornography or "romance novels?" Have you exposed yourself to any sexually oriented material? Did you put yourself in a situation with a member of the opposite sex that could appear to be compromising, even though it may not have been?

14. Have you shared your faith? In what ways? How can you improve? Have you had an opportunity to share with a non-Christian?

15. How well are you handling your finances right now? Have your financial dealings been questionable?

16. Have you been trustworthy? Have you lied? Stolen? Cheated? Been dishonest or manipulative? Have you elevated yourself over another for your own personal agenda? What about your language and attitude?

17. Have you allowed the media and its distortions in TV, music, and movies to unduly influence you? What about peer pressure?

18. Have you been prideful? Have you been guilty of gossip or anger? Slandered? Shown Indifference? Been greedy? Not controlled your tongue? (This hinders people from knowing and trusting Christ the most!)
19. Have you demonstrated a servant's heart? How so? What have you done for someone else this week?
20. Did you struggle with a disappointment this week? How did you handle it?
21. Have you respected and treated your classmates, co-workers, and peers graciously by showing them compassion and the love of God in your words and deeds? What can you do to enhance these relationships?
22. How is your level of character according to the comparison of Gal. 5:22-23 versus Gal. 5:19-21?
23. How did you practice *joy* this week? Have you had a thankful attitude toward God? Have you struggled with anger toward God? How so? What can you do about it?
24. Have you taken care of the temple of the Holy Spirit with rest, sleep, exercise, healthy eating, etc? What about addictions, gluttony, or substance abuse?
25. Has your thoughts been kept pure?
26. Are you giving to the Lord's work with your time, talents, and treasures? What about financially?
27. What do you need to do to improve your relationships with God and with others?
28. What do you see as your number one need or struggle for this next week?
29. Have you compromised your integrity in any way, or lied about the above questions?
30. How can this group help you?

Take it slow and easy. Don't try, or even expect, to immediately delve into the deepest, darkest corners of your life. Begin by having your close friends hold you accountable for things like praying regularly and integrity issues. As you see the benefit and results of this, you will also be building up trust, which is necessary for accountability in more personal and private areas.

If you need further help in this area, seek a qualified and trusted pastor or Christian counselor. Also, seek someone to whom you can be accountable.

Do not just trust yourself; have a small group or mentor ask you these questions on a regular basis!

When I kept silent, my bones wasted away through my groaning all day long (Psalm 32:3).

If you fall away from these questions, or refuse to have someone hold you to them, then Satan will have placed a foothold in your life. These questions are not just for the pastor or church leader; they are for all Christians who want to live a life of integrity and significance. The failure to have accountability will produce sin. At that point, it is not a question of *if* you may fall, but, rather, *when* you will engage in sin and destroy everything in your life. The relationships and ministry God has given you, as well as your family and those around you for generations to come will be destroyed. Yes, there can be restitution and restoration, but the cost can never be completely repaid. Just look at King David; his sin had dire consequences with which we still live.

"The highest proof of true friendship is the intimacy that holds nothing back and admits the friend to share our inmost secrets."—Andrew Murray

The Christian life offers glaring, empirical proof that *all of us make many mistakes,* (James 3:2) and we are grateful for the forgiveness offered to us through Jesus Christ (1 John 2:1)!

He committed no sin, and no deceit was found in his mouth. 1 Peter 2:22

APPENDIX III
SCRIPTURE REFERENCES

OVER 2,000 SCRIPTURAL REFERENCES!

Below are the Scripture References for Building Healthy Relationships for each chapter and section. For deeper insights, self-study, and in leading Bible studies, look them up, read them, and then ask these essential inductive questions:

1. What does this passage say?
2. What does this passage mean?
3. What is God telling me?
4. How am I encouraged and strengthened?
5. Is there a sin in my life for which confession and repentance is needed?
6. How can I be changed so I can learn and grow?
7. What is in the way of these precepts affecting me? What is in the way of my listening to God?
8. How does this apply to me? What will I do about it?
9. What can I model and teach?
10. What does God want me to share with someone?

For even a deeper study, see the book *Into Thy Word: How to Do An Inductive Bible Study.* The book is available at intothyword.org as well as a downloadable "Chart" and "Cheat Sheet" with all the tools you need to take these Scriptures and study them in-depth in your personal devotions or lead others to do so in your teaching, Bible study, or sermons!

PREFACE

The Journey of Love and Relationships: Numbers 6:24-26; Joshua 1:8; Psalm 32:8; 119:9, 24; Proverbs 6:22-23; 12:4; 28:20; 31:10; John 8:31-32; Colossians 1:3-6; 3:5-17; 2 Timothy 3:16-17; 2 Peter 1:4

CHAPTER I

Preparing for Relationships with the Right Mindset This chapter is the template to the rest of this book. These Biblical principles are where our focus is to be: Proverbs 12:4; 28:20; 31:10; 2 Corinthians 5:11-21; Colossians 1

1 Right Biblical Mindset: John 3:30; Galatians 2:20-21; Philippians 3:1-21; Colossians 1:3-6, 15-29
2 Kingdom of God: Isaiah 9:1-7; 24:14-25; 29:18; 31:1-32; 35:4-6; 40:1-11; 42:1f; 61; Matthew 3:2; 4:23; 5:3,10,19-20; 6:10; 33; 7:21; 10:7; 13:24-47; 23:13; Mark 9:42-47; Luke 4:14-21; 16:1-12; Romans 1:21; 13:1-7
3 Immediate Revelation: Psalm 19; Isaiah 44:9-20; Acts 14:8-19; 17:16:34; Romans 1:18-23; 2:14-15; Colossians 3:5
4 Special Revelation: Psalm 119; John 17:17; 1 Thessalonians 2:13; 2 Timothy 3:15-17; 2 Peter 1:20-21
5 More Kingdom of God: Psalm 10:16-18; Daniel 2:44; 4:34; Isaiah 9:6-7; Matthew 3:1-12; 4:23; 5:6, 17-20; 24:14; 28:18-20; Luke 9:1-12; 11:14-20; 16:1-12, 16; 17:21; 22:16-30; John 18:36; Acts 20:25; 28:23-31; Colossians 1:13; 28-29; Galatians 3:16; 26-29; Ephesians 2:11-18; 3:6-15; Hebrews 1:8-14; 2 Peter 3:13-14; Revelation 5:9-10; 7:9; 17:14; 19:16; chaps. 21-22
6 Fullness: Psalm 9:18; 37:4; 40:17; 86:1; 107:9; 109:22; Jeremiah 22:15-16; 31:14; Joel 2:26; Mark 7:1-13; Matthew 5:3, 6; 6:33-34; 7:13-14; 13:40-43; 16:24-27; 25:31-34; 28:18; John 4:13-14; 6:35; Romans 6: 12, 19-23; 8:32; 9:30-31; Galatians 2:20-21; 5:19-21; Ephesians 5: 15-21; Colossians 1:1-23; 15:23-28; 2 Timothy 1: 12,18; 4:8; 2 Peter 1:10-11; 3:10-13; James 1:22-25; Revelation 1:9; 21:1-22:5
7 Work of Jesus Christ: Luke 17:20-21; John 18:36; Acts 2:36; Romans 14:17; Ephesians 1:20-23
8 Saved By the Grace: Isaiah 57: 15; 66:1-2; Luke 18:13; Galatians 2:20-21; Ephesians 2:8-9
9 Joy: John 14:16-26; 16:12-15; 17:17; Ephesians 1:13-14; 4:30; Colossians 3:15-16

10 Reconnection and Confession: Judges 17:6; 1 Samuel 7: 2-10; Romans 12:1-3; 2 Corinthians 5:9-21; Colossians 1: 9-14; 1 Thessalonians 4:1-8
11 Confess Your Sins to God: Romans 14:12-13; Galatians 6:1-5; Ephesians 6:21; 1 Peter 4:10-11
12 Learn About Yourself: Proverbs 1:5-7; 3:11-12
13 Putting It All Together: 2 Corinthians 5:14-15; Galatians 5:22-25

CHAPTER II

The Quest for Authentic LOVE: Mark 12:28-31; John 13:1-5, 34; Romans 5:8; 1 Corinthians 13; 1 John 4:7-12
1 How Is Love Spelled Out in the Bible: Psalm 23:6; Hosea 1:1; Matthew 5:44; 22:34-40; Mark 12:28-31; John 3:16; 7:38; 13:34-35; 21:15; Romans 1:31; 12:10; 1 Corinthians 13; Ephesians 5:33; 1 Thessalonians 1:3; 2:8; 3:6; 12; 4:9-10; 5:8; 13; 2 Timothy 3:3; 1 John 2:16; 1 John 4: 7-12
2 What Love Is: 1 Corinthians 13; 1 John 4:7-12
3 Patient: Psalm 33:20; Matthew 27:14; Romans 5:3; 12:12; Galatians 5:1; Colossians 1:11; James 1:3-4,12; 3:17; 5:10-11
4 Kind: Romans 12:10; Ephesians 4:11-15, 32; Philippians 1:6; 2:13; 1 Peter 4:10; Hebrews 10:24
5 Not Envious: Proverbs 14:30; 1 Corinthians 12:15-16; Philippians 4:12-13; James 3:16
6 Not Boastful: Proverbs 13:10; 16:18; Matthew 7:5; 1 Corinthians 12:25-25; Ephesians 3:18-19; 1 John 1:6-7
7 Not Proud: Job 41:34; 2 Chronicles 26:16; 32:26; Psalm 10:4-5; 18:27; 31:18; 56:2; 59:12; 62:10; 73:6-12; 101:5; 131:1; 6:17; Proverbs 8:13; 11:2; 13:10; 16:18; 21:4; 24; 29:23; 30:13; Isaiah 2:11-21; 13:19; 16: 6; 23:9; Ezekiel 28:2; Obadiah 1:3; 1 Corinthians 1:6; 2 Corinthians 5:12; 7:4; Galatians 6:4; (these are just a few!)
8 Not Rude: 1 Corinthians 11:18-22; Philippians 2:1-5
9 Not Self-Seeking: Proverbs 10:12
10 Not Easily Angered: Proverbs 12:16; Ecclesiastes 7:9; Matthew 5:22; Romans 12:19; Ephesians 4:26-18; James 1:19-21
11 No Record of Wrongs: Matthew 18:21-35; Mark 11:25; Hebrews 13:21-21
12 Not Delight in Evil: Isaiah 40:11; Matthew 9:36; 18:12-13; 23:37; Mark 1:41; Hebrews 4:15; 5:2

13Rejoices in Truth: Romans 12:10; 1 Peter 2:17; James 2:1-9

14Always Protects: Isaiah 42:2-3; Matthew 11:28-30; John 14-15; 2 Corinthians 1:3-7; 7:6-7

15Always Hopes: Psalm 31:24; 33:22; 71:14; Romans 12:12; Hebrews 6:11-12; 18-20; 17:7

16Always Perseveres: Psalm 86:12; Matthew 5:16; John 13:34-38 Romans 5:5; 15:7; 1 John 4:7-12

17God's Love Must be Our Model for Life: Romans 1:21; 5:1-5; 1 Corinthians 15:56; 1 John 4:7-12

18Love Is a Spiritual Fruit: Colossians 3:12-14; 1 Thessalonians 4:9-10; 5:8-13

CHAPTER III

The Myths of Love: Deuteronomy 6:5; Joshua 24:14 -15; Isaiah 44:9-20; John 21:16; Romans 8; 13:11-14; 1 Corinthians 7:32-35; 13; 2 Corinthians 1:21-22; 5:5 Galatians 5:5; Colossians 3:5; 1 John 4:7-12

CHAPTER IV

Kindness, Making Love Real in our Lives: John 14-15; Romans 1:16-17; 2:1-17; 8; 11:16-24; 12:9-21; Galatians 5:19-23; Ephesians 4:24-5:7; Colossians 3:12-14; 1 John 3:16-23; 1 Peter 1:5-11

1 Positive Examples: Genesis 39:21-23; Joshua 2:4-16; Ruth 2:8-16; 3:15; Luke 7:2-6; and Acts 24:23; 27:3, 43

2 Negative Examples: Genesis 21:9-14; 37:12-36; Exodus 5:6-18; Luke 22:64; and John 19:3

3 When o be Kind, Matthew 3:12; 18:9; 25:41-46; Luke 16:24; Mark 9: 43-48; Ephesians 5:1-2; Revelation 14:11

4 Consideration: Proverbs 3:5; Leviticus 19:34; Deuteronomy 22:1; Luke 6:34-35; 1 John 3:16-23

5 Imitators of God: Romans 12:17-21; Galatians 3:2-3; Ephesians 4:31-32- 5:2

6 When Not to be Kind: Matthew 21:12; 23:15-27; John 2:15; James 1:19

7 Kind to Enemies: Leviticus 19:34; Deuteronomy 22:1; Luke 6:34-35

CHAPTER V

Understanding the Importance of Being Good: Amos 5:15; Proverbs 25:22; Matthew 19:16; Romans 12:17; 2 Corinthians 5:20; 6:6; Galatians 5:17-22; Ephesians 4:1-6; 5:8-9; Colossians 3:12-17; 1 Peter 3:11; 2 Peter 1:3-8

1 Righteousness: 1 Samuel 26:23-24; Proverbs 13:6; 21:21; Isaiah 32:16-17; 42:6-8; Matthew 5:6; Romans 1:17; 3:21-26; 14:17-18
2 Joseph: Genesis 37-50
3 Virtue in Action: Psalm 34:8; 119:103; Proverbs 25:22
4 Goodness in Action: Romans 6:5-8; Ephesians 4:20-24; Colossians 3:5-17
5 Power of our words: Psalm 19:14; 51:10; 141:3; Proverbs 4; 25:11; Matthew 12:33-35; Mark 7:21; 12:29-31; Luke 6:45; 2 Corinthians 3:2; Ephesians 4:29-32; Philippians 4:8; Colossians 3:5-17; 4:6; James 3:9-12
6 Communicate: Mark 12:29-31; Romans 12:2; 2 Corinthians 10:5; 11:3; Philippians 4:8-9; 1 Peter 1:13-14; James 3:1-12
7 Character: Ruth 3:11; John 14-15; Acts 17:11-12; Romans 5:1-5; 1 Corinthians 15:33-34

CHAPTER VI

"ATTITUDE" The Prelude to Effective Relationships: Romans 12; Galatians 2:20-21; Philippians 2; 3:1-14; Ephesians 5:8-14; James 1:2; 4:10

1 Humility: 1 Kings 8:58; 2 Chronicles 7:14; 34:27; Psalm 10:17; 25; Proverbs 16:19; 22:4; 29:23; Matthew 5:3; 18:4; 23:12; Luke 22:27; Colossians 1:18; Philippians 2:5-9; 4:4-7; James 4:6-10; 1 Peter 5:3-6
2 Pride: Proverbs 3:7; Matthew 23; Luke 6; Philippians 1:2-8
3 Emotions: Matthew 11:28-30; Romans 12:21; Ephesians 4:31-32; Philippians 2:1-4; James 1:2-8
4 Communication: Proverbs 15:28; 16:32; 18:13; 25:28; 29:20; Luke 8:18; Romans 5:5; 12:10; Ephesians 4:15, 25-27; Colossians 3:13, 19; 4:6; Hebrews 3:7, 15; 1 Peter 1:22; 3:8; James 1:19; 1 John 3:16

CHAPTER VII

The Character of Friendship: Proverbs 18:24; 27:17; Matthew 5-7; Luke 15:1-2; John 13:34-35; 15:13-17; John 14-15; Romans 12; Hebrews. 13:2; 1 Peter 4:9

1 Rotten Fruits: 1 Samuel 25:9-13; 2 Samuel 10:1-5; Luke 9:51-56; John 1:11; Galatians 5:19-22; James 2:1-6
2 Friendship Factor: Genesis 18:1-8; Proverbs 18:24; Matthew 7:1-6; Luke 10:29-37; 10:38; 14:7-14; John 3:16-17; 8:47; 13:34-35; 15:13-17; Ephesians. 5:14; James 1:19-25; 5:13-16; 1 John 4:7-19; 3 John 1:2-4; James 1:19-25

Chapter VIII

Build a Good Personality: Matthew 7; John 15; Galatians 6:1-2
1 To Improve Our Personality: Matthew 4:18-20; 5:22, 37; 12: 33-37; 15:1-20; 2 Corinthians 12:20; Ephesians 4; 1Timothy 1:10; James 3:6; Revelation 21:8
2 Our Commitment to Christ: Joshua 1:8; Psalm 1; 42:1; 63:1; Matthew 6:33; Mark 1:16; 8:34; 12:30; John 15:1-11; 17:3; Romans 8:29; 12:1, 2; 1 Corinthians 10:31; 2 Corinthians 5:15; Philippians 1:21; Revelation 4:10-11; 5:12
3 Commitment to the Body of Christ: John 13:33-15:12, 18; 17:21; Ephesians 4:11-16; Colossians 1:28, 29; 2 Timothy 2:2; Hebrews 10:24, 25
4 Commitment to the Mission of Christ: Genesis 12:1-3; Daniel 12:3; Proverbs 11:30; Matthew 9:37-ff; 28:19; Mark 1:17; 12:31; 6:15; John 17:34; Acts 1:8-28:30; 2 Corinthians 5:18-20; Galatians 6: 3-5, 10-ff
5 Mature Christian: Matthew 11:25-30; 12:33; John 1:12; 3:16; Romans 10:9; 1 Corinthians 12-14; Ephesians 4:7-15; 5:18;1 Timothy 3:14-16; James 4:6; 2 Peter 1:5-7; Revelation 3:20

Chapter IX

Courtship Anyone?: Genesis 24; Book of Ruth; Job 31:1; Psalm 119:9; Proverbs 4:23; 5:15-23; 6:27; 31; Ecclesiastes 3:5; Book of Song of Solomon; Hosea 2:19-23; Malachi 4:6; Matthew 7:24-27; Mark 9:42-48; Luke 9:23; Romans 13:12-14; 1 Corinthians 6:18-20; 7:1-2, 32-39; 9:25-27; 2 Corinthians 11:2; Ephesians 5; 6:1; Philippians 1:9-11; Colossians 4:6; 1 Thessalonians 4:3-8; 2 Timothy 2:22; 2 Peter 1:5-7

CHAPTER X

Preparing for a Successful and Happy Marriage: Galatians 2:20-21; 2 Corinthians 6:14-15; Colossians 3; 1 Thessalonians 3: 11-13; 4:1-8; James 1:1-12

1 Submission: 1 Corinthians 7; Ephesians 5; Colossians 3:18-21; Galatians 2:20-21; 5:22-26; 1 Thessalonians 3: 11-13; 4:1-8; 1 Peter 3:1-7
2 Preparing for Marriage From the Perspective of Christ and the Church: 1 Kings 12; Amos 3:3; Matthew 5:32; 19:9; 1 Corinthians 13:4-7; Ephesians 5; Colossians 3; Revelation 21:1-2
3 Marriage Verses: Genesis 2:24-24; Proverbs 24:3-4; 1 Corinthians 7; 13; Galatians 5:22-23; Ephesians 5:21-33; 1 Thessalonians 4:3-8; 1 John 4:7-12
4 Passion: Song of Solomon 2
5 Commitment: Song of Solomon 8: 6-7
6 Fidelity: Proverbs 5:15-20; 1 Corinthians 7:1-16
7 Model of Love: 1 Corinthians 13
8 Roles of Marriage: Ephesians 5:21-33
9 Communication: Colossians 3:16
10 Harmony: 1 Peter 3:1-9
11 Husband's role: 1 Timothy 3:1-7
12 Wife's role: Proverbs 31:10-31
13 Honor: Hebrews 13:4
14 Character: Colossians 3:12-17
15 Listening: James 1:19-25

CHAPTER XI

How to set Boundaries: 1 Corinthians 6:18; 1 Thessalonians 5; 2 Timothy 2:22, Hebrews 13:4

1 Self-Control: Proverbs 16:32; 25:28; Romans 13:12-14; 1 Corinthians 6:12; 9:25-27; Galatians 5:22-23; 1 Thessalonians 5: 22; Titus 2:12; Hebrews 12:2; 2 Peter 1:5-7
2 Positive Examples from Scripture: Genesis 39:6-18; 2 Samuel 16:5-13; Daniel 1:8-16
3 Negative Examples from Scripture: Genesis 3:1-7; Numbers 20:7-12; 2 Samuel 13:1-19; 1 Kings 21:1-7

4 Boundaries in Dating and Sex: Psalm 55:16; Proverbs 6:32-35; 16:32; Ecclesiastes 4:8-10; Matthew 11:28-30; John 21:15-19; Hebrews 13:4; 1 Peter 5:1-2

CHAPTER XII

What the Bible Says About Sex and Romance: Proverbs 6:25-29; Matthew 5: 27-32; 19:4; Romans 1: 27; 8; Ephesians 4:19-24; Colossians 3:5; 1 Thessalonians 4:3-8; 1 John 2:16-17

1 Sex is a Bond: Genesis 2:24-25; 34:1-3, 8; Proverbs 5:15 -22; Romans 8:12-17; 1 Corinthians 6: 12-20; 7:3-5; 2 Corinthians 10:5-6; Ephesians 1:3; 2:4-10; 5:30-32; Colossians 3:1-4; Hebrews 13:4
2 Knowing That God Made Me: Genesis 2; Matthew 19:4
3 Sex: Genesis 2:24; Exodus 20: 14; 17; Job 31:1; Proverbs 5:15- 21; 6:25-29; Song of Solomon; Matthew 5: 27-28; 19:5; John 14: 21-24; Ephesians 5:23-33; 1 Corinthians 7:1-9; Ephesians 4:19; 5:22-33; 1 Peter 3:7-12
4 God's Standards: Ruth 4:8-10; 1 Peter 3:7-12
5 Lust: Proverbs 6:25-29; Job 31:1; Matthew 5: 27-32; 19:4; Romans 1: 27; 8:12-17; Ephesians 1:3; 2:4-10; 4:19-24; Colossians 3:1-5; 1 Thessalonians 4:3-8; 1 John 2:16-17
6 Marriage: 1 Corinthians 7:1-7; Ephesians 5:22-33

CHAPTER XIII

Learning to See in Relationships: Proverbs 5:19; 31: 30-31; Song of Solomon 2:8-17; 4:1-16; 5:2; Ecclesiastes 9:9; Acts 2:46; 1 Corinthians 7:2-5; 13; 2 Corinthians 6:14

1 Fellowship: Acts 2:42-47; 2 Corinthians 6:14-18; 8:1-9
2 Intimacy: Genesis 1:28; 2:24; 4:1; 24:67; Deuteronomy 24:5; 1 Peter 3:7
3 In Love: Proverbs 5:3; 31: 30-31; John 14-15; Galatians 2:20-21; Ephesians 5:22-33; Philippians 3:10

Chapter XIV

The Call of Forgiveness: Psalm 32; Matthew 18:21-35; 2 Corinthians 5:21
1 What Forgiveness Looks Like: John 13:34-35; Ephesians 4:29-32
2 Forgiveness is Hard: Isaiah 55:8-9
3 Forgiveness is Complete: Colossians 3:12-14; Galatians 2:20-21
4 Forgiveness is Costly: Luke 6:27-31; John 3:16
5 Forgiveness Pursues: Proverbs 25: 21-22; Hosea 2:14-15; Romans 12:19-20; Galatians 5:19-20
6 Forgiveness Is Continual: Luke 17:3b-4; Colossians 3:13
7 What Forgiveness Is Not: Job 5:2; Romans 8:28-39; 2 Timothy 4:14-15
8 How do I know I have forgiven someone properly: Romans 3:22-24; 1 Peter 2:23-24
9 The Biblical Steps In Forgiving: Proverbs 10:12; 17:9; Job 11:12-15; Jeremiah 9:23-24; Romans 3:22-24; 12:2, 19; 2 Corinthians 7:10-13a; 2 Corinthians 7:8-11; 1 Peter 4:7-8

Chapter XV

How to Understand, Solve, and Prevent Conflict: Genesis 4; Proverbs 3:4-6; 18:13; Matthew 7:5; 15:18-20; 18: 15-20; Luke 19:1-9; Romans 8:28-29; 1 Corinthians 6:1-8; 10:31-11:1; 13; Galatians 5; Ephesians 4:22-32; 5:1;
Philippians 2:3-6; 4:2-9; James 4:1-3; 1 John 14:15
1 Why We have Conflicts: Mark 12:30-31; Romans 8; 1 Corinthians 7; 1 Peter 1: 13-16; James 4:1-4
2 Types of Conflict: Proverbs 16:18; Mark 3:25; Galatians 6:1-5
3 Proper Attitude and Motives: Romans 12:17-21
4 Be Prepared Spiritually: Romans 12:17-21
5 Cultivating a Biblical Solution: Proverbs 3:4; Matthew 7:3-4; 15:18-19; James 5:16
6 Essential Points: Psalm 103:12; Proverbs 11:29; 15:12; 32; 19:11; Isaiah 43:25; Matthew 15:19; 18:15; Luke 15:11-24; 17:3; 1 Corinthians 6:1-8; 13:5; 2 Corinthians 12:9-10; Galatians 2:20-21; 6:1,9; Philippians 2:4-5; Colossians 3:12-14; James 1:19-25
7 ABC's of Conflict Communication: Proverbs 19:11; Ephesians 4:29; Matthew 18:15-17
8 You Are Christ's Loved One: 2 Corinthians 12:9-10

9 Conflict is an Opportunity: 1 Corinthians 6:1-8

10 Listening: Proverbs 28:13; James 1:19-25; 1 John 1:8-9

11 Understand Forgiveness: Psalm 103:12; Isaiah 43:25; 1 Corinthians 13:5; Colossians 3:12-14

12 Communication: Luke 15:11-24

13 Commit to a Positive Solution or Understanding: James 4:1-12; Matthew 15:18-19

14 Break Down the Issue: Matthew 7:12; 22:39; Romans 12:18; 1 Corinthians 13:5; Philippians 2:3-4; 2 Timothy 2:24-26; 1 Peter 1:13-14

15 Marriage Problem: Matthew 7:3-5; 2 Corinthians 3:18

16 Agreeing to disagree: Romans 12:17-18

17 Dealing with Difficult People: 1 Samuel 24:1-22; Psalm 10; 37; Isaiah 59:1-2; Matthew 5:48; Luke 6:27-31; Romans 3:23; 6:23; 12:14-21; Ephesians 4:29; Colossians 3:1-4; Hebrews 12:6; 1 Peter 2:12 -19; 3:15b-16

18 Satan Thrives on Conflict: Romans 8:12-14; James 4:7-8

19 Preventing Conflict: Jeremiah 2:13; John 4:10

CHAPTER XVI

Loneliness: Deuteronomy 4:31; 31:6; 33:27; 1 Samuel 12:22; Psalms 27:10; 46:1; 147:3; Proverbs 18:24; Isaiah 41:10; 54:10; Jeremiah 17:14-17; John 14:1,18; 14:1-6; 14:26-28; 15:12-19; 16:1-16; Romans 8:35-39; 1 Corinthians 3:11; 10:4; Ephesians 2:20; Colossians 4; Hebrews 13:5-6; James 1:22-25; 1 Peter 2:4-6; 5:7

1 The Sands of Loneliness: Proverbs 18:24; Matthew 7: 26-27; 11:28-37; Mark 15:34; John 15:12-14, 17; 2 Corinthians 5:20-21; Galatians 2:20-21

2 Storms Cannot Buffet Those in Christ: 2 Kings 6:16-16, 32; Psalm 4:8; 29:3-4; 42:7; 65:5-7; 89:9; 107:23-30; Proverbs 19:23; 30:4; Job 12:22; Matthew 8: 23-27; Mark 1:22, 27; 2:10; 4:35-41; Luke 8:8, 18-25; John 1:15; 4:6; 11:35-38; chaps. 14-15

3 God's Care For Us: Genesis 2-3; Job 14:16; Psalm 34:18; 51:17; 56:8; 63:1-3; 68:5-6; 139; Isaiah 43:2-5; Matthew 10:30; 11:28-37; Mark 15:34; Luke 16:10; 19:17; John 7:17; 10:3; 14:12; 2 Corinthians 5:21; Galatians 2:20-21; Philippians 2:10-13; 4:19; Hebrews 2:10,17-18; 4:15-16; 12; 13:5; 1 John 1:7

4 How Can I Get Reconnected?: Psalm 23; 40:8; 68: 6; Proverbs 25:12;

27:17; Isaiah 41:10; Jeremiah 17:14; Hosea 4:6; Matthew 11:29; 28:18-20; Mark 12:29-31; Acts 1:4-14; 2:42-47; Romans 5:3-5; 1 Corinthians 10:13; 13;11:1; Colossians 3:12-17; 1 Thessalonians 5:12-16; 2 Timothy 4:9-11; Hebrews 4:15-16; 10:23-24; 13:5

Chapter XVII

How to Destroy a Relationship: John 3:5; Romans 3:23; 1 Corinthians 4:6; 5:2; 13:4; 2 Corinthians 5:12; 10:17-18; Galatians 6:1-5; Colossians 1:18; 2 Timothy 3:2-5; James 1:9-10; 4: 1-6 ; 1 Peter 5:5; Revelation 3:17

1 Relationship Breakdown: Proverbs 13:12; Matthew 5: 1-12; John 16:33; Acts 20:31; Romans 6:11; 15:5-7; 1 Corinthians 12:26; 2 Corinthians 2:1-4; 4:6; 5:2, 12; 10:17-18; Galatians 6:1-8; Ephesians 1:3-7; 4: 2, 11-16, 25-32; Colossians 2:13,14; Ephesians 1:3-5; 4:2, 11-15; 26; 1 Thessalonians 2:7-8; James 1:9-10, 19; 4:1-11, 29; 1 Peter 1:22-2:10; 4:7-11; 29; 5:5

2 Pride: Job 35:12-13; 40:12; 41:34; 2 Chronicles 26:16; 32:26; Psalm 10:4-5; 18:27; 31:18; 56:2; 59:12; 62:10; 73:6-12; 101:5; 119:21; 131:1; 6:17; Proverbs 3:34; 8:13; 11:2; 13:10; 16:5,18; 17:4; 21:4; 24; 27:2; 28:25-26; 29:23; 30:13; Isaiah 2:11-21; 5:21; 13:19; 16: 6; 23:9; Ezekiel 28:2; Obadiah 1:3; Habakkuk 2:4; Mark 9:35; Luke 16:15; John 5:44; Romans 1:21-32; 12:16;1 Corinthians 1:6; 2 Corinthians 5:12; 7:4; Galatians 6:4 and these are just a few!

3 Defensive Mechanisms: Proverbs 17:4; Matthew 7:1-5; 21-23; 25:31-33; Luke 15:17-19; John 5:22

4 Defensiveness: Proverbs 17:14; John. 3:5; 13:34, 35; Ephesians 4:15; 2 Timothy 2:23-24; 4:1-2; 1 Peter 5:5

5 Contempt: Psalm 94:4; 18:25-26; 62:12; Proverbs 27:15; 29:9; Matthew 7:1-5; John 5:24; 16:33; Romans 2: 1-16; 1 Corinthians 3:18; 4:17; 2 Timothy 2:22-26; 2 Peter 2:10

6 Criticism: 2 Samuel 6:20; Psalm 15; Proverbs 17:27-28; 26:18-20; Philippians 2:3-6; James 3:13-4:2

7 Withdraw: Matthew 5: 13-16; John 1:15; 16:33; Galatians 6; Colossians 1:13; James 1:5-8; 1 Peter 2:9

8 Getting Over It: Job. 23:10; 36:5; Psalm 19:12-14; 139:23-24; Proverbs 25:15; Jeremiah 17:9-10; Romans 5:3-5; 1 Corinthians 12:26; 13:4-8; 2 Corinthians 2:1-4; Galatians 6:3-5; Ephesians 4:15, 32; 5:1-2. 28-29; Philippians 1:27-30; 1 Thessalonians 5:16-18; Ephesians 4:31-32; Hebrews 12:15; 1 Peter 2:17, 3: 7

9   Disappointments: Psalm 136; 142:1-7; Proverbs 3:5-6; 20:30; 23:10; Isaiah 26:3; Matthew 6:33; 21:21-22; John 7:17-18; Romans 8:28-29; 2 Corinthians 1:9; 4:7-12; Philippians 1:27-28; James 1:4-8; 1 Peter 1:6-7

10 Building Healthy Relationships: Genesis 4:4-7; Psalm 23:4; 27:1-14; Proverbs 1:7; 3:3-10; 12:25, 28; 25:15; Isaiah 1:10-15; Jeremiah 6: 20; Amos 5:21-24; Matthew 5:11-12; John 3:5; 8:12; 1 Corinthians 3:16-17; 10:23-24; 2 Corinthians 3:16-17; 4:6; 9:12-13; Ephesians 4:15, 5:8-9; Philippians 1:27-30; 2:3-8, 14-15; Colossians 4:6; Hebrews 11:6; James 1:17;1 Peter 1:22-23; 2:9-12, 21-27; 1 John 4:7-12

CHAPTER XVIII

How to deal with Anger: Job 5:6-7; 14:1; Proverbs 14:29; 15:18; 16:32; 27:12; 28:1-3; 29:11; 22; Ecclesiastes 7:9; Matthew 6:34; 18:15-17; 21:12-13; John 2:13-16; Romans 1:18; 6:11; 1 Corinthians 10:13; Galatians 6:1-2; Ephesians 1:7; 4:25-27; Colossians 2:13-14; James 1: 1-3, 19-21; 1 Peter 5:8-9

1. Negative Examples From Scripture: Genesis 4:1-14; 34:13-31; 49:5; Numbers 20:10-12; 1 Samuel 17:28-32; Acts 24:24-26

2. Positive Examples From Scripture: Exodus 17: 10-13; 22:22-24; Numbers 22:20f; 31:1; Nehemiah 5:6-7; Matthew 4:1-11; 5:23-26; 21:12-13; Mark 3:5

3. Pride Is the Root of Anger: Genesis 4:4-7; Psalm 37:8; Proverbs 6:16-19; 8:13; 15:8; Isaiah 1:10-15; Jeremiah 6: 20; Amos 5:21-24; Matthew 5:17-26; John 3:5; Romans 1: 18-32; 12:18-21; Galatians 5:19- 21; Ephesians 4:31; 1 Peter 1:22-23; 3:7

4. Pride: Job 41:34; 2 Chronicles 26:16; 32:26; Psalm 10:4-5; 18:27; 31:18; 56:2; 59:12; 62:10; 73:6-12; 101:5; 131:1; 6:17; Proverbs 8:13; 11:2; 13:10; 16:18; 21:4; 24; 29:23; 30:13; Isaiah 2:11-21; 13:19; 16: 6; 23:9; Ezekiel 28:2; Obadiah 1:3; 1 Corinthians 1:6; 2 Corinthians 5:12; 7:4; Galatians 6:4 (and these are just a few)!

5. Righteous Anger: Matthew 21:12-13; Romans 12:3; Ephesians 4:26-27; Galatians 5: 19- 23; Ephesians 4:26-27

6. Destructive Nature of Anger: Psalm 37:8; Proverbs 6:16-19; Romans 12:18-21; Galatians 5:19- 21; Ephesians 4:31; 1 Peter 3:7

7. Handling Anger: 1 Samuel 31:4; Psalm 4:4; 10:1-18; 103: 11-12; Proverbs 3:31; 4:23; 10:18; 14:17, 29; 15:1,18; 16:14, 32-35; 27:4; 29:11, 22; Ecclesiastes 7:9; Zephaniah 3:8; Matthew 5:23-24; 43-46;

6:12; 7:1-5,11; 18:15; John 3:5; Acts 24:16; Romans 12:2,17-21; 2 Corinthians 5:7; 16-19; Ephesians 4:15,22-27, 32-5:2; Philippians 2:4; 4:13, Colossians 3:8, 16; Hebrews 4:12; James 1:19, 20; I Peter 1:22-23; 4:8-16; 5:6-7, 16

8. Self Control: Proverbs 16:32; 25:28; Romans 13:12-14; 1 Corinthians 6:12; 9:25-27; 1 Thessalonians 5: 22; Titus 2:12; Hebrews 12:2; 2 Peter 1:5-7

9. Symptoms: Genesis 13:7; 2 Samuel 6:20; The Book of Ruth; Psalm 94:4-7; 141:3; Proverbs 12: 25-28; 17: 14; 18:2; 25:15; 26:18; 27:15; 29:9; Matthew 5:17-26; 12:34; Mark 7:21; 12:29-31; Luke 6:45; John 1:14; 1 Corinthians 3:18-23; Ephesians 4:11-15, 24-32; Philippians 2:3-8,14-15; 4:8; Colossians 3:8-14; 4:6; 1 Timothy 5:13; 2 Timothy 2:23-24; 3:13; Hebrews 12:15; James 3:1-12; 1 Peter 1:22; 2:17, 21-27; 2 Peter 2:10-11; 3: 7; 1 John 3:16

10. Compassion: Job 29:13; Psalm 136; Proverbs 17:4-5; Isaiah 40:11; Matthew 9:35-36; Mark 1:41; 9:41; Luke 10:25-37; 19:4; John 7:17-18; Romans 2:4; 12:1; Ephesians 4:23; 1 Thessalonians 5:14; James 1:5-8; 1 Peter 3:8

Chapter XIX

Relationships in the Workplace: Genesis 1-3; Psalm 24:1; 1 Corinthians 7:23; 2 Corinthians 9:6-15; 10:1-6; 11:1-3; Romans 8:17; Ephesians 4:1-6; 6:5-8; Colossians 1:21-23; 3:17-24; 1 Peter 2:9-21

1. God's Call For the Employee: Genesis 1:26-28; Exodus 23:12; 35:2; Proverbs 10: 4, 26; 22:29; 24:30-34; 25:13; Ecclesiastes 2:4; 5:12; 10:10; Matthew 18: 23-34; Luke 16:10-12; 1 Corinthians 7:23; Romans 12:11; Ephesians 4:28; 6:5-8; Philippians 2:1-11; Colossians 3: 17, 22-25; 2 Thessalonians 3:6-15; 1 Timothy 6:2, 17; Titus 2:9-10; 1 Peter 2:18-20

2. God's Call For the Employer: Leviticus 19:13; Deuteronomy 24:4, 4-15; Proverbs 27:18; Malachi 3:5; Luke 10:7; 1 Corinthians 9:6-12; Ephesians 6:8-9; Colossians 3:17; 4:1-2; 1 Timothy 5:17-18; James 5:4-5

3. God's Call For the Workplace: Ecclesiastes 2:4; 4:7-8; Colossians 3:22-25

4. We are called to work with respect and honor to God and others: Genesis 2: 15; 3: 15; Proverbs 6:6-8; 10:4-5,26; 12:9; 13:4; 14:23;

18:9; 22:29; 31:11-31; Ecclesiastes 3:22; 5:12; Ephesians 4:28; 1 Timothy 5: 8!
5. We Are Called to Work with Integrity: Proverbs 10:2; 15:27; Jeremiah 22: 13; Ephesians 4:28!
6. We Are Warned About Laziness: Exodus 20:9-11; 23:12; 34:21; Proverbs 16:27; 18:9; 19: 15; 22:13; 24:30-34; 1Thessalonians 4: 11, 12; 2 Thessalonians 3:7-15!
7. We Are Called to Honor Just Remuneration: Proverbs 3:27, 28; 27:18; Luke 10:7; 1Timothy 5: 18; James 5:1-5
8. The Dangers: Romans 12:1-2; 2 Peter 1:3-4
9. Building Better Relationships: Proverbs 10:4, 5, 2:11; 12:24; 13:4; 15:19; 18:9; 19:15; 24:30-32; Galatians 6:9; Colossians 3:23-25; 1 Timothy 6:1-2; Titus 2: 9-20; James 1:8
10. Emotional Stress: Proverbs 12:24; 13:4; 19:15; 24:30-32; Jeremiah 29:10-14; Colossians 3:23; Romans 12:1-2; Galatians 6:9; Philippians 4:11-13; Titus 2: 9-20; 1 Timothy 6:1-2; James 1:8; 2 Peter 1:3-4
11. Fear: 1 Kings 19: 1-18
12. Fatigue: Numbers 11:10-17
13. Frustration: Jonah 1-4
14. Excited: Genesis 1: 26-28; Proverbs 22:29; Ecclesiastes 10: 10; Isaiah 40:31; Luke 16:10-12; Romans 12; 1 Corinthians 3:16-17; 6:19; 2 Corinthians 6:16; Galatians 5:22-23; Philippians 3: 13-16; Colossians 3:23; 1 Timothy 6:17-19; Hebrews 10:25; 1 Peter 1:3-4; 1 John 1: 9

CHAPTER XX

Putting it all together: Psalm 1; 15; 40:8; John, chapters 13-15; Romans 5:8; 1 Corinthians 13; Galatians 5:22-23; Colossians 3:15
1 We Are Called To a Relationship: Ezekiel 43:7-9; 48:35; John 8:34; 14:2, 23; 15; Colossians 1:24
2 Living Our Lives Worthy: John 13:5; 2 Corinthians 12:10: Galatians 2:20-21; Philippians 1:27- 2: 11; 3:10; Colossians 1:24-27; Titus 2:11-14; Hebrews 2:14-18
3 Building Your Life On the Rock of the Word: Numbers 32:23; Proverbs 9:1-18; 24:3; Isaiah 25:4-5; 28:14-18; Ezekiel 33:30-33; *Matthew 7: 24-29*; 8:24-25; 13:1-23; Romans 2:4-6; 2 Corinthians 5:10-11; 1 Thessalonians 2:23; Hebrews 9:27; James 1:22-25

4 Not As the Scribes: Matthew 5:22-44; 6:1-8, 19, 25; 7:23-24; 23; Mark 1:21-22; 6:2

5 We Have to Produce Relationships; They Do Not Just Happen: Genesis 29; Deuteronomy 31:6; Psalm 147:1-3; Proverbs 4:34; Isaiah 40:29-31; Ecclesiastes 9:10; 2 Corinthians 9:6; Colossians 3:23; Philippians 3:13-14; Philippians 4:13; 2 Thessalonians 3:10-13

6 Take Up the Cross: Deuteronomy 6:4-7; 13:6-11; 2 Maccabees 7:22-23 (apocrypha); Matthew 10: 34-42; 11:29; 18:1-6; Luke 14:25-33; John 3:29-30; Romans 6:11-14; 1 Corinthians 1:30; 2 Corinthians 1:20; 12:9; Galatians 1:10; Ephesians 6:10; Colossians 1:27; 2:6-7; Philippians 2:12-13; 1 Thessalonians 4:3; 5:23-24; 1 Timothy 5:8; James 1:2-4; 1 Peter 1:3-11

7 What Does This Come Down To?: Genesis 1:26-27; 2:18-24; Deuteronomy 4:9-10; 5:29; 31:11-13; Judges 2:6-13; Jeremiah 17:14; Psalm 2:8; 78:5-8; 127:1; Matthew 16:24; 28:20; Luke 9:23; John 1:1-3; 3:30; 13:20; 16:12-13; Acts 20:28; Romans 7:4, 18; 1 Corinthians 3:11; 10:4; 2 Corinthians 11:2; Galatians 2:20; Ephesians 1:7, 20-22; 2:20; 5:23; Colossians 1:16-18; 2:4-10; 3:11; 1 Timothy 6:14-15; Hebrews 1:2,6; 13:5; 1 Peter 1:18-19; 3:22; Revelation 1:5; 5:11-12; 7:9-10

And he is the head of the body, the church; he is the beginning and the firstborn from among the dead, so that in everything he might have the supremacy. Colossians 1:18

Appendix IV
THE "*ONE ANOTHER*" PASSAGES

Bible passages essential for us to understand and develop healthy relationships by knowing we are called to *One Another*:

1. Love One Another: John 13:34-35; 15:12, 17; Romans 12:10; 13:8; 14:13; 1 Thessalonians 3:12; 4:9; 2 Thessalonians 1:3; 1 Peter 1:22; 1 John 3:11, 3:22; 4:8; 23; 4:7, 11-12; 2 John 1: 5
2. Serve One Another: Galatians 5:13; 21; Philippians 2:3; 1 Peter 4:9; 5:5
3. Accept One Another: Romans 15:7, 14
4. Strengthen One Another: Romans 14:19
5. Help One Another: Hebrews 3:13; 10:24
6. Encourage One Another: Romans 14:19; 15:14; Colossians 3:16; 1 Thessalonians 5:11; Hebrews 3:13; 10:24-25
7. Care For One Another: Galatians 6:2
8. Forgive One Another: Ephesians 4:32; Colossians 3:13
9. Submit to One Another: Ephesians 5:21; 1 Peter 5:5
10. Commit to One Another: 1 John 3:16
11. Build Trust with One Another: 1 John 1:7
12. Be Devoted to One Another: Romans 12:10
13. Be Patient with One Another: Ephesians 4:2; Colossians 3:13
14. Be Interested in One Another: Philippians 2:4
15. Be Accountable to One Another: Ephesians 5:21
16. Confess to One Another: James 5:16
17. Live in Harmony with One Another: Romans 12:16
18. Do Not be Conceited to One Another: Romans 13:8
19. Do Not Pass Judgment to One Another: Romans 14:13; 15:7
20. Do Not Slander One Another: James 4:11
21. Instruct One Another: Romans 16:16

22.   Greet One Another: Romans 16:16; 1 Corinthians 1:10; 2
        Corinthians 13:12
23.   Admonish One Another: Romans 5:14; Colossians 3:16
24.   Spur One Another On Toward Love and Good Deeds: Hebrews
        10:24
25.   Meet with One Another: Hebrews 10:25
26.   Agree with One Another: 1 Corinthians 16:20
27.   Be Concerned for One Another: Hebrews 10:24
28.   Be Humble to One Another in Love: Ephesians 4:2
29.   Be Compassionate to One Another: Ephesians 4:32
30.   Do Not be Consumed by One Another Galatians 5:14-15
31.   Do Not Anger One Another: Galatians 5:26
32.   Do Not Lie to One Another: Colossians 3:9
33.   Do Not Grumble to One Another: James 5:9
34.   Give Preference to One Another: Romans 12:10
35.   Be at Peace with One Another: Romans 12:18
36.   Sing to One Another: Ephesians 5:19
37.   Be of the Same Mind to One Another: Romans 12:16; 15:5
38.   Comfort One Another: 1 Thessalonians 4:18; 5:11
39.   Be Kind to One Another: Ephesians 4:32
40.   Live in Peace with One Another: 1 Thessalonians 5:13
41.   Carry One Another's Burdens: Galatians 6:2

APPENDIX V
ABOUT INTO THY WORD MINISTRIES

Your word is a lamp to my feet and a light for my path. Psalm 119: 105

The *Into Thy Word Ministries* vision is to provide Christians with the most effective tools and the most effectual means possible to better understand and apply God's Word to their lives. Our call is a dedication to teaching people all over the world how to study the Bible in a simple, clear, and concise way! Our passion is to glorify Christ (Colossians 1). Currently, we are training thousands of pastors and church leaders all around the world. We do this through seminars, missionary efforts overseas, church leadership consulting, curriculum development, and our interactive website resources! *Into Thy Word* (*ITW*) was founded in 1988 at Richard's home church in Pasadena California under Pastor Paul Cedar who is the founder and Director of "Mission America." *ITW* was an outgrowth from Richard's seminar on "How to do Inductive Bible Study." There are currently over 3,500+ ITW associates who personally distribute our Discipleship tools and curriculums in over 80 countries through CDs, booklets, and electronically. In 2000, Richard was further challenged by Pastor Paul and Billy Graham to take this ministry fulltime; thus, started *ITW*'s passionate efforts of training pastors and missionaries fulltime overseas, targeting Russia, China, and India. We incorporated (pending 501-3c) as a ministry with the launch from our interactive website, again, at the personal request of Billy Graham.

One of the great tragedies of the church today is that fewer and fewer people are reading the Bible. Fewer and fewer people are living the life of a disciple of Jesus Christ than ever before. As Christians living in America today, we tend to be more concerned with who is coming to our church and how many are coming than with making disciples, which we are called first and foremost to do.

We believe that the lack of Bible study and Bible knowledge is one of the root causes of the problems that most Christians face, because without this knowledge, they are unable to make healthy and wise decisions. It is also one of the root problems that our *churches* face. Our churches are riddled with conflict and strife thereby pushing people away when we are called to be a light in darkness, salt to a flavorless world, and a haven of rest. Yet, we choose to ignore our call and rather place our focus upon our selfish needs and quests, when it needs to be upon the foot of the cross, who Christ is, and what He did for us as revealed in His Word.

Because of the aforementioned reasons, we have remained committed to Christ and His call to *Into Thy Word Ministries*. We at *ITW* are committed to teaching people how to find the time for Him, how to be His disciples and how to understand His Word. In so doing, we believe that the church will flourish in power and commitment for our Lord's glory! Then, we can be the light in darkness, the flavor, and the rest in the midst of life's harshness. We can be the people of God so we can do the work of God!

You can Partner with us by:

1. **PRAYER** - Personal and professional-so the word gets out about why learning how to study the Bible is important. In Matthew 9:37, 38 Jesus said, the harvest is plenteous, but the laborers are few. We need dedicated missionaries to teach biblical exegetical methods to pastors overseas, and we need people to help with administration and fundraising. We have many other places of opportunity, too.
2. **GIVE** - We are missionaries, and ITW is a mission endeavor. We receive no salary while carrying out Christ's Great Commandment and Great Commission, and this requires money. With few exceptions, most of us could give more for the Lord's work.
3. **HELP** - We are always looking for people to help us with administration, fundraising, and translating our "Pastor Training Packs" into different languages. We are always looking for people to distribute them, too!
4. **PROMOTE** - By spreading the word about Into Thy Word, how people can get more out of their Bible, and receive free, quality discipleship tools!

If you feel that you could be a part of this plan, any gift that you give would be extremely appreciated. If you feel led to support us, you may give "online" or conventionally. A onetime gift or an ongoing monthly commitment of your choice is greatly needed. Your financial gift will be the tool that God uses to keep this vital ministry going all over the world, but it is your ongoing prayers that will give us the strength, protection, and encouragement we need to be an impact.

Please consider helping us spread the word about God's Word, as we teach biblical principles as well as how people can get more out of their Bible and how they can grow in Christ through our ministry!
Need discipleship materials? Does your church have you down? Do you need help and insights to know how to lead biblically, or some encouragement to keep steady in the faith? Then check out our website; we have over 700 articles of solid biblical curriculums designed to help people grow in Him!

You may also see "About" on our Website for more information, how to contact us, our statement of faith, and how you can better understand His Word.

THANK YOU for your support!

Into Thy Word Ministries
www.intothyword.org
info@intothyword.com

The LORD bless you and keep you; the LORD make his face shine upon you and be gracious to you; the LORD turn his face toward you and give you peace. Numbers 6:24

Appendix VI

ABOUT THE MAN BEHIND THE WORDS

Let me understand the teaching of your precepts; then I will meditate on your wonders. Psalm 119:27

Richard Joseph Krejcir lives in Southern California and is married to the beautiful MaryRuth. He is committed to prayer, spiritual growth, and integrity. He is the Director of *Into Thy Word Ministries*, a missions and discipling ministry, with a call upon his heart to bring discipleship materials to pastors and everyone who needs them both here and overseas. He is the author of numerous articles, curriculums, and the book, *Into Thy Word*, and is also an ordained pastor, teacher, and speaker. He is a graduate of Fuller Theological Seminary in Pasadena California (M.Div., Master of Divinity) and Canbourne University in London, England (Ph.D., Doctor of Philosophy in Practical Theology). He has amounted over 20 years of pastoral ministry experience, mostly in youth ministry, including serving as a church growth consultant.

Richard has been teaching inductive Bible study principles at camps, conferences, and churches all over the world since 1979. He does this to give people opportunities and tools so they can learn how to gain those life-impacting insights from the Bible. Richard has been personally discipled by some of Christendom's greatest thinkers and leaders, including Francis A. Schaeffer, Dr. Walter Martin, Chuck Miller, Ralph Winter, and Robert Boyd Munger, as well as other great and godly men. His main influencers have been Schaeffer as well as Oswald Chambers and Charles Haddon Spurgeon. Richard has learned and remains committed to teaching people how to find the time for Christ, how to be His disciple, and how to understand His Word better.

The following are essential to the Christian's walk of faith, which Richard strives to the fullest to obey and practice daily:

1. A caring, effective love relationship with Jesus Christ as LORD.
2. A lifestyle dedicated to obeying God's Will.
3. Daily devotional times, prayer, and studying of God's Word.
4. A joyful love and willingness to serve our Lord, even through personal sacrifice.
5. A witness for Christ without hypocrisy.
6. A firm desire to be God's child through trust and obedience.
7. A working faith in God's promises for all daily needs and in all situations.

But whatever was to my profit I now consider loss for the sake of Christ. What is more, I consider everything a loss compared to the surpassing greatness of knowing Christ Jesus my Lord, for whose sake I have lost all things. I consider them rubbish, that I may gain Christ and be found in him, not having a righteousness of my own that comes from the law, but that which is through faith in Christ—the righteousness that comes from God and is by faith. I want to know Christ and the power of his resurrection and the fellowship of sharing in his sufferings, becoming like him in his death, and so, somehow, to attain to the resurrection from the dead. Philippians 3:7-11

9 781413 771794

Mzilikazi wa Afrika's achievements include:

2014: Elected as a board member of the Global Investigative Journalism Network (GIJN).

2014: Taco Kuiper Award for Investigative Journalism joint-runner-up.

2014: Standard Bank Sikuvile Journalism Award: Investigative Journalism joint-winner.

2013: Vodacom Journalist of the Year Award winner.

2013: Vodacom Print News Journalist of the Year Award winner.

2013: Global Shining Light Award winner (Brazil).

2013: A speaker at the Global Investigative Journalism Conference (Brazil).

2012: Standard Bank Sikuvile Journalism Awards: South African Story of the Year winner.

2012: Standard Bank Sikuvile Journalism Awards: South African Journalist of the Year winner.

2012: Standard Bank Sikuvile Journalism Awards: Investigative Journalism winner.

2012: Taco Kuiper Award for Investigative Journalism winner.

2011: Vodacom Journalist of the Year Award winner.

2011: Vodacom Print News Journalist of the Year Award winner.

2011: Vodacom Journalist of the Year Regional winner.

2011: Taco Kuiper Award for Investigative Journalism winner.

2011: Mondi Shanduka Newspaper Awards: Investigative Journalism finalist.

2011: Mondi Shanduka Newspaper Awards: Hard News Story winner.

2010: Released the EP *Zvinosiririsa* (Ocha Records).

2010: Released the EP *Umoja/The Flute Song* (Ocha Records).

2010: Released the EP *Ancestral Calling* (Nulu Music).

2009: Released the double album *Tamanini* (Soul Candi Records).

2009: Released the international EP *Mahuwelele Remixes* (Ocha Records).

2008: Released the album *The Icon* (Universal Music).

2007: A researcher for *The Dream Deferred* by Mark Gevisser.

2005: Released the album *Dance or Die!* (Gallo Records)

2005: Authored the chapter "Investigative Journalism" in *Changing the Fourth Estate – Essays on South African Journalism* (Human Science Research Council (HSRC)).

2005: Released a debut album *Afrika* (Gallo Records).

2003: Guest Speaker at the International Conference for Investigative Journalism (Denmark).

2003: International Consortium of Investigative Journalism Award finalist (USA).

2003: *Sunday Times* Journalist of the Year winner.

2003: Lorenzo Natali Investigative Journalism Prize finalist (Belgium).

2003: John Manyarara Investigative Journalism Award winner (Namibia).

2002: Vodacom Journalist of the Year Regional Award winner.

2001: Sunday Times Story of the Year winner.

2001: Mondi Paper Newspaper Award: South African Story of the Year winner.

2001: Mondi Paper Newspaper Award: News Writing winner.

2001: The Nat Nakasa for Media Integrity Award winner.

2001: Awarded Honorary Citizenship of Nebraska State (USA).

2001: US Foreign Exchange Fellow for Investigative Journalism Scholarship (USA).

2001: Harry Brittain Fellowship (England).

2000: *Sunday Times* Story of the Year winner.

1999: *Sunday Times* Journalist of the Year winner.

1999: Foreign Correspondence Association finalist.

1999: South African Courageous Journalism Award winner.

1999: Nat Nakasa for Media Integrity Award winner.